Practical Conflicts
New Philosophical Essays

Practical conflicts pervade human life. Agents have many different desires, goals, values, commitments, and obligations, all of which can come in conflict with each other. The agent facing a conflict, therefore, finds herself in a difficult predicament. How can practical reasoning help to resolve practical conflicts?

In this collection of new essays, various distinguished philosophers analyze the diverse forms of practical conflicts. Their aim is to provide a comprehensive basis for understanding the sources of practical conflicts, to investigate the challenge they therefore pose to an adequate conception of practical reason, and to assess how that challenge can be met. Practical conflicts thereby provide a lens through which questions about the scope of practical reason come into focus.

These essays will serve as a major resource for students of philosophy but will also interest students and professionals in related fields of the social sciences, such as psychology, political science, sociology, and economics.

Dr. Peter Baumann is Lecturer in Philosophy at the University of Aberdeen.

Dr. Monika Betzler is Assistant Professor of Philosophy at the University of Göttingen.

Practical Conflicts

New Philosophical Essays

Edited by

PETER BAUMANN

University of Aberdeen

MONIKA BETZLER

Universität Göttingen

CAMBRIDGE
UNIVERSITY PRESS

PUBLISHED BY THE PRESS SYNDICATE OF THE UNIVERSITY OF CAMBRIDGE
The Pitt Building, Trumpington Street, Cambridge, United Kingdom

CAMBRIDGE UNIVERSITY PRESS
The Edinburgh Building, Cambridge CB2 2RU, UK
40 West 20th Street, New York, NY 10011-4211, USA
477 Williamstown Road, Port Melbourne, VIC 3207, Australia
Ruiz de Alarcón 13, 28014 Madrid, Spain
Dock House, The Waterfront, Cape Town 8001, South Africa

http://www.cambridge.org

First published 2004

Printed in the United States of America

Typeface ITC New Baskerville 10/13 pt.   *System* LaTeX 2_ε [TB]

A catalog record for this book is available from the British Library.

Library of Congress Cataloging in Publication Data

Practical conflicts : new philosophical essays / edited by Peter Baumann
and Monika Betzler.
p. cm.
ISBN 0-521-81271-2 – ISBN 0-521-01210-4 (pbk.)
1. Practical reason.   2. Conflict (Psychology)   I. Baumann, Peter.   II. Betzler, Monika.
BC177.P72   2004
128′.4 – dc22   2003061213

ISBN 0 521 81271 2 hardback
ISBN 0 521 01210 4 paperback

Contents

Foreword

The idea for this anthology grew out of many discussions and jointly taught seminars on matters of values, autonomy, practical reasons, and rational choice at the Philosophy Department at Göttingen University (Germany).

All of the papers collected in this anthology are original contributions except Christine Korsgaard's "The Myth of Egoism," which was delivered as the 1999 Lindley Lecture at the Department of Philosophy at the University of Kansas. We thank Christine Korsgaard and the Department of Philosophy for allowing us to reprint the lecture here, which, so far, has been accessible only to a relatively small audience.

Many people have encouraged us to pursue this book project. We are particularly grateful to the contributors and special thanks go to Rüdiger Bittner and R. Jay Wallace for their ongoing support and many helpful suggestions. Many thanks go to Jon Cameron for producing the index. We also thank Terence Moore of Cambridge University Press for his valuable guidance during the preparation of this volume.

Introduction:

Varieties of Practical Conflict and the Scope of Practical Reason

Peter Baumann and Monika Betzler

Practical conflicts pervade human life. They arise in various domains, take many different forms, and pose a challenge, in varying degrees and intensities, to the rationally deliberating agent.

In this collection, analyses of practical conflicts in the various forms and domains in which they arise are gathered together for the first time. The aim is to provide a comprehensive basis for understanding their exact sources, the challenge they therefore pose to an adequate conception of practical reason, and how (ultimately) this challenge can be met – if, in fact, it can be met. Practical conflicts thereby provide a lens through which questions about the scope of practical reason come into focus.

There are many different reasons for action that can conflict with one another. The list of items that give rise to potentially conflicting reasons is long and might even appear open-ended. Consider, for example: desires, preferences, emotions, interests, goals, plans, commitments, values, virtues, obligations, and moral norms. After all, agents have many different desires, goals, and values; they subscribe to a variety of ideals and principles and accept different normative or moral commitments. Because all these different reasons are action-guiding claims, we call conflicts between them "practical conflicts." In contrast, the conflicts that arise, for example, between scientific theories and contradictory empirical evidence are often described as "theoretical" – having more to do with reasons to believe something and leaving the connection with action rather remote.

We focus on practical conflicts and, in particular, those faced by single agents, while neglecting interpersonal conflicts that involve problems of social coordination: These are being faced by more than one agent, and they cannot be dealt with from the perspective of only one agent.[1] Single-agent conflicts pose a special challenge to rational deliberation from the agent's perspective and therefore qualify as a distinct field of study.

In their most general form, practical conflicts consist in the fact that the agent cannot act on all of her reasons for action: The agent has a reason to do A, and has a reason to do B, but cannot act on both of them.[2] In such situations, it would seem, therefore, that practical conflicts offer incompatible guidelines as to how the agent should act. Given the circumstances, the constraints on time, and her limitations in effort or ability, she cannot concurrently satisfy, pursue, or act on all of her reasons for action, even though each of the conflicting reasons qualifies as good in some way, applies to the situation, and thus seems to have normative force. The agent facing a conflict, therefore, finds herself in a difficult predicament, and is often unguided as to how (or whether) to act.

Closer investigation is required in order to explain why exactly an agent is confronted with such a conflict, and what she can do with regard to its resolution. As it will emerge, practical conflicts come in different kinds, but most of them give rise to questions about the scope of practical reason. This gives particular importance to the topic of this volume. Whether certain kinds of conflicts limit the scope of practical reason, or whether substantial assumptions about practical reasons and practical reasoning prove wrong in light of such conflicts, are questions that the study of practical conflicts across domains should help us confront anew.

Very often, there is an easy or even trivial answer to the question "What shall I do?" I want to have the cake and eat it, too. Since my desire to eat the cake is much stronger than my desire to keep it, I can easily solve the "problem." This does not require much deliberation. It is fairly obvious which reason proves better for the agent, and the cost of not pursuing the other reason is negligible. The agent is not "conflicted" in any interesting sense of the word and it would be very misleading to say that she needs to engage in practical deliberation. Therefore such trivial cases do not deserve to be called "practical conflicts."[3]

Practical conflicts pose a more or less severe challenge to the deliberating agent, and they are much more difficult to solve than trivial cases such as the one about the cake. Consider the following examples:

1. Mary is trying to finish some work. She is getting tired and feels like having a break, but she also wants to finish. She can't do both. She has conflicting desires.

2. Jack is already late for his appointment when he runs into a good friend who happens to need his advice immediately. Jack cannot both talk to his friend and be on time for his appointment. He is faced with two conflicting normative commitments.

And there are even more severe cases:

3. Ann may be torn between two incompatible goals that are both highly valuable: to dedicate herself entirely to her career or to lead a happy family life. She might pick one over the other but never systematically resolve the essential tension between the two conflicting ideals about how to lead her life. In that case, the importance of the conflicting issues may not allow for a fully satisfying or "complete" solution.

4. Or to take a moral problem: Should I be honest with my friend and tell him unpleasant news or spare his feelings? Here, again, it is difficult to assess which reason is stronger. Even if I come up with an answer, I may harm my friend no matter what I do.

There are hard, at times tragic, cases of which some think that there is no fully satisfying solution, or at least no fully satisfying solution available to us given our cognitive and other limitations. There simply is no resolution without remainder to be found, and acting on one of the options results in grave losses or harm caused by forgoing the other option. Possibly, the conflict may turn out to be a real quandary, and in the example above Ann may not be able to resolve the conflict at all. A practical conflict is considered genuine if the agent cannot in principle find a solution.

It remains controversial as to whether there are unsolvable practical conflicts of this kind, particularly insofar as such conflicts pose a serious challenge to the deliberating agent who faces them, and thus challenge the claims of practical reason to unrestricted scope. If our reasons for action conflict, and if we find ourselves unable to come up with an all-things-considered resolution and act accordingly, then practical reason lacks, to some extent at least, the action-guiding force it is supposed to have. It is thus of major importance for an adequate theory of practical reason to tackle these problems if we are to be guided by the best possible reasons or, for that matter, if we are to be guided by reasons at all. The debate over whether there is a right way to reason in light of practical conflicts and, consequently, to resolve them or not largely depends on what practical reasons are, how we as agents can reason about them, and how practical reason is thought to operate with regard to a conflict among reasons. Such questions have not yet received sufficient attention. The analysis of practical conflicts across domains presented in this volume demonstrates that the challenge they pose depends on respective conceptions of practical reasons, and practical rationality more generally. At the same time, the diversity of different types of conflicting reasons that is examined in this volume helps us see more clearly what the exact conditions (if any) are under which our deliberative capacities can be put to work.

Practical conflicts pose particular problems for the morality, well-being, and autonomy of an agent, and these are the major domains in which they arise. Conflicting moral principles make demands on the agent that cannot all be fulfilled. In this predicament the agent is forced to make a decision under pain of potential immorality.[4] Or so, at least, it would seem. In a similar manner, when we are confronted with a number of conflicting values, it would seem that our well-being (as a function of the successful pursuit of our goals) is undermined. And if our motives remain conflicted, we not only remain divided selves (perhaps even to the extent that our personhood is threatened), but we also do not sufficiently – that is, autonomously – guide ourselves. Moral conflicts[5] (such as Jack's conflicting commitments to talk to his friend or to make it to his appointment[6]), conflicts of value[7] (such as Ann's problem of choosing between career and family), and conflicts of the will[8] (such as that of Mary, who wants to finish her work, but also feels like having a break) have therefore given rise to a variety of controversies: controversies about the potential for moral principles to be action-guiding, controversies about the commensurability of values, and controversies about the conditions of self-control and autonomy.

We can distinguish between different substantive features that can generate a practical conflict: Either different evaluative properties engender different and therefore potentially conflicting reasons or a single evaluative property gives rise to conflicting reasons. More precisely, there are (1) conflicts between moral and nonmoral reasons,[9] (2) conflicts between desires and values,[10] and (3) conflicts between reasons derived from a single source. In short, there are conflicts of moral reasons, conflicts of desires, and conflicts of values.

The often-quoted story about Gauguin arguably offers an example of a conflict between moral and nonmoral reasons. He may be torn between his project to go to the Fiji Islands and paint and his esteemed sense of loyalty to his family.

Weakness of will and other problems of self-control typically account for conflicts between desire and value: An agent may give in to a desire that she would prefer to suppress or to not even possess, or she may subscribe to a value she does not really care to be guided by. Consider the smoker who has an urge to smoke and yet subscribes to the value of leading a healthy life or the person who thinks that leading a religious life is valuable and yet cares about many things that are incompatible with such a life.

Mary's conflict of desires (to work or not work), Jack's conflict of obligations (to talk to his friend or to make his appointment), or Ann's conflict of values (a career or a happy family life) represent single-source conflicts.

Given the incompatibility of conflicting reasons, and considering their different substantive features and inherent diversity, it seems particularly difficult for practical reason to assess their relative weight or stringency and issue an action-guiding verdict. What do the agent's deliberative capacities enable her to do in light of her conflicting desires, virtues, goals, values, principles, or moral norms? How can she reason about conflicts between her moral and nonmoral reasons or between her desires and values, and rationally resolve the conflict between them?

Different theories of autonomy, well-being, and ethics in general have taken quite different positions on the challenge posed by practical conflicts. In fact, practical conflicts arouse philosophical perplexity to the extent that the resolutions recommended by these theories does not seem to eliminate the conflict. The puzzle that causes this perplexity concerns the apparent rift between the common belief in the action-guiding or agent-forming force of practical reason and the various ways in which practical conflicts seem to undermine the scope of that force. It is not only that several substantive features of practical conflicts can be distinguished; a distinction can also be drawn between two main views about practical conflicts, that is, between those who believe in the unrestricted scope of practical reason and those who question that claim to unrestricted scope.

The most familiar classical theories of practical reasoning, such as Kantianism, Humeanism, and consequentialism,[11] typically hold that practical conflicts can be resolved, all things considered. They focus on various kinds of conflicts, but it is the assigned task of practical reason either to preclude conflicts or to guide clearly their resolution. Such theories are ideal in the sense that they have never really dealt much with the practical conflicts and the challenge they present. Given the widespread difficulties of actually solving many practical conflicts, such theories may appear overly optimistic. Let us call the view that practical conflicts can be completely resolved "rationalism." Even though classical rationalist theories differ as to what qualifies as practical reasons and what practical reason exactly amounts to, they all provide standards of rationality that are supposed to help us tackle various practical conflicts.

According to a standard interpretation of Kant's ethical theory, for example, being rational entails that we are autonomous and morally guided. As reflective beings, we give ourselves the universal law of practical reason (i.e., the Categorical Imperative), which in turn endorses or rejects our given motives.[12] The Categorical Imperative, thereby, clearly adjudicates any conflicts between our moral and nonmoral motives by applying certain standards of consistency on action, eventually turning our moral motives into conclusive reasons for action. Kant's theory of practical reason (on a standard interpretation) clearly guides the resolution of any conflict between nonmoral motives and morality because the relation between morality and reason is conceived of as analytical. Practical reason thus qualifies immoral motives as irrational.

Hume's conception of practical reasoning, by contrast, precludes conflicts between rational and irrational motives by strengthening the divide between reason and the passions.[13] He relegates reason to the domain of the theoretical, while the passions qualify as arational "original existences" pertaining to the practical domain. Reason thus cannot criticize the agent's motives, but can only determine means to the desired ends. Conflicts arise only between incompatible desires, and they are settled according to their relative strength. As long as an action satisfies the agent's strongest desires, given her beliefs about the facts, it qualifies as rational. Conflicts between desires that an agent values and desires that she would rather lack – that is, conflicts of the will – cannot be captured by the standard Humean model.

Rationalism appears particularly attractive if one holds some kind of value monism. Consequentialist theories (such as utilitarianism or rational choice theory, not to mention the Humean model) subscribe to it, albeit in different forms.[14] Practical reasons are generated here by valuable states of affairs – desire satisfaction, expected utility, or the fulfillment of informed desires – and their value is weighed and estimated according to a common evaluative standard. Nevertheless, the different versions of value monism share the assumption that conflicting desires, values, or moral reasons can be ranked ultimately as to their strength or weight, and the relevant values can thus be maximized or satisfied.[15]

Classical decision theory in particular provides us with specific standards of rationality. These standards prescribe the strict ordering of preferences and thus exclude the possibility of conflicts among preferences. A set of axioms ensures that a rational agent's preferences will constitute such an ordering among the options she faces.[16] The axioms of completeness and transitivity in particular imply that there is always at least one best option. According to the axiom of completeness, the comparative values of alternative options are captured in a threefold relation. It entails that for any pair of options, one option is always either better or worse than the other in the pair or is equally good. The transitivity assumption states that if the first option is better than the second, and the second option is better than the third, then the first option is better than the third. This entails that the common evaluative standard by which the options are compared is exhaustive. The application of these standards is supposed to yield the rational resolution of any conflict between desires broadly understood. If it were to fail, we would seem to face a conflict on pain of irrationality.

Decision theory also elaborates the Humean approach in that intentional action always reflects the agent's strongest desires, together with her beliefs about the probabilities of the outcomes. Hence, an agent always does what she believes will be best – a view that leaves no room for conflicts of the will. This raises the basic question of whether this approach is really adequate to account for the full range of phenomena to which a theory of rational choice must apply.

In the meantime, various explanations have been offered as to why it proves difficult, if not impossible, to balance conflicting reasons so as to arrive at an "all things considered" solution and eventually act on it. Alternative approaches suggest that classical rationalist theories are unsuited to meet the problem presented by many practical conflicts.

Many critics of the classical rationalist picture maintain instead that practical conflicts reveal the limitations of practical reason in the various areas we have just sketched. How restrictive these limitations are is a matter of controversy. If conflicts are not just a rare exception and if they often cannot be solved (or at least not fully solved), then fundamental questions about the scope of practical reason are raised. Some think that many practical conflicts cannot be entirely resolved by any standard conception of practical reason.

According to these authors, not the Categorical Imperative, nor the Humean model of rational action, nor value monism, nor the completeness and transitivity axioms represents a standard of rationality that lets us adequately tackle the problems posed by many different practical conflicts. All of these either seem to offer unduly stringent requirements or lack the resources to rationally resolve many practical conflicts.

Let us call this alternative view the "skeptical view,"[17] since critical opponents of rationalism share a certain skepticism about the claim of practical reason to unrestricted scope.

The basic assumptions about practical reason in the various rationalist approaches just sketched has thus been subject to influential objections that sometimes have led to alternative conceptions of practical reason. Some protagonists of the skeptical view may agree with rationalists in holding that there is some legitimate way of rationally choosing between conflicting reasons and consequently acting on one of them. However, they are skeptical of the standards of rationality provided by rationalism and typically give up the basic assumptions shared by many rationalist theories according to which a conflict must be resolved either by comparing the relative weight of the conflicting reasons or by assigning categorical weight to a certain type of reason. They take rationalist theories to either underdetermine or overdetermine the rational resolution of many practical conflicts. In the first case, they leave us at a loss as to how to resolve certain conflicts; assigning a relative weight to conflicting reasons just cannot be all that we have to do in order to reason practically about many conflicts. And even in cases in which we are able to assess the relative weight of conflicting reasons, the conflict cannot always be entirely resolved. After all, we often cause harm, forsake values, or remain conflicted about what to value, all things considered.

In the case of overdetermination, conflicts that do not meet the proposed requirements of rationality are relegated to the irrational domain. It is open for debate, however, whether such conflicts are clearly irrational or whether the proposed requirements of rationality that result in that verdict call for revision. The dispute between rationalists and their critics thus grows out of a puzzle about the adequate scope of practical reason. Facing practical conflicts in their variety can help us shed more light on this puzzle.

Along these lines, skeptics typically examine different forms that practical conflicts can take – forms of conflict that seem particularly resistant to a complete resolution. So far, they have focused on cases in which determining the categorical force of a reason, or assessing the relative weight of the conflicting reasons as to whether they are stronger than one another or of equal strength, is considered as either (1) not enough or

(2) impossible to achieve. We are unable to resolve the conflict of reasons with respect to a common evaluative standard. Our rational capacities, therefore, are taken to be clearly restricted in light of many practical conflicts.

For example, in the case of conflicting moral reasons, we may conclude that the conflicting reasons are equally strong, and no further moral criterion enables us to decide between them. A person might see two young children about to drown in a river. She might not be able to save them both, and her reason to save one is not better or worse than her reason to save the other.[18] Many believe that such a person faces a moral dilemma: She ought to save the one child, and she ought to save the other child, but she cannot save both of them. No matter what she does, she seems to breach an obligation,[19] and wrongdoing appears inescapable.[20]

But even if she finds one conflicting reason more compelling than the other and so has no problem deciding what to do, such serious cases of moral "sacrifice"[21] still leave her deeply conflicted. She has reason to regret that she could not act on the other reason, even if it was clearly weaker. Take, as one such example, Winston Churchill's alleged decision to let the Germans bomb Coventry to prevent much greater harm.

Reactive emotions, such as regret and feelings of guilt, are often taken to indicate that the rational resolution of moral conflicts cannot entirely eliminate them. Our capacities to rationally resolve a moral conflict are therefore considered to be limited. Some maintain that they simply cannot undo the binding force of moral reasons that we respond to in reactive emotions.[22]

Others hold that the relative weight of conflicting reasons cannot be assessed because they are, at times, incommensurable. If there is incommensurability of reasons, then an assessment of the relative weights of conflicting reasons is, in principle, impossible. One has to distinguish between two different types of incommensurability. In the first case, neither is one reason better than the other, nor are they equally good with respect to some common standard or value.[23] Consequently, we are unable to completely resolve conflicts between reasons with incommensurable evaluative properties.

Ann's difficult decision between career and happy family life might qualify as a typical case here: Her options may be so radically different that it would be false to say that one is either better than the other or is equally good.[24] If there is no dimension whatsoever that allows Ann to rank her options, she cannot come up with an all-things-considered judgment as to how she should act.

Others maintain that there are cases in which incommensurability arises because it is indeterminate whether one reason is better than another or is equally good. According to some semantic indeterminists, there are cases that show that the application of such comparatives is vague:[25] It is neither true nor false that a comparative value relation holds between two items, because it is neither true nor false that a comparative term applies. For example, the application of an ordinary English comparative such as "more pleasant" allows for borderline cases in which it is indeterminate whether, say, spending an evening at the movies is more pleasant than spending an evening with friends in a pub.[26] Thus, the comparative "more pleasant" gives rise to incommensurability.

Those who believe that there are different substantive features that generate reasons typically argue for the trumping force or "overridingness" of certain types of reason over other conflicting ones. Moral reasons typically enjoy such a normative status over nonmoral reasons. They are thought to have overriding significance.[27] Similarly, cognitive states, such as beliefs about the good, are thought to guide rationally noncognitive motives. The classical account of weakness of will thus takes beliefs or judgments about the good to provide the authority necessary to qualify desires that deviate from them as irrational.

Critics of the rationalist picture have increasingly attacked these orthodox claims. Along these lines, the universal normativity of moral reasons is put under doubt.[28] If moral reasons lose their authoritative force, the question seems to remain open as to how conflicts between moral and nonmoral reasons can be resolved. More important, the amoralist does not even stand convicted of some error of reason. And, indeed, it seems much more plausible to suppose that immoral reasons are not irrational.

In the same vein, it has been questioned whether there is such a close rational connection between an agent's beliefs about the good and her desires, such that acting against her own best judgment (as weakness of will is defined) appears to be a form of irrationality. Instead – as some maintain – her beliefs about the good may prove to be erroneous, and her noncognitive states may reveal what she really values.[29]

Ultimately, the various debates and problems just sketched reflect the larger struggle as to how to come to terms with practical conflicts. The philosophical interest of moral dilemmas, value commensurability, moral normativity, and weakness of will lies in their bearing on how various kinds of reasons can be rationally assessed such that they issue in rational choice.

A number of different views on how rationalist or skeptical we should be about the resolution of practical conflicts are offered in this volume. Its contributors present novel analyses on what the adequate standards of practical reason could be in the light of practical conflicts, and what exactly their various sources are that render them ineliminable. They investigate in more detail conflicts between moral and nonmoral reasons (Velleman, Korsgaard, Chang), moral conflicts (White, Schaber, Elster), conflicts of desires (Richardson, Levi, Baumann), conflicts between values and desires and the connection of conflicts to free will and self-control (Mele, Guckes), and conflicts of reasons more generally (Raz, Betzler). In the remainder of this introduction, we survey the different contributions to this collection and highlight their respective approach to practical conflicts with regard to the task practical reason is thought to fulfill or to fail to fulfill given the conditions of conflict.

To avoid the skeptical view and its repercussions on the scope of practical reason, those who believe in the rational resolution of practical conflicts argue that objections to it can be accommodated within a broadly rationalist framework. Accordingly, practical reason is taken to provide means that allow one to assess conflicts and issue conclusive reasons for action.

Opinions diverge as to how best to do this, and suggestions made by Christine Korsgaard, David Velleman, Henry Richardson, Ruth Chang, and Isaac Levi cover a broad range of possible new approaches to various kinds of practical conflicts. Each of these responses represents a development within rationalist thought that goes far beyond classical formulations of rationalism and early rationalist responses[30] to the challenge that the skeptical view poses. What remains rationalist about all of them is that they do not share the belief that practical conflicts block rational choice. Instead, they propose more sophisticated standards of rationality. In light of the difficulty of resolving many practical conflicts, these standards are supposed to help assess conflicting reasons and consequently to guide action. A fresh look is taken at conflicts between moral and nonmoral reasons, conflicts of desires, and conflicts of values. To resolve conflicts between moral and nonmoral reasons, rationalists have to show how moral reasons can be normative and therefore overrule or trump conflicting nonmoral reasons.

Recall that Kant conceived the relationship between rationality and morality as analytical, and thereby precluded any irresolvable conflict between moral reasons and reasons favoring our well-being. Being guided by morality entails being free from irresolvable conflicts of practical reasons. What seems particularly hard to defend for the Kantian is the claim that any conflict between moral and nonmoral reasons can be clearly resolved. Kant's account is particularly vulnerable to two objections: (1) being immoral does not seem necessarily irrational, and (2) the reasons we have for the pursuit of our own well-being undoubtedly have motivating force, while moral reasons can often lack that force.

David Velleman and Christine Korsgaard present two broadly Kantian arguments relating how it is possible for moral reasons to provide a normative standard, despite their frequent conflict with reasons of self-interest.

In his chapter, "Willing the Law," Velleman devotes himself to the first objection and offers what he calls a "concessive" Kantian interpretation as to how wrongdoing conflicts with our practical reason. While Velleman takes an immoral act to be rational in-itself, he views it as the act of an irrational agent. The conflict arises between immoral projects (though rational in themselves) and the Categorical Imperative (as a commitment to humanity expressing the fundamental moral identity of a person). The contradiction in the will of an immoral person lies in the fact that she could not rationally choose to be or continue to be such a person. Even if (in a particular moment) an agent's reasons are not up to her and she (thereby) may lack sufficient reason for acting morally, she is still responsible for getting into conflicting projects. Conflicts of this kind cannot be solved easily, since they presuppose a psychological change in the agent, which cannot be effected at will. Velleman suggests that such conflicts can be overcome only by an "irrational leap to a greater rationality" pertaining to the reasons arising from one's underlying identity as a rational human being.

Christine Korsgaard devotes herself to the second objection against the Kantian interpretation, according to which it is hard to see why moral reasons should be normative. In her chapter, "The Myth of Egoism," she attacks what some think is a major source of conflict, that is, the tension between egoism and morality as two conflicting principles definitive of practical reason. The "egoistic principle" of practical reason is supposedly compatible with the view that all practical reasons are instrumental and all motivation is grounded in desire. Many philosophers believe that the egoistic principle has an advantage over the moral one since it more obviously meets the naturalistic requirement of internalism, that is, that practical reason has the capacity to motivate.

Against these claims, Korsgaard shows that the egoistic principle (as a form of instrumentalism) is based on false assumptions about the nature of practical reason. In the case of a conflict between egoistic and moral reasons, practical reasoning must resort to some normative standard to weight and balance them – a standard that egoism as such cannot provide. The importance of one's egoistic project is determined by the goodness of the reason promoting it, and such a project requires the possibility that we be motivated by pure practical reason in exactly the same way that moral action is motivated. It is only *what* practical reason tells us to do that is different in both the moral and the egoistic cases.

Whereas Korsgaard's and Velleman's Kantian reinterpretations pertain to questions of either why moral reasons enjoy priority in a conflict with nonmoral reasons (deriving from our desires and goals) or why nonmoral reasons do not provide a better normative standard (as some maintain), Henry Richardson offers an Aristotelian answer to the question of how we can rationally deliberate and eventually resolve conflicts between the reasons derived from our desires. While Humean versions of practical reason force us to think about our desires only in terms of their objects and their strength, in his chapter, "Thinking about Conflicts of Desire," Richardson shows that these attributes of desires are not sufficient for making sense of conflicts among desires, let alone for determining an adequate account of how to proceed rationally when they conflict. According to the Aristotelian interpretation proposed by Richardson, desires have a further dimension of "place" within an agent's conception of the good that is tolerant of the fact that conceptions of the good have not been fully worked out. In unreflective cases, perception (*phantasia*) indicates the respect in which a desire is taken as good, but this feature may become the subject of deliberative reflection. This reflection, in turn, helps to guide the agent's revision of his desires.

While Richardson, by introducing a further respect under which desires can be evaluated, centers on the question of how the conflicts of reasons generated by various desires can be rationally resolved, in "Putting Together Morality and Well-Being," Ruth Chang proposes a novel account of how conflicting values can be rationally accommodated so as not to issue in conflicting reasons for action. Chang defends the thesis that for any given conflict between particular moral and prudential values, there is some other more comprehensive value (often nameless) that includes the conflicting values as "parts" and in terms of which the conflict between them can, in principle, be rationally resolved. She argues that the conflicting values at stake and the circumstances in which they figure underdetermine the relative weights of those values. Hence, what matters in a choice must have content beyond that which is given by the values at stake. Moreover, if disagreement about what matters in a choice is to be possible, this further content must go beyond their mere weighting. Chang argues that it is in virtue of a nameless value that (in a particular case) a moral value has whatever normativity it has in the face of conflict with a prudential value, and that nameless value provides what matters in that choice. Chang's nameless value account offers a value-based resolution of practical conflicts between more particular values, and thus supports the claim that any choice between conflicting reasons is justified only if a common evaluative standard is found that enables the assessment of their relative betterness.

Conversely, Isaac Levi defends the view that conflicts of practical reasons can be rationally resolved without assessing their relative betterness, thus loosening the rationality conditions defended by a standard account of rational choice theory. In his chapter, "The Second Worst in Practical Conflict," he rebuts two widespread prejudices of classical decision theory that he qualifies as "absurdly stringent" constraints on rational choice. Against the first prejudice, which states that rational agents have strict preference orderings and therefore always choose for the best (all things considered), Levi defends the view that agents can rate two options as equally optimal and yet choose rationally. He considers the second prejudice, which maintains that the preferences of rational agents are revealed by their choices (a prejudice that is also prevalent in the belief-desire theory of action explanation), to be derived from the temptation to think of rationality as hyperbolic maximization. In the course of his article, he particularly devotes himself to the kind of practical conflict that arises when several dimensions of value are of concern to the decision maker and defends a new criterion of choice that he calls "V-admissibility." According to this criterion, an option that comes out optimal in keeping with at least one possible standard of evaluation in the partial ordering[31] is deemed admissible. Levi shows how, contrary to "V-maximality," V-admissibility can accommodate the kinds of conflicts that emerge when the distinction between cases where one of three options is second worse or second best is relevant. He thus introduces a standard of rational choice that can also tackle conflicts between cardinal value structures.

Since our rational capacities turn out to be more flexible and varied than perhaps expected, the appeal of rationalism and the underlying idea that we can resolve practical conflicts rationally persists in different variants. Yet recent contributors to these debates disagree about how we can rationally assess the competing reasons. According to these new developments pertaining to the rational resolution of practical conflicts, practical reason turns out to be a capacity that not only lets us apply given standards, but also enables us to come up with appropriate standards for different conflict situations. More precisely, practical reason is differentiated into two kinds. The first kind allows us to balance our momentary reasons for action, while the second pertains to our rationality as persons, arising from our underlying identity as human beings (Velleman). Practical reasoning does not just serve to uncover our desires. Instead, it must resort to a normative standard provided by pure practical reason with regard to the balancing of our desires (Korsgaard). Practical deliberation in the face of rational conflicts must resort to our perception of how desires have a place in our conception of the good and consequently guide the revision of our goals (Richardson). Practical reason lets us conceive comprehensive, often nameless, values that contain (in part) conflicting values, but that also contain normative standards as to how the conflicting values are to be compared (Chang). In conflicts between cardinal value structures, practical reason provides us with V-admissibility as a sufficient criterion of rational choice. It entails that an option comes out optimal if it is in keeping with at least one way of evaluation in the partial ordering (Levi).

Even if we can find other more sophisticated and flexible ways in which we can approach conflicting reasons that will yield rational standards of comparison or resolution, it will still remain controversial whether practical conflicts can entirely be eliminated. One reason for this may be the indeterminacy of comparison. Another possible reason is that no standard of comparison can eliminate the losses of values, harms, and inner divisions that are typical of practical conflicts. Furthermore, practical reasons may be of such a nature that we are in principle unable to respond to their binding force once they conflict.

As a result, the most obvious alternatives to any new version of rationalism are attempts that are realist about the persisting force of reasons not acted on, indeterminist about our standard of comparison, or otherwise skeptical about the perfect action-guiding force of practical reason. Yet there is a shift in emphasis away from general doubts about the scope of practical reason to a more detailed analysis of the specific conditions that render the rational resolution of conflicts difficult or inadequate. That renders the skeptical approaches more varied. The chapters by Joseph Raz, Nick White, Alfred Mele, Peter Schaber and Jon Elster, along with our own contributions, indicate this. They examine moral conflicts, conflicts of reasons more generally, and conflicts between different evaluative attitudes. These authors cast light on practical conflicts from a different perspective and examine in more detail what remains in the way of any rational resolution. They agree to a large extent with rationalism that the rational resolution of conflicts is possible, but that rational resolvability does not entail that conflicts are entirely eliminated. In many cases, in addition to the difficulty of finding the means to resolve practical conflicts, the force of conflicting reasons not acted on may remain. Further analysis is offered as to what characterizes practical conflicts that practical reason cannot do away with.

In his chapter, "Personal Practical Conflicts," Joseph Raz distinguishes between two theoretical questions with regard to practical conflicts: Is there a right action in conflict situations, implying that reasons deriving from different, distinct values may be compared in strength, weight, or stringency? And, what is unfortunate about such conflicts? Conflicts are unfortunate only where doing one's best is not good enough, and where the agent is blameless. Raz describes such conflicts as "normative" if there are more reasons than it is possible to conform with, or, at least, to conform with in full. It is this impossibility of perfect conformity with reasons that characterizes what is unfortunate about conflicts (even though it does not exclusively pertain to conflicts and does not thereby define them).

This characterization assigns practical reason the role of recognizing and responding to reasons. Reasons for action are thus taken as evaluative facts favoring action. If something is to qualify as a reason, it must entail that we should conform to it. Given this conception of practical reasons, we are in a genuine conflict if reasons demand incompatible actions. The rational resolution of such a conflict cannot eliminate the binding force of reasons that require conformity.

Monika Betzler's chapter, "Sources of Practical Conflicts and Reasons for Regret," puts the argument from reactive emotion under closer scrutiny. The argument demonstrates that the resolution of practical conflicts, which gives rise to such reactive emotion, is rationally underdetermined. Whereas previous views dictating what precisely regret reveals about the reasons not acted on prove to be mistaken, Betzler's analysis attempts to specify what reasons there are for us to be susceptible to regret. A more thorough analysis of the objects of regret reveals that rational regret responds to forgone commitments. What makes regret compatible with having rationally resolved a conflict is the fact that commitments are connected with two kinds of reasons, notably (1) reasons favoring the commitment in the first place, and (2) reasons deriving from such commitments. Even though the reasons favoring our commitments can be balanced, and conflicts between them rationally resolved, the commitments engendered valuable pursuits that often continue to give us reasons to value them. Regret is justified despite the rational resolution of conflict insofar as it responds to what we still consider valuable but can, given the limitations on time and ability, no longer act on.

While Raz and Betzler both identify and describe various kinds of reasons not acted on that continue to stay in force such that the agent is rationally required to respond to them, the papers by White, Baumann, Mele, Schaber, and Elster focus on various distinct conditions that make the rational resolution of conflict hard, if not inconceivable.

Drawing on Plato's and Socrates' thought on the unity of virtue, Nick White's chapter, "Conflicting Values and Conflicting Virtues," examines what forms conflicts between goods can take. He identifies two distinct questions that need to be answered in order to account for the difficulty of resolving many practical conflicts. On the one hand, we need to ask whether or not there is any reason to believe that a virtue (as a trait that is good) can come in conflict with other virtues. Yet, on the other hand, he shows that we also need to investigate whether or not the particular traits that we identify as virtues conflict with each other. What initially looks like a question about the intrinsic value of a good (taken by itself in a given practical conflict) really involves evaluating that good with respect to context, covering value, and the situation within which the evaluation fits. Thus, for White, the indefiniteness of the conditions under which an evaluative standard could be determined is the main difficulty not sufficiently attended to in the current discussion.

Peter Baumann's chapter, "Involvement and Detachment: A Paradox of Practical Reason," deals with what, according to him, constitutes an interesting but worrisome paradox of practical reason. This paradox is structurally analogous to the well-known preface paradox for beliefs and could be called a "preface paradox for goals." It concerns conflicting types of reasons for action and has to do with the conflicting attitudes a rational agent apparently has toward his own goals. On the one hand, agents do not have an indefeasible reason not to want that all their goals will be realized. Is it not almost trivially true that we are very much "involved" with and committed to the realization of our goals? On the other hand, Baumann argues, an agent does indeed have indefeasible reason not to want that all her goals be realized: If a person's life were completely successful (in every respect), it would lose its point. As reflexive beings, we are also somehow "detached" from and not fully committed to our goals. However, if all this is true, we do, of course, face a contradiction. After discussing various objections, Baumann concludes that it is not at all clear where we should look for a solution to the paradox.

Alfred Mele's chapter, "Outcomes of Internal Conflicts in the Sphere of *Akrasia* and Self-Control," examines more thoroughly the conditions under which agents confronted with internal practical conflicts either succumb to temptation or master it. Drawing from his previous work on action theory, he proposes a principled way of distinguishing various kinds of conflicts of the will. Agents either intend to act in accordance with a decisive belief that favors acting and then backslide due to competing intentions or they fail to make the transition from decisive belief to intention. Furthermore, given one's own standards, one can also change one's decisive belief resulting from motivational bias, or sometimes motivation can bias our beliefs. By introducing results from the psychological literature, Mele shows how these conflicts come about. As it turns out, in many cases agents are not helpless victims of strong temptations but fall prey to various forms of biases that have a disproportionate influence on the formation and retention of beliefs about what action is best. Mele thus provides a psychologically more adequate analysis of the sources of inner conflicts. This does not preclude their rational resolvability but, on the contrary, elucidates the constraints involved with rational self-control.

Not White, nor Baumann, nor Mele questions the rational resolvability of practical conflicts in general, but each focuses on specific kinds of problems pertaining to its difficulty. Similarly, Peter Schaber and Jon Elster are concerned with moral dilemmas, and both explore under what conditions such dilemmas arise.

Peter Schaber's chapter, "Are There Insolvable Moral Conflicts?," presents an analysis of the conditions that must hold for moral conflicts to be reasonably called "insolvable" so as not to issue in categorical prescription on action. He demonstrates that conflicts of this kind are best conceived as conflicts between moral reasons. If there are further reasons contrary to weighing the moral reasons at stake, then moral reasons can be considered practically incommensurable. Yet conflicts between incommensurable moral reasons turn out to be nonresolvable only if these reasons are "symmetrical." In most cases, however, they are asymmetrical, and the agent can arrive at an all-things-considered judgment regarding what he ought to do.

In "Moral Dilemmas of Transitional Justice," Jon Elster focuses on a field of study that has, so far, received no attention within the debate on practical conflicts. He is particularly concerned with conflicts arising in the political realm and investigates the kinds of moral dilemmas and conflicts of justice that arise in the transition process from predemocratic regimes to democracy. Drawing extensively from empirical material (e.g., concerning the restoration or introduction of democracy in many European countries and Japan after 1945, in Eastern European countries after 1989, or recently in South Africa), he shows how our intuitions remain mute or torn with regard to our ability to come to terms with the predemocratic past. The historical evidence casts light on how irresolvable dilemmas arise between procedural and substantive, consequentialist and nonconsequentialist principles of justice regarding the compensation of suffering, the restitution of property, and the assessment of personal responsibility in trials for wrongs committed under predemocratic regimes. While there is no formula for balancing conflicting principles, Elster reckons that either principle is defensible up to a point, though either becomes absurd if taken to the extreme.

Such more critical approaches, then, differ from those that focus exclusively on the possibility of rational resolution to practical conflicts in two respects. They either

1. center on the various conditions that account for the difficulty of rationally resolving many conflicts – for example, a lack of a definite standard for rational comparison (White), contradictory attitudes toward goals (Baumann), how bias affects our ability to make choices about how best to act (Mele), and how changes in institutional conditions can result in the application of conflicting principles of justice (Elster), or
2. subscribe to the view that there are reasons that remain in force despite the potential difficulty of a rational resolution to a practical conflict.

This view stems from the idea that there is something unfortunate about conflicts even if they can rationally be resolved. What remains unfortunate is attributed to reasons that in general we cannot perfectly conform to (Raz), to particular kinds of reasons that remain in force due to valuable pursuits engendered by our commitments (Betzler), or to incommensurable moral reasons that are symmetrical (Schaber). However, none of these accounts is incompatible with the rationalist view that the rational resolution of practical conflicts is largely possible.

While critics of rationalism present various arguments specifying why and under what conditions the rational resolution of conflicts is inadequate or simply not enough, it has rarely been acknowledged (at least not in this context) that the limitations posed by practical conflicts might also yield advantages.

In Barbara Guckes's chapter, "Do Conflicts Make Us Free?," the question is raised as to what extent genuine practical conflicts provide us with the sole conditions under which it is intelligible to consider ourselves free and responsible agents. She draws on the recent incompatibilist debates on free will, which stipulate that an agent can act freely only in genuine conflicts. Genuine conflicts present the only conditions under which a person seems free (i.e., indetermined) to act either way between two conflicting alternatives, yet with the capacity to control his respective choices in accordance with his reasons. Hence, the lack of stronger action-guiding reasons may leave us with a pocket of freedom. After discussing various recent incompatibilist theories (attempting to show how an agent can be free, i.e., indetermined in the face of conflicting options, and yet in rational control of her action), Guckes agrees that, if we can act freely at all, we can do so only in practical conflicts. She concludes, however, that none of the theories succeed in showing how it is possible for an agent to rationally control an indetermined action. Hence, even practical conflicts do not seem to yield the pocket of freedom that we had hoped for.

To be sure, the contributions to this collection are not the only possible answers to the intricate problems that practical conflicts continue to pose. However, we believe that they cover a broad range of new analyses that provide a better understanding of the sources and conditions under which practical conflicts arise and that they also clarify how we should conceive the challenge to the scope of practical reason and how it can eventually be met.

In addition to conflicting desires, moral obligations, or values, we encountered conflicts between moral and immoral motives (Velleman, Korsgaard), conflicts of virtues (White), conflicts of commitments (Betzler), conflicts of attitudes toward goals (Baumann), and conflicts of justice (Elster). Our initial thesis stated that further analysis of the sources of practical conflicts provides the key to understanding what role practical reason can play with regard to them. This volume contains various suggestions regarding a more adequate conception of the sources of practical conflicts that enable us to spell out more clearly what practical reasoning can achieve. Tentatively, we may conclude from the contributions collected in this volume that investigations into the rational resolvability of conflicting motives or values either

1. concentrate on further specifications or broadenings of reason-providing features (features that lead us rationally to resolve

conflicts and to produce assessments of betterness (Richardson, Chang, Levi)) or

2. focus on the conditions that render reasons normative, despite possible hurdles and difficulties (e.g., the rationality of persons and the normativity of pure practical reason (Velleman, Korsgaard)).

Analyses of the conditions that make it systematically hard to resolve conflicts or that reveal potential resolutions to practical conflicts as inadequate concentrate either

3. on the question of how reasons continue to remain binding (Raz, Betzler, Schaber) or

4. on the sources preventing us from assessing what we (as deliberating agents) should do, all things considered (White, Baumann, Mele, Elster).

We hope that the focus on practical conflicts presented in this volume will help to show that there are more refined ways practical reason can be put to work. Potentially, our discussions reveal that there is (as Bernard Williams once pointed out) another "deliberative route,"[32] if not various deliberative routes, that our reasoning can take in light of the various conflicts we can imagine. Furthermore, the fact that some conflicts remain difficult to resolve may more clearly reveal the way in which practical reasoning remains constrained. The contributions to this volume indicate that the dispute between rationalists and their critics has become more intricate. But what divides them is the perspective they take on practical conflicts and the assumptions those conflicts are based on regarding the relationship between practical reasons, their reason-providing sources, and the task of practical reason. Future research may provide us with further insights into the conditions of that relationship.

Notes

We are grateful to Carla Bagnoli, Rüdiger Bittner, Christian Budnik, Jon Cameron, Barbara Guckes, Henry Richardson, Vicki Velsor, and R. Jay Wallace for helpful comments on earlier drafts of this introduction.

1. See McConnell 1988: 25, who characterizes interpersonal moral conflicts thus: "one agent, P_1, ought to do a certain act, say A, a second agent, P_2, ought to do a different act, say B, and though each agent can do what he ought to do, it is not possible both for P_1 to do A and for P_2 to do B" (see also Marcus 1980: 121f.). Many interpersonal conflicts are not moral conflicts (see, e.g., some of the coordination problems in game theory), and many moral

conflicts are, of course, not interpersonal conflicts (in the sense above), since a single agent can face a moral conflict.

2. This tentative explanation should not be taken as a definition. The conflict of reasons must also be so serious that the agent is conflicted, and therefore starts to deliberate (we return to this point below).

3. Applying the term "practical conflict" to trivial cases such as the one above would "inflate" the meaning of the term: Almost every decision situation would constitute a practical conflict. This use of the term would, of course, not be illuminating at all.

4. See, e.g., Walzer 1972/73: 166.

5. See the contributions in Gowans 1987 and Mason 1996. See also Sinnott-Armstrong 1988.

6. Or conflicts of virtues: A person might, for instance, be both courageous and kind; on one particular occasion, however, it might not be possible to act on both virtuous dispositions.

7. See, e.g., Nagel 1979; Williams 1981; Stocker 1990.

8. See, e.g., Mele 1987; Fischer and Ravizza 1998. For an overview of the problem of weakness of will, see Walker 1989.

9. We certainly do not want to say that all practical conflicts are clearly either moral or nonmoral conflicts; perhaps there are even no, or only very few, clear and pure cases of moral or nonmoral conflicts. Perhaps the moral or nonmoral character of a practical conflict is nothing but a matter of degree. Be that as it may, the distinction itself seems very helpful.

10. See, e.g., Watson 1975; Frankfurt 1988a; Velleman 1992; Bratman 2000.

11. Obviously, there are many more theories of practical reason. However, the ones mentioned are not only the most widespread ones in contemporary practical philosophy. They are also the main target of those who claim that practical conflicts reveal the limited scope of practical reason.

12. See Kant, *Grundlegung zur Metaphysik der Sitten*, Books 1 and 2.

13. See Hume, *A Treatise of Human Nature*, Book II, iii.

14. See, for example, Mill, *Utilitarianism*. Even though Mill distinguishes between two different kinds of pleasure, pleasure still represents the only value. Sidgwick, *The Methods of Ethics*, believes that there is always a more general and more authoritative value to be found that allows one to assess seemingly conflicting values. See Griffin 1986: chs. 1–2, for an account of informed desire satisfaction. See also Hume, *A Treatise of Human Nature*, Book II.iii. Slote 1985 argues, however, that utilitarianism can allow for the possibility of genuine practical conflicts.

15. See, e.g., Slote 1989.

16. See von Neumann and Morgenstern 1953: 26–7; Sen 1970: 8f.; Savage 1972: 18.

17. See, e.g., Berlin 1969; Williams 1973; Nagel 1979; Raz 1986; Wiggins 1997.

18. See, e.g., Conee 1989: 139f.

19. Some assume that there are moral dilemmas:

> (1) An agent S ought to do A and S ought to do B but S cannot do (both A and B).

If one adds two further, rather plausible assumptions, a contradiction can be derived. First, the "agglomeration principle" tells us that

(2) If S ought to do A and if S ought to do B, then S ought to do (both A and B).

(1) and (2) imply

(3) S ought to do (both A and B).

Another very plausible principle tells us that

(4) *Ought* implies *Can.*

(3) and (4) imply

(5) S can do (both A and B),

which contradicts (1). Hence, we have to give up at least one of the three assumptions: that there are moral dilemmas, that the agglomeration principle is true, or that *ought* implies *can*. See, among many: Williams 1973 and the contributions in Gowans 1987 and Mason 1996.

20. See, e.g., Walzer 1972/73; Gowans 1994; Greenspan 1995.

21. See Lukes 1997.

22. See Williams 1973: 177ff.; Marcus 1980; Sinnott-Armstrong 1988: 44ff.; Hurka 1996; Bagnoli 2000.

23. See Raz 1986: ch. 13; Griffin 1986; Stocker 1990: chs. 4 and 5; Anderson 1993: ch. 3; Richardson 1994: ch. 5; Richardson 2001; Broome 1999; also see the overview in Chang 1997a and the anthology Chang 1997b. One could also say: If neither option A nor option B is better than the other, and if there is or could be a third option C such that C is better than A but not better than B, then A and B are incommensurable (see Raz 1986: 325f.). Incommensurability is not compatible with one of the crucial assumptions of rational choice theory: the connectedness or completeness axiom (see, e.g., Luce & Raiffa 1957: 23, 25): An agent either prefers one of two options to the other or is indifferent between the two options. However, incommensurability is compatible with the absence of a common unit of measurement. For example, there is no common scale of measurement shared by the option to throw oneself into the mud and the option to have a nice cup of coffee; however, there is no doubt that under normal circumstances one would clearly prefer the latter to the former.

24. Some philosophers think that there is a fourth possibility. See, e.g., Griffin 1986: 81ff. for his account of "rough equality." See Chang 1997a: 25–7 and Chang 2002: ch. 5 for her account of "parity." We focus here on the usually held position that there are only three possibilities.

25. See Seung and Bonevac 1992; Broome 1997; Endicott 2000.

26. Broome 1997 argued that comparative terms in a natural language such as English can never determinately fail to apply.

27. Kantian as well as utilitarian approaches have derived the normative standing of moral reasons from different connections to value, such as our rational nature (Kant) or the promotion of well-being (utilitarianism). These connections lend moral considerations their normative force.

28. See, e.g., Foot 1978: 151ff.; cf. Lawrence 1995 and Frankfurt 2000. According to Raz 1999: chs. 11–13, moral reasons stem from a radically heterogeneous

group of values. Hence, there is no substantive unity to morality as a normative domain.

29. See, e.g., Frankfurt 1988b; McIntyre 1993; Arpaly 2003: ch. 2. Some propose to describe weakness of will in terms of value incommensurability: The agent acts on one value commitment that remains incommensurable with the value commitment she has to disregard in her decision. See, e.g., Nussbaum 1986: chs. 2–4; Wiggins 1991.

30. See, e.g., Watson 1975 with regard to a rational resolution of conflicts of the will; Hare 1981 and Donagan 1987 with regard to the rational resolution of moral dilemmas; and Griffin 1986: 81ff. with regard to forms of comparability.

31. A relation is a partial ordering of a domain A if and only if the relation is reflexive, antisymmetric, and transitive in A.

32. Williams 1995: 38 suggested that reasoning in the case of practical conflicts amounts to a new deliberative route opposed to mere means-end reasoning.

Bibliography

Anderson, Elizabeth. 1993. *Value in Ethics and Economics*. Cambridge, Mass.: Harvard University Press.

Arpaly, Nomy. 2003. *Unprincipled Virtue*. New York: Oxford University Press.

Bagnoli, Carla. 2000. Value in the Guise of Regret. *Philosophical Explorations* 3: 169–87.

Berlin, Isaiah. 1969. *Four Essays on Liberty*. Oxford: Oxford University Press.

Bratman, Michael. 2000. Valuing and the Will. *Philosophical Perspectives* 14: 249–65.

Broome, John. 1997. Is Incommensurability Vagueness? In Ruth Chang (ed.), *Incommensurability, Incomparability, and Practical Reason*. Cambridge, Mass.: Harvard University Press, 67–89.

Broome, John. 1999. Incommensurable Values. In John Broome, *Ethics Out of Economics*. Cambridge: Cambridge University Press, 145–61.

Chang, Ruth. 1997a. Introduction. In Ruth Chang (ed.), *Incommensurability, Incomparability and Practical Reason*. Cambridge, Mass.: Harvard University Press, 1–34.

Chang, Ruth (ed.). 1997b. *Incommensurability, Incomparability and Practical Reason*. Cambridge, Mass.: Harvard University Press.

Chang, Ruth. 2002. *Making Comparisons Count*. New York and London: Routledge.

Conee, Earl. 1989. Why Moral Dilemmas Are Impossible. *American Philosophical Quarterly* 26: 133–41.

Donagan, Alan. 1987. Consistency in Rationalist Moral Systems. In Christopher W. Gowans (ed.), *Moral Dilemmas*. Oxford: Oxford University Press, 271–90.

Endicott, Timothy. 2000. *Vagueness in Law*. Oxford: Oxford University Press.

Fischer, John Martin, and Mark Ravizza. 1998. *Responsibility and Control*. Cambridge: Cambridge University Press.

Foot, Philippa. 1978. *Virtues and Vices*. Oxford: Blackwell.

Frankfurt, Harry. 1988a. Freedom of the Will and the Concept of a Person. In Harry Frankfurt, *The Importance of What We Care About.* Cambridge: Cambridge University Press, 11–25.

Frankfurt, Harry. 1988b. Rationality and the Unthinkable. In Harry Frankfurt, *The Importance of What We Care About.* Cambridge: Cambridge University Press, 177–90.

Frankfurt, Harry. 2000. Rationalism in Ethics. In Monika Betzler and Barbara Guckes (eds.), *Autonomes Handeln.* Berlin: Akademie Verlag, 259–73.

Gowans, Christopher W. 1994. *Innocence Lost.* An Examination of Inescapable Wrongdoing. New York: Oxford University Press.

Gowans, Christopher W. (ed.). 1987. *Moral Dilemmas.* Oxford: Oxford University Press.

Greenspan, Patricia S. 1995. *Practical Guilt: Moral Dilemmas, Emotions, and Social Norms.* New York: Oxford University Press.

Griffin, James. 1986. *Well-Being: Its Meaning and Measurement.* Oxford: Oxford University Press.

Hare, Richard M. 1981. *Moral Thinking: Its Levels, Method, and Point.* Oxford: Clarendon.

Hume, David. 1978. *A Treatise of Human Nature,* 2nd ed., ed. Peter H. Nidditch. Oxford: Clarendon.

Hurka, Thomas. 1996. Monism, Pluralism, and Rational Regret. *Ethics* 106: 555–75.

Kant, Immanuel. 1902ff. *Grundlegung zur Metaphysik der Sitten.* In Immanuel Kant, *Gesammelte Schriften* (Akademie-Edition). Berlin: G. Reimer.

Lawrence, Gavin. 1995. The Rationality of Morality. In Rosalind Hursthouse, Gavin Lawrence, and Warren Quinn (eds.), *Virtues and Reasons: Philippa Foot and Moral Theory.* Oxford: Clarendon, 89–147.

Luce, R. Duncan, and Howard Raiffa. 1957. *Games and Decisions. Introduction and Critical Survey.* New York: Wiley.

Lukes, Steven. 1997. Comparing the Incomparable: Trade-offs and Sacrifices. In Ruth Chang (ed.), *Incommensurability, Incomparability, and Practical Reason.* Cambridge, Mass.: Harvard University Press, 184–95.

Marcus, Ruth Barcan. 1980. Moral Dilemmas and Consistency. *Journal of Philosophy* 77: 121–36.

Mason, Homer E. (ed.). 1996. *Moral Dilemmas and Moral Theory.* Oxford: Oxford University Press.

McConnell, Terrance C. 1988. Interpersonal Moral Conflicts. *American Philosophical Quarterly* 25: 25–35.

McIntyre, Alison. 1993. Is Acratic Action Always Irrational? In Owen Flanagan and Amélie Rorty (eds.), *Identity, Character, and Morality.* Cambridge, Mass.: MIT Press, 379–400.

Mele, Alfred. 1987. *Irrationality.* New York: Oxford University Press.

Mill, John Stuart. 1998. *Utilitarianism.* Oxford: Oxford University Press.

Nagel, Thomas. 1979. The Fragmentation of Value. In Thomas Nagel, *Mortal Questions.* Cambridge: Cambridge University Press, 128–41.

Neumann, John von, and Oskar Morgenstern. 1953. *Theory of Games and Economic Behavior.* Princeton, N.J.: Princeton University Press.

Nussbaum, Martha. 1986. *The Fragility of Goodness.* Cambridge: Cambridge University Press.

Raz, Joseph. 1986. *The Morality of Freedom.* Oxford: Clarendon.

Raz, Joseph. 1999. *Engaging Reason.* Oxford: Oxford University Press.

Richardson, Henry. 1994. *Practical Reasoning about Final Ends.* Cambridge: Cambridge University Press.

Richardson, Henry. 2001. Commensurability. In *The Encyclopedia of Ethics,* 2nd ed., ed. L. C. Becker and C. B. Becker. London: Routledge, 258–62.

Savage, Leonard. 1972. *The Foundations of Statistics.* New York: Dover.

Sen, Amartya. 1970. *Collective Choice and Social Welfare.* San Francisco, Calif.: Holden-Day.

Seung, T. K., and Daniel Bonevac. 1992. Plural Values and Indeterminate Rankings. *Ethics* 102: 799–813.

Sidgwick, Henry. 1981. *The Methods of Ethics,* 7th ed. Indianapolis, Ill.: Hackett.

Sinnott-Armstrong, Walter. 1988. *Moral Dilemmas.* Oxford: Basil Blackwell.

Slote, Michael. 1985. Utilitarianism, Moral Dilemmas, and Moral Cost. *American Philosophical Quarterly* 22: 161–68.

Slote, Michael. 1989. *Beyond Optimizing: A Study of Rational Choice.* Cambridge, Mass.: Harvard University Press.

Stocker, Michael. 1990. *Plural and Conflicting Values.* Oxford: Oxford University Press.

Velleman, David. 1992. What Happens When Someone Acts? *Mind* 101: 461–81.

Walker, Arthur F. 1989. The Problem of Weakness of Will. *Nous* 23: 653–75.

Walzer, Michael. 1972/73. Political Action: The Problem of Dirty Hands. *Philosophy and Public Affairs* 2: 160–80.

Watson, Gary. 1975. Free Agency. *Journal of Philosophy* 72: 205–20.

Wiggins, David. 1991. Weakness of Will, Commensurability, and the Objects of Deliberation. In David Wiggins, *Needs, Values, Truth: Essays in the Philosophy of Value,* 2nd ed. Oxford: Basil Blackwell, 239–67.

Wiggins, David. 1997. Incommensurability: Four Proposals. In Ruth Chang (ed.), *Incommensurability, Incomparability, and Practical Reason.* Cambridge, Mass.: Harvard University Press, 52–66.

Williams, Bernard. 1973. Ethical Consistency. In Bernard Williams, *Problems of the Self.* Cambridge: Cambridge University Press, 166–86.

Williams, Bernard. 1981. Conflicts of Value. In Bernard Williams, *Moral Luck.* Cambridge: Cambridge University Press, 71–82.

Williams, Bernard. 1995. Internal Reasons and the Obscurity of Blame. In Bernard Williams, *Making Sense of Humanity and Other Philosophical Papers.* Cambridge: Cambridge University Press, 35–45.

2

Willing the Law

J. David Velleman

Kant believes that we must come up against practical conflicts in order to feel the normative force of morality, because that force consists in our own unwillingness to live with practical conflicts of two kinds: contradictions in conception and contradictions in the will. Every instance of immorality is, according to Kant, an instance of one or the other conflict; and only by recognizing and recoiling from these conflicts do we come under the guidance of morality. Because these conflicts are contradictions, they are conflicts of reason, and their instances are irrational as well as immoral. We come under moral guidance, then, in recognizing and recoiling from conflicts of practical reason.

I am going to argue against Kant's account of contradictions in the will, and in favor of an alternative account, which I shall call "concessive." My arguments will imply that Kant is wrong about one of the ways in which wrongdoing is irrational, and hence about one of the ways in which we are guided by morality.

Kant is committed to the proposition (i) that wrongdoing entails irrationality in the agent, since a perfectly rational agent always does the right thing. He is also committed to the more specific proposition (ii) that wrongdoing entails irrationality in the action, since the balance of valid reasons for acting always favors doing the right thing. The latter, more specific proposition has often been the target of criticism.[1] The reasons there are for an agent to act seem to depend on aspects of his circumstances and psychological makeup that cannot be guaranteed to harmonize with what's right. A particular agent can therefore be a "hard case" in the sense that the right act is one that he has no reason to perform.[2] A proposition to which Kant is committed thus appears to be false.

In the debate over this proposition, Kantians have pointed out that a person can indeed be a hard case in the sense that he is not moved by reasons for him to do right; but in that instance, he is not exempt from those reasons but rather irrationally insensitive to them.[3] What depends on the agent's psychological makeup, then, is whether he is rational in responding to reasons for doing right, not whether such reasons apply to him.

Although I have in the past seconded this response to the critics of Kantianism,[4] I am also tempted to make a more concessive response. I am tempted to concede that an agent may do something wrong, not because he is insensitive to reasons for doing right, but because he has no such reasons. Yet having conceded that an agent can lack sufficient reason for doing the right thing, I would insist that such an agent is nevertheless irrational. I am therefore inclined to assert proposition (i) but deny (ii). The resulting view is what I shall call "concessive Kantianism."

My goal in this chapter is not so much to defend concessive Kantianism as to explain it and to show that it may in fact be implicit in a prominent reconstruction of Kantian ethics. I'll begin by explaining how an immoral act can be rational in itself while being the act of an irrational agent. The explanation will be that an agent can be irrational by virtue of having a problematic set of reasons for acting, even though he proceeds to take the course of action favored by the balance of those reasons. The result is a rational act performed by an irrational agent.[5]

This explanation commits me to evaluating an agent as rational or irrational on the basis of the reasons that he has for acting. It therefore commits me to holding an agent responsible for the reasons available to him. After offering a rather breezy defense of this commitment, I'll point out that it originates in the moral psychology of Kant's *Groundwork*. Indeed, Kant himself is committed to holding an agent responsible for his reasons in an especially rigorous way, and here is where my version of Kantianism makes its characteristic concession. I'll try to explain why my concessive way of holding an agent responsible for his reasons should be preferred to Kant's. Finally, I'll argue that this concessive version of Kantianism is implicit in the reconstruction of Kantian ethics recently offered by Christine Korsgaard in the symposium on her Tanner Lectures (1996b).

The upshot will be a novel account of contradictions in the will – the second and, I think, less obvious kind of practical conflict that we are enjoined to avoid in Kantian ethics. I call the account novel not to boast but to concede that it is historically inaccurate. Then again, maybe Kantian ethics could do with a little less historical accuracy.

AN IRRATIONAL SORT OF PERSON

Let me turn, then, to my exposition of the view that I call concessive Kantianism. And let me begin by illustrating the view with an example borrowed from Bernard Williams:[6]

Suppose, for example, I think someone . . . ought to be nicer to his wife. I say, "You have a reason to be nicer to her." He says, "What reason?" I say, "Because she is your wife." He says – and he is a very hard case – "I don't care. Don't you understand. I really do not care." I try various things on him, and try to involve him in this business; and I find that he really is a hard case: there is *nothing* in his motivational set that gives him a reason to be nicer to his wife as things are.

Here an orthodox Kantian may insist that the man doesn't need his "motivational set" to give him a reason for being nicer: He already has plenty of reasons. What his motivational set must give him is a motive responsive to those reasons, a motive in the absence of which the agent counts as irrational. The possibility that I am now entertaining, however, is that the agent may not have any reason for being nicer to his wife, and this because of his motivational profile. Given the sort of man he is, he may in fact have no reason to be nicer. But the sort of man who has no reason to be nice to his wife, I want to say, is an irrational sort of man to be.

How can someone be irrational when he is nevertheless acting on the balance of reasons that apply to him? How can he be irrational for failing to have the right reasons? The answer is that there is more than one way to be irrational.

On the one hand, a person is irrational if he lacks some capacities or dispositions that are essential to the activity of practical reasoning. If someone lacks the ability to recognize which considerations are the stronger reasons for him to act, or a disposition to be guided by such considerations, then he is deficient as a practical reasoner and hence irrational. On the other hand, a person can be irrational because his situation or personality presents him with reasons that hinder practical reasoning, without necessarily undermining his capacities as a reasoner.

Consider a person who is torn between two conflicting projects. He aspires to great wealth and success, for example, while also seeking a simple life of reflection and self-cultivation. He may be perfectly capable of

weighing the reasons that issue from these ideals, and perfectly responsive to the force of those reasons. Indeed, long experience with difficult
choices may have made him unusually adept at the art of deliberation.
Yet there is something irrational about being so conflicted, about holding
on to goals that cannot be jointly attained.

This example, underdescribed though it is, suggests that Williams's
hard case has been described even less adequately. Not even the most
demanding Kantian would balk at the idea of two people's having no
reason to be nice to one another, even if they happen to be married.
The Categorical Imperative doesn't require that everyone be nice to everyone else, and marriage is a context in which people can lose their
reasons for being nice. But in such cases, people have usually lost
their reasons for being married, or for living together in circumstances
that provide opportunities for being nice or the reverse. What Williams's
example invites us to imagine, I think, is a case in which a man isn't as
nice to a woman as he should be in light of their remaining together
as husband and wife. For some reason – and we imagine that the man
has a reason – he stays in the marriage while treating his wife as would
be appropriate only for a stranger or even an enemy. And now we have
imagined an agent who is, in some way that remains to be described,
committed to conflicting projects. Something in his life gives him reason
to be married to a woman to whom he is unsympathetic or even hostile,
and so there must be an underlying practical conflict of some sort.

One might argue that the man is failing to act on the reasons that
apply to him, because each of his conflicting projects gives him reason
to abandon the other. But reasons for abandoning a project tend to undermine the reasons that issue from it, and so the agent's reasons for
abandoning either project are undermined by his reasons for abandoning the other. The man's problem is not that he's inappropriately hostile
in light of his commitment to the relationship, since he has reason to
give up the relationship in light of his hostility; nor is the problem that
he's inappropriately committed to the relationship in light of his hostility,
since he has reason to give up the hostility in light of the commitment.
His problem is that he has gotten himself into a bind, which is a problem
merely in light of his being an agent.

We can thus describe this agent's problem in terms that abstract from
the particulars of his case: He is irrationally conflicted. This description
specifies the form of the agent's motivational set but not its content.

One might insist that the irrationality of being conflicted does too
depend on the content of the agent's motivational set. Being conflicted

is irrational, one might say, only because it frustrates the pursuit of a higher order end that any agent must have, the end of attaining his lower order ends. This end gives any agent reason to avoid having lower order ends that cannot be jointly attained, and hence to avoid conflicts. But this way of stating the problem is misleading and consequently unpersuasive. Can't an agent's motivational set fail to include the higher order motive that would give him the requisite end? What if an agent cares about his several ends but not about the master end of their joint attainment?

What's misleading about this statement of the problem is that, in mandating a higher order end, it seems to be mandating a motive, as an element of the agent's motivational set; whereas an agent's motivational set is supposed to represent the contingent, individually variable input to his practical reasoning. This statement of the problem therefore invites the question why an agent must have a motive toward attaining his lower order ends.

Yet if ends are conceived as variable between agents, because of arising from their individual motivational sets, then each agent must have something else – a project, it might be called – that isn't an end in this sense. An agent must have the project of coping with, or doing justice to, the reasons that issue from his motivational set (or from anywhere else, for that matter). The reasons there are for him to act define a practical problem for him, and he must have the project of solving such problems, if he is to be a rational agent. This project isn't an end because it isn't just given to the rational agent by the contingent elements of his motivational set; it's a prerequisite for his being a rational agent, who can regard his motivational set (or anything else) as a source of reasons.

So even if we start from the assumption that reasons for acting must issue from the projects represented in the agent's motivational set, we end up at the realization that an agent must have at least one additional project, simply by virtue of being an agent – namely, the project of coping with the reasons that issue from his motivational set, a project that requires a motivational set that issues in reasons with which he can cope. Since the reasons that issue from deeply conflicting projects are extremely difficult to cope with, being conflicted is a hindrance to the project of practical reasoning itself.

I want to say that this hindrance to the project of practical reasoning renders the conflicted agent irrational. In so saying, however, I seem to be blaming a difficult situation on its victim. How can an agent be irrational for facing a difficult practical problem?

At this point, a contrast with theoretical reasoning might be helpful. In theoretical reasoning, we must cope with the various reasons for belief that confront us – the evidence, the arguments, our prior assumptions, and so on. Our task is to arrive at a belief that accommodates these reasons as well as possible, as if it were the solution to a set of simultaneous equations. Some sets of equations admit of an obvious solution and are therefore easy to solve; but other sets admit of no solutions, in which case we are obliged to discount some of our evidence, discard some of our assumptions, or otherwise adjust the set of reasons to be accommodated.

In theoretical reasoning, our task is to cope as best we can with whatever reasons the world serves up to us. A difficult theoretical problem is an inscrutability in the world, not an irrationality in ourselves. But in practical reasoning, the reasons with which we must cope, the simultaneous equations that we must solve, are served up by our personalities and circumstances, which are partly our own responsibility. The man in Williams's example didn't just wake up in a bind: he probably got himself into a bind, by ignoring signs of trouble, shirking crucial choices, and making fateful compromises over time. More importantly, he can and ought to get himself out of his bind, though doing so will also take time. For he can and ought to resolve the conflicts in himself, by altering his motives or his circumstances, or both. So whereas a theorist with deeply conflicting evidence is merely unfortunate, an agent with deeply conflicting projects may be rationally criticizable, insofar as he is responsible for getting into, and is in any case responsible for getting out of, his own deliberative difficulties.

One might object that the epistemic agent can also avoid deliberative difficulties, simply by closing his eyes to recalcitrant evidence or closing his ears to distracting hypotheses. But such maneuvers would defeat the purpose of theoretical reasoning, which is to arrive at the truth, or at least at the hypothesis that best accounts for the phenomena, where the truth and the phenomena are fixed by the way the world is. By contrast, the purpose of practical reasoning is not just to cope with reasons that are fixed by the agent's current motives and circumstances, since changing his motives or circumstances often remains one of the agent's options, a possible outcome of his practical reasoning. The epistemic agent's predicament is defined by what the world is like, and he must cope with that predicament, because he cannot change it. But the practical agent's predicament is defined by what his life is like, and one of the resolutions available to him is to change his life. The practical agent can therefore be held rationally responsible for getting himself into, or not getting himself out of, the wrong predicaments, predicaments that are wrong in the sense that they confront him with a problematic set of reasons.

Kant is committed to holding an agent responsible for the reasons that apply to him. This commitment appears in Kant's doctrine of willing the law.

An agent wills the law, according to Kant, when he wills his maxim in the form of a law for all rational agents; and his maxim is a principle of practical reason, specifying a proposed course of action and his reasons for taking it.[7] The agent wills that the principle of taking that course for those reasons be valid for any rational agent, as it would have to be in order to be rationally valid at all, even for him.[8] Thus, when the agent acts for reasons, he acts on the basis of considerations that he has willed to be valid as reasons, for himself or anyone else.

In the form enunciated by Kant and adopted by contemporary Kantians, the doctrine of willing the law does not fit the process that I have imagined as making an agent responsible for the reasons that apply to him. But that orthodox form of the doctrine is also flawed, in my opinion; and its flaws turn out to coincide with its differences from the process that I have imagined. In my opinion, my concessions to the critics of Kant turn out to be an improvement over the orthodoxy.

In the process that I imagined above, an agent is responsible for the reasons that apply to him insofar as he is responsible for his personality and his circumstances, which at any particular time determine the set of applicable reasons. But the agent's responsibility for his reasons, in my conception, does not involve the capacity to decide, at a particular moment, which reasons apply to him. His personality and his circumstances determine the set of applicable reasons in a systematic way that is not up to him;[9] and because he cannot change his personality or his circumstances on the spot, he cannot immediately change the reasons that apply to him, either. He is responsible for the reasons that apply to him only because his choices over time have shaped, and will continue to shape, the attitudes, traits, and circumstances that determine the set of applicable reasons.

By contrast, Kant's doctrine of willing the law seems to imply that an agent is in a position simply to will that particular considerations have validity as reasons – as if their rational force were up to him. This implication follows from a combination of passages, as follows. First, Kant defines the will as "the capacity to act *in accordance with the representation* of laws, that is, in accordance with principles"; he adds that "[s]ince *reason* is required for the derivation of actions from laws, the will is nothing other than practical reason."[10] Kant subsequently asserts that "every rational being having a will" must exercise that will under the idea of freedom, because the will consists in practical reason and "[r]eason must regard itself as the author of its principles."[11] Thus, in any being with a will, practical reason must derive actions from laws of which it regards itself as the author; and those laws, as we have seen, are universalized principles of acting in particular ways for particular reasons. Any rational being must therefore purport to originate the principles expressing the validity of his own reasons for acting.

As I have said, I think that the orthodox Kantian doctrine of willing the law is flawed. I think that practical reason need not – indeed, cannot – regard itself as the author of its principles, because an agent cannot regard himself as originating the validity of his reasons for acting. I will now try to explain this flaw in the Kantian view and how it can be corrected.

The flaw in this conception of practical reason is that it cannot explain how an agent is guided by reasons for acting. The volition in which the agent wills the universal validity of his reasons is the same as the volition in which he wills his action, since his decision to act for those reasons "contains in itself its own universal validity for every rational being"[12] or is "also included as universal law in the same volition."[13] Because the agent's decision to act for reasons contains or includes his willing the validity of those reasons, it cannot be guided by any prior recognition of their validity. All that guides the agent's decision, according to Kant, is his recognition that he is not precluded from willing the universal validity of his reasons for acting. In framing his decision, the agent is not bound by any antecedently valid principles of practical reasoning other than the principle of framing his decisions as principles whose universal validity he can simultaneously will.[14]

Critics of Kant have long complained that when the Categorical Imperative is so understood, it does not constrain the agent's choices in the determinate way that morality constrains them, because it constrains their form but not their substance. I am not sympathetic to this complaint when it is directed against Kantianism as a moral theory, since I think that an important part of morality is precisely a constraint on the form rather than the content of the will. But I am sympathetic to the complaint when it is directed against Kantianism as a theory of practical reason. In this capacity, the Categorical Imperative implies that the reasons for an agent's decision must be reasons whose validity is willed in that very decision. And a decision that wills the validity of its own reasons cannot be guided by a recognition of their validity.

The only guidance available for such a decision is the guidance of the Categorical Imperative itself, which rules out deciding to act for reasons whose universal validity cannot simultaneously be willed. Within this purely formal constraint, the agent can decide to act for any reasons that he thereby wills to be universally valid. But how can the agent regard his decision as being guided by reasons whose validity he regards as being conferred on them by that very decision? How can he actually *be* guided by reasons so regarded?

A deeper aspect of this problem is that the validity of reasons is not the sort of thing that we ordinarily conceive as being subject to the will at all. A reason for acting is a consideration that purports to justify acting, and a valid reason is a consideration that, if true, really does justify what it purports to. But to justify something is to show (at least prima facie) that it is just, in the archaic sense of being in accordance with a *jus*, or rule of correctness. Hence a consideration justifies an action by tending to show that it would be a correct thing to do. How can the agent decide whether a consideration tends to show that a particular action would be correct?

If Kant were to acquiesce in this manner of speaking, he would point out that we are puzzled by the notion of an agent's deciding the justificatory force of reasons only because we assume that they must exert that force in relation to antecedently fixed rules of correctness for action. Perhaps we are improperly assimilating the case of action to that of belief, in which reasons must exert their justificatory force in relation to the antecedently fixed rule that a belief is correct only if true. A believer is in no position to decide which considerations shall have validity as reasons for belief, because he cannot decide which considerations show a belief to be correct in relation to the rule of truth. But in the practical case, the agent can decide the validity of reasons, Kant would argue, because he decides the rules of correctness as well: The autonomous agent adopts his own rules of correctness for action, subject only to the proviso that he adopt them in universal form, avoiding any rules that he cannot thus universalize.

Thus, Kant would say, we were puzzled about willing the law only because we had too narrow a conception of this process, as a process of willing merely that particular considerations should count as showing an action to be correct. That conception left us wondering how an agent could possibly decide the import that particular considerations would have for the correctness of an action. The answer is that we need a broader conception of willing the law, as a process of willing the rules of correctness themselves, and only thereby willing the validity of the associated reasons. The agent wills that actions of a particular kind shall be correct in circumstances of a particular kind – which amounts to willing that consideration of the circumstances shall tend to justify the actions.

Unfortunately, this clarification doesn't solve the problem. If one's actions are subject to no fixed rules of correctness other than a rule for willing what those rules of correctness shall be, then one cannot really place one's actions under rules of correctness after all, since one's latitude in willing those rules reveals that, when it comes to actions, anything goes. How can one make an action correct in the circumstances by willing it to be correct, given that one could equally have conferred such correctness on a different action? Willing the law now looks like an empty exercise in self-congratulation – a matter of ruling one's choice to be correct so that one can pat oneself on the back for choosing correctly.

Of course, Kant will respond that not *quite* anything goes when it comes to actions, because in willing rules under which his actions are correct, the agent is restricted to rules that he can will in universal form. Perhaps the rules that he adopts can be rules of correctness because they have been constrained by the master rule of universalization – that is, by the Categorical Imperative. Yet this response brings us back to the problem of empty formalism, regarded again as a problem in the Kantian conception of practical reason. When the agent doesn't know what to do, he looks for reasons to guide him; but all he finds, according to Kant, is a set of actions that (under some description) he could will to be universally correct in circumstances that (under some description) are similar to his. Even if we believe that this set would exclude any morally impermissible actions, we must doubt whether the agent can will distinctions of correctness among the remaining, permissible alternatives. Within the constraints of the Categorical Imperative, the agent appears to face an arbitrary choice among various universal rules, which would specify various actions as correct in light of the circumstances, variously considered, thereby constituting different considerations as reasons for taking different actions. Having decided to act under one of these rules, how can the agent regard it as conferring correctness on his action, or normative force on his reasons, given that he has simply adopted it from among various rules that would have constituted other permissible actions as correct, and other considerations as reasons?

Let me repeat that this problem is more difficult for a Kantian conception of practical reason than it is for Kantian ethics. The availability of many act descriptions that the agent could consistently incorporate into a universal law is not necessarily a problem for the Categorical Imperative in its capacity as a test of morality. The test of the Categorical Imperative applies to any description under which the agent proposes to act, and it yields an up-or-down verdict on the permissibility of acting under that description. Once the agent has discovered which of the available acts would be permissible, and which would not, he has completed the moral reflections required of him, according to Kant. But having sorted the available acts into the permissible and the impermissible, the agent has not yet completed his practical reasoning about which of the permissible acts to perform. He must still choose one of the permissible acts rather than the others, and he must choose it for reasons. (If he didn't have to choose on the basis of reasons, then his choice wouldn't have been constrained by the Categorical Imperative, since the necessity of choosing for reasons is what generates the need to universalize.) The problem is that the reasons favoring one permissible act or the other are reasons that the agent himself must will into validity as he chooses between them. So how can he look to the validity of these reasons as a basis on which to choose?

One might think that the problem is solved by the additional constraint of hypothetical imperatives, which require the agent to will adequate means to his ends. Yet hypothetical imperatives, too, are merely formal constraints that provide only minimal guidance. They require only that an agent either abandon an end or adopt adequate means to it; and in the latter case, only that he adopt some adequate means or other. Of course, many philosophers believe that such formal constraints exhaust the guidance available from practical reason, which does no more, in their view, than enforce consistency on an agent's choices. But this solution is not available to Kant, precisely because he regards every rational choice as adopting not just a particular action but a corresponding rule of correctness, which is more specific than the purely formal imperatives that constrain it. In choosing among the actions conducive to his ends, the agent must will a law conferring correctness on actions like his in circumstances like his, so that his choice is derived from a law of which he can regard himself as the author. (Otherwise, he wouldn't qualify as choosing at all, and unchosen behavior, not purporting to embody a rule, would not have to be universalizable.) [15]

Thus, the agent still appears to be engaged in an empty form of self-congratulation. The rule of correctness that ought to be the basis for a choice is only willed into force as the choice is being made. The problem is how the basis of a choice can be willed into being by the same volition as the choice itself.[16]

KORSGAARD'S CONCESSIVE VERSION OF KANT

Christine Korsgaard grapples with these problems in her Tanner Lectures, where she offers her own model of willing the law.[17] I am going to argue that Korsgaard comes close to adopting what I call concessive Kantianism; but first I'll need to explain how the relevant criticisms bear on Korsgaard's version of Kantian ethics.

In Korsgaard's version of Kantian ethics, willing the law is a matter of adopting a self-conception, or "practical identity." Korsgaard derives the notion of practical identities from the phenomenology of reflective agency:[18]

When you deliberate, it is as if there were something over and above all of your desires, something which is *you*, and which *chooses* which desire to act on. This means that the principle or law by which you determine your actions is one that you regard as being expressive of *yourself.* To identify with such a principle or way of choosing is to be, in St. Paul's famous phrase, a law to yourself.

Because an agent identifies with the principle that dictates his choice, the principle can actually be expressed as a self-conception:

An agent might think of herself as a Citizen of the Kingdom of Ends. Or she might think of herself as someone's friend or lover, or as a member of a family or an ethnic group or a nation. She might think of herself as the steward of her own interests, and then she will be an egoist. Or she might think of herself as the slave of her passions, and then she will be a wanton. And how she thinks of herself will determine whether it is the law of the Kingdom of Ends, or the law of some smaller group, or the law of egoism, or the law of the wanton that will be the law that she is to herself. (101)

As we have seen, the law with which the agent identifies, by adopting one of these self-conceptions, is in fact a principle of choosing to act in particular ways under particular circumstances – circumstances that the law constitutes as reasons for acting in those ways. Thus:

That you desire something is a reason for doing it from the perspective of the principle of self-love.... That Susan is in trouble is a reason for action from the perspective of Susan's friend; that the law requires it is a reason for action from the perspective of a citizen, and so forth. (243)

In sum, an agent adopts a principle that determines what counts as a reason, but he adopts that principle in the form of a conception of himself as someone's friend, or as a citizen of a nation, or whatever.

Korsgaard's lectures seem to equate practical identities with principles of choice. She appears to say that adopting the identity of Susan's friend just consists in identifying with particular principles of choice, such as the principle of helping Susan when she's in trouble. This view implies that insofar as the reason-giving import of Susan's troubles depends on whether the agent is her friend, it depends on whether the agent adopts particular principles of choice, including the principle that explicitly specifies her troubles as reasons. The view therefore implies that the agent can decide whether Susan's troubles have reason-giving force for him, simply by deciding whether to adopt a principle conferring such force upon them.

COHEN'S OBJECTION AND THE BEGINNING OF KORSGAARD'S REPLY

In the symposium on Korsgaard's lectures, G. A. Cohen objects that a law adopted at will by the agent can just as easily be repealed by the agent and therefore fails to bind him in any meaningful way: "[A]lthough you may be bound by a law that you can change, the fact that you can change it diminishes the significance of the fact that you are bound by it. There's not much 'must' in a 'must' that you can readily get rid of."[19] To say that "there's not much 'must'" is to say that almost anything goes, and so Cohen's objection to Korsgaard resembles the one that I raised earlier against Kant. In either case, the objection is that being adopted at will would drain rules or laws of any significant normative force.

Korsgaard's answer to this objection shows that her conception of willing the law already differs from the conception that I have attributed to Kant. Her answer begins with a point that Cohen himself has acknowledged, "that even if I can change the law that I make for myself, I remain bound by it until I can change it" (234). What this point reveals is that in Korsgaard's model, an agent's decision is constrained, not only by the principle of choice that he wills in making that very decision, but also by principles that he has willed on previous occasions. And the latter principles are antecedently available to guide the agent's present decision, unlike the principle that he wills in making the decision itself.

An agent can thus be guided, in making his present decision, by reasons whose validity he has willed in the past. Each time he has made a choice in the past, he has willed and thus committed himself to a principle dictating similar choices in similar cases, including cases that he might encounter in the future. If he now encounters such a case, he will be bound by his former commitment to that principle of choice. In time, the agent will find himself encumbered with commitments to many principles, of which it is likely that some will apply to any particular case he may encounter; and he remains encumbered by those commitments until he revokes them. On any particular occasion, the relevant principles will constitute various considerations as reasons for him to act.

With this background in place, Korsgaard is now in a position to answer Cohen's objection. The objection, remember, was that even if a principle adopted by the agent is binding until revoked, it does not significantly bind him given that he is empowered to revoke it. Korsgaard's answer to the objection is this: "[I]f I am to be an agent, I cannot change my law without changing my mind, and I cannot change my mind without a reason." Hence "we cannot change our minds about just anything" (234). Korsgaard derives this answer from the results of an earlier discussion, in which she put the point as follows:

If I am to regard *this* act, the one I do now, as the act of my *will*, I must at least make a claim to universality, a claim that the reason for which I act now will be valid on other occasions, or on occasions of this type. . . . Again, the form of the act of the will is general. The claim to generality, to universality, is essential to an act's being an act of the will.

A couple of paragraphs ago I put into the objector's mouth the claim that when I make a decision I need not refer to any past or future acts of my will. But now we see that this turns out to be false, for according to the above argument it is the claim to universality that *gives* me a will, that makes my will distinguishable from the operation of desires and impulses in me. If I change my mind and my will every time I have a new impulse, then I don't really have an active mind or a will at all – I am just a kind of location where these impulses are at play. And that means that to *make up my mind* even now – to give myself a reason – I must conceive of my reason as an instance of some general type. Of course this is not to say that I cannot ever change my mind, but only to say that I must do it for a reason, and not at random. (231–32)

We'll need to spend a moment analyzing this passage in order to understand Korsgaard's conception of willing the law.

In this passage, Korsgaard observes that making up one's mind requires one to adopt some stable or settled practical stance, which must consist in more than an occurrent impulse. From this observation, she infers that making up one's mind requires one to have a general principle, which will embody one's made-up mind. The conclusion of this inference has both subjective and objective aspects. The subjective aspect is that in order to *view* oneself as making up one's mind, one must view oneself as instituting a stable practical stance; and one must attain this view by framing one's decision in the form of a general principle that purports to cover occasions beyond the present. But one can thus purport to make up one's mind without actually succeeding, since the purportedly stable stance that one has instituted may consist in a general principle that one might instantly revoke at any time. Objectively speaking, then, making up one's mind requires not only that one's practical stance purport to cover future occasions but also that it really have some stability across the occasions that it purports to cover.

Korsgaard's argument continues from the latter, objective condition on making up one's mind. Before one can change one's mind, one must have succeeded in making it up one way or another, so that there is something for one to change; and in order to have made up one's mind one way or another, one must have arrived at a stance with some real stability. Hence one cannot change one's mind if it is unduly changeable, since what is unduly changeable does not amount to a made-up mind, to begin with. Changing one's mind entails becoming differently *minded*, which requires being antecedently minded in some determinate way, which in turn requires being resistant to undue change.

According to Korsgaard, this restriction on undue changes of mind restricts one to changes of mind for which one has a reason. What she says is that one must change one's mind "for a reason, not at random." Her thought appears to be that change at random is undue change, which made-up minds tend to resist, and that the opposite of change at random is change for a reason. If one changes one's mind at random, then it will not really have been made up, in the first place, and to that extent won't amount to a mind to be changed. But if one changes one's mind only for a reason, then one's mind, though proving to have been changeable, will not have been unduly so, and hence will really have been made up, after all. The requirement to have a reason for changing one's mind ensures that a change will amount to a transition between determinate ways of being minded rather than a dissolution of determinate mindedness altogether.

But now the problem of empty formalism reemerges. For if one's change of mind is not an undue change so long as it is based on a reason, then the ready availability of reasons will take the bite out of any restriction on changes of mind. In order to change his mind for a reason, the agent need only make the change under cover of a relevant principle, which will constitute some considerations as the requisite reasons. Of course, the agent may already be committed to principles about how and when to change his mind; but those principles will themselves be subject to reconsideration and revision, provided only that their revision be adopted under a yet further principle.

Let me clarify the problem by summarizing how it has arisen. Kant says that when an agent decides to take an action, he must will not just the action but also a relevant principle of correctness, which constitutes particular considerations as reasons for taking the action. We worried that giving the agent this much latitude to bless his own actions as correct, and thus to constitute considerations as reasons for taking it, would undermine the very possibility of correctness in actions, or of normative force in reasons for acting. When Cohen expressed this worry, in response to Korsgaard's reconstruction of Kant, her answer was that the agent's latitude is significantly restricted by the blessings he has conferred on actions in the past, whereby he committed himself to principles of correctness, and hence to reasons for acting, to which he remains committed.

What worries us now is that the agent's latitude cannot be restricted by past commitments, precisely because it undermines those commitments as well. No rational commitment is so binding that it cannot be revoked for good reasons – that is, on the basis of considerations tending to show that revoking it would be correct. Hence the agent's latitude to confer correctness on actions, and thus to constitute considerations as reasons, cannot be restricted by past commitments, because it includes latitude to confer correctness on the act of revoking those commitments, and thus to constitute reasons for revoking them. Although the agent has committed himself by blessing his actions in the past, he can always revoke those commitments under cover of a new blessing. *The problem is that reasons are too easy for the agent to conjure up, and so the solution cannot be that once having conjured them up, he needs a reason for conjuring them away.*[20]

THE REST OF KORSGAARD'S REPLY

Korsgaard's version of Kantian theory has various additional resources for addressing this problem. After I describe those resources, I will argue that they add up to what I call the concessive response to critics of Kant – the response that accepts the proposition designated (i) in my introduction, while rejecting the proposition designated (ii). (I do not claim that Korsgaard herself would add things up in the same way.)

The first of these resources is the claim that, with one important exception, the principles willed by an agent must be endorsements of his antecedent impulses toward acting:[21]

[T]he contrast between being motivated by reason and being motivated by affection . . . is, on my view, incoherent. To be motivated "by reason" is normally to be motivated by one's reflective endorsement of incentives and impulses, including affections, which arise in a natural way. (127)

The exception to this generalization is the case in which action is required or forbidden by the Categorical Imperative:[22]

It is only in cases of reflective rejection that the impulse to act or refrain has to "come from reason." For example, when I discover that my impulse to break a burdensome promise must be reflectively rejected, that discovery itself must be the source of a new impulse, an impulse to keep the promise. This second impulse is strictly speaking what Kant called "respect for law." But respect for law more generally is expressed by the standing commitment to act only on morally endorsable impulses. (127, n. 41)

Korsgaard thus arrives at what she calls a "double-aspect" theory of reasons for acting. Except in cases of acting purely out of respect for law, acting for a reason involves acting on the conjunction of an impulse and an endorsement of that impulse, which consists in a principle of acting on impulses of its kind. Although Korsgaard sometimes says, "A reason is an endorsement of an impulse" (154), her considered view is that a reason consists in the conjunction of the two: "Neither the incentive nor the principle of choice is, by itself 'the reason' for the action; rather, the reason is the incentive as seen from the perspective of the principle of choice" (243).

The upshot is that Korsgaard believes reasons for acting to be determined by the agent's motivational set, after all. The vast majority of reasons for acting are impulses as endorsed by principles of choice. The only exceptions are reasons that consist in laws that require the rejection of particular impulses as reasons. Thus, all reasons involve the endorsement or rejection of impulses, and to that extent, all reasons are impulse-based.[23]

Furthermore, Korsgaard believes that the impulses in an agent's motivational set are under his control to some small extent:

Our contingent practical identities are, to some extent, given to us – by our cultures, by our societies and their role structures, by the accidents of birth, and by our natural abilities – but it is also clear that we enter into their constitution. And this means that desires and impulses associated with them do not just *arise* in us. When we adopt (or come to wholeheartedly inhabit) a conception of practical identity, we also adopt a way of life and a set of projects, and the new desires which this brings in its wake.... The motives and desires that spring from our contingent practical identities are... in part the result of our own activity. (239–40)

Insofar as an agent is responsible for adopting identities and the motives that they entail, he is also responsible for the range of reasons that will be available to him. But his ability to alter the range of available reasons is limited. He can alter the range of available reasons only by adopting, shedding, or somehow modifying his practical identities, and this process takes time. Hence he cannot alter the available reasons on the spot: "Although I have just been suggesting that we do make an active contribution to our practical identities and the impulses that arise from them, it remains true that *at the moment of action these impulses are the incentives, the passively confronted material upon which the active will operates*" (240–1, emphasis added).

Finally, Korsgaard believes that the motives and principles associated with an agent's contingent practical identities can be genuinely normative even if they are ultimately in conflict with the Categorical Imperative. Discussing the case (introduced by Cohen) of a man whose practical identities include that of a Mafioso, Korsgaard says:

It would be intellectually tidy, and no doubt spare me trouble from critics, if I... said that only those obligations consistent with morality are "real" or in Cohen's phrase "genuine." Then I could say that it seems to the Mafioso as if he had an obligation to be strong and in his sense honour-bound, but actually he does not. I could say that there's no obligation here, only the sense of obligation: no normativity, only the psychic appearance of it.... But I am not comfortable with this easy way out, for a reason related to one of Cohen's own points – that there is a real sense in which you are bound by a law you make for yourself until you make another.... There is sense in which these obligations are real – not just psychologically but normatively. And this because it is the endorsement... that does the normative work. (257)

The endorsement that "does the normative work" of obligating the mobster to his mob is embodied in the principles that make up his identity as a Mafioso – principles of perfect loyalty to the mob and perfect ruthlessness to outsiders. And these principles underlie not only the mobster's obligations, when he is tempted to be less than completely loyal or completely ruthless, but also his reasons for being loyal or ruthless on occasions when he isn't tempted to be otherwise. If these principles can lend normative force to the obligations, then they must also be able to lend normative force to the associated reasons.[24]

Korsgaard believes that the normative force of these reasons, like that of the associated obligations, can ultimately be undermined by the mobster's more fundamental identity as a human being who must act for reasons, the identity that consists in his commitment to the Categorical Imperative: "If Cohen's Mafioso attempted to answer the question why it matters that he should be strong and in his sense honour-bound even when he was tempted not to, he would find that its mattering depends on the value of his humanity, and if my other arguments go through, he would find that that commits him to the value of humanity in general, and so to giving up his role as a Mafioso" (256). But Korsgaard does not say that the existence of this latent conflict between the mobster's commitment to humanity and his commitment to the role of a mobster already undermines the normative force of the latter commitment, even before the conflict is discovered and the latter commitment revoked. On the contrary, she says that the latter commitment gives rise to genuinely normative obligations.

The resulting view severely constrains an agent's latitude in constituting and reconstituting reasons for acting. Reasons for him to act must consist in impulses endorsed by principles; his impulses are "passively confronted material" that he cannot change at the moment of action; and his principles can be revised only on the basis of reasons, which themselves require passively confronted impulses and/or conflicting principles to dictate the revision. Hence the agent cannot simply conjure up reasons for acting, or reasons for revising his principles, since he is confined in both instances to reasons based either on impulses already available in his motivational set or principles already available among his practical identities. Changing the set of available reasons therefore requires substantive psychological change, which the agent cannot effect at will.

In sum, we can no longer object that anything goes for a rational agent. His psychological makeup now provides substantive constraints on his practical reasoning, and so his practical reasoning is no longer an empty form. At the same time, however, the agent's practical reasoning is no longer guaranteed to encounter a set of reasons that weighs in favor of moral action. That's why I think that Korsgaard's view has become concessive.

WHY KORSGAARD'S VERSION OF KANTIANISM IS CONCESSIVE

Consider again the mobster introduced by Cohen. This man may have inherited the practical identity of a mobster from his family, or adopted that identity on his own, or acquired it through some combination of these processes. In any case, his acquisition of that identity will have entailed the acquisition of associated desires and impulses, such as the desire to kill anyone who threatens the interests of the mob. When anyone threatens those interests, the desire to kill him will unavoidably arise as "passively confronted material on which [the mobster's] will operates." And his identity as a mobster will include principles endorsing such desires as reasons for acting. As endorsed by those principles, his murderous desires will have genuine normative force as reasons for the mobster to act. He will therefore have genuine reasons for committing murder.

To be sure, the mobster also has countervailing reasons, based in his fundamental identity as a human being, as expressed in the Categorical Imperative. But these reasons weigh against acts of murder only indirectly, by committing him to "giving up his role as a Mafioso." They are reasons for him to revoke his commitment to that more particular identity, which turns out to conflict with his underlying identity as a human being, and so they are reasons for him to become someone who no longer has reasons for committing murder. The mobster is irrational to commit murder, not because he doesn't have reasons for committing such an act, but rather because he has reasons against being the sort of person who has those reasons.

One might think that the mobster's fundamental commitment to his humanity, as expressed in the Categorical Imperative, militates directly against acts of murder, thus overriding the reasons generated by his identity as a mobster. The Categorical Imperative does militate directly against particular immoral acts in Kant's own version of the theory. Unfortunately, Korsgaard's version of the theory has eliminated the mechanism by which it militates against those acts.

In Kant's theory, the Categorical Imperative rules out particular acts only by ruling out the volitions behind them; and it rules out those volitions by requiring every volition to include not just the description of an action but also a universalized maxim of acting under that description – what Korsgaard calls a principle of choice. In order to commit a murder, the agent must will not just the particular killing but, at the same time, a principle of killing. And willing such a principle turns out to involve a contradiction. Because Kant's theory requires the agent to will the particular act only in conjunction with a principle, the contradiction involved in willing such a principle stands in the way of willing the act.

In Korsgaard's version of the theory, however, the agent may already be committed to the relevant principle by virtue of having adopted it earlier and not repealed it since. In that case, there would seem to be no need for him to will the principle afresh in acting on it again. Indeed, he would seem to be in no position to will the principle any more, given that he is already committed to it: He can no longer will it to be a law for him, because it already is one, whether he likes it or not. And if his volition to act need not encompass his principle as well, then the contradiction involved in willing the principle cannot pose any rational obstacle to the act.

Imagine that Kant himself wrote in Korsgaard's language of self-constitution. In that case, Kant would say that the Categorical Imperative requires that, in choosing to kill, the agent adopt the identity of a killer, by adopting a general principle of killing. Kant would add that adopting the identity of a killer entails a contradiction that consequently stands in the way of choosing to kill. But Korsgaard's view is that the agent may already *have* the identity of a killer, and so the contradiction that would be involved in adopting that identity no longer stands in his way.

The result of retroactively imposing Korsgaard's terminology on Kant himself is a theory of radical self-constitution: With every act, the agent re-adopts the relevant identities all over again, reconstituting himself as a killer with every killing, as a friend with every act of friendship, and so on. This theory raises the problem of empty formalism precisely because it has the agent reinventing himself from the ground up with every choice. Because the agent can reinvent himself, he can rewrite the set of available reasons, and so almost anything goes. Korsgaard solves the problem of empty formalism by restricting the scope of the self-constitution that accompanies a particular choice: The agent approaches each choice with antecedently fixed identities, which he can revise only within constraints fixed, in part, by those identities themselves. Unfortunately, this solution to the problem of empty formalism removes the mechanism by which the Categorical Imperative militates against individual actions, since the Imperative militates against actions only by requiring them to include bits of radical self-constitution that would be contradictory. I therefore suspect that Korsgaard cannot avoid the concessive version of Kantian theory, in which moral considerations do not necessarily provide sufficient reasons against immoral acts.

This concessive version of Kantian theory has the strength of entailing weaker consequences than the orthodox version. It doesn't imply that every agent, on every occasion, has reasons for acting that on balance forbid committing murder. It concedes that the first-order reasons available to a particular agent on a particular occasion – the reasons for choosing one action over another – may on balance favor his committing murder. It merely adds that someone who finds himself with such a set of first-order reasons will also have higher-order reasons for changing the reasons available to him, by changing himself. And then it adds the further concession that changing himself will take time.

Korsgaard puts the point like this:

> I am certainly not suggesting that the *rest of us* should encourage the Mafioso to stick to his code of strength and honour and manfully resist any wanton urges to tenderness or forgiveness that threaten to trip him up. The rest of us should be trying to get him to the place where he can see that he can't see his way to this kind of life anymore. (257)

In order to maneuver the Mafioso out from under the force of reasons for committing murder, then, we would have to "get him to a place" from which he could see something that he can't currently see from the place he's in, at the moment of pulling the trigger. Indeed, we'd have to get him to a place where he could turn around and see that he couldn't find his way back, a place that would therefore have to be far removed, in the space of reasons, from the place he currently occupies. Such changes of perspective cannot be brought about on the spot, when push has already come to shove, or shove to shoot.

Because this concessive Kantianism entails weaker consequences than the orthodoxy, it is harder to attack and easier to defend. Although Korsgaard suggests that it will evoke "trouble from critics," it will in fact disarm the traditional critics of Kant, who can no longer adduce the usual "hard cases" as counterexamples. The existence of hardened immoralists, who have no first-order reasons for doing the moral thing on some occasions, is perfectly compatible with the concessive version of Kantian theory. Critics will therefore have to go further afield for their counterexamples.

Here is a problem, though. If Korsgaard's version of the theory doesn't bring the Categorical Imperative to bear on particular murders, but only against being a person who has reason to commit them, then maybe it doesn't condemn murders as immoral; maybe all that it condemns as immoral is a willingness to acquire, or an unwillingness to shed, the identity of a murderer. This leniency may be implicit in Korsgaard's description of how "the rest of us" should regard the Mafioso. When she says that we "should be trying to get him to the place where he can see that he can't see his way to this kind of life anymore," perhaps she means that we should blame him for going astray in life but not for pulling the trigger here and now.

Note that *this* moral theory wouldn't fit my model of concessive Kantianism, since it would preserve the equivalence between morality and rationality in action. The mobster would have sufficient reason to commit murders, but the murders that he committed would not in themselves be immoral; what's immoral would be his acquiring or failing to shed the identity that provides his reason for murdering, and this act or omission would indeed be contrary to the balance of reasons for him to act. So the fact would remain, as stated in proposition (ii), that wrongdoing entails irrationality in action; the extension of the term "wrongdoing" would merely have shrunk, to include primarily acts of self-constitution rather than garden-variety, first-order acts.

But surely Korsgaard's concession to the normativity of the Mafioso's commitments is not meant to imply that they are normative in the moral sense. I assume that Korsgaard believes the mobster's killings to be morally wrong, even though he has normatively potent reasons, and perhaps even obligations, to commit them. I assume that when she recommends coaxing the Mafioso into a different "place," she doesn't mean that this therapeutic approach should preempt moral condemnation of his actions. The therapeutic approach is the only way to reason with the mobster, given that his existing identities support only a defective set of reasons; but gently reasoning him out of his identity as a mobster is meant to be compatible, I assume, with uncompromising condemnation of what that identity leads him to do.

I have no idea whether these suggestions capture Korsgaard's intentions, but I think that they capture what is plausible in her treatment of the case. And they imply that Korsgaard has brought us to a version of Kantian ethics in which morality and rationality really do come apart. In this version of Kantianism, which really is concessive, what rationality recommends on a particular occasion is that an agent do what he has the strongest reasons for doing, even if those reasons arise from an identity that's irrational for him to have. But morality requires an agent *not* to do things for reasons that arise from irrational identities: Morality requires him to act only on reasons that he could rationally have.

If this theory is right, then what becomes of reasons for being moral?

The theory insists that every agent has reasons for being a sort of person who has reasons for acting morally. In this sense, it insists on reasons for *being* moral. And the reasons for being moral, in this sense, are the ones defined by Korsgaard's version of contradictions in the will: They are reasons that arise from underlying conflicts between immoral identities and the Categorical Imperative, which expresses the fundamental identity of a person. Because of these conflicts, being an immoral person is an irrational way of being a person, and so it isn't a way that any person could rationally choose to be, or to continue being. Therein lies the contradiction in the will of an immoral person, according to concessive Kantianism.

But concessive Kantianism doesn't insist on reasons for *acting* morally – not, at least, for agents who have failed to heed their reasons for *being* moral. If an agent has overlooked or tolerated the contradictions involved in having an immoral identity, he may then have insufficient reason for acting morally, according to this theory. This much the theory concedes, not only to the critic of Kant, but also to the immoralist.

Even so, the theory has one remaining resource for softening this concession. It can point out that acting morally represents, as it were, a higher rationality – a rationality of acting on the reasons of one's ideally rational self rather than one's actual selves. What morality requires one to do may not be what one actually has reason for doing, but it is what one could have reason for doing if one had a rational set of reasons.[25] And the same cannot be said for immoral actions. To be sure, it's rational to act on the reasons one actually has, even if they favor acting immorally. But to act instead on reasons that it would be rational to have is not exactly irrational: it is rather extrarational, above and beyond the call of practical reason.[26]

Consider again how the Mafioso might find his way out of the bind created by his immoral identity. As Korsgaard points out, he might reason his way out, but only by way of a long and subtle train of reasoning, which is unavailable in the heat of the moment. Yet even in the heat of the moment, the mobster might simply step out of his bind: The scales might fall from his eyes, and he might drop his gun and walk away, never to return to his life of crime. (Of course, this sudden change of practical identities might not be accepted by his former associates without help from the Witness Protection Program.) In the latter case, I would say, the mobster would not be acting on the balance of reasons that were currently available to him. Rather, he would be rejecting some of the reasons available to him, thereby reconstituting his current set of reasons.

As I have said, the act of reconstituting his current set of reasons is not supported by the overall balance of reasons in that set. Shedding his identity as a mobster would be a betrayal of the mob and hence of the commitments fundamental to that identity. Hence it is not a rational step for the agent to take, all things considered. But the act of reconstituting his set of reasons is indeed supported by a crucial subset thereof – namely, the reasons arising from his underlying identity as a rational human being. And the agent can act on that subset of reasons while holding the others in abeyance; for he can think of himself merely as a human being, reflecting with critical detachment on his more specific identities. Thus, he can tentatively suspend his identity as a mobster for the sake of considering whether to reject it altogether.

Even this tentative suspension of an identity would not be rational for the agent, all things considered. His commitments to the mob strongly militate against even toying with the idea of betrayal. But he can still toy with the idea, albeit irrationally. Indeed, he can *literally* toy with it, by playing or pretending for a moment that he isn't committed to the mob. He can imagine himself to be only a part or aspect of everything that he is, so as to make believe that he is deciding from scratch what to be.[27]

Let me repeat that toying with an idea in this fashion would be an irrational process, since it would require the agent to pretend that he didn't have commitments and reasons that he actually has. But this irrational process would enable the agent to become a more rational person, who wasn't caught in a bind of conflicting reasons. The process would therefore constitute an irrational leap to a greater rationality – a leap of faith in the possibility of being more rational. Kant might call it a leap of faith in oneself as a person.

Notes

This chapter develops a suggestion that I make at the end of "The Self as Narrator," a paper on Dan Dennett's conception of the self (to appear in *Autonomy and the Challenges to Liberalism*, ed. Joel Anderson and John Christman (forthcoming)). Audiences to which I presented that paper have helped me to write this one; they include the philosophy departments at the University of Pittsburgh, the University of Maryland (College Park), and the University of Chicago. I am also grateful to Jerry Cohen, Tamar Schapiro, Nishiten Shah, and Ralph Wedgewood for comments on earlier drafts.

The issues discussed here are treated in terms that are less scholarly, but possibly clearer, in my "Brief Introduction to Kantian Ethics," which will appear in a volume of essays entitled *Self to Self* (forthcoming, Cambridge University Press). Until that volume appears, that essay will be posted on my Web page: http://www-personal.umich.edu/~velleman/.

1. See, e.g., Foot 1978a, 1978b; Williams 1981, 1995.
2. The phrase "hard case" comes from Williams 1995: 39.
3. See Korsgaard 1986.
4. See Velleman 1996.
5. A similar thesis is defended by Michelle Mason in her doctoral dissertation, "Moral Virtue and Reasons for Action"(2001); see esp. ch. 2.
6. 1995: 39. I have omitted a parenthetical remark that the "ought" in this passage is used "in an unspecific way" – which means, I take it, a way that isn't specifically moral. I have followed Williams in this respect by speaking of actions as "right" and "wrong" in senses that aren't necessarily moral.
7. For this conception of maxims, see, e.g., Korsgaard 1996a: 13: "Your maxim must contain your reason for action: it must say what you are going to do, and why."
8. In many formulations, the Categorical Imperative appears to require only that the agent be *able* to will that his maxim become a universal law. But the best justification for requiring that he be able to will the universalization of his maxim is that he must actually will it, or at least regard himself as willing it. And this necessity is indeed asserted in Kant's Formula of Autonomy: "The principle of autonomy is . . . : to choose only in such a way that the maxims of your choice are also included as universal law in the same volition" (*Groundwork of the Metaphysics of Morals*, 47 [4: 440]). See also 45 [4: 437–8], "the basic principle, act on a maxim that at the same time contains in itself its own universal validity for every rational being," and 46 [4: 438–9], "act in accordance with the maxims of a member giving universal laws for a merely possible kingdom of ends." (Note that in the last quotation, what is qualified as merely possible is, not the agent's willing of his maxim as a law, but the kingdom of ends that would exist if the law were universally obeyed.)
9. I haven't specified how the agent's motivational set determines the set of applicable reasons, because I disagree with Williams and other so-called internalists on this question. In particular, I don't believe that reasons applicable to an agent are dependent on his motivational set, as conceived by Williams, for their capacity to influence the agent's behavior.
10. *Groundwork*, 24 [4: 412]; see also 36 [4: 427].
11. *Groundwork*, 54 [4: 448].
12. *Groundwork*, 46 [4: 438–9].
13. *Groundwork*, 47 [4: 440].
14. See *Groundwork*, 40 [4: 442]: "[T]he human being . . . is subject *only to laws given by himself but still universal* and . . . he is bound only to act in conformity with his own will, which, however, in accordance with nature's end is a will giving universal law."

15. See the quotation from pp. 231–2 of Korsgaard's Tanner lectures (1996b), on p. 40 [of the present volume].

16. I think that there are cases in which practical reasoning takes this puzzling form, but they aren't cases that support the Kantian conception. For they are clearly unsuited to be a model of practical reasoning in general.

When you are tempted to eat or drink too much, to work or exercise too little, to shirk a social obligation or make an undue imposition – in short, to indulge yourself in some way – you tend to look for aspects of the occasion that make it unusual, precisely so that you can endorse such self-indulgence only on similarly unusual occasions, while continuing to condemn it more generally. These circumstances needn't be ones that you antecedently regard as positive reasons for self-indulgence: they may be as trivial as the fact that it's Tuesday. Yet if you allow yourself, say, to overeat in light of the fact that it's Tuesday, then you seem to make its being Tuesday a reason for allowing yourself to overeat. You thus seem able to choose what shall count as a reason for your action on this occasion and others like it.

I think that when you preemptively excuse or rationalize an action by finding an acceptable principle for it, you may indeed be in the position of willing the law; and your principle may indeed have justifying force insofar as you accept it under the constraint of having to accept it in universal form. Not just anything goes when it comes to self-indulgence, only those things which you're willing to accept as going in general – including, perhaps, overeating on Tuesdays, but not overeating every day. And because you've confined yourself to what you're willing to accept as going in general, you seem to be justified in letting it go today. So you seem to have willed your action into being correct, and your circumstances into being reasons for it.

Although such cases exemplify the Kantian conception of willing the law, they don't lend that conception much support. For they are cases not so much of adopting reasons as of adopting excuses or pretexts – cases in which your principles at best permit you to do something but don't positively guide you to do it. Again, your reasoning in these cases may be an adequate model of moral reasoning, insofar as moral reasoning is just a matter of asking, "May I?" But practical reasoning is not in general permissive, not just a matter of asking, "May I?" It's a matter of asking what you should do from among the many things that you may. Practical reasoning must give you a positive basis for choosing among the many morally permissible actions, and cases in which you adopt principles for permitting or excusing self-indulgence cannot be a model for such reasoning.

17. Korsgaard 1996b.

18. Korsgaard 1996b: 100. All parenthetical references from here on are to this volume.

19. Cohen 1996: 170.

20. The problem of empty formalism runs even deeper than Korsgaard's conception of practical reason: It runs all the way down to the agent's conception

of his own agency. For in Korsgaard's version of Kant, principles of choice are constitutive not only of practical reasoning but of the agent himself. Korsgaard puts the point most clearly in a recent article:

> To conceive yourself as the cause of your actions is to identify with the principle of choice on which you act. A rational will is a self-conscious causality, and a self-conscious causality is aware of itself as a cause. To be aware of yourself as a cause is to identify yourself with something in the scenario that gives rise to the action, and this must be the principle of choice. . . . You regard the choice as yours, as the product of your own activity, because you regard the principle of choice as expressive, or representative, of yourself. . . . Self-conscious or rational agency, then, requires identification with the principle of choice on which you act. (1999: 26)

Yet if the person casts himself as author of his actions by identifying with the principles that generate those actions, then how does he cast himself as the author of his principles, as Kant says he must? The answer would seem to be that he generates the principles of his actions from antecedent principles with which he also identifies. Yet this regress of principles cannot go on forever; and where it ultimately stops is at the Categorical Imperative, which is the principle simply of deriving things from principles – a purely formal principle, from which no particular substantive principles can be derived.

So here is the problem: Somewhere between the agent's commitment to the Categorical Imperative and his authorship of a particular action, he must acquire substantive principles without having prior principles sufficiently substantive to generate them. And those substantive principles, to which his action will be ultimately attributable, will not be attributable to him as their author. The empty formalism of the Categorical Imperative thus seems to have emptied human action of a responsible agent. (Readers of Harry Frankfurt may recognize this problem as the infinite regress of higher-order identifications)

21. Korsgaard bases this claim on her interpretation of Kantian ethics as a "reflective endorsement" theory. "That after all is the whole point of using the reflective endorsement method to justify morality: we are supposing that when we reflect on the things which we find ourselves inclined to do, we can then accept or reject the authority those inclinations claim over our conduct and act accordingly" (1996b: 89).

22. The passage quoted here expresses Kant's view. Korsgaard's view is that the impulse that Kant attributed to the Categorical Imperative can also be generated by the agent's other, contingent practical identities:

> In some cases our conception of a contingent practical identity will give rise to new motives in a way that parallels the generation of the motive of duty by the thought of the categorical imperative. You may be tempted to do something but find that it is inconsistent with your identity as a teacher or a mother or a friend, and the thought that it is inconsistent may give rise to a new incentive, an incentive not to do this thing. (239–40)

23. Why must the will operate on the agent's antecedent impulses? In a recent paper, Korsgaard answers as follows: "According to Kant you must always act on some incentive or other, for every action, even action from duty, involves

a decision on a proposal: something must suggest the action to you" (1999: 26). Yet in the Tanner Lectures, Korsgaard points out that an action can be suggested, not just by the agent's impulses, but by other agents (1996b: 139–40). And we might wonder, more generally, why a faculty that can be the author of its own principles cannot be the author of its own suggestions, too. This aspect of Kantian moral psychology seems undermotivated, to say the least.

24. Korsgaard describes the relation between obligations and reasons as follows:

> To make a law for yourself . . . is at the same time to give expression to a practical conception of your identity. Practical conceptions of our identity determine which of our impulses will count as reasons. And to the extent that we cannot act against them without losing our sense that our lives are worth living and our actions are worth undertaking, they can obligate us. (129)

25. Why do I say "what one *could* have reason for doing. . . . "? The reason is that if one has an irrational set of reasons, then there is no particular set of reasons that one would necessarily have if one had a rational set instead. There is no particular identity that the Mafioso would necessarily adopt instead of his identity as a mobster. There are many ways for him to be moral, and morality requires only that he adopt one of them.

26. What I'm suggesting, then, is that although the moral act is not always rationally required, under concessive Kantianism, it is at least rationally supererogatory.

27. For further discussion of this process, see Velleman 2002b. I discuss another instance of the same process in Velleman 2002a.

Bibliography

Cohen, G. A. 1996. Reason, Humanity, and the Moral Law. In Christine Korsgaard, *The Sources of Normativity*. Cambridge: Cambridge University Press, 167–70.

Foot, Phillipa. 1978a. Are Moral Considerations Overriding? In Philippa Foot, *Virtues and Vices*. Berkeley: University of California Press, 181–88.

Foot, Phillipa. 1978b. Morality as a System of Hypothetical Imperatives. In Philippa Foot, *Virtues and Vices*. Berkeley: University of California Press, 157–73.

Kant, Immanuel. 1997. *Groundwork of the Metaphysics of Morals*, tr. Mary Gregor. Cambridge: Cambridge University Press.

Korsgaard, Christine. 1986. Skepticism about Practical Reason. *Journal of Philosophy* 83: 5–25.

Korsgaard, Christine. 1996a. An Introduction to the Ethical, Political, and Religious Thought of Kant. In Christine Korsgaard, *Creating the Kingdom of Ends*. Cambridge: Cambridge University Press, 3–42.

Korsgaard, Christine, (with G. A. Cohen, Raymond Geuss, Thomas Nagel, and Bernard Williams). 1996b. *The Sources of Normativity*, ed. Onora O'Neill. Cambridge: Cambridge University Press.

Korsgaard, Christine. 1999. Self-Constitution in the Ethics of Plato and Kant. *Journal of Ethics* 3: 1–29.

Mason, Michelle. 2001. Moral Virtue and Reasons for Action. Ph.D. dissertation, University of Chicago.

Velleman, J. David. 1996. The Possibility of Practical Reason. *Ethics* 106: 694–726.

Velleman, J. David. 2002a. Identification and Identity. In Sarah Buss and Lee Overton (eds.), *Contours of Agency: Essays on Themes from Harry Frankfurt.* Cambridge, Mass.: MIT Press, 91–123.

Velleman, J. David. 2002b. Motivational by Ideal. *Philosophical Explorations* 5: 89–104.

Williams, Bernard. 1981. Internal and External Reasons. In Bernard Williams, *Moral Luck.* Cambridge: Cambridge University Press, 101–13.

Williams, Bernard. 1995. Internal Reasons and the Obscurity of Blame. In Bernard Williams, *Making Sense of Humanity and Other Philosophical Essays.* Cambridge: Cambridge University Press, 39–45.

3

The Myth of Egoism

Christine M. Korsgaard

Man does not pursue happiness. Only the Englishman does that.
Friedrich Nietzsche[1]

Many philosophers believe there is a principle of practical reason that directs the rational agent to maximize the satisfaction of his own desires and interests. I will call this "the egoistic principle," and the person who believes in it an "egoist." Some philosophers believe that conformity to the egoistic principle is equivalent to the pursuit of happiness, or – if these are different – to the pursuit of the individual's own good. In the social sciences, especially economics, it is widely believed that some form of the egoistic principle is both normative and descriptive: that is, that it tells us not only how we should act, but also how, at least in clear-headed moments, we do act. Philosophers who endorse this view sometimes take the egoistic principle to be *definitive* of practical rationality, and therefore suppose that the way to show that we have "reason to be moral" is to show that conformity to moral requirements will somehow maximize the satisfaction of our own desires and interests.

This is not, of course, how the rationality of morality has been understood in either the Kantian or the rationalist tradition. Both Kant and Sidgwick, for instance, claimed that the moral principle is a principle of reason in its own right.[2] But they also accepted the idea that something like the egoistic principle is a normative rational principle.[3] For Sidgwick, the egoistic principle is a rival to the moral principle of utility. Kant's various remarks about the nature of happiness are not entirely consistent, but at one point he defines it as "the sum of satisfaction of all inclinations" (G 4: 399).[4] Kant thinks that the rationality of pursuing one's own happiness is represented by the imperative of prudence, which he sometimes appears to believe governs the conduct both of wicked people all the time and of good people once the demands of morality are satisfied.[5] But both those who think that the egoistic principle is definitive of rationality and those who think there is a separate rational principle of morality commonly believe that the egoistic principle has an advantage over the moral one. The egoistic principle, they suppose, more obviously meets the requirement of internalism – that is, the requirement that practical reasons must be capable of motivating us – since the egoistic principle essentially tells us to do what we want most. Even Kant believed that imperatives of prudence are hypothetical imperatives whose normativity can be established just as easily, and on essentially the same grounds, as that of instrumental principles. Contemporary egoists go one step further, and suppose that egoism is an expression of the instrumental principle itself. Egoism sees itself as a naturalistic view, which requires no extravagant assumptions about the metaphysics of the good or the possibility of pure practical reason.

In this chapter I will present some reasons for doubting these familiar views. In Part I, I will examine some possible views about the normative foundations of the egoistic principle. I will argue that the view that egoism is a form of instrumentalism is based on a pair of false assumptions about the nature of practical rationality. When we abandon these assumptions, it becomes clear that the idea of a maximum of satisfaction is a substantive conception of the good. Egoism, I will argue, is essentially a rationalistic position: its normativity is grounded in a non-natural conception of the good, and its psychology requires the possibility of motivation by pure practical reason. In Part II, I will take a closer look at the content of this conception of the good. I will ask what exactly we must mean by a "maximum of satisfaction" if that idea is to ground a principle which is at once both plausibly rational and distinctively egoistic. I will argue that the relevant conception of the good is one recognizably grounded in the psychological assumptions of classical eighteenth-century British empiricism. Egoism therefore requires a familiar empiricist conception of the good, whose normativity can be defended only on rationalist grounds. It does not therefore follow that it is an incoherent position. It does however follow that it cannot be defended on any of the grounds which egoists usually offer in its favor.

I. NORMATIVE FOUNDATIONS FOR THE EGOISTIC PRINCIPLE

Instrumental Egoism

Not everyone believes that any argument needs to be made for the normativity of the egoistic principle. Characteristically, philosophers and social scientists who believe that the egoistic principle is definitive of practical rationality also consider themselves to be instrumentalists about practical reason. That is, they endorse the view that the only principle of practical reason is the principle that directs us to take the means to our ends. For shorthand, I am going to call this position "instrumental egoism" and the person who believes it an "instrumental egoist." Instrumental egoists usually also believe that the instrumental principle itself is either obviously normative or does not need to be normative, since we are in fact motivated to act in accordance with it. Elsewhere I have argued, as against that last view, that the instrumental principle is normative and that an account of its normative force is therefore required.[6]

However that may be, the view that egoism is a form of instrumentalism is incoherent on its surface. The instrumental principle tells us only that we must take the means to our ends; it says nothing whatever about what our ends should be. It therefore does not say either that we ought to pursue a maximum of satisfaction, or that we ought to prefer that maximum to the satisfaction of particular desires in cases of conflict. Since egoism requires us both to pursue a specific end and to prefer that end to all others, it has to go beyond the theory that all practical reasons are instrumental.

But instrumental egoists deny that the egoistic principle requires you to pursue a specific end. Happiness in the egoist's sense is supposedly not a specific end: it is just the maximum realization of the ends you already have. And more generally, all that the principles of rational choice do is apply some formal structure to the ends, whatever they might be, that are fed into its formulas. It is neutral about the good – or so its defenders claim.

I think that there is a mistake here like the one that John Stuart Mill makes in his proof of the principle of utility. Mill says that the only thing that "proves" that anything is desirable and therefore good is that it is desired. Each person desires his own happiness, so the sum of everyone's happiness is desirable and therefore good.[7] But, we may object, at least for all we know, no one desires the sum of everyone's happiness, so if only desire makes for desirability, what makes the sum desirable? Mill wants to mean that each *part* of it is desired, by the person whose happiness it is.[8] But of course a maximum does not include its parts in *that* way: maximizing happiness is not like adding one acre of ground to another that adjoins it. Conflicts are possible, and if the calculation turns out so, I may have to sacrifice my happiness in order to maximize the total, and then where is my part? In the same way, if my happiness consists in the maximum satisfaction of my desires, it is unlikely to include the satisfaction of each of my desires. And just as the individual person whose happiness is sacrificed for the sake of overall utility seems to have some right to protest, so also the individual desire whose satisfaction is sacrificed for the sake of overall happiness seems to have some right to protest. There are moments when the question "why should I be prudent?" is as much in need of an answer as its more famous cousin.

Why then does the instrumental egoist suppose that it is possible to believe both in instrumentalism and in egoism? How can he even imagine that these two positions are compatible? The instrumental egoist has to believe both that people do in fact desire maximum satisfaction and also that no real conflict can possibly arise between a person's desire for this maximum and her desires for particular things. One way to reach that conclusion is to suppose that satisfaction itself is the *only* thing which people want for its own sake, and that all desired objects are wanted as mere means to satisfaction. That is the view famously attacked as incoherent by Bishop Butler, on the grounds that an object cannot give us satisfaction unless we want it for its own sake.[9] I propose to set it aside here, not merely on the good Bishop's authority, but also because it so *obviously* involves a substantive, and controversial, conception of the good. I believe that the more common assumption behind instrumental egoism is that what a person *really* wants, deep down, just *are* the things that are consistent with or part of her happiness. According to this view, once you have understood that something would be detrimental to your happiness, you will cease to desire it. Our desires, when we are clearheaded, accord with prudence.

With that idea in mind, the instrumental egoist treats the possibility that someone might desire something inconsistent with her happiness as if it were exactly on a par with the possibility that she might miscalculate or simply make a factual error. Suppose someone mistakes white vinegar for vodka. "You do not *really want* to drink *that*," we say to her; and she does not; we are absolutely right. The instrumental egoist must suppose that it is true in *just that way* that the addict does not *really want* the heroin, or that the angry person does nor *really want* to break the window, or that the adulterer does not *really want* to have the affair that will destroy his marriage. In these cases, the instrumental egoist must say, the person's mind is so clouded by addiction, rage, or lust that he is unable to identify what he really wants.

But considered as a psychological hypothesis, the idea that human beings "really" have all and only these domesticated desires seems not only false but hilarious. As Bishop Butler wrote in his *Sermons*:

> Men daily, hourly sacrifice the greatest known interest to fancy, inquisitiveness, love, or hatred, or any vagrant inclination.[10]

Someone who says the addict does not "really want" the heroin must be using "want" in some specialized sense, for in one familiar sense he very obviously does want it.

In my view, if we are tempted to think that the addict does not really want the heroin, that temptation must be *based on* our belief that it is irrational for him to want it, together with a certain conception of rationality. It is the hallmark of a rational agent, one may suppose, that his desires are directed and reshaped by his rational deliberations. So if the addict were thinking rationally, he would not want the heroin. But even if that is right, we cannot allow the egoist to posit that this reshaping has happened before the deliberation ever *starts*: that is, that his "real" desires somehow *already* accord with the results of his deliberations.

This is the first of the two false assumptions about practical rationality that I mentioned at the outset of this essay: the view that practical reasoning really just serves to uncover our "real" desires. On this assumption, what we call "practical reason" is actually a form of theoretical reasoning about our psychology. This view is not one to which people openly subscribe, but rather an unconscious assumption which shows up in the way they argue, and we will see it at work again later on.[11] But practical deliberation is not aimed at psychological knowledge: its conclusions are not just *reminders* of what we already want, deep down. It is rather a way of determining what is good for us, what we ought to want.

In any case, the belief that it is irrational for someone to want heroin cannot be *based* on the instrumental principle, since is a belief about what his ends should be. So if the instrumental egoist asserts that the addict does not "really want" the heroin, there must be a substantive view about what it is rational to want hiding under the cover of that word "really." This is what enables the instrumental egoist to imagine that the only really *practical* reasoning going on here is instrumental.

This is even clearer when the egoist reverts to the use of that dangerous word "interests." Until now I have been talking about desires and interests as if these ideas were interchangeable, but in fact this is correct only if we take the word "interest" in a rather peculiar sense. When we say that someone "has a desire" for something, we are naturally understood as talking about an item in his natural psychology, an urge, or an attraction, or a disposition to find the object pleasurable, or something of that sort.[12] We may then see the principle of maximizing satisfaction as a principle of naturalistic construction, which applies a maximizing formula to certain items regarded as naturally or prima facie good, with the individual's happiness or overall good coming out as the result of the exercise. Let me call that result "the maximum compossible set" of the objects of desire. The items from which the set is constructed must have some sort of prima facie normative *weight* – given by how strongly you desire them, for example – so that we can perform a maximizing operation. But they do not yet have what we might call a normative *ranking* – that is, we have not yet decided which of them you ought to pursue in preference to which. It is the point of the maximizing operation to *assign* them a normative ranking. It is important not to get confused about this: the prima facie weights do not settle the question of the normative ranking, since, for instance, a very strong desire may have to be suppressed (given a low or negative ranking) for the sake of maximizing the total. Now when we say that someone "has an interest" in something, we may not be referring to a natural psychological item, or at least not to one not yet normatively ranked, for the phrase "has an interest" is also used in a way that already implies a normative ranking. In this sense, when we say that someone "has an interest" in something, we imply *that reason favors his pursuing it over other options.* If we suppose that reason favors the satisfaction of those desires whose objects fit together into the maximum compossible set, then *those* are the desires in whose satisfaction you "have an interest," and the idea of maximizing the satisfaction of your *interests* just says the same thing twice over. This is why the word "interest" is dangerous. The normative use of the word "interest" gives the formulation "maximizing the satisfaction of one's interests" an agreeably rational ring, but in fact the egoist cannot mean "interest" in this normative sense without reducing his principle to an empty tautology.

Some rational choice theorists like to use the word "preference" (maximize the satisfaction of one's preferences) but in my view this is even more misleading, for "preference" carries the idea of a comparative ranking on its *surface.* Of course it may not be a comparative *normative* ranking, but if that is not what it refers to then it must refer to a comparative natural ranking, perhaps one based on the comparative strength of desire. So why not say so? If the idea of egoism is that we can generate the notion of a person's good or of his happiness simply by performing a maximizing operation on some naturally existing items, it is really better to keep this clearly before our minds by calling those items "desires." But if we stick to "desire" and keep in view that we are talking about some natural psychological items, then the claim that a person's "real desires" are directed to all and only those things which are consistent with his happiness seems patently false.

At this juncture it may be useful to review the points I have just made. Instrumental egoism is inconsistent on its surface. I have suggested that what enables people even to imagine that it might be right is that they make an implicit assumption – the assumption that people "really want" the things that make them happy, that is, that accord with their maximal satisfaction. Reasoning about how to get what you ("really") want and reasoning about how to promote your maximal satisfaction therefore coincide. This assumption, I have argued, is in turn based on a false view of the role of practical reason – the view that practical deliberation "uncovers" our real desires – together, of course, with certain background assumptions about what those real desires must be.

But there is a second and even more serious problem with the assumption behind instrumental egoism. If it were true that we really desired all and only those things that are consistent with our happiness, egoistically understood, then we would automatically conform to the dictates of the egoistic principle, not because it is rational to do so, but because we would naturally want to. If someone did act against his own best interests, this would not be because he failed to conform his will to the egoistic principle, but rather because he was making some mistake in his calculations, and did not understand where his interests really lay. But if this were so, what need would there be for an egoistic principle of *practical* reason?

The point I am making turns on the distinction between making a mistake and true practical irrationality – that is, violating a principle of practical reason. When a person's action is based on a mistake, the person does the wrong thing, objectively speaking, but that does not show that the person is truly irrational. A person who adds a little dry vermouth and some olives to a glass of white vinegar, believing it to be a glass of vodka, is not doing anything irrational, for by her own lights the action makes perfectly good sense. There is nothing amiss with her motivation, nothing – if I may put it this way – wrong with her will: it is only her factual judgment that needs correcting. According to the assumption behind instrumental egoism, a person who desires to take heroin must suppose that it is consistent with his happiness to take it; otherwise he could not even imagine that he really desires it. But that means he *is* conforming to the egoistic principle, by his own lights. His problem therefore is not true practical irrationality, but simply mistaken judgment. The mistake may have its source in his addiction – it may some-how be caused by the addiction – but what the addiction causes is not practical irrationality; it is bad theoretical judgment. But if people cannot ever be guilty of violating the egoistic principle by their own lights, then it is not a rational principle. It is simply a description of the inevitable effect that a certain kind of judgment has on the human will: prove to us that something is contrary to our happiness and we will forthwith cease to desire it.

This is the second of the two false assumptions about practical rationality that stand behind instrumental egoism: the view that rational principles are *essentially* descriptions of the *effects* that certain judgments have on the will. This assumption is also behind the commonly held view, mentioned earlier, that the instrumental principle is either already normative or does not need to be normative, because people actually are motivated to take the means to their ends. According to this view, if someone fails to take the means to an end, we are entitled to conclude either that he does not really want the end after all, or that he is mak-ing a mistake about how to promote it. But prove to him that the action will promote his end, and he will forthwith be motivated to do it. So no one ever violates the requirement of instrumental reason by his *own* lights. The principle of instrumental reason turns out to be essentially a description of the *effect* that means/end judgments have on the human will.[13]

The trouble with this conception of rationality is that it cannot support the normative use of "ought." For according to this view, if I say to you "you really ought to see a dentist about that tooth" all that I mean – *all* – is that if you came to understand that a visit to the dentist is essential to the achievement of an end requisite for your happiness, you would in fact be motivated to go. The rational judgment is not really a recommendation, but rather a sort of hypothetical prediction. And it is *not* that I predict you would be motivated to go if you understood that going would promote your happiness because you would then see that you have a *reason* to go. It is not *that*, for on this view the claim that you have a reason to go *just amounts to* the claim that if you made the judgment you would in fact be motivated to go. So it turns out that what looks like the normative "ought" is really just a version of the "ought" of expectation. On this view, saying of someone on the brink of toothache that he ought to go to the dentist is exactly like saying of someone who is late that he ought to be home by now. Given human nature, we would have predicted that the person on the brink of toothache would be motivated to go to the dentist; just as given the distance, we would have predicted that the person who left the office an hour ago would be home about now. If these predictions turn out false we know that something has gone wrong. But what has gone wrong can no more properly be described as a failure of practical reason in the first case than in the second.

The inadequacy of the view is clear from this fact: there may be many principles which accurately describe the way human beings are characteristically motivated. And this conception of rationality leaves us with no way of distinguishing which ones are principles of reason and which ones are not. We *can* reliably predict that people will be motivated to take the means to their ends. But suppose that we also could reliably predict that when criticized people will cry and stamp their feet. We would not be tempted to think that it follows that such behavior is rationally required of us.

The Imperative of Prudence

We might at first think that a better account of the normativity of the egoistic principle is available in the *Groundwork of the Metaphysics of Morals*. Kant recognized both that the imperative of prudence, as he called it, is not the same as the instrumental principle and that it stands in need of a normative foundation. In the second section of the *Groundwork*, Kant proposes that there are three kinds of practical imperatives. First there are rules of skill or technical imperatives – that is, instrumental principles. Second there are counsels of prudence or pragmatic imperatives, which direct us to pursue our own happiness, identified, as I mentioned earlier, with "the sum of satisfaction of all inclinations" (G 4: 399). And finally of course there are commands of morality, or categorical imperatives (G 4: 416).

Kant appears to leave room for the normativity of prudence, for in the *Groundwork* at least he seems to believe that we do not inevitably follow imperatives of prudence by our own lights. One of the four examples he uses in the first section of the *Groundwork* to explicate the difference between acting from duty and acting from inclination concerns a man who is tempted to imprudence; when prudence fails to govern him, morality steps in. Kant says:

To assure one's happiness is a duty (at least indirectly); for, want of satisfaction with one's condition... could easily become a great *temptation to transgression of duty*. But in addition, all people have already... the strongest and deepest inclination to happiness because it is just in this idea that all inclinations unite in one sum. However, the precept of happiness is often so constituted that it greatly infringes upon some inclinations, and yet one can form no determinate and sure concept of the sum of satisfaction of all inclinations under the name of happiness. Hence it is not to be wondered at that a single inclination, determinate both as to what it promises and as to the time in which it can be satisfied, can often outweigh a fluctuating idea, and that a man – for example one suffering from the gout – can choose to enjoy what he likes and put up with what he can since, according to his calculations, on this occasion at least he has not sacrificed the enjoyment of the present moment to the perhaps groundless expectation of a happiness that is supposed to lie in health. But even in this case, when the general inclination to happiness did not determine his will... there is still left over here... a law, namely to promote his happiness not from inclination but from duty; and it is then that his conduct first has properly moral worth. (G 4: 399)

Unfortunately – but interestingly – the example is muddled. Kant portrays the man as falling into doubt about whether the imperative of prudence that forbids the unhealthy treat is well-founded or not, being based on "the perhaps groundless expectation of a happiness that is supposed to lie in health." Obviously, if there were *good reason* to doubt whether forgoing the unhealthy treat is a means to happiness, then the man's resistance to the imperative that forbids the unhealthy treat would to that extent be *rational*. And in that case the indirect duty to pursue one's happiness would no more forbid the unhealthy treat than the imperative of prudence does. It seems likely that what Kant is really thinking is that the man has a tendency to rationalization. "Oh, how does anyone know that health really leads to happiness anyway?" he says to himself, licking his lips at the thought of the treat. And then the thought of his duty stiffens his resolve. Even then it is not clear how exactly the example is supposed to work, since the rationalization works against the thought of duty in the same way it works against the thought of prudence. But at all events the case does show that Kant thought one could resist the normative force of prudence when that force "infringes upon some inclinations." And indeed this is necessary to his account, for Kant recognizes that a principle cannot be normative unless it is possible to violate it. Imperatives are addressed to creatures who can violate them and so they are normative:

All imperatives are expressed by an *ought* and indicate by this the relation of an objective law of reason to a will that by its subjective constitution is not necessarily determined by it. . . . They say that to do or omit something would be good, but they say it to a will that does not always do something just because it is represented to it that it would be good to do that thing. (G 4: 413)

How then is the normativity of prudence to be established?

Rules of skill, or principles of instrumental reason, are hypothetical imperatives, taking the form "if you will this, then you must also will that." According to Kant their normative force is based on the principle that "whoever wills the end also wills (insofar as reason has decisive influence on his actions) the indispensably necessary means to it that are within his power" (G 4: 417). This principle, Kant claims, is analytic, because "in the volition of an object as my effect, my causality as acting cause, that is, the use of means, is already thought" (G 4: 417). To will something is not merely to desire it, but to set yourself to bring it about – that is, to cause it – and so willing something essentially involves determining yourself to use the means to it.

Imperatives of prudence, Kant claims, are also hypothetical imperatives, arising from the fact that we necessarily will happiness. He says:

There is, however, *one* end that can be presupposed as actual in the case of all rational beings . . . and therefore one purpose that they not merely *could* have but that we can safely presuppose they all actually *do have* by a natural necessity, and that purpose is *happiness.* (G 4: 415)

And therefore:

If only it were as easy to give a determinate concept of happiness, imperatives of prudence would agree entirely with those of skill and would be just as analytic. For it could be said, here just as there: who wills the end also wills (necessarily in conformity with reason) the sole means to it that are within his control. (G 4: 417–18)

We run into problems, however, when we try to make out what Kant could possibly mean when he claims that we "have" the end of happiness by a natural necessity. He could mean either that we necessarily *will* happiness, or that we necessarily *desire* it, but there are difficulties either way. On the one hand, if he means that we necessarily *will* happiness – that is, we necessarily choose it, when no moral obligation prevents us – the claim seems to be contrary to his own views about our essential freedom of the choice of ends. In the *Metaphysics of Morals* Kant says:

An end is the object of the choice (of a rational being), through the representation of which choice is determined to bring this object about. – Now, I can indeed be constrained by others to perform *actions* that are directed as means to an end, but I can never be constrained by others *to have an end*; only I can *make* something my end. (MM 6: 381)

Here Kant argues that adopting an end is an internal action to which we cannot be compelled; hence it must be a free act. Although his contrast here is between freedom and constraint by other people, the claim that "only I can make something my end" seems equally to exclude ends determined by nature. More generally, Kant's argument for the moral law starts from the definition of a free will as one that is not determined by any law outside itself, and involves the premise that we must regard ourselves, insofar as we are rational, as having free wills. We choose maxims for ourselves autonomously, and our ends are chosen as part of our maxims. The idea that we necessarily will happiness seems inconsistent with all of this.[14]

On the other hand, if all Kant means is that we cannot help but *desire* happiness, it is puzzling that he singles out a special sort of imperative to guide our pursuit of this desired end. For in the first place, there are many things, most notably the satisfaction of our physical needs, which we cannot help but desire, but Kant does not single out special imperatives for them. In the second place, and more importantly, mere desires for ends do not support hypothetical imperatives, which are based on the principle that whoever *wills* an end wills the means, and therefore cannot be derived from mere desires. Desiring an end does not analytically involve the thought of "my causality as an acting cause," in the way that willing an end does. And in the third place, the mere *desire* for happiness would be only one desire among others, which would have to compete for our attention with other, more particular, desires and ends. In fact, even if Kant did have an argument to show that we necessarily *will* happiness as an end, it would not automatically follow that we should always rationally prefer it to more particular ends; nor does Kant give any argument at all to that effect. Happiness would at most be established as one end among others. And if there were a principle of practical reason, an imperative, directing us both to *have* happiness as an end and to *prefer* happiness to every other end, that principle would seem to lie somewhere in between Kant's two categories of hypothetical and categorical imperatives. Unlike a hypothetical imperative, it would command us to pursue a certain end no matter what else we happened to want; but unlike a categorical one, it would hold only conditionally, since our pursuit of this end would have to give way to moral considerations.[15]

Of course Kant might after all mean that we always do pursue happiness, by our own lights, at least when not forbidden by duty. Later he seems to come around to this view, for in *the Metaphysics of Morals*, after arguing that "what everyone wants unavoidably, of his own accord, does not come under the concept of duty" (MM 6: 386), Kant says:

Since it is unavoidable for human nature to wish for and seek happiness, that is, satisfaction with one's state, so long as one is assured of its lasting, this is not an end that is also a duty. (MM 6: 387)[16]

But if we cannot have a duty to pursue our own happiness because we inevitably do pursue it, then neither can there be an imperative of prudence, for the same reason. So this leaves us back where we were.

A Kantian Conception of Rationality

Perhaps it will seem that in making this argument I am rejecting the very idea of a theory of rationality that is at once both normative and descriptive. For I am insisting that if we necessarily do conform to a certain principle, then it cannot be normative. But the lesson need only be that that correlation must be understood in a different way. We can suppose that rational principles are descriptive of rational procedures or activities, and of human beings insofar as we engage in those procedures or activities. This is a view most naturally associated with Kant. Kant's account of the imperative of prudence in the *Groundwork* does not yet, in my view, express his mature conception of rationality.[17]

Kant views reason as the *active* aspect or dimension of the human mind, that is, as its power of self-determination. The principles of reason describe the active contribution of the mind to belief and to action. They are procedures we follow in determining our beliefs and actions, insofar as we are rational. A comparison may help to show why this makes them both normative and descriptive. The principles of English grammar are both normative and descriptive because they describe procedures we follow in constructing our sentences insofar as we are speaking English.[18] To speak English is essentially to be guided by those principles; we may say that being guided by those principles is constitutive of speaking English. In the same way, the most general function of the mind is to think, and to think is essentially to be guided by the principles of logic. According to Kant, the mind is also faced with the more specific task of constructing a unified conception of the world from the phenomena, and to do this is to be guided by the principles of the understanding. And the mind is faced with the task of choice or volition, of the determination of our actions; and to will is to be guided by the principles of practical reason.

The important thing to emphasize about this conception of rationality is that rational principles describe activities: they tell us what the rational mind as such *does* with certain items that are given to it, rather than merely describing the effect which those items will have on the mind. The principles of logic and the canons of evidence describe what the thinker as such *does* with the incoming evidence: arriving at a belief through reasoning is an active process, a process by which the mind determines itself to a conclusion. Rational principles may be seen as *directions* in the most literal way. Given P and *if P then Q* infer Q: modus ponens is a direction for thinking. We can predict with some confidence that the rational mind when confronted with this argument will believe Q, but it is certainly not inevitable. And if the mind does believe Q when faced with the argument, that is an *effect* of its rationality, not the *essence* of its rationality. Inferring Q from P and *if P then Q* is no more the same as merely being caused to believe it than jumping off a cliff is the same as merely being caused to fall off of it, for the aspect of self-determination is missing. What makes your beliefs logical is not that *they* conform to the rules of logic, for you could believe P, Q, and *If P then Q*, and never notice any connection between them. Nor is it that believing the premises causes you to believe the conclusion, for this too could happen without your notice. What makes your belief logical is that you *put* the two premises together in the way required by modus ponens, and so *cause yourself* to believe it. In the same way, the principles of practical reason describe what the *will* as such does with certain items, say beliefs and desires, that are given to it. Volition, the determination of our actions, is an active process, a process by which we cause ourselves to act. It is not just something that happens in us or to us. The instrumental principle, for instance, on this view, is an *instruction* for willing: if you are to *will* the end, rather than merely wishing for it or wanting it, and these are the means, then you must determine yourself to take these.

Now it may seem as if there is something paradoxical about this conception of rationality. The principles of practical reason govern action. Yet I am claiming that reasoning *itself* must be seen as a kind of action, in order to capture the element of self-determination that is essential to volition. If reasoning must be seen as a kind of action, what captures the element of self-determination that is essential to reasoning itself? Do we need some deeper sort of rational activity that in turn captures that? A regress obviously threatens. We are here confronting one of the deepest problems of philosophy, the problem of identifying the exact nature of the self-determination that distinguishes actions and activities from mere events. This problem rests behind the persistent philosophical temptation to try to reduce both action and reason, as forms of self-determination, to special forms of causation. One expression of that temptation is what I have identified as the second false assumption about rationality, the view that the principles of reason merely describe the effects that certain judgments have on the will or the mind.

Kant offers us a way to block the regress. To explain it, it will be helpful to distinguish between a weaker and a stronger version of the Kantian conception of rationality. According to both versions, the principles of reason are principles of rational activity, principles that describe the mind's active contribution to thinking or volition. The stronger version adds a further thought, namely, the thought that we can derive the *content* of the principles of reason from this very conception of what they are. The principles of reason, on this view, are not just principles that direct us to do this or that, but principles whose content captures the very essence of activity or self-determination. Consider once more the way I formulated the instrumental principle a moment ago: If you are to *will* the end, rather than merely wishing for it or wanting it, then you must determine yourself to take the means. Seen this way, the instrumental principle is intended to capture something about the very essence of volition, in particular what makes volition different from mere desire. You are not *willing* the end at all unless you determine yourself to cause the end to come about, that is, to use the means. The categorical imperative, in its universal law formulation, wears this thought on its face, for what it tells us to do is to give ourselves a law – that is to say, what it tells us to do is to determine ourselves. The Kantian arguments for these principles are meant to establish that you succeed in exercising the self-determination that is the essence of volition only to the extent that you follow these principles.[19]

Now let me return to a point I made earlier. I argued that if we support instrumental egoism with the view that people do not "really want" things that are inconsistent with their happiness, we must say that people who pursue ends which are in fact inconsistent with their happiness are guilty of mistake, of bad theoretical judgment. But I also said that the mistake might be caused by the agent's condition – by addiction or rage or lust, for instance. Whereas the instrumental egoist regards these conditions as causes of confusion, making people unable to see what they really want, the Kantian will say that they are, directly, causes of true practical irrationality – or to put the same point another way, conditions that undermine our power of self-determination. We do not have to suppose, as the instrumental egoist does, that the addict's condition makes it impossible for him to *understand* that there is good reason for him not to take heroin. We can say that his addiction makes it impossible, or maybe just hard, for him to guide himself in accordance with that reason. Or rather, if we do imagine that he says to himself, at least at very the moment when he takes the stuff, that it is consistent with his happiness – for I am inclined to think that something like that does happen – we can see that as *rationalization*. That is, if he says to himself that just now, this time, just once, it really is good for him, or anyway not bad, to take the drug, we can see that as an attempt to conceal his failure of self-determination or self-control from himself, rather than seeing it as a mistake that causes behavior which is not actually irrational by his own lights. So the order of what happens is different. The instrumental egoist says that the addiction causes an error of judgment which in turn leads to conduct which only looks practically irrational from the outside, but which is not really so by the addict's own lights. The Kantian says instead that the addiction causes genuinely, inwardly, practically irrational conduct – causes a defect in the will – which the agent then scrambles to *rationalize* by the invocation of the mistaken belief.

Apart from the fact that this second way of seeing the situation is consistent with the possibility of practical reason, while the first way is not, the second way seems to me to be getting things the right way around. In fact there is room here for an interesting account of what rationalization is and why it is so pervasive. Because we are self-conscious we are faced with the task of self-determination, both of our beliefs and of our actions. It is a task that requires a degree of vigilance and self-command that is often beyond our powers. The need to maintain the fiction that we are always in control, both in our own eyes and in those of others, is a deep human drive. Think of the difficulty older people have in admitting they have dozed off for a moment. Or the temptation to make an awkward physical movement look as if it were some sort of deliberate step. Or the temptation, in the heat of argument, to defend a thesis just because it has somehow fallen out of your mouth, and someone else has objected to it. Get a person to do some odd action under the influence of post-hypnotic suggestion, and then ask him why he did it. He will not say "I do not know." He will make up a plausible story and tell himself as well as you that that is what he had in mind. The use of rationalization to conceal our failures of self-determination in thought and action from ourselves is all of a piece with these things, an attempt to maintain the appearance of perfect self-command.

Implications of the Kantian Conception for Egoism

In this chapter I am not going to argue for the stronger version of the Kantian conception of rationality, the version that derives the content of rational principles from the very idea of self-determination. But I cannot resist mentioning one ramification of that view for rational egoism. I hope that you can at least see how someone might be tempted to think that the categorical and hypothetical imperatives are principles that capture the very essence of self-determination. But it is not even remotely plausible to suppose that *the egoistic principle* captures the very essence of self-determination. That is, it is not plausible to think that you only succeed in exercising self-determination if you aim to maximize the satisfaction of your desires; or that you are not really willing at all unless *what you will* is maximum satisfaction. If we accept the stronger version of the Kantian conception, then the egoistic principle simply seems to be *the wrong sort of thing* to be a principle of practical reason. To put the point in somewhat more old-fashioned Kantian terms, the egoistic principle is concerned with the *content* of the will, not with the very *form* of willing.

But as I said, I do not propose to argue for the stronger version of the Kantian conception here. I do mean to argue, however, that in order to get the normative "ought" we need to see the principles of reason, as Kant does, as principles that describe mental activities, and not just the effects of judgments on the will. But even this weaker version has important implications for the way we conceive of rational egoism. For if we accept it, there are certain elements of Kantian moral psychology that we must accept along with it.

In Kantian moral psychology, the mind determines itself by operating in accordance with a rational principle on certain items that are given to it. The rational principle is descriptive of the mind's activity, of what it does with the items given to it. In the case of practical principles, some of these items have a prima facie motivational force: they present a possible action to the will as eligible. Kant calls such a motivational item an "incentive." Desires, in Kant's view, function as incentives. So every willed action involves both an incentive and a principle: something presented to the will, on which it then acts. If a desire directly caused a person to act, there would be no contribution from the agent's own activity or self-determination, and so it would not be a case of volition. Suppose that an agent experiences a desire, and acts on it. To the extent that the agent determines himself, he *takes* the desire to be a reason to act; and that is not the same as its causing him to act. We may represent this fact – the contribution of his own activity – by saying that it is his *principle* to do what he wants. The principle describes his activity. If we want to reserve that troublesome word "motive" for what actually produces the outward act, then it is not quite right to say his desire is a motive. His desire is an incentive. His motive is, speaking very roughly, that he takes the desire to be a reason.

This has two implications. The first is that rational egoism is not the same as the thesis that only desires are motives. In fact it is inconsistent with that thesis. If desires produced human actions directly, without the intervention of principles, we would not be practically rational in any sense, egoistic or otherwise.[20] The second implication is less obvious. It is that rational egoism is not the same as the thesis that only desires are incentives. It is also inconsistent with that thesis.

I can most easily bring out the reason for this by means of a comparison. As an internalist, Kant supposed that the moral law applies to us only if respect for law can serve as an incentive for the will. The reason is simple. Suppose that your principle is to act only on a maxim that can serve as universal law. Suppose also that, with some ordinary desire serving as the incentive, you formulate a maxim that turns out to be incompatible with that principle. Wanting to spend the day at the beach, you are tempted to break your promise to help your neighbor paint his house on the first sunny day. You test your maxim, it is rejected, and you therefore do help your neighbor to paint his house as you had promised. If rational action always involves both an incentive and a principle, what is your incentive for doing that? What presents "keeping your promise" to your mind as an eligible action? According to Kant, it is respect for law, the moral law's operation as its own incentive. In other words, the thought that you are required to keep a promise can itself serve as the incentive for keeping it. This is what Kant means by being motivated by pure practical reason – that the thoughts generated by the rational principle can serve as incentives for the will.

In a similar way, if there is an egoistic principle of practical reason, it must be capable of generating an incentive of its own, an incentive for doing those things which we must do if we are to maximize our satisfactions, and which we do not otherwise want to do. Suppose for instance you are tempted not to go to the dentist, since you are afraid of the drill. Let us suppose that the egoistic principle says that you must go, since your desire to avoid the toothache ahead gets a higher normative ranking than your desire to avoid the drill now. It is no use insisting that the incentive you act on when you conform to the egoistic principle is your desire to avoid the toothache ahead, for if that were a sufficient incentive to get you to go to the dentist, you would not have been tempted to violate the egoistic principle in the first place. To suppose that your desire to avoid the toothache ahead is, *after all,* strong enough to overcome your fear of the drill is to revert to a version of the first assumption about rationality I criticized. It is to suppose that the role of practical deliberation is to uncover the psychological facts, to show you that you already, deep down, prefer to brave the dentist than to face the toothache later. We have seen that that assumption is not warranted. Your incentive must rather be provided by the thought that it is better for you overall if you go to the dentist. So *rational* egoism is not compatible with the view that only desires can serve as incentives. Only completely wanton action is compatible with that. Rational egoism requires the possibility that we can be motivated by pure practical reason, in exactly the same way that morality does. It is only *what* it tells us to do that is different.

The Realist Egoist

We have seen that the egoistic principle cannot be reduced to the instrumental principle. If it is a rational principle at all, it must be a principle in its own right. If it is to be a normative principle, associated with a normative ought, the egoistic principle must describe a rational activity. So in order to determine whether the egoistic principle is a normative principle, we need a way to identify rational activities. The stronger version of the Kantian conception, which tries to derive the content of rational principles from the very idea of self-determination, gives us one way of doing that, but we have seen that it is not a promising route for the egoist to take. The remaining option seems to be a form of realism. Just as realists think that following the principles of logic and the canons of evidence is guiding yourself in matters of belief by the aim of achieving the True, so they may think that following the principles of practical reason is guiding yourself in matters of action by the aim of achieving the Good. A person's happiness is *her own good,* so of course it is normative for her. Or perhaps it is just plain *good,* and so normative for us all.

Now it is important to see that by itself, this sort of move does not get us to rational egoism. Suppose that we say that a person's happiness is good for her (or just good, it does not matter for this argument), meaning that maximum satisfaction is good for her. It seems natural to give one of two explanations of what makes happiness in this sense good. The first is that the satisfaction of each of her desires is a good thing for her, so that by maximizing her satisfactions she is maximizing good things. The second is that her happiness is good because she in fact desires it, and so good for her for the same reason that each of the objects of her particular desires is good for her. In whichever of these ways we establish the goodness of happiness, we get the result that each of the person's particular desires has the same kind of normative claim on her that her happiness does. So if the aim of maximizing satisfaction comes into conflict with the aim of satisfying one of her desires, she now has a normative reason to do each of these things, and she needs some further reason to prefer the maximum satisfaction to the particular satisfaction. The problem of why she should be prudent, which before seemed to be a problem about *whether* there is a normative principle of prudence, has simply reappeared in the guise of a conflict among a plurality of normative principles.

Now perhaps you will agree that this problem does arise for someone who claims that happiness is good because we desire it, and therefore places happiness exactly on a footing with the other objects of desire. But you may be tempted to think it does not arise for someone who claims that happiness is good because the satisfaction of each of her desires is a good thing, and therefore that happiness is a maximum of good things. For it is obvious that a maximum of good things is better than any one good thing, on the principle that more is better. But recall that we are not claiming that satisfaction is the only thing you want for its own sake, so we are not talking here about getting more of the only thing you want. You also want the particular objects of your desires. So the trouble with this argument is that it does not explain the authority of the egoistic principle, but rather simply asserts it. The imprudent person is not denying that he will get more satisfaction if he acts prudently – he is asking why he therefore has a reason to do so, especially since he may have to give up something else he wants.[21]

There is one final move available to the realist egoist, though. Earlier I claimed that behind instrumental egoism stands a certain psychological thesis, namely the thesis that people only *really want* what is consistent with their happiness. The realist egoist can transform this thesis into a view about what is *really good*. He can say that only the maximum compossible set of the objects of a person's desires, and the various objects that are parts of that set, are really good. So only those desires whose satisfaction is consistent with happiness have normative standing, and others do not. By turning that thesis into a thesis about the good, rather than a thesis about real desires, the realist egoist escapes the problems I mentioned earlier. He avoids the charge of domesticating human psychology, since he is no longer making a psychological claim. And he also avoids the charge of emptying the principles of practical reason of their normative content, by making us incapable of disobeying them. He is not claiming we can be *motivated* only by the good, for we have non-normative desires that also move us.

But he avoids these charges at the cost of giving up the view that the egoistic principle is a principle of naturalistic construction, and embracing in its place a pure form of dogmatism. For now the good is not constructed out of items regarded as naturally or prima facie good. The realist egoist can no longer explain the goodness of happiness in terms of the goodness of satisfying desires, in either of the ways I mentioned above. For now he has embraced the view that not every satisfaction is good, and more generally that not everything a person desires is good. This form of egoism is a top-down version, which tells us that it is prima facie rational to be motivated by our desires only *because* the maximum compossible set of their objects is the Good.

On this view, the good for a person *just is* the maximum compossible set of his desires. This is not because the maximum compossible set is necessarily *what he wants most*, for we have dropped the assumption that an agent always *actually* prefers his happiness to any particular desired end, in order to secure the normativity of the egoistic principle. Nor is it because it includes *most of what he wants* – for we have dropped the assumption that an agent's wanting something is in itself the source of a normative claim, in order to avoid generating a plurality of normative claims that will conflict with that of the egoistic principle itself. The claim that the maximum compossible set of one's desires is the good is therefore a dogmatic claim. The answer to the question why you should be prudent is simply that prudence is the pursuit of the maximum compossible set and that *just is* your good. This position appears to be logically unassailable, but that is no reason to pass out cigars. All dogmatic positions are logically unassailable.

So egoism is a dogmatic rationalist view, which derives the normativity of its principle from a substantive conception of the good. Let us now look more closely at this conception.

II. THE CONTENT OF THE EGOISTIC PRINCIPLE

Balancing and Particularity

I want to begin this part of the chapter by saying something about the intuitive ideas that the egoistic principle is meant to capture. By way of approach to one of these ideas, notice that there is widespread agreement that reason requires us to take the means to our ends. But many people believe that this by itself does not capture the demands of instrumental reason. Surely we should take the most efficient means, and there are problems about how those are to be specified; and of course there are the notorious problems about how to handle risk when we are pursuing ends under uncertainty. Many people think of solving these problems as part of working out the correct formulation of the instrumental principle.

Actually, however, these problems are generated by the same very basic idea that also seems to stand behind the egoistic principle. To formulate this idea, I will use the word "project" as a neutral term for anything that gives you a reason, whether it is a goal you are pursuing, a principle you live by, a cause you adhere to, your standing concern for the welfare of a friend, or whatever. I will speak of "promoting projects" and ask you to remember that promoting a project need not always involve pursuing a goal. The basic idea I have in mind is that you have more than one project and rationality requires you to take into account the impact which promoting one project will have on the others. Considerations of efficiency and caution spring from this idea in a generalized form: if you have reason to minimize your expenditure of time and resources, it is for the sake of your other projects, not for the sake of the project you are promoting right now.

I am going to call this basic idea the requirement of balancing – meaning that whenever we make a choice, we are required to balance the reasons stemming from the project we are now pursuing against the reasons stemming from our other projects.[22] The idea that there is a requirement of balancing is an important element in egoism, but there is nothing inherently egoistic about it. The belief in egoism also seems to import another idea, which is that the overall good you are pursuing or constructing when you engage in this balancing is particularly your own. I am going to call that idea the idea of particularity. The familiar ambiguity in the term "prudence" picks up both the ideas of balancing and particularity: people are described as prudent when they remember to attend to interests they will have in the future as well as the ones they have now, and also when they seem to be especially attentive to their own good.[23]

There is room for disagreement about how exactly the egoistic principle captures the idea of particularity – about what it is that makes egoism *egoistic*. What makes the successful pursuit of a project a part of my own good? Is it just that the project is mine, or is there some subset of my projects whose success constitutes "my own good"? Or is it rather something about the *way* the egoist proposes to meet the requirement of balancing, which is by maximizing his own satisfaction? On the first of these options, the idea of particularity is supposed to be captured by the kind of items that go into the egoistic calculation – they are mine, my desires, my projects, my personal concerns. The egoist reasons from egoistic materials. On the second, the idea of particularity is supposed to be captured by the structure or form of egoistic deliberation: it is because *satisfaction* is the basis for assigning weights to the items in the egoistic calculation that egoism counts as a pursuit of the agent's own good. The egoist reasons about a general range of materials, but reasons in a specifically egoistic way. In what follows, I will examine each of these possibilities in turn.

Reasoning from Egoistic Materials

First, are the materials that go into egoistic reasoning somehow inherently egoistic? For instance, is the egoist pursuing his own good because the incentives on which the egoistic principle operates are his desires? The trouble with this thought is that the word "desire" either refers to a particular kind of incentive, or it does not. If the word "desire" refers to anything that can serve as an incentive for the will, or perhaps we should say any incentive except those generated by the egoistic principle itself, then all of one's incentives are trivially "desires," and nothing is added to the idea of balancing. On the other hand if "desire" refers to some particular kind of incentive, say those that are associated with appetite or pleasure, then we are owed an explanation of why the egoistic principle commands us to promote projects grounded in this particular kind of incentive in preference to or at the expense of other projects. Whatever that explanation might be, it will not refer to the fact that the other incentives are not *your own*, but rather to the fact that the other incentives are not *desires*. There is no obvious sense in which a principle like that is either rational or egoistic.

A more tempting option is that it is not the bare fact that something is a desire but its content that is relevant. In his essay "Egoism and Altruism" Bernard Williams proposes that we can isolate a category of egoistic desire by means of a device intended to isolate the content of a desire. The device is to represent the desire in this way:

I want that (. . . . .)

where what we put in the parentheses is a description of the desired state of affairs. Then we can say that a desire is egoistic if the self appears somewhere in that description:

I want that (. . . . I . . . . . .)

Williams calls such a desire an I-desire.[24]

But actually this device does not seem to capture the intuitive idea of egoism. In fact what it seems to capture is rather the idea of narcissism. For instance, someone in the grip of a pathological case of remorse or masochism might want that he should suffer. Or someone might want to be the author of some good thing of which he himself may never get the benefit, like someone who wants to be the one who discovers a cure for cancer. And then there are the desires we would most naturally formulate not in terms of "I" but in terms of "my own," like the godfather's desire that his own family should remain in power or the patriot's desire that his own country should be free. Or suppose an artist wants his own paintings to make the world a more beautiful place. Are these desires egoistic? They contain a self-reference, but they certainly do not all concern things that you want *for yourself* in any intuitive sense. Of course we could say that a desire is only egoistic if the person wants something good for himself but then we cannot use these desires to *define* the notion of a person's good.

Nevertheless, let us suppose that the device does pick out a category of egoistic desire. Now we must be careful to avoid a confusion. Psychological egoism, in one of its many forms, is the view that human beings have only egoistic desires. Those who believe it usually also believe that all human projects are grounded in desire. If these things were true, you would always pursue things you wanted for yourself, and the requirement of balancing would require you to pursue your own overall good. But this would not be because it is rational to pursue your own good as such. The only rational element in this picture is the requirement of balancing, which is not essentially egoistic; the egoism here is psychological. If the requirement of balancing has only egoistic materials to work on, it commands the pursuit of your own good by default, and not because a focus on your own good is rational.

So if the question of *rational* egoism is even going to come up, we must suppose that human beings have both egoistic and non-egoistic projects. Suppose you want things both for yourself and for others, and perhaps have some impersonal desires for states of the world in general. According to this view it is a requirement of reason that you should prefer those things you want for yourself to the things you want for others or impersonally, no matter how badly you want those other things. Why would this be rational? Do not be tempted by the thought that your I-desires are favored by reason *because* they are the ones directed to your own good. The claim here is not that you first form some conception of the good, and then form egoistic desires by applying it to your own case. If that is the way it is, the good is not a maximum of satisfaction, but something else altogether, which desire merely aims at. This version of egoism is rather the view that your good is *constituted* by the maximum compossible set of the objects of your I-desires, *whatever* those happen to be, and even if they include things like wanting yourself to suffer.

That is not very plausible. But in any case it is not the route that most egoists take. Social scientific egoists, in particular, have insisted that they can be neutral about what sorts of elements may go into the maximum compossible set. If this is right, then what is egoistic about egoism must be the form of balancing that it directs us to do. It must be that it is the pursuit of satisfaction.

The Pursuit of Satisfaction

The view that we are to maximize the satisfaction of our desires is ambiguous, because the idea of "satisfaction" is ambiguous. "Satisfaction" may refer either to an objective or a subjective state. Objective satisfaction is achieved when the state of affairs that you desire is in fact realized. For instance, you want your painting to hang in the Metropolitan Museum of Art, and it does. Obviously, you could achieve the satisfaction of your desire in the objective sense without knowing anything about it: you may never know that your dream of artistic fame has been realized. Subjective satisfaction by contrast is a sort of pleasurable consciousness that objective satisfaction obtains. You know that your picture has been hung in the Museum, say, and you feel good about it; you reflect on the fact with pleasure. Although subjective satisfaction is pleasurable, it is important to distinguish it from pleasure in general, and in particular from pleasure that is caused by the satisfaction of a desire by any route whatever.[25] Egoism is not supposed to be the same thing as hedonism. Subjective satisfaction is a specific kind of pleasure, pleasure taken in the knowledge or belief that a desire has been satisfied.

Now someone who deliberates with the aim of achieving the maximum sense of subjective satisfaction over the whole course of his life seems to be in a recognizable sense egoistic. His conduct is governed by the pursuit of something that will be experienced as a good by himself. But there is a problem about saying that he is rational. Subjective satisfaction is the pleased perception of objective satisfaction and so is conceptually dependent upon objective satisfaction. And so, one would think, its importance must be dependent on the importance of objective satisfaction as well. There would be something upside down about thinking it mattered that you should achieve subjective satisfaction independently of thinking that it mattered that you should achieve objective satisfaction. You can see the problem by imagining a case in which they pull apart. John Rawls used to tell the following story in his classes.

A man is going away to fight in a war, in which he may possibly die. The night before he leaves, the devil comes and offers him a choice. Either while he is away, his family will thrive and flourish, but he will get word that they are suffering and miserable; or while he is away his family will suffer and be miserable, but he will get word they are thriving and happy. He must choose now, and of course he will be made to forget that his conversation with the devil and the choice it resulted in ever took place.

The problem is obvious. The man loves his family and wants them to be thriving and happy, and this clearly dictates the first choice, where his family thrives but he believes they do not. But the goal of achieving subjective satisfaction seems to favor the second choice, where he gets to enjoy the satisfaction of believing they thrive when actually they do not. So here we have *rationality* dictating the choice of a pleasing delusion over a state of affairs which the man by hypothesis genuinely cares about. He must care about it, or he could not get the subjective satisfaction: that was Butler's point. The pursuit of subjective satisfaction in preference to objective satisfaction can lead to madness, in the literal sense of madness: you can lose your grip on *reality*.

So suppose instead that we take the claim that we should maximize our satisfaction to be a claim about objective satisfaction. Now we run into a new problem. The idea of *maximizing* objective satisfaction makes no obvious sense. Even supposing that we had some clear way of individuating and so counting our desires, nobody thinks that maximizing objective satisfaction is rational if that means maximizing the raw number of satisfied desires, for everyone thinks that our desires differ greatly in their importance and centrality to our lives. Maximizing satisfaction must have something to do with giving priority to the things that matter more to us. So we need some way of assigning prima facie weights or measures of some kind to our desires or more generally to our projects before we know how to maximize satisfaction. And these weights or measures must be based either on reason or on our psychology.

Suppose first that the weights are grounded in reason: we ask how strong a reason, relatively speaking, is provided by each of our projects. There are two things we might mean by this. First, we may be asking how important the project is to our happiness, how much of a contribution it makes. As I have already suggested, when I talked about the danger-ous word "interest," the egoist cannot use this measure going in to his calculations, for it is precisely this measure that is supposed to emerge from his calculations. Finding out how to maximize satisfaction is sup-posed to *tell* him which projects he must give priority to if he is to be happy. Second, we may be asking how strong a reason the project pro-vides by some other rational measure, some measure that may derive in part from rational considerations or convictions other than those spring-ing from the egoistic principle itself. For instance one may hold the view that reasons deriving from morality or, say, friendship are weightier than reasons deriving from personal comfort. Roughly speaking, the measure of a project's importance is given by how good a reason there is to pro-mote it. Provided we have a theory of practical reason rich enough to assign such measures, this is certainly an intelligible procedure. But it is not egoistic, for this is simply the procedure of determining what we have most reason to do. In other words, this is simply the requirement of balancing, taken all by itself, and in its most starkly formal sense. Fur-thermore, and importantly, if we are going to allow the initial measures to reflect rational considerations, we must leave it open whether it will turn out that balancing will take a maximizing form or not. For perhaps some reasons are unconditional and some are not, or perhaps some are by their nature lexically prior to others. If these things are so, balancing requires us to take them into account. Balancing is a matter of maximiz-ing only if we start with items that vary only in a raw commensurable weight.

So if we are to get a distinctively egoistic principle, and not just the requirement of balancing, it seems as if the initial weights we assign to our projects must be based on something psychological, something about our own attitudes towards them. An initial temptation is to turn back to the idea of subjective satisfaction, which may seem like the relevant sort of quantum. Although we can agree that it is objective satisfaction that matters, the test of how much it matters is subjective: that is, it is how much subjective satisfaction we would experience if we knew that the desire were objectively satisfied. But the problem of the conceptual dependence of subjective satisfaction upon objective satisfaction again arises. Surely the degree of our subjective satisfaction should depend on how important the objective state of affairs is to us, and not the reverse. Subjective satisfaction cannot serve as an independent measure.

This means that the measure must be provided by some subjectively identifiable or anyway psychological quantum other than the degree of satisfaction. In other words, it has to be something roughly along the lines of intensity of desire. In this case egoism is normally misdescribed, for conformity to the egoistic principle will really lead to a maximum of *satisfaction* only on the hypothesis that the degree of subjective satisfaction exactly corresponds to the intensity of the desire which gets satisfied. This was indeed the assumption of the British empiricists who originally brought us this theory. "Every affection," Hume declares, "when gratified by success, gives a satisfaction proportioned to its force and violence."[26] We need not linger over the question whether that is true, because it is inessential to the theory. The essential idea is that egoism is egoistic because the measure of a desired object's prima facie weight is how badly you want it. It is as if adding up all the intensities of your particular desires produces, in the case of the maximum compossible set, a single desire for the set as a whole with such a high degree of intensity that it *transmutes* into normative force.

However that may be, the use of intensity of desire as the measure means that the egoist cannot have the neutrality he often claims about the kinds of items that go into the calculation. In fact a dilemma faces the egoist here. On the one hand, we may allow the items that go into the calculation to get their initial weights from any source, including normative sources such as personal commitments or the other principles of reason. This gives us the desired neutrality, but in that case what is supposed to be the egoistic principle is really just the requirement of balancing, and the form that that requirement takes will not necessarily be a maximizing one. Or we may insist that the items going into the calculation are items of a quite particular kind, psychological items with a measurable intensity or some other introspectively accessible psychic magnitude that reflects our personal attitudes. Then we get egoism, but we do not get the desired neutrality. To this extent, the egoistic principle cannot after all be detached from its origins: it is a child of introspective psychology, grounded in the British empiricist theory of happiness or the good.

CONCLUSION

Let me now sum up my conclusions. Egoism is not consistent with instrumentalism or with the view that human beings are motivated only by desires. Like any substantive theory of what it is rational to do, egoism requires the possibility of motivation by pure practical reason. The egoistic principle differs from the categorical imperative by having a different content, not by the kind of motivation it involves. The egoistic principle tells us that we must treat a certain conception of the good as having normative authority over our conduct. This conception of the good is not philosophically neutral, nor is it merely the result of imposing a little order on the natural prima facie goods that it starts from. In fact, if the arguments of both parts of this chapter are correct, egoism must be based on a rational intuition that happiness as it was conceived by the British empiricists is the Good, and is therefore the source of a normative principle. I therefore think that Nietzsche was right in the *Twilight of the Idols* when he dismissed rational egoism as a myth. Man does not pursue happiness, at least as happiness must be conceived by the rational egoist. Only the Englishman does that.[27]

Notes

This chapter was originally presented as the 1999 E. H. Lindley Lecture at the Department of Philosophy at the University of Kansas on October 21, 1999.

1. *The Twilight of the Idols,* Maxims and Arrows, number 12.
2. Sidgwick is a utilitarian about the content of the moral principle, but his account of its normative foundation is rationalistic. See Sidgwick 1981, esp. book III, ch. XIII. Eighteenth-century rationalists, such as Clarke and Price, think that moral principles are rational principles, and tend to see the principle of rational self-interest as a branch of duty. For them the rival of morality is not rational self-interest but passion, vice, and corruption. But twentieth-century ethical rationalists like Ross and Prichard seem to hold the view that duty and interest are different forms of reason.
3. I say "something like the principle of egoism" because Sidgwick thinks of egoism as a principle of maximizing one's own pleasure or "agreeable

consciousness" rather than of maximizing the satisfaction of one's desires. See Sidgwick 1981.

4. References to Kant's works are inserted into the text, using an abbreviation for the title of the work followed by the volume and page number of the Prussian Academy Edition (1902ff.; reprint of vols. 1–9 by de Gruyter) found in the margins of most translations. The translations I have used are those of Mary Gregor, published in the series Cambridge Texts in the History of Philosophy. G stands for *Groundwork of the Metaphysics of Morals* (1785; Cambridge: Cambridge University Press, 1998); C2 for *The Critique of Practical Reason* (1788; Cambridge: Cambridge University Press, 1997); and MM for *The Metaphysics of Morals* (1797; Cambridge: Cambridge University Press, 1996).

    Kant's remarks on happiness are not easy to reconcile with one another. Elsewhere in the *Groundwork* Kant says that happiness is "an ideal of the imagination" or "an indeterminate concept" because I cannot be sure which elements I should include in it in order to achieve "a maximum of well-being in my present condition and in every future condition" (G 4: 418). In these passages Kant portrays the agent as wondering which ends to will as the elements of happiness – whether to will health, wealth, or knowledge, say. What seems to make these elements candidates for inclusion in the happy life is not that they are the objects of the agent's own inclinations but that they are the sorts of things that usually bring about, or constitute, "well-being." Sometimes these remarks are interpreted hedonistically – happiness is not the satisfaction of inclination but pleasure, to which the satisfaction of inclination is related causally. This is in part because Kant makes other remarks that seem to call for a hedonistic interpretation, most notably the parallel remarks in the *Critique of Practical Reason* (C2 5: 23–6). In another passage, Kant defines happiness as an ideal in which "all inclinations unite in one sum" (G 4: 399), suggesting that happiness is not just a maximum of satisfaction but rather an ideal of having *everything* one wants. And it is arguable (although I will not argue it here) that the argument of the Dialectic of the *Critique of Practical Reason* makes best sense if happiness is understood as success in attaining one's willed ends. These are all different ideas.

5. That is, Kant thinks this if we suppose that the principle of self-love, which according to Kant governs the evil will, dictates something like the maximization of a person's satisfaction. Kant does sometimes seem to think of the principle of self-love that way, in particular in the opening sections of the *Critique of Practical Reason*. But at other times, in particular in the first section of the *Groundwork*, he seems to think of it more as a "wanton" principle, the principle of (unreflectively) following the desire of the moment. I have argued that this is how it should be understood in 1996a: esp. 208–12.

6. In Korsgaard 1997.

7. See Mill 1979: ch. IV, esp. 34.

8. Mill actually says this is what he meant in a letter to Henry Jones:

    As to the sentence you quote from my *Utilitarianism*, when I said that the general happiness is a good to the aggregate of all persons I did not mean that every human being's happiness is a good to every other human being; though I think, in a good state of society & education it would be so. I merely meant in this particular sentence to argue that since A's happiness is a good, B's a good, C's a good, &c, the sum of all these goods must be a good.

(Mill 1972: 1414). I owe the reference to Charlotte Brown and Jerome Schneewind.

9. See Butler 1983: Sermon IV (originally Sermon XI), esp. 47–9.
10. Butler 1983: preface, 21.
11. The assumption that practical reasoning reveals our "real" desires to us is an expression of romantic metaphysics in the most literal sense, and it is tempting to speculate that its influence on Anglo-American philosophy springs from Hegel. The distinction that Aristotle and Kant make between theoretical and practical reason is elided by the assumption. But it may also be an expression of the empiricist view, found for example in Hume, that "reason" just is "the discovery of truth and falsehood" (*A Treatise of Human Nature*, 458).
12. The word "desire" is a source of confusion in philosophy because of the many ways it is used. The idea voiced in the text – that "desire" refers to an item in one's natural psychology – might be disputed, or anyway deemed misleading, by philosophers who think desire is a response to the perception of reasons. The instrumental egoist, however, needs to understand the idea of desire naturalistically, since he thinks there are only instrumental reasons.
13. The two false assumptions may be thought related: it is because the instrumental egoist supposes that the conclusion of practical reasoning uncovers your real desire that he supposes it will cause a motive in you. But I am not certain of this. Consider the theoretical analogues of the two false assumptions. The analogue of the first assumption would seem to be the view that logical reasoning is actually a sort of empirical reasoning that uncovers our "real" beliefs – or, alternatively, a Platonic view that makes all a priori reasoning a matter of recollection. The analogue of the second false assumption is that logical reasoning is a matter of the (merely causal) effect of certain conjunctions of judgments on the mind. The first assumption seems to me to be more commonly made about practical reasoning than about theoretical reasoning, and made as a way of making all reasoning seem theoretical. But as I will suggest later, I think the second assumption is commonly made about both kinds of reasoning. This makes me think the two errors may have separate sources.
14. Hannah Ginsborg (1998) argues that Kant's view is that we are free to act against our happiness only when the moral law demands it. There are certainly passages in his works that can be taken to support that view. But I do not see how it can be squared with the claim that we "act under the idea of freedom." Admittedly, the foundational argument in the *Critique of Practical Reason* is often thought to be different from, and to represent a rejection of, the foundational argument of the *Groundwork*, and in the second *Critique* Kant does not appeal to the thesis that we act under the idea of freedom. In fact he argues there that our freedom is revealed to us only by the experience of moral obligation: we know we are free to act against even our strongest desire, since we know that we can do what we ought (C2 5: 29–31). Morality is the *ratio cognoscendi* of freedom, although freedom is the *ratio essendi* of morality (C2 5: 4n.). But the freedom thus revealed

must be general. For even here Kant argues that freedom is the *ratio essendi*
of morality – the moral law applies to us because we have free will, not the
reverse. For more on these arguments see Korsgaard 1996b and 1998.

15. This discussion is largely lifted from Korsgaard 1998.

16. It is unclear whether Kant means to imply that the duty to pursue happiness
can only be an indirect one (not an end in itself, but only a means to the
avoidance of temptation) or whether he has changed his mind about the
duty to pursue one's own happiness altogether. But either way he now seems
to think we do inevitably pursue happiness.

17. I make a similar argument – that Kant's account of instrumental imperatives
in the *Groundwork* does not represent his mature view – in 1997: 239–40.

18. I owe the example to Barbara Herman.

19. I say "to the extent" because it is important to this account that self-
determination can be partial and therefore defective. Something must
count as trying to determine yourself and failing, for example willing the
end but failing to will the means. Otherwise it will be impossible to violate
practical imperatives: you will either determine yourself successfully or not
at all. To see the importance of this, consider the comparison to language
again. If you violate the rules of English, there is a sense in which we might
say, "You are not speaking English." But in another sense, if you were not
speaking English, the rules of English would not apply to you and so you
would have done nothing amiss. If not speaking English at all were the only
alternative to speaking English perfectly, the rules of English would not be
normative, since the moment they failed to be followed they would also fail
to apply. But of course that is not how it is: you can certainly violate a rule
of English and still be, recognizably, trying to speak English. What matters
is that your efforts at speaking are generally guided, even if unsuccessfully,
by the rules. This is what makes normativity possible.

20. Actually, something stronger is true: there would be no actions. A movement
caused by a desire or a passion is not an action. Blushing, trembling, and
salivating are not actions. This is not to say that one must employ rational
principles in order to act; the other animals act. But in their case instincts
play the role of principles: they determine what the animal does with the
sensory and desiderative inputs that assail it. See Korsgaard 1998: esp. 49–54.

21. To see this, recall the comparison to Mill. The argument for the principle
of utility depends on the idea that each person's happiness is a good and
therefore the utilitarian must grant that each person's happiness is the
source of a normative claim. Again what we get in the first instance is a
plurality of normative principles, one for each person's happiness, and
one – assuming that adding makes sense – for the total. Someone who
challenges the principle of utility when his own happiness is to be sacrificed
is not denying that there will be more total happiness if we follow the
principle of utility. He is asking why he therefore has a reason to give up his
own happiness, which the utilitarian must agree is also a good.

22. Is the principle of balancing, taken by itself, a principle of reason? Let me
first back up. In Korsgaard 1996c and 1997 I argue that the principle of
instrumental reason is normative on the grounds that it is a constitutive

principle of willing. I mean this in a strong sense of constitutive: there is a sense in which acting on the principle of instrumental reason *gives* you a will, that is, an agency that is unified and distinct from the particular incentives over which it has authority. More precisely, it makes you such an agency. The general idea is that if you were swayed from the pursuit of an end *whenever* you experienced an incentive (say, difficulty, boredom, temptation) that made you reluctant to take the means to that end, you could not be said to have a will to pursue the end – or taking the point generally, to have a will at all. Since you would be moved by any incentive or impulse that came along, you would not be distinct from your impulses, and so would be a sort of disunified heap of impulses. (In 1996c and 1999 I make a similar argument about the principle of universalization.) The principle of balancing also seems necessary to secure the unity of your will, at a sort of next level up from the instrumental principle: we might say that without it, you are a mere heap of projects, each wholly engrossing you, and so in effect being you, at the moment of its ascendancy. This is vague and I am not perfectly happy with it, but it may be taken to indicate that unlike the egoistic principle, the principle of balancing *is* the right sort of thing to be a rational principle. For the relevant arguments see Korsgaard 1996c: section one of the reply, esp. 225–33; 1997: esp. 245–50; and 1999: esp. 23–7.

23. My attention was drawn to this by Nagel 1970: 36.
24. See Williams 1973. My discussion throughout this paper owes much to Williams. Williams borrows the device of the I-desire from Anthony Kenny (1963).
25. See note 26.
26. Hume 1975: 281–82. Hume, following Butler (that is, following the argument mentioned in note 9 above), is arguing that satisfying the passion of benevolence makes at least as much of a contribution to your own happiness as satisfying a less altruistic desire. Like Butler, Hume goes on to throw certain pleasures into the calculation along with that proportional satisfaction – the immediate feeling of benevolence, which he says is "sweet, smooth, tender, and agreeable" (282), the pleasing consciousness that we have done well, and so forth. The argument is hedonistic, and satisfaction is thrown as one of the relevant pleasures; and yet it follows from the argument that we could not get the satisfaction if we acted for the sake of the satisfaction *rather than* for the sake of helping the other. If this argument were intended to motivate an agent, authentic benevolence and the desire for one's own satisfaction and pleasure would have to be combined somehow in the agent's motivation. With a theory of volition such as the Kantian account described in this chapter, we might explain how this combination is possible. The benevolent person *desires* the other's good for its own sake, but he *chooses* to act on that desire rather than some other desire because of its special advantages. But Hume and Butler do not have a theory of volition, so their accounts leave it unclear how we could be moved at one and the same moment by the desire for another's good and the desire for our own. I do not consider this to be a problem for Hume, since in his case I think the argument is not intended

to motivate; its aim is rather to establish congruence between the moral and the self-interested points of view. (See Charlotte Brown's unpublished paper "Hume Against the Selfish Schools and the Monkish Virtues," and my own account in 1996c: secs. 2.2.4–7, 60–6.) But it may be a problem for Butler.

27. The argument of this chapter may leave the reader with a pair of related worries. First, one may wonder why, if the idea of rational egoism is as confused as I have claimed, the temptation to believe in the egoistic principle is so strong and so perennial. Second, and more importantly, one may wonder where the argument leaves the idea of happiness or the individual human good, and the rationality of pursuing that good. I have not discussed hedonism much in this paper, but like many of my readers I do not find it plausible, at least in its modern, Benthamite form. But if we reject both hedonism and the desire-satisfaction model, it may seem as if we are left with only a kind of "external realist" conception of the individual's good or happiness. On such a conception, the good is something defined independently of the individual's natural desires and capacities for interest and enjoyment. This seems absurd, since most of us believe that a person's good or happiness must be something *necessarily* capable of motivating, interesting, or pleasing him. And of course there is a connection between these two worries, for the unpalatability of external realism about happiness or a person's good has something to do with the perennial temptation to believe in egoism. To do justice to these questions would require another paper, and it is a topic I hope to take up on some future occasion. For now I will only indicate where I think the answer lies. The ancient Greeks, especially Aristotle, offer a conception of the human good which is psychologically grounded, but which cannot be identified with either the desire-satisfaction model or Benthamite hedonism. The rough idea is that happiness rests in the excellent activity of our healthy faculties, an activity that we necessarily experience as pleasurable, although not because it is the cause of a pleasant sensation. I believe some version of this conception can be shown to be much more plausible than its modern, less sophisticated, alternatives. See Aristotle's *Nicomachean Ethics* and the discussion of pleasure and pain in Korsgaard 1996c: secs. 4.3.1–10, 145–53.

Bibliography

Aristotle 1984. *Nicomachean Ethics*, tr. W. D. Ross, rev. J. O. Urmson. In *The Complete Works of Aristotle*, Revised Oxford Translation, ed. Jonathan Barnes. Princeton, N. J.: Princeton University Press.

Brown, Charlotte. Hume Against the Selfish Schools and the Monkish Virtues. Unpublished manuscript.

Butler, Joseph. 1983. Fifteen Sermons Preached at the Rolls Chapel. In Joseph Butler, *Five Sermons Preached at the Rolls Chapel and a Dissertation upon the Nature of Virtue*, ed. Stephen Darwall. Indianapolis, Ind.: Hackett.

Ginsborg, Hannah. 1998. Korsgaard on Choosing Non-Moral Ends. *Ethics* 109: 5–21.

Hume, David. 1975. *Enquiry Concerning the Principles of Morals*, 3rd ed., ed. Peter H. Nidditch. Oxford: Clarendon.

Hume, David. 1978. *A Treatise of Human Nature*, (2nd ed., ed. Peter H. Nidditch). Oxford: Clarendon.

Kant, Immanuel. 1902. *Gesammelte Schriften*. Berlin: G. Reimer.

Kenny, Anthony. 1963. *Action, Emotion, and Will*. London: Routledge.

Korsgaard, Christine M. 1996a. From Duty and for the Sake of the Noble: Kant and Aristotle on Morally Good Action. In Stephen Engstrom and Jennifer Whiting (eds.), *Aristotle, Kant, and the Stoics: Rethinking Happiness and Duty*. New York: Cambridge University Press, 203–36.

Korsgaard, Christine M. 1996b. Morality as Freedom. In Christine M. Korsgaard, *Creating the Kingdom of Ends*. New York: Cambridge University Press, 159–87.

Korsgaard, Christine (with G. A. Cohen, Raymond Geuss, Thomas Nagel, and Bernard Williams). 1996c. *The Sources of Normativity*, ed. Onora O'Neill Cambridge: Cambridge University Press.

Korsgaard, Christine M. 1997. The Normativity of Instrumental Reason. In Garrett Cullity and Berys Gaut (eds.), *Ethics and Practical Reason*. Oxford: Clarendon, 215–54.

Korsgaard, Christine M. 1998. Motivation, Metaphysics, and the Value of the Self: A Reply to Ginsborg, Guyer, and Schneewind. *Ethics* 109: 49–66.

Korsgaard, Christine. 1999. Self-Constitution in the Ethics of Plato and Kant. *The Journal of Ethics* 3: 1–29.

Mill, John Stuart. 1972. The Later Letters of John Stuart Mill, 1849–1873, ed. Francis E. Mineka and Dwight N. Lindley. In *Collected Works of John Stuart Mill*, vol. XVI. Toronto: University of Toronto Press.

Mill, John Stuart. 1979. *Utilitarianism*. Indianapolis, Ind.: Hackett.

Nagel, Thomas. 1970. *The Possibility of Altruism*. Princeton, N.J.: Princeton University Press.

Nietzsche, Friedrich. 1968. *Twilight of the Idols*. In Friedrich Nietzsche, *Twilight of the Idols and The Anti-Christ*, tr. R. J. Hollingdale. Harmondsworth: Penguin.

Sidgwick, Henry. 1981. *The Methods of Ethics*, 7th ed. (1907). Indianapolis, Ind.: Hackett.

Williams, Bernard. 1973. Egoism and Altruism. In Bernard Williams, *Problems of the Self*. Cambridge: Cambridge University Press, 250–65.

4

Thinking about Conflicts of Desire

Henry S. Richardson

Nothing is more familiar: One wants one thing and wants another, but cannot have both. The problem also has a less objectual, more behavioral guise, as when one wants to do one thing, do another, and cannot do both. Most generally, perhaps, we may mark out a propositional form of desire conflict: One desires that p, desires that q, and recognizes that both propositions cannot obtain.[1] In whichever form, desire conflicts pervade our daily lives. That is not in itself a big deal: To say this is hardly to side, yet, with Isaiah Berlin on conflicts of Values.[2] Whatever he meant by clashing Values, he presumably did not have in mind that between a sensible family station wagon and a sporty two-seater, nor that between attending the department meeting and watching one's child play soccer, nor yet that between one's sister hosting one for the holidays and one's brother doing so. I want to focus on the conflicts of desire that are pedestrian and pervasive, rather than the ones that are portentous and potentially problematic. While the latter are important for ethics and value theory, even the simpler, more basic conflicts put our understanding of desire under significant pressure.

In addition to facing conflicts of desire daily, we also constantly deliberate about how to resolve them. That is not to say that it is easy: We may feel torn about what sort of car to buy, about how to juggle professional and familial responsibilities, or about the best way to plan our holidays. Sometimes, we let inertia or someone else decide these matters for us, and sometimes we cannot decide at all. Often, however, we will deliberate about these issues and come to a decision about how best to resolve our conflicts of desire.

I lay down these undeniable commonplaces about desires – that they pervasively conflict and that we often deliberate in terms of how to resolve their conflicts – at the outset, as it will turn out that they pose an important challenge to an influential way of thinking about desire. It is my claim that in order to make adequate sense of these fundamental phenomena, we need to depart radically from the simple, dyadic functionalist way in which desire has, of late, mainly been understood by philosophers. On this understanding, desires are distinguished along two dimensions: They have different objects and different strengths. To make better sense of conflicts of desire, I argue, we need to return to a richer interpretation of desire more along the lines of Aristotle's, which adds a third dimension that serves to "place" the desire in a hierarchy of ends. What I criticize, then, is not functionalism, as such – for it seems plausible to understand Aristotle as a functionalist, too, in some sense[3] – but the two-dimensionality of most modern functionalist understandings of desire.

According to modern functionalist accounts, a desire is a psychological state that serves a dual role as both a disposition tending to produce an action and a rationalizer of the action produced. It both tends to give rise to the action and, by being directed toward a state at which the action also aims, helps to explain or to rationalize the action.[4] In so operating, a desire is thought of as paired with a belief: A desire that p is paired with a belief that by φ-ing, one will help bring it about that p, thereby tending to produce and rationalize the action of φ-ing. So much can be said without assigning any kind of priority to desire or to belief. Different functionalists then develop this basic idea in various ways, sometimes treating desire as the driving element, with beliefs merely ancillary to them, and sometimes granting a greater role to beliefs as judgments.[5]

Those unwilling simply to take on board the commonsense distinction between belief and desire may ask for a philosophically rigorous way to distinguish these two mental states. Their distinct functional contributions are sometimes explained by reference to the idea of "direction of fit." A belief must fit the world, but the world must fit a desire. As Michael Smith has rather starkly glossed the contrast, "a belief that p tends to go out of existence in the presence of a perception with the content that not p, whereas a desire that p tends to endure, disposing the subject to bring it about that p."[6] While I cast some doubt on the adequacy of this way of distinguishing the two kinds of state, it may serve to help provide some initial orientation to those unwilling to take on board the commonsense notions.

Returning to the simple functionalist characterization of desire itself, it is important to note that if we set aside any issue about whose desire it is, it follows that there are only two dimensions essential to any desire: an object that indicates the direction of its tendency and a weight that indicates its strength.[7] Accordingly, one problem that one might have with the model of practical reasoning suggested by this account of desire is that it will rely on a notion of "balancing" desires that is either empty (the "weights" simply reflecting the decisions once made) or illusory (the "weights" being purported to be accessible to the agent for purposes of deliberating), as well as being resistant to more subtle, principle-based modes of reasoning.[8] I have prosecuted that line of criticism elsewhere.[9] Here, I want to pursue some difficulties that arise instead with regard to the other aspect of the simple functionalist characterization of desire: its implications about the objects of desire.

Issues about how to understand the objects of desires arise as soon as we begin to reflect on the potential form of conflicts between them. Clearly, most conflicts of desires have a contingent basis, but is it possible for the conflict to reflect a logical contradiction? Bernard Williams was skeptical:

The contingent root of [a] conflict may, indeed, be disguised by a use of language that suggests logical impossibility of the desires being jointly satisfied; thus a man who was thirsty and lazy, who was seated comfortably, and whose drinks were elsewhere, might perhaps represent his difficulty to himself as his both wanting to remain seated and wanting to get up. But to put it this way is for him to hide the roots of his difficulty under the difficulty itself; the second element in the conflict has been so described as to reveal the obstacle to the first, and not its own real object. The sudden appearance of help, or the discovery of drinks within arm's reach, would make all plain.[10]

The crucial point to note here is how Williams's justified refusal to take self-ascriptions of desire as definitive causes trouble. He is right that we cannot simply trust agents to give us reliable descriptions of what it is that they desire – not just because they are often insincere or unwilling to trust us, but also because they are often unclear in their own minds about what it is that they desire. If we cannot trust self-reports to describe or individuate the objects of desires for us, however, we must find a theoretical basis for doing so.

In what follows, I begin by examining the sort of account of the objects of desire that seems to follow from the simple, dyadic functional characterization of desire. This will be seen to go in two potential directions, depending on whether the objects of desire are taken to be as the agent implicitly takes them as being or rather as the agent would take them to be after completely thinking all relevant matters through. On the first variant, as Philip Pettit and Michael Smith have argued, desires so understood are too crudely individuated to be generally appropriate elements in deliberation. But if that is so, then we will have difficulty accounting for deliberation about conflicts of desires. On the second variant, which exploits the flexibility of taking desire to have propositional objects, while desires would be as eagerly welcomed as any fairy godmother would be if she ever showed up, they are equally fictional as any Sleeping Beauty. Hence, as I argue, neither the idealized nor the nonidealized way of thinking about the objects of desire supported by the dyadic functional characterization can well cope with deliberation about conflicts of desire. While I would not suggest that we deliberate *only* about desires, we can and must deliberate about our desires sometimes, especially when they conflict. A philosophical theory of desire that cannot well account for how we do so is seriously defective.

This complaint would not be conclusive if we had no better way of thinking about desires. Perhaps we are, in fact, simply in a muddle when it comes to our conflicting desires. But there is, I urge, an alternative understanding of desire – one that gets beyond the two-dimensionality of the simple functional characterization – that can generate a better interpretation of the ways we deliberate when faced with conflicts of desire and affords a better basis for preparing to understand autonomy.

DESIRE'S OBJECT AS OUT OF PLACE IN DELIBERATION?

In this section I present Pettit and Smith's argument against generally accepting nonidealized desires into the foreground of deliberation. As they urge, it is one thing to suppose that combinations of belief and desire must be operating in the background every time someone (intentionally) acts, and quite another to take an agent's deliberation always to proceed via a recognition of how belief and desire combine to support acting in a certain way. They affirm, as relatively noncontroversial, what they call "the intentional conception of human beings," according to which pairs of desires and beliefs are always operating when someone acts; they also accept, for the sake of argument, "the deliberative conception of human beings," according to which "action usually issues from the belief that there is a justifying reason . . . for the choice."[11] Yet this leaves open the question, as they point out, of what the relation is between the reasons on which agents act and the underlying desires. In particular, must agents take their desires to be their reasons for acting?

Supposing that they must, Pettit and Smith argue, would impose a counterintuitive shape on the scope of our desires. By the "scope" of a desire, they mean its aim as tested across intertemporal and counterfactual variation.[12] Williams's simple example of the thirsty recliner has prepared us to understand what they mean by this. One of the surface facts of that case is that this agent desires to get up. What the miraculous appearance of drinks at his elbow would make plain, however, is that he wants to get up only because he wants a drink: Counterfactual variation of the facts helps us hone in on what he "really" wants. But, Pettit and Smith argue, taking desires as they ordinarily appear to us into the foreground of deliberation will impose an unacceptable view of the scope of some of our desires.

The reason this will happen, as Pettit and Smith lay it out, hinges on their definition of bringing a desire into the foreground of deliberation. For a given choice, "the desire for [state of affairs S] figures in the foreground if and only if the agent reaches that choice via the recognition that he has that desire and that the option has the desirable property – the property justifying its choice – of promising to satisfy the desire."[13] But this means, in turn, that the scope of the desire, as it operates in deliberation, will be unacceptably shaped around the idea of answering to the agent's desire, suggesting that the agent would not pursue this course of action in those possible worlds in which he or she did not desire S.[14] And while this may be a plausible rendering of the reason-giving scope of some desires – they suggest the craving for a smoke – others will pick out reasons that are not so easily undercut by counterfactually subtracting the desire. Here Pettit and Smith give two examples: the desire to do one's duty and the desire to submit an interesting paper for publication. What one wants when one wants to do one's duty is not counterfactually conditioned on one's wanting so to act: What one wants is to do one's duty whether or not one is so inclined. What one wants when one desires to publish an interesting article is not dependent on the continuation of the desire to publish it, but rather on whether the ideas in it are really new and interesting. In these latter sorts of case, giving a foreground role to the thought "I desire S" will distort the deliberation of the agent and misapprehend the reasons that the underlying desire actually reflects.

I take it that Pettit and Smith's argument places a large obstacle in the way of anyone who seeks to explain desire's role in deliberation. Reacting to it, moral realists, anti-Humean cognitivists, and others may want to say, "Aha, we told you so: Desires are not reasons." That would be too hasty a reaction, however – and not only because we ultimately want to know how it is that we deliberate about conflicts of desire. It is too hasty also because there remain two important ways to see desires as shaping the reasons taken up in deliberation, compatibly with the simple functional characterization of desire. First, desire might operate largely in the background of deliberation, being taken up explicitly as reason-giving only in cases such as the craving for a smoke. Second, desire might be idealized so that, after all, taking it into the foreground would present all considerations in the right shape, giving each the correct counterfactual scope (by whatever lights the uncorrected desires were deemed, when brought to the fore, to fail).[15]

Pettit and Smith argue for the first, backgrounding option. Although human intentional action is to be understood in terms of the functional combination of belief-desire pairs of the kind I have described, deliberation is not to be conceived as generally taking up desires as reasons or even as adequately scope-defining halves of a belief-desire reason. Their objection to foregrounding desires, again, is that doing so will generate improper counterfactually contoured objects in many cases.

THE PROBLEM WITH BACKGROUNDING DESIRES

The world is saturated with potential desirability, from careers to types of cocoa bean. Not to mention the potential undesirability of owning a clunky station wagon, missing a child's soccer game, or offending one relative by going to another's for the holidays. (For present purposes, it does not matter whether we think of these goods and ills as residing, objectively, in the world or as being projected onto it by our myriad actual and potential desires. Indeed, one of the philosophically important features of the intentional conception of human beings, as Pettit and Smith develop it, is that the role in which it casts functional combinations of beliefs and desires is compatible with at least some sorts of cognitivist value metaphysics as well as with noncognitivism.[16]) What does matter here is that we cannot live our lives by attending evenhandedly to all the potential considerations that there are. Our desires must either constitute or else carve out a manageable subset of these potential considerations so as to guide our choices of careers, cars, and chocolates.

This fact generates a problem for the idea of backgrounding desires. In many ways, this problem is the flip side of the problem of counterintuitive scope identified by Pettit and Smith in the cases of doing one's duty and submitting interesting articles. Suppose that my schedule affords me a few hours' leisure after dinner. There are all sorts of ways I might use the time: by going drinking with friends, watching basketball on television, going to the ballet, reading a good novel, and so on. In cases such at this, it would be crazy *not* to foreground one's desires. One needs to give due prominence to such thoughts as "I want to catch the NCAA finals, but I have no desire to go drinking." Otherwise, the decision-problem in any such case would be overwhelming. Furthermore, giving each consideration just such scope as it would have independently of one's desires would have implications just as counterintuitive as letting commitment to duty be conditioned on one's desires. It would be to fail to give due prominence to the set of worlds in which, like the actual world, one feels like watching basketball. Hence, backgrounding dyadic functional desires yields problems in deliberation that parallel the problems with foregrounding them.

To be fair to Pettit and Smith, I should note that by "backgrounding desire," they mean "recognizing that desire need not always enter the foreground of deliberation." Sometimes it will appropriately enter, sometimes not. If we could reliably tell, for any given desire or its object, whether the desire were properly brought into the foreground, then we could steer between the twin rocks of focusing too little on what we want and focusing too much on it. But there seems to be no general basis for determining whether a given desire ought to be foregrounded. Objective reasons might, promiscuously, be seen lurking under most any desire. One might take it that there is objective reason to publish interesting ideas, but equally that there is objective reason to read great novels. For an enormous range of such issues, it seems to be rationally permissible either to take such (purportedly) objective considerations as being regulative in one's life or not. As Harry Frankfurt would put it, this is partly a matter of what one cares about.[17] Yet we cannot first settle what we care about, and then proceed to deliberate about how to resolve our conflicts of desire. That is because our conflicts of desire – certainly, at any rate, our more significant ones – force us to reconsider what it is that we do care about. What place these considerations deserve – whether foreground or background – seems to be something that we have to settle in deliberation, rather than being something that can be settled on general, philosophical grounds.[18]

With regard to background and foreground, then, the dyadic functional characterization of desire puts us in a no-win situation. Forced to think in terms only of a desire's object and its strength, we are here having to try to settle in terms of each desire's object whether it belongs in the foreground or not; yet this is an issue that we would in fact be in a good position to settle only at the end of the day, after already having resolved the conflict of desire in question. For instance, suppose that I want to focus on my research but that I also want to be department chair, as there are some departmental reforms I would be excited to undertake. Suppose, however, that I also foresee becoming bored and frustrated with the chairmanship job before its three-year term is up, at which time I would no longer want to carry out its duties. How should I conceive of the reasons on the side of service? Is their correct scope one on which they withdraw or recede at that future time in which I am no longer desirous of reforming, or does the prospect of reform put forward an objective reason that I should treat as having the same force independently of what I feel like doing? In such a case, the answer to this sort of question simply is not antecedently clear: Answering it is part and parcel of attempting to deliberate about and resolve the conflict of desire at issue. Yet while the dyadic functional characterization of desire opens us up to pitfalls on either side, highlighting the potential problems with either taking the agent's desiring into the scope or not doing so, it offers no help to our attempts to resolve such questions.

IDEALIZING DESIRES DOES NOT HELP

If desires as they are cannot be brought into the foreground without yielding distortion, the other alternative to backgrounding them is to suppose them to be corrected or idealized in such a way that this sort of distortion would not result from bringing them into the foreground. To see how this idealization might go, we should first start considerably farther back than the cases of doing one's duty and submitting interesting articles. Just as the thirsty recliner may characterize his desires in a way that fails to get at the root of what is going on, so, too, more pervasively an agent may characterize his or her desires in ways that suggest false generalizations across possible worlds while failing to suggest the right ones.

In the functionalist tradition, where the dyadic characterization of desire we are working with arises, it is natural to think of the objects of desire in terms of its satisfaction conditions. Further, in line with Smith's gloss of desire's "direction of fit," it will make sense to think of the object of desire in terms of some proposition, p, the obtaining of which tends to make the desire (for p) go away. In the right way, of course: A kick in the

stomach will make a desire for chocolate go away, but ought not be taken
to satisfy that desire. What, exactly, "the right way" amounts to need not
concern us here. One approach is to appeal to the idea of reinforcing an
underlying disposition: "A desire is satisfied iff its going away reinforces
the disposition to act in the way that caused it to go away."[19] However
one spells out the conditions for making the desire go away in the right
way, it is likely that agents will often mistake what they are, and hence
mischaracterize their own desires. There is so much of which we are
ignorant. Sometimes we will be overly specific: One will think that one
wants a ketch, when really any single-masted sailboat would equally satisfy
him. Another will take herself to want chocolate, when carob would do
just as well. And sometimes we will overgeneralize. One will think he
likes dogs and wants to own one, whereas it is really only dachshunds that
he desires. Another will suppose herself to want chocolate, when really
only 73.5 percent bittersweet cocoa from Venezuelan beans would satisfy
her. And we have not even mentioned the complexities that arise from
the interaction of these various objects of desire in different contexts
(consuming Venezuelan bittersweet on a ketch cruising the Venezuelan
coast may have quite different effects than consuming it while walking
one's dachshunds on a gray winter's day in New England).

   Mind-boggling as these complexities of the objects of desire may be,
the so-called theory of rational choice has made us familiar with the sort
of idealization that would prevent them from posing a problem. The sort
of rational choice theory I mean is that which confines itself to a fairly
modest set of axioms – such as that of transitivity – that together ensure
that agents' preferences will constitute an ordering across the options
they face. Yet the crudity of agents' actual understanding of their options
often gives rise to cases of apparent intransitivity and of other violations of
the axioms. Here is an example from Broome:[20]

Maurice prefers visiting Rome to mountaineering in the Alps, and he prefers
staying at home to visiting Rome. However, he does not prefer staying at home to
mountaineering; if he had a choice between those two alternatives, he would take
the mountaineering trip. So Maurice's preferences are intransitive. Write "*M*"
for mountaineering, "*R*" for visiting Rome and "*H*" for staying at home. Since
Maurice prefers R to M and H to R, transitivity requires him to prefer H to M.
And he does not. . . .
   Maurice's claim to rationality is this. Mountaineering frightens him, so he
prefers visiting Rome. Sightseeing bores him, so he prefers staying at home. But
to stay at home when he could have gone mountaineering would, he believes,
be cowardly. That is why, if he had the choice between staying at home and
going mountaineering, he would choose to go mountaineering. (To visit Rome

when he could have gone mountaineering seems to him cultured rather than cowardly.)

Let us distinguish four alternatives where previously I distinguished only three: M, mountaineering; R, visiting Rome; H_1, staying at home without having turned down a mountaineering trip; and H_2, staying at home having turned down a mountaineering trip. H_2, Maurice believes, would be cowardly, and H_1 would not. . . . So this example poses no threat to the transitivity axiom, after all.

Such cases of apparent intransitivity, as well as more complex ones involving gambles, such as the Allais paradox, generate, within decision theory, pressure to idealize desires, or their expression in preferences, so as to be sure that they are fine-grained enough to mark all such distinctions among options – without, of course, getting so fine-grained as to postulate a distinction where no relevant one exists.[21] All that we need suppose is that the agent has "completely thought through" all of the factors that matter regarding what he or she wants, including all of the ways they interact across possible worlds.[22]

This sort of idealization would generate a basis for deliberation that would be freed from many of the problems that arise from individuals' imperfect understandings of what it is that they want. Would it help with the kind of problem that Pettit and Smith identify, though, in cases such as wanting to do one's duty? Perhaps not. Their problem seems to arise not from a crude version of the proposition, p, that characterizes the object of one's desire, but rather from taking the fact that one *desires that* p into the foreground of one's deliberation. Still, here is one way that this idealizing route might cope with such cases. The problem situations regarding this desire are those possible worlds in which one does not desire to do one's duty. What does one's desire to do one's duty commit one to saying about such cases? Fiddling with the precise delineation of the object of this desire will not help get around this problem, but it is conceivable that fiddling with the content of all of one's competing desires would do the trick. The thing about the moral desire is that it is categorical. Hence, complete thinking that incorporated it would build an implicit reference to it into every other desire one has – just as Maurice's concern for cowardice got built into, and hence partitioned, the object of staying at home. If every other desire's object is thus divided as between, say, eating Venezuelan bittersweet in a way that does not violate my duty (to exploited rainforest peons, for instance) and eating Venezuelan bittersweet in a way that does violate my duty, then it may turn out that the deliberative damage done by the counterintuitive shape of thinking directly about one's desire to do one's duty will be adequately compensated for by adjustments elsewhere in one's system of desires.

Whether this idealizing response to Pettit and Smith would work will not, in the end, matter, as this approach has other difficulties that I will now highlight. If it did not work even as a first line of defense here, then we could take it that there are two independent problems with bringing desires of the dyadic functionalist sort into the foreground of deliberation: that of getting the right characterization of each desire's object and that arising from attending, in deliberation, to one's desiring as such. But for present purposes let me suppose that the idealizing solution is equally successful as the backgrounding one in avoiding the problems of counterintuitive scope.

The backgrounding proposal clashes head-on with our need to take up conflicting desires in deliberation, but the idealizing approach is hardly any better when it comes to deliberating about desires. I have argued elsewhere that such idealized approaches cannot in general count as apt models of deliberation, as they assume that the serious deliberation has already been concluded.[23] This point holds a fortiori about deliberation addressed to conflicts of desire. Whenever desires conflict, we have strong reason to examine matters closely to see whether we have gotten to the root of the relevant concerns and whether we have characterized the competing considerations correctly. If he fails to do that, Williams's thirsty recliner will remain stuck in a quandary that he might have escaped simply by asking someone to bring him a drink. In the case of contingent conflicts of desire, there is also always the possibility of shifts in the object of one or the other that will effect a compromise. Perhaps I can watch just the more exciting second half of the NCAA playoff game and still get that paper revised. The whole thrust of the idealizing approach, as is plain from its development within preference theory, is to arrive at an all-things-considered ordering of alternatives. If that is really what one has, then one will no longer face conflicts of desires: One will simply consult one's ordering, which will have already resolved all such potential conflicts. Hence the idealizing route escapes the problems with foregrounding desires only at the cost of rendering itself useless to deliberating about conflicts of desire.

AN ALTERNATIVE CONCEPTION OF DESIRE

The simple functional characterization of desire, with its two dimensions of direction and strength, may be well suited to explaining human action from, as it were, the outside. What we have just seen, however, is that it is not well suited to being taken up within our deliberations. A fully adequate account of desire ought to serve in both capacities, but in this chapter, I simply develop an account that fits better with the nature of deliberation. In this section, I set out a competing characterization of desire – one with roots in Aristotle – that adds a third dimension, which I will call "place." The dimension of *place* indicates something about the location of the desire's object within the agent's values or ends. I postpone a fuller explanation of my choice of label; first, to put myself in the position of being able to explain this dimension of place any further, I need to say more about the general philosophical motivations of this alternative conception of desire.

The modern, functionalist characterization of desire arose within theories that aspired to do more than simply give a general account of what belief and desire are. They aimed to put us in a position to explain or "rationalize" particular actions in terms of particular desires. This is the aim of the Davidsonian interpreter, who seeks to make sense of interlocutors' particular actions by factoring their psychological states into two, a conative one and a cognitive one. The aim of attributing particular desires is even more obvious in the case of the decision theorist who aspires to quantitative definiteness. Think of Ramsey's famous method for eliciting preferences and beliefs about probabilities from choice behavior. By eliciting preferences about certain complex, constructed alternatives ("gambles"), the theorist can – on the supposition that the individual is fundamentally "rational" in the sense of maximizing the expected value of their choices – factor the grounds of preference into two components, desire and belief, and also assign numerical values (unique up to a linear transformation) to those components.[24] In this process, the decision theorist is fundamentally uninterested in how the agent actually arrived at his or her choices. Hence, it is not surprising that this account of desire or preference is not particularly useful in deliberation. But now the new point to which I draw your attention is that such theorists seem to be sacrificing realism about deliberation for the sake of definiteness, even quantitative definiteness, with regard to the operation of these psychological states in particular instances of action. And the reason I stress this is that the Aristotelian psychology to which I now turn is associated with a quite different set of philosophical aims.

Aristotle's account of desire is shaped by the fact that he calls on the notion to help explain the self-movement of animals.[25] Animals move, but, then again, so do leaves and planets. Something is going on in animals that leads us to say that they move themselves – that they move "of their own accord." Well, they act as they desire. To say this is implicitly to accept a hypothesis about what is going on when animals move themselves. It is to say something in response to Aristotle's superficially odd question, "What is it that moves the animal in the case of progressive movement?"[26] The question is not as odd as it sounds, for if we are to be able to understand self-movement, or even hold firm to the contrast between something moving itself and something simply being blown in the wind, then we will have to say something about what is going on within the animals that are moving themselves.[27] This framing concern with something akin to autonomy – a kind of proto-autonomy we share with other animals – will turn out to yield an importantly more sophisticated conception of desire than that provided by modern functionalism.

As always, the shape of potential explanations depends on the characterization of the phenomena to be explained. As Aristotle approached the problem of accounting for self-movement, he argued that the phenomenon exists in a true form only in those animals that have senses capable of perceiving objects at a distance. Sighted and hearing animals can move themselves, whereas the "imperfect" (*atelês*) animals that have only the senses of touch (and taste, we might add) can do so only indefinitely, without any definite aim or direction.[28] This suggests that desire necessarily depends on the deliverances of perceptual faculties.

This observation about the correlation between self-movers and those capable of perceiving objects at a distance seems to have helped inspire Aristotle's account of desire's role in action. Metaphorically, at least, he casts desire as a proto-movement, a kind of reaching out toward an object presented as good by perception. In his account of animal action, there are three main components: (1) the object of desire, perceived as good, (2) the perception (*phantasia*) by means of which it is perceived as good, and (3) the desire for it. As between the desiderative and perceptual capacities, there is a marked division of labor: Whereas the "epistemic" side "is never moved but remains at rest," desire is both moved and moving.[29] Metaphorically, at least, desire is a kind of movement toward an object that is, at least metaphorically, distant. Desire gets the ball of action rolling toward a target one has perceived as good.[30]

Since there is much not to like in this Aristotelian account, we must begin to sort what is illuminating in it from what is not. Its implication that everything for which we reach we perceive to be good has been questioned.[31] Abstracting from that claim, however, the suggestion that perception and imagination play an essential role in orienting desire seems correct, and all we will need is the less objectionable claim that the agent takes the object of desire to be good or attractive in some respect.[32] Aristotle's account of desire is put forward as part of a metaphysical account (as we would call it) of a kind of motion. As such, it is full of obscurities. Indeed, one might say, as a backhanded compliment, that one of its virtues is that it is sufficiently committal to enable one to locate some precise points where questions about the relation between body and soul become pressing.[33] More specifically, however, Aristotle's account of desire is also part of an account of *self*-movement. As such, it gives an enduringly important emphasis to what appears good or attractive to the agent.

Although this broadly Aristotelian view is metaphysical, it is so only in a *general* way. It aims to put before us a general picture of what goes on when animals such as ourselves move themselves. It does not aim, in the first instance, to give an account of particular actions, perceptions, or desires. If a more particular account were wanted, the natural route, for Aristotle himself, at least, would be to start with the good of a given sort of animal, and then consider the extent to which an individual animal either correctly apprehends that good or instead is led into certain mistakes, perceiving as good things that are bad and perceiving as bad things that are good.

Let me now try to abstract the Aristotelian account of desire somewhat from its original formulation. In contrast with the dyadic functionalist characterization, the Aristotelian conception of desire casts it as one of *three* interrelated psychological (functional[34]) states: a *belief* that I can φ, a *perception* (*phantasia*) that φ-ing would be good in some respect r, and a *desire* to φ on account of r – or not to φ in light of some r' perceived as bad. The point of adding in the belief is to make explicit that the function of perception, on the Aristotelian account, is not to provide the "premise of the possible" – or at any rate is not limited to that. Hence, for animals with belief, we can separate that function. The crucial role of perception, differentiating this view from the dyadic functionalist characterization, is that of placing or locating some feature of the action in respect to the agent's conception of the good. (Aristotle, of course, would go on to give an objective account of an agent's good, but I do not think we need to build in any further cognitivism here, beyond what is already implied by the idea of perception, to make out the distinctive conception of desire that Aristotle offers us.) Because of the richer constellation of psychological states in which desires are enmeshed, on this account, desires will correspondingly have three dimensions: an object and a strength, as in the dyadic conception, and additionally one pertaining to the respect in which the object of desire is perceived to be good.

This triadic Aristotelian account of desire has considerable common-sense appeal. Indeed, I would suggest that it is an even better fit with folk psychology – for whatever that is worth – than is the dyadic functionalist belief-desire story. So: a piece of chocolate cake in a store window looks so delicious I come to want it; I believe I can afford it, so I buy it. I recognize that I could desert my post, but see that option as cowardly, and hence do not want to take it. Note, too, that this dimension that places the action within an intelligible conception of the good also snuck into Broome's commonsense descriptions of the reasoning that might lead one from the circular ordering of H over R over M over H to the coherent ordering of H_1 over R over M over H_2. In the example, Maurice prefers Rome as a haven for the cultivated to mountaineering, which is frightening, prefers staying home to going to boring old Rome, and yet prefers mountaineering as a way to prove or express his courage over staying home and being cowardly. There is nothing particularly mysterious or novel in this account, only the familiar structure of everyday practical reasoning.

What the Aristotelian three-dimensional account of desire allows, however, is integrating desire into the reasoning that underlies such refinements of commitment as that of Maurice, rather than limiting desire to being expressed in the two-dimensional orderings that result from and are revised by such refinements. In this way, the Aristotelian view facilitates an accounting for everyday reasoning involving conflicting desires, whereas the dyadic functionalist view does not. The reason for the former's superiority in this respect is that its dimension of place is tolerant of the fact that actual agents have not yet fully worked out their conceptions of the good. Let me explain.

In the case of the thirsty recliner, Williams suspects that the surface characterization, which depicts him as harboring desires that conflict with logical necessity, has not gotten to the bottom of things. To get to the bottom of things, agents guided by the dyadic functionalist characterization face a daunting task: They need to provide a completely thought-through conception of the way their final ends work out and work together in all contexts of action, such that the only work needed for the belief component of the functionalist pair is to indicate which of the ranked alternatives is possible. On the Aristotelian view, in sharp contrast, perception's role is to indicate the place within the agent's conception of the good to look in working such things through: See *deliciousness*, see *cowardice*. The dimension of place thus guides the agent's revisions of his or her aims. On the dyadic functionalist approach, the agent is pushed to *replace* an initial, imperfect characterization of a desire's object or scope (*to get up from my chair*) with another one that gets to the root of things (*to get a drink*). On the Aristotelian approach, one starts with a richer characterization (*to get up from my chair in order to get a drink*) that one can rest with – as in this case – or that, more importantly, indicates lines for potential refinement.

Speaking of getting up in order to get a drink, I have arrived at a way of articulating the dimension of place that is specific to human beings: a teleological one. It is important to recognize, however, that even without drawing on the concept of pursuing one thing for the sake of another, which serves to make an agent's conception of the good explicit, the conceptual resources offered by the Aristotelian account of desire are considerably richer than those offered by the dyadic functional characterization. This richness arises from the dimension of place, which invites a second semantic objection that opens up a potential logical space between the action toward which the agent is tending and the aspect in which that action appears good to the agent. Each of these dimensions being a proper component of desire, on this view, we do not have either to hypothesize an ideal "complete thinking" or to keep desire in the background of deliberation in order to avoid being stuck with a counterintuitive or wrong characterization of the desire's object. Rather, the dimension of place signals that this characterization is a work in progress and indicates the lines by which progress might be made. While having an explicit conception of ends can facilitate this sort of progress, even rats, which may try to pursue a certain path through a maze as a way of getting to some food, can correct themselves once they learn that food is no longer available by that route.

For human beings, who do deploy the teleological concepts of end and means, the logical space between the description of the pursued action and the aspect under which it is perceived to be good can be explicitly captured in terms of the question of whether the action, as described, is sought for its own sake. In the case of final ends, sought for their own sakes, the description of the desired action – in the dimension of scope – *coincides* with the aspect under which it appears good – in the dimension of place. Furthermore, the shapes of the desire in each of these two dimensions coincides in terms that are explicitly conceptualized along these lines by the reflective agent. The agent takes them to coincide.[35]

At this point, I must face two threshold objections. The first is that while Aristotle's attempt to account for animals' self-movement may have helped to explain why he ended up with a triadic concept of desire, having that philosophical motivation is not necessary to adopting the richer notion. In particular, modern functionalists could easily refine their views by adding the dimension of place. To this my response is just that if they do so, they are abandoning the dyadic view I am criticizing in favor of the triadic one I am recommending. I would welcome their company. My tale about Aristotle's philosophical motivations, however, was in part by way of warning or concession: For it seems that enriching the concept of desire in the way I am recommending may well put beyond reach the kind of quantitative definiteness and particularity at which Ramsey, for instance, aimed. I myself think that would be no great loss, but functionalists who would like to join the triadic camp should take note.

Second, it will be objected that – unless we are quite lax about multiplying metaphysical items beyond necessity – what can be said on this Aristotelian account can also be said in simpler terms using the dyadic functional characterization. Revisit Williams's thirsty recliner. One simply needs to get down to what the agent really desires, or desires "at root." Unless the third Aristotelian dimension can be shown to carry out some further function, then it ought to be regarded as an idling wheel, a useless appendage. It is in the course of answering this objection that I will finally explain why I have chosen the term "place" to label the dimension introduced into the Aristotelian account of desire by the importance of perceiving the object of desire as good or attractive.

In the case of something I pursue as a final end, scope and place coincide: I desire to φ in light of it appearing good in some respect r, where r just is *that this would be to φ*. Importantly, however, for these two aspects to coincide does not mean that their functional distinctness disappears. As the case of actions sought for their own sake reminds us, action descriptions can themselves mark out aspects of desirability. This fact, combined with a constraint I will come to shortly, combine to generate an ordering among our ends that is not an ordering of strength. Consider the following: (1) Maurice, we may suppose, values, for its own sake, acting courageously. (2) He also seems to be drawn to mountaineering partly for the sake of expressing or exercising his courage. (3) Although his courage seems somewhat borderline, he might further desire mountaineering for its own sake. However it may be with regard to the third assertion, if the first two facts are true, then it is incoherent to suggest that (4) he also exercises his courage for the sake of mountaineering.

Why is this? The dyadic functional characterization cannot explain this limitation on the possibilities, for if (3) is true, then both acting courageously and mountaineering count as things that Maurice "really wants," and it should not matter in which order they are put. That the intuitive notion of pursuing one thing for the sake of another does tend to build asymmetric orderings indicates that something else must be going on conceptually, besides just picking out what is really wanted. This asymmetry cannot come from the dimension of strength, either, for (2) is compatible with a mountaineering desire being stronger than any desire to be courageous.

What tends to generate this lack of symmetry, I suggest, is that the dimension of place serves to indicate how to regulate the pursuit of the indicated action.[36] It indicates at least a rough place within the agent's conception of the good to look in modulating the way one pursues the desired action. It is primarily with regard to that aspect of one's conception of the good that one would settle any further questions that arose, for instance, in carrying out a plan of so acting. If Maurice wants to go mountaineering as a way of expressing courage, then he will not sign up for a hiking tour that hauls him up easy pitches frequented by little old ladies out bird-watching. There are, indeed, a whole host of possible ways in which mountaineering might fail to test or exhibit courage. The point of the regulation is not so much to narrow down to one specific description of the desired action (*mountaineering with no little old ladies in sight and no...*), but rather to guide the agent's potential deliberation about how to carry out any mountaineering plan. In accepting this way of regulating his mountaineering pursuits, Maurice indicates that he would not regulate his pursuit of courageous action by, say, being concerned with courage only when he is in the mountains. Here, my suggestion is that the asymmetry is needed to preserve the clarity of what regulates what.

A desire's place, then, is its place in an organism's good. In humans, this place may be explicitly conceptualized by the agent as its place within the agent's conception of the good. If that agent's conception of the good has built up any teleological hierarchies of pursuit, then this place may be a place in one such hierarchy. On the Aristotelian three-dimensional characterization, the concept of desire clearly does not presuppose that the agent has developed a conception of the good, let alone that the agent has constructed linked hierarchies of pursuit, but it just as clearly lends itself to being integrated into such articulated conceptions of the good. And this possibility makes it far better suited than is the dyadic functional characterization to providing an adequate account of deliberating about conflicting desires.

The great advantage of the three-dimensional conception of desire, when it comes to conflicting desires, is that the dimension of place indicates potential lines along which to seek a deliberative resolution of the conflict. This dimension provides a conceptual platform for the possibilities of reasonable compromise that, as I noted earlier, exist, but that remain simply offstage as far as the dyadic functional characterization is concerned. With this abstract possibility in mind, we may return to some of our earlier examples.

In Williams's case, of course, the path for deliberation is obvious: If I want to stay seated as a way of maintaining my comfort but want to get up as a way of getting a drink, I must search my context for potential ways of getting a drink without getting up. "Waiter!"

In the case of the conflict between watching the NCAA basketball play-offs and revising a paper, the potential for compromise has again already been signaled, but let me spell out how the dimension of place helps. Suppose that I want to get the paper revised because I have promised to deliver it to certain colleagues in a few days (I desire doing so as a way of fulfilling this expectation or commitment). And suppose that I want to watch the playoffs because I really like viewing exciting basketball (I desire it as a way of viewing some particularly exciting hoops). Then, as noted, I may use the latter dimension of place to narrow my viewing time down to the more exciting second half of the game, thereby (I may hope) leaving myself enough time to meet my paper deadline.

Hence, rather than either indicating inappropriate ways to deliberate about conflicting desires (as the unidealized version of the dyadic functional characterization does) or failing to indicate any ways to deliberate about conflicting desires (as the idealized version of the dyadic functional characterization does), the Aristotelian three-dimensional conception of desire suggests some fully appropriate and fruitful modes of deliberating about conflicts of desires.

Please note, however, that the fact that such modes of compromise among conflicting desires is often reasonable does not imply that it always is, nor that the Aristotelian conception will indicate that it is. Suppose, for instance, that we simply vary the psychological suppositions slightly about the conflict between revising a paper and watching basketball. Suppose that watching basketball is something that I desire, not as a way of seeing some exciting sports, but rather as a way of putting myself in a position of giving a full report on the game to my son, who is otherwise occupied the relevant evening. If that were the place of my game-watching desire, then watching only half of it might not do, and I might find myself in a real quandary.

Once we are well ensconced within explicit human deliberation framed by at least fragmentarily explicit conceptions of the good, then the vocabulary of "place" may well seem awkward. We might instead find it more natural to speak of "the reason why" I want to watch basketball or – slightly more archaically – the end for the sake of which I want to do so. I have no brief against these other ways of speaking, but part of my reason for insisting on the role of the dimension of place in the desires of nonhuman animals, to whom things can appear good or bad, was to indicate that we can build up to a position that licenses us to use the richer vocabulary – of "reasons why" or "ends" – if only we start with a conception of desire that is richer than the dyadic functional characterization. I do not claim that reasons or ends are simply Aristotelian three-dimensional desires, taken up more explicitly.[37] What I do claim is that this conception of desire well lends itself to being taken up in deliberation employing the ideas of ends or reasons.

Furthermore, the deliberative prominence of the dimension of place cancels any worries about foregrounding desire. Take the case of the desire to do one's duty, for instance. The counterintuitiveness of bringing a dyadic functionalist desire to this effect into the foreground arises from the fact that doing so loses touch with the fact that the virtuous agent – the one who wants to do the right thing – in effect desires to do so for its own sake. If that is so – if the agent takes this commitment to be appropriately self-regulating – then that will be captured in this desire's dimension of place, which indicates that the agent means to give this commitment a place in his or her deliberations even in those possible occasions in which she does not desire to do the right thing.

OBJECTIONS AND CONCLUSION

This view will generate many objections. Having just come back to the role of *phantasia* within this Aristotelian psychology, let me start with one addressed to that. If we understand *phantasia* as perception, that implies the existence of the object perceived. We seem at least to be talking about objects that the agent takes there to be. Yet commonly, desire's role is to spur us to produce objects or bring about states of affairs that do not yet exist. Hence, a psychological state that incorporates an essential role for perception cannot be desire.

The answer to this first objection is that *phantasia*'s role must be understood more broadly and in a more behaviorally focused way, as presenting a respect in which a possible action appears good or attractive to the agent. Possible actions never already exist. Some possible actions aim at obtaining standard mid-sized objects for the agent, such as glistening slices of chocolate cake. In such cases, perception of a more literal sort will play a role. Other possible actions aim at securing states of affairs, and still others are activities pursued for their own sakes. In neither of these latter two cases may the role of *phantasia* in desire be understood along such literally perceptual lines. In humans, this dimension of place can be explored through what Dewey described as the imaginative rehearsal of proposed action.[38] In other animals, perhaps such things go on less explicitly.

This degree of laxity in describing what goes on in other animals will generate a further objection, which is that I have mischaracterized the disagreement between the three-dimensional Aristotelian conception of desire and the dyadic functional one. Not only is the Aristotelian conception more complex, it is also not really functionalist. I have offered no counterpart to Ramsey's elegant method for factoring the psychological states generating choice into desires and beliefs, and it does not seem likely that any such way of moving from choice behavior to the attribution of psychological states will be in the offing for the Aristotelian view. Accordingly, that view must be seen as indulging in metaphysical speculation about psychology of a kind that functionalists had hoped to avoid.

Perhaps so, but to address this issue fairly, one must note that Ramsey's decision-theoretic strategy runs into trouble with actual human choice, which appears empirically to violate some of the decision-theoretic axioms, such as transitivity. Here, the decision-theorist can retreat to the idealization of completely thought-through preferences, thus purchasing nonontological propriety at the cost of becoming practically and empirically irrelevant. Alternatively, the functionalist will at least need to avail him- or herself of attributions of counterfactually characterized commitment, so as to begin to get at the "root" of what people desire or choose. At the end of the day, it may be that the Aristotelian view, in the absence of any counterpart to a method such as Ramsey's, may have to rely more on the agent's own introspective (which is not to say incorrigible) understandings than a strict functionalist would like. For one whose primary interest is in understanding the role of desire in deliberation – as opposed to accounting for how material beings can deliberate – this reliance on first-personal understandings should not be considered a problem.

Finally, take a somewhat more specific objection that combines aspects of the two we have just considered. It is not just that the Aristotelian conception of desire fails to suggest an operational method for attributing the states of belief, *phantasia*, and desire that it postulates; it also clashes with the fundamental notion that belief and desire have opposite directions of fit. This will be so even if *phantasia* is understood as being more akin to imagination than to perception: For the *phantasia* that p can be undercut only by the fact that not-p, whereas the desire that p, it is supposed, tends to be maintained in the presence of the fact that not-p. And even though the Aristotelian account theoretically acknowledges that the desire and the *phantasia* are different mental states, my emphasis on the role of desire's dimension of place has tied the two awfully close together.

Guilty as charged. It is true that the three-dimensional Aristotelian conception disturbs the idea that belief and desire may be differentiated neatly in terms of opposite directions of fit.[39] That this is so is most obvious if we look at the explicit, reflective states that take up Aristotelian desire into a conception of the good. A reflectively endorsed or held state, such as an agent's commitment to an end, will involve both a forward-directed commitment to act in certain ways and an evaluative judgment that its dimension of place appropriately regulates the relevant range of future deliberations. As such, an end will have both of the counterfactually expressed directions of fit that Smith identifies. Nor is there any paradox or contradiction in this fact – along the lines of both tending to persist and tending to disappear in the presence of belief that not-p – since one of these directions will bear on the desire's scope and the other will bear on the desire's place.[40] Two directions, but pertaining to two different objects or propositions: a coherent result that suggests that the idea of direction of fit is less useful than has been thought.

Accordingly, while the Aristotelian three-dimensional conception of desire will understandably make contemporary functionalists a bit nervous, it suffers no incoherence and indulges in no great metaphysical extravagance. It is well at home in our commonsense understandings of ourselves, as I have shown – though a long period of philosophical ascendancy of the dyadic functionalist characterization has pushed it aside for a while. But the far superior ability of desires on the Aristotelian conception to be taken up in sensible and sound deliberations about conflicting desires – the fact that this conception enables us to represent the considerations at play in such conflicts without giving them counter-intuitive shape and in a way that suggests fruitful avenues for reasonable compromise – more than compensates for any weakness that its dependence on first-personal understandings may involve.

Notes

I thank both Monika Betzler for her extremely helpful detailed comments and the members of the Philamore group for their searching criticism and insightful advice.

1. The distinction between objectual, behavioral, and propositional ways of representing desire is developed in Audi 2001: 91. I follow Audi in treating "wanting" as a synonym of "desire."
2. See Berlin 1988.
3. See Nussbaum and Putnam 1992.
4. See Pettit and Smith 1990: 565–6. In my discussion, I assume that what they call "the intentional conception of human beings," according to which actions are to be explained in terms of belief-desire pairs that rationalize them, is at least more correct than is an account that would scrap even this thin accommodation of folk psychology.
5. For a sketch of a belief-desire model in which beliefs, as practical judgments, play a more prominent role, see Davidson 1980: 286.
6. Smith 1994: 115. Smith characterizes this gloss as an approximation that would have to be complicated to account for issues involving choice under risk and uncertainty.
7. This point is noted in Scanlon 1998: 50.
8. See ibid.
9. I have criticized the idea that balancing competing aims plays a useful role in practical reasoning in a range of essays, from Richardson 1990 to Richardson 2000.
10. Williams 1973: 167.
11. Pettit and Smith 1990: 566.
12. See ibid.: 575.
13. Ibid.: 568.
14. At 576, Pettit and Smith make a separate argument that desiring S in the actual world cannot be all that is required to underwrite the idea of "promising to do best by one's desires" in any possible world.
15. A third possibility would be to attempt to show that, at bottom, we really only desire one kind of thing, such as pleasure, and hence deliberate by commensurating all of the options in terms of that good. As I have argued in Richardson 1994: sec. 17, this suggestion would distort the account of our deliberation in other respects, as values are not in fact commensurable in this way.

16. See Pettit and Smith 1990: 569–70.
17. See Frankfurt 1988.
18. Smith (1994: 158–61) sketches an attractive account of how individuals deliberate "by trying to integrate the object of [a] desire into a more coherent and unified desiderative profile and evaluative outlook" (159). My claim would be that the alternative conception of desire I defend here lends itself far more easily to this sort of holistic elaboration than does desire as Smith himself describes it.
19. Whyte 1991: 67, whence also the example of being kicked.
20. Broome 1991: 100–1.
21. Broome compellingly argues that there must be limits on individuating options, or "requirements of rational indifference," to prevent the axioms of rational choice theory from being vacuous, and he interestingly points out that these stand as a kind of limit to the extreme Humean claim that there are no rational constraints on the content of desires. See Broome 1991: 104–7.
22. On the issue that "incomplete thinking about the possible courses of action" poses for preference theory, see Sen 1982: 61.
23. See Richardson 1994: sec. 15.
24. The fundamental idea of this approach goes back to Frank P. Ramsey's *Truth and Probability*. Ramsey's approach is clearly expounded and freed from some needless metaphysical baggage in Jeffrey 1983: ch. 3.
25. In characterizing Aristotle's account, I am drawing on Richardson 1992a. In that interpretive essay, I contrast two variants of the Aristotelian view, one that looks to the object of desire to individuate desires, and one that takes desires as occurrent states individuated just fine as they are. In the present context, the worry introduced by Williams's case provides reason for setting aside the latter variant and concentrating on the first – which, I have argued, is also better supported by the text of *De anima*.
26. Aristotle, *De anima*, 432b13–4 (*ti to kinoun to zôion tên poreutikên kinêsin*).
27. To say that we must look inside is not to imply that looking outside is irrelevant; indeed, human autonomy – a paradigm or strong case of self-movement – may depend on certain relations to community norms, as I have argued in Richardson 2001.
28. The "indefinitely" at *De anima* 434a4 is thus illuminatingly read by contrasting it with the kind of definite limitation provided by the ends of movement. See *De motu animalium* 700b16–17 (tr. Nussbaum): "All animals impart movement and are moved for the sake of something, so that this is the limit of their movement, the thing for-the-sake-of-which."
29. Respectively: *De anima* 434a16 (tr. J. A. Smith), 433b16.
30. Aristotle uses the simile of a ball at *De anima* 434a13, at least according to some of the extant manuscripts.
31. See Stocker 1979.
32. I do not, in the end, think that the notion of an agent's conception of the good can be understood without reference to the potential objectivity of that agent's good, but this conceptual dependence on an objective idea of goodness may not factor through to each case of individual action.

33. One such point is Aristotle's account of the "innate breath" (*sumphuton pneuma*) in ch. 10 of *De motu animalium*, on the obscurities of which see Nussbaum 1978: essay 3. Of course, my aim in this chapter is to put the Aristotelian conception of desire to work in reconstructing deliberation about conflicts of desires, not to try to resolve any aspect of the mind-body problem.

34. As will become clear, it is not the *functionalism* of the simple functional characterization to which I object but its *simplicity* – specifically, its limitation to the two dimensions of strength and scope.

35. On the distinction between conceptualized and nonconceptualized desire in Aristotle, see Labarrière 1984 and Tuozzo 1994.

36. Here I arrive, by a slightly new route, at a qualified version of the explanation of the antisymmetry of pursuit that I offered in Richardson 1992b (attributing the view to Aristotle) and in Richardson 1994: sec. 7 (abstracting the view from Aristotle's text).

37. An end, for instance, has an aspect of motivational commitment, expressible counterfactually and addressed along its dimension of place, that is not implied by desire as such.

38. See Dewey 1967: 132–3.

39. I have developed this point a bit more fully in Richardson, forthcoming.

40. On the contradiction involved in attributing both directions of fit to one state, where each direction bears on the same propositional object, see Smith 1994: 119. Here I am indebted to Little 1997: 63–4. Note that I am not here attempting to address the issue between the Humean and the cognitivist.

Bibliography

Aristotle. 1984. *The Complete Works of Aristotle: The Revised Oxford Translation*, ed. Jonathan Barnes. Princeton, N.J.: Princeton University Press.

Audi, Robert. 2001. *The Architecture of Reason: The Structure and Substance of Rationality*. Oxford: Oxford University Press.

Berlin, Isaiah. 1988. On the Pursuit of the Ideal. *New York Review of Books*, 17 March: 11–18.

Broome, John 1991. *Weighing Goods: Equality, Uncertainty, and Time*. Oxford: Basil Blackwell.

Davidson, Donald 1980. *Essays on Actions & Events*. Oxford: Oxford University Press.

Dewey, John. 1967. *Human Nature and Conduct* (vol. 14 of *The Middle Works, 1899–1924*; ed. Jo Ann Boydston). Carbondale: Southern Illinois University Press.

Frankfurt, Harry G. 1988. *The Importance of What We Care About: Philosophical Essays*. Cambridge: Cambridge University Press.

Jeffrey, Richard C. 1983. *The Logic of Decision*, 2nd ed. Chicago: University of Chicago Press.

Labarrière, Jean-Louis. 1984. Imagination humaine et imagination animale chez Aristote. *Phronesis* 29: 17–49.

Little, Margaret Olivia. 1997. Virtue as Knowledge: Objections from the Philosophy of Mind. *Nous* 31: 59–79.

Nussbaum, Martha Craven. 1978. *Aristotle's* De motu animalium: *Text with Translation, Commentary, and Interpretive Essays*. Princeton, N.J.: Princeton University Press.

Nussbaum, Martha C., and Hilary Putnam. 1992. Changing Aristotle's Mind. In Martha C. Nussbaum and Amélie O. Rorty, *Essays on Aristotle's* De anima. Oxford: Oxford University Press, 27–56.

Pettit, Philip, and Michael Smith. 1990. Backgrounding Desire. *Philosophical Review* 99: 565–92.

Ramsey, Frank P. 1988. Truth and Probability. In Peter Gärdenfors and Nils-Eric Sahlin (eds.), *Decision, Probability, and Utility: Selected Readings*. Cambridge: Cambridge University Press, 19–47.

Richardson, Henry S. 1990. Measurement, Pleasure and Practical Science in Plato's *Protagoras*. *Journal of the History of Philosophy* 28: 7–32.

Richardson, Henry S. 1992a. Degrees of Finality and the Highest Good in Aristotle. *Journal of the History of Philosophy* 30: 327–52.

Richardson, Henry S. 1992b. Desire and the Good in *De anima*. In Martha C. Nussbaum and Amélie O. Rorty (eds.), *Essays on Aristotle's* De anima. Oxford: Oxford University Press, 381–99.

Richardson, Henry S. 1994. *Practical Reasoning about Final Ends*. Cambridge: Cambridge University Press.

Richardson, Henry S. 2000. Specifying, Balancing, and Interpreting Bioethical Principles. *Journal of Medicine and Philosophy* 25: 285–307.

Richardson, Henry S. 2001. Autonomy's Many Normative Presuppositions. *American Philosophical Quarterly* 38: 287–303.

Richardson, Henry S. Forthcoming. Satisficing: Not Good Enough. In Michael Byron (ed.), *Satisficing*. New York: Cambridge University Press.

Scanlon, Thomas M. 1998. *What We Owe to Each Other*. Cambridge, Mass.: Harvard University Press.

Sen, Amartya. 1982. *Choice, Welfare, and Measurement*. Cambridge, Mass.: MIT Press.

Smith, Michael. 1994. *The Moral Problem*. Oxford: Blackwell.

Stocker, Michael. 1979. Desiring the Bad: An Essay in Moral Psychology. *Journal of Philosophy* 76: 738–53.

Tuozzo, Thomas M. 1994. Conceptualized and Unconceptualized Desire in Aristotle. *Journal of the History of Philosophy* 32: 525–49.

Whyte, J. T. 1991. The Normal Rewards of Success. *Analysis* 51: 65–73.

Williams, Bernard. 1973. Ethical Consistency. In Bernard Williams, *Problems of the Self: Philosophical Papers 1956–1972*. Cambridge: Cambridge University Press, 166–86.

5

Putting Together Morality and Well-Being

Ruth Chang

It seems an inevitable fact of life that morality sometimes asks us to do something that requires a sacrifice in our own well-being. Should we keep a promise to accompany a friend to the dentist or go off to hear a rare performance of our favorite artist? Go out of our way to help a stranger in distress or hurry on our way to an important business meeting? Give a certain percentage of our income to charity or fund our own nest egg? Conflicts between moral and prudential values are thought to raise concerns about the normativity of morality and the scope of practical reason. If being moral involves making one's life go worse, why should one be moral? And if conflicts between moral and prudential values are genuine, how in such cases can practical reason guide decision about what to do?

Both worries stem in part from an alluring picture of the relationship between morality and prudence. On this picture, moral and prudential values issue from two "fundamentally distinct points of view," points of view so different that there is no more comprehensive point of view from which values from the one point of view and values from the other can both be given their normative due.[1] For example, from the moral point of view, I should send my year-end bonus to Oxfam, but from the prudential point of view I should invest the money in my own retirement. It seems that there is no more comprehensive point of view from which I can properly consider the reason-giving force of both sorts of consideration. If there is no such comprehensive point of view, then why should I do anything other than what makes my life go best? And, more generally, if the reason-giving force of a value is relative to the point of view from which it issues, then how are values from one point of view normatively "put together" with values from a fundamentally different one? Unless values from fundamentally distinct points of view can be put on the same normative page, there can be no rational resolution of conflicts between them.[2]

A significant part of moral philosophy has been occupied with this question of putting together morality and well-being. Values that are "put together" are normatively related to one another in the context of practical choice – they have what one might call "relative normative weight": One value outweighs, overrides, trumps, ties with, or is in some other way normatively related to the other.[3] If moral and prudential values have normative weight vis-à-vis one another, then it is in virtue of those relative weights that it is sometimes rational to be moral even though that makes one's life go worse and, more generally, that conflicts between them are rationally resolved as they are.

The aim of this chapter is to propose for consideration a new approach to putting together morality and well-being, one that, I believe, provides the basis for a unified account of the relative normative weights of *any* values that might figure in practical conflict. My proposal is that for any given conflict between particular moral and prudential values, there is some more comprehensive value – what I elsewhere call a "covering value" – that includes the conflicting values as "parts" and is that in virtue of which the conflict is rationally resolved if it is rationally resolvable. For example, the prudential value p of building a financial nest egg gives me a reason to invest the bonus in my pension, while the moral value m of aiding starving children around the world gives me a reason to send it to Oxfam instead. On the proposed view, there is some more comprehensive value V with p and m as parts that accounts for the reason-giving force of m in the face of conflict with p and determines the rational resolution of the conflict between them if there is one. This is not to say that there is a single more comprehensive value in virtue of which all conflicts between morality and prudence can be resolved, but only that for each such conflict, there is some or other more comprehensive value in virtue of which there is a rational resolution. And talk of one value being a "part" of another should not be taken to presuppose that values are "out there" or, worse, that they are entities with spatial extension. One value w being "part" of another value v requires no more than that being w contributes constitutively to being v.

Now these more comprehensive values that put together moral and prudential values are unusual in that they are, at present, typically nameless.[4] Because they have no names, it is easy to look right through them, though, as I try to show, they play a crucial role in determining the rational resolution of conflicts between moral and prudential values. In claiming that nameless values "determine" rational resolution, I do not mean to imply that a rational deliberator must appeal to such values in order to arrive at a rational resolution; a rational agent might correctly arrive at a rational resolution of a conflict by appeal to authority or some form of deliberation that makes no reference to that in virtue of which there *is* a rational resolution. My suggestion is that however someone might arrive at a rational resolution, its being rational holds partly *in virtue of* a more comprehensive nameless value.

My case for the "nameless value approach" centers on two arguments. The first provides a prima facie case; there *are* cases of value conflict whose rational resolution is very plausibly determined by a more comprehensive value that has the conflicting values as parts, and it is not clear how conflicts between moral and prudential values can be relevantly distinguished from them. Without a clear basis for distinction, we have reason to think that just as there is a more comprehensive value that accounts for rational resolution in the one kind of case, so, too, is there in the other. The second maintains that a careful examination of the role of circumstances shows that if circumstances are to play a role in determining the relative normativity of the values at stake, there must be something with content beyond those values and circumstances in virtue of which the values have the relative weights that they do. That thing with further content, I argue, is a nameless value that has the conflicting values as parts.

Whether in the end one believes that there are such nameless values depends on whether more traditional accounts of rational conflict resolution can do the job of putting together values instead. I therefore present the arguments for my approach in the context of examining problems for what I take to be its leading competitor. Even if at the end of the day one remains skeptical of nameless values, the case for them, I believe, raises a serious challenge to the usual way in which the determination of rational conflict resolution is understood.

I have set up the problem and its solution as involving *values* – very broadly understood to include disvalues, duties, obligations, rights, and so on. But the key idea behind the proposal is that resolution of conflicts between any type of consideration – whether they be values, desires, reasons, ends, and so on – holds in virtue of a more comprehensive consideration that includes the conflicting considerations as parts.[5] Since I believe the right way to understand conflict and its resolution is in terms of "values," broadly understood, I frame the discussion in these terms.

Moreover, although the values on which I focus are *moral* and *prudential*, the arguments do not turn on any of their special features and can in principle be generalized to other values. Thus, there may be nameless values that put together rights and utility, efficiency and beauty, and perhaps even theoretical values such as ontological economy and explanatory simplicity. The suggestion is not that *any* two named values can be put together by a nameless one but rather that values that appear to raise problems for practical (and perhaps theoretical) reason because they issue from fundamentally different points of view may in fact be put together by more comprehensive nameless values. This account allows us to maintain quite generally that conflicts between values are resolved, if resolvable at all, in virtue of more comprehensive values that have those conflicting values as parts.[6]

OTHER APPROACHES

Attempts to account for how moral and prudential values are put together are legion, but the main contenders can be roughly grouped into three categories.[7] First, there is the "single point of view" approach, which holds that moral and prudential values are put together by being subsumed under a single point of view: The moral or prudential point of view is the "more comprehensive" point of view that includes the other; or there is some third, more comprehensive point of view that includes both; or there is a "view from nowhere," a maximally perspectiveless objective point of view that transcends all other points of view, from which the relative weights of all moral and prudential values are given.[8] The second approach is "procedural"; it holds that values – which must ultimately be understood in terms of conative states – are put together by a putatively value-neutral procedure, such as "cognitive psychotherapy" or "procedural deliberative reflection" so that one value is taken to have greater normative weight than another in virtue of being an output of this procedure.[9] And finally, there is what we might call, as a reflection of its ubiquity, the "orthodox" approach. On this approach, values once fully understood *put themselves together*. Nothing more than the values at stake themselves – perhaps in conjunction with a "supplementary" factor to be explained shortly – is needed to account for their normative relations. Values might be likened to physical forces; just as it is a fact about a particular electromagnetic force that it interacts in a certain way with a particular gravitational force, it is a fact about a particular moral value that it normatively interacts in a certain way with a particular prudential value.[10]

I am, somewhat dogmatically, going to set aside the first two approaches. The procedural approach has long been attacked by those who claim, essentially, that neutral procedures for sanitizing desires will not yield the "oughtness" of normativity; something substantive must be assumed.[11] It seems to me that the attacks are sufficiently successful to warrant casting about for a different approach. And while the single-point-of-view approach might in the end be correct, in the current stage of debate there are methodological grounds for setting it aside. This approach denies the intuitive understandings of moral and prudential values that seem to underwrite the special difficulty in the first place, namely, that they do not issue from a common point of view. However, other things being equal, when a demand for explanation is underwritten by a natural, intuitive understanding of the phenomena at issue, we should take that demand at face value and attempt to satisfy it before dissolving the problem on the controversial grounds that the intuitive understanding is mistaken.

This leaves the orthodox approach as the main alternative to my own. According to this approach, relative normative weight is in some sense "built into" the values themselves; values give rise to reasons that already are on the same normative page.[12] Some who take this approach think that moral values always override prudential ones; others think that moral values sometimes outweigh prudential ones and that sometimes the reverse is true; still others conclude that a proper understanding of morality and prudence shows that there is little or no genuine conflict in the first place – morality is sufficiently attentive to individual interests to include most prudential values, or well-being is sufficiently capacious to include most moral ones.[13]

The orthodox approach comes in two varieties: the "simple" version, which holds that the values at stake alone account for their own relative normative weights, and the "sophisticated" version, which holds that the values in conjunction with a supplementary factor determine their relative weights. According to the first, the values put themselves together apart from any consideration of the circumstances in which they figure, and according to the second, circumstances, purposes, principles, or a theory of value work as supplementary factors to help values put themselves together. "Circumstances" should be understood throughout this paper to include only *nonevaluative* or *nonnormative* considerations, such as the fact that the next train for Trenton leaves in an hour but not the fact that the train conductor is kind.

Proponents of the sophisticated version come in many stripes. "Specificationists," for example, think that circumstances of a choice situation help to specify or to fill out the values at stake in a way that delivers the normative relations among them.[14] "Coherentists" or "interpretivists" argue that by considering the contours and application of related values in a range of other circumstances, a coherent or best theory of a broad range of values emerges in terms of which their relative normative weights are determined.[15] Others think that principles, such as "Family and friends first" or "The greater one's distance from the victim, the less stringent one's duty to save her," help account for why some values, such as the value of human life, may give rise to a stronger reason in one circumstance but a weaker reason in another.[16] And still others maintain that the aim or purpose of a choice, understood in conjunction with the values at stake, determines how those values normatively relate in that case.[17]

Circumstances, purposes, principles, and theory are "supplementary" factors on these views in that it is only because the values are as they are that these factors help to determine the weights of those values in the way that they do. It is in some sense the values themselves that are the primary determinants of rational choice. This idea of being the primary determinant might be likened to being the cause of an event. Striking the match causes the match to light, while the presence of oxygen is a supplementary factor that plays a background role in accounting for the match's being lit. In the same way, it might be thought that values are determinative of their own relative weights, while the circumstances in which they figure, the purpose of choice, the principles that apply in the circumstances, or a theory of value play a background role in helping to account for those weights.[18]

It is worth noting that if either the orthodox or nameless value approach is correct, talk of "points of view" is a red herring. For both approaches grant, for the sake of argument, that moral and prudential values might issue from fundamentally different points of view but insist that this is no block to putting those values together. If this is right, then it might be wondered why it *seems* that issuing from fundamentally different points of view, that is, from points of view that are not subsumed by some single more comprehensive point of view, raises a problem for putting values together. I believe the appearance of difficulty might be explained by a failure to distinguish between a value "per se" and a value qua instance of a *type* of value. A point of view is an evaluative stance from which the normative weights of all values of a *type* can be given. Conflicts of values, however, involve values per se and not essentially values *as* values of a certain type. Thus, even if there is no more comprehensive point of view that gives the relative weights of every moral and prudential value

as values of the "moral" type and values of the "prudential" type, a particular moral value – not essentially conceived as a value of the moral type –
may normatively relate to a particular prudential value – not essentially
conceived as a value of the prudential type. Putting together particular
moral and prudential values in this way is putting together morality and
well-being in the way that counts.[19]

A Prima Facie Case

A conflict between values occurs whenever one value favors one of two
conflicting options, another value favors the other, and yet both values
are "at stake" in the choice. Values are at stake if they are in some intuitive sense what the choice is about, and thus they are not excluded,
canceled, or bracketed as irrelevant to the choice. The values at stake
can be understood as either the generic values relevant to the choice
(e.g., beneficence) or the particular instantiations of those values borne
by the alternatives (the particular beneficence of x). In the simplest form
of conflicts we take as our focus, certain moral and prudential values are
at stake, and the moral values favor one alternative, while the prudential
values favor the other.[20]

In every conflict situation there is something that "matters" in the
choice. I will stipulate that what matters in a choice is to be understood
as that in virtue of which a choice is rational. If one is faced with a choice
between Ayer and Wittgenstein, for example, which one rationally should
choose is a matter of what matters in the choice between them. If what
matters is philosophical talent, one should choose Wittgenstein; if what
matters is ability to entertain at a cocktail party, one should choose Ayer.
Whatever else may matter in the choice, the values at stake will always
matter.[21] I also assume that what matters in one choice may be different
from what matters in another choice, though we return to this assumption
below. According to the orthodox approach, what matters in any given
case is given by the values at stake themselves, perhaps supplemented by
circumstances, purposes, principles, or a theory of value. According to the
nameless value approach, what matters is given by a more comprehensive
value with the values at stake as parts.

We – philosophers at least – have ways of indicating what one rationally
should choose without explicitly specifying what matters in the choice.
We say that one should choose the option that one has "most reason to
choose, all things considered" or is "best or good enough with respect to
choiceworthiness" or is "what one ought to do" where the ought is the
general ought of practical reason. Each of these locutions is a placeholder

for different things that matter in different choice situations. Sometimes an alternative will be most choiceworthy because it is the socially just course of action; sometimes an alternative will be what one has most reason to choose, all things considered, because it is best with respect to cost, efficiency, and pleasantness. On the orthodox approach, these placeholders hold the place of a list of the values at stake, perhaps supplemented by some factor; on the nameless value approach, they hold the place of a more comprehensive value with the values at stake as parts.

It is useful, given our focus on conflicts between moral and prudential values, to stipulate a placeholder – call it the somewhat unlovely "prumorality" – as holding the place of whatever matters in particular conflicts between moral and prudential values. Like "all things considered," prumorality holds the place for different considerations in different choice situations. In some cases, prumorality may stand for something that includes the moral value of saving a human life and the prudential value of achieving a lifetime goal, and in other cases, something that includes different moral and prudential values. It should not be thought that by naming a placeholder as that which matters in a conflict we have stacked the deck in favor of finding that prumorality is a value. As a stipulated name for whatever matters in a choice, prumorality may hold the place of nothing more than a list of the values at stake, supplemented or not.

Thus the issue between the orthodox and nameless value approaches can be put as follows: In any given conflict between moral and prudential values, is prumorality a placeholder for a possibly supplemented list of the moral and prudential values at stake or for a more comprehensive nameless value that has those values as parts?

Now there is an intuitive line of argument that suggests that prumorality is, indeed, a placeholder for more comprehensive values with moral and prudential values as parts. Start with the thought that many value conflicts have a straightforward rational resolution, and, in many of these, it is perfectly clear that the resolution is determined by a more comprehensive value that gives what matters in the choice. Suppose you are a member of a philosophy appointments committee whose task is to fill a vacant chair in your department. There are only two candidates for the post: Aye, who is quite original but a historical troglodyte, and Bea, who is singularly unoriginal but is a bit more historically sensitive than Aye. In all other respects, the two are equally matched.[22] Originality favors choosing Aye; historical sensitivity favors choosing Bea; and both are at stake in the choice. It is perfectly clear that one rationally ought to choose Aye. In virtue of what does Aye's originality and historical sensitivity have the relative weight it does against Bea's originality and historical sensitivity such that it is rational to choose Aye? The natural, intuitive answer is that these weights are determined by a more comprehensive value, namely, philosophical talent, which gives what matters in the choice and determines the normative relations among its component values. Philosophical talent is that in virtue of which the normative weights of those component values are related as they are in the circumstances. There is more reason to choose Aye than Bea because the particular bundle of originality and historical sensitivity Aye bears makes her more philosophically talented than the particular bundle of originality and historical sensitivity Bea bears.

Next, consider what looks to be a parallel case involving a conflict between moral and prudential considerations. Suppose you are a keen athlete who has entered a major marathon race. The day of the race comes and you are running well. As you approach the last mile, you realize in a wave of excitement that you are in the lead position. Suddenly you spy a stranger who is flailing about in a nearby pond. If you stop to help him, you will lose the race; if you don't stop, he will drown. Stopping to help has the moral value of saving a human life; carrying on has the prudential value of winning the race. We can rig the details of the case so that the prudential disvalue of failing to stop is insignificant – perhaps you don't give a toss about morality, and since no one will know that you failed to save the stranger, failing to stop will have only a slight negative effect on your well-being. Both the moral and prudential values are at stake in the choice. Yet it seems clear that the reason to save the stranger is weightier than the reason to carry on in the race. You rationally ought to stop and save the stranger.[23]

The question for the orthodox approach, then, is: Why should what accounts for the rational resolution of this case be any different from what accounts for the rational resolution of the philosophy case? In both cases we have a conflict of values; in both the conflicting values matter in the choice; in both we have rational resolution of that conflict; and in both that rational resolution plausibly proceeds by one value having greater normative significance than the other. In the philosophy case, it is clear that the greater weight of one value is determined by a more comprehensive value that includes the values in conflict. Why not think that in the drowning case there is similarly a more comprehensive value that accounts for the greater significance of the moral value of saving the stranger over the prudential value of winning the race?

As a first reaction, it might be insisted that the question rides on a false presupposition: easy cases of conflict between morality and prudence are an illusion – it is false that there is more reason to save the drowning stranger than to win the race. Sidgwick, for example, thought that there was no way to bring such values together in practical reason. But Sidgwick's skepticism was founded on his own confessed inability to see how moral and prudential values might be put together, not on an a priori argument that they could not be. Indeed, if Sidgwickian skepticism is right and easy cases are an illusion, we should nevertheless be able to explain what it is about such cases that makes them different from the philosophy case, a case whose ease of resolution is *not* an illusion. The demand for explanation stands.

A more promising line of explanation might appeal to the fact that there is a more comprehensive value in the philosophy case because the values at stake are not all that different, while in the drowning case, the moral and prudential values at stake are so different that there is no more comprehensive value that has them as parts. But what is meant here by "so different"?

One possible view would have it that values are so different if conflicts between them are intractable. But moral and prudential values are not like this; as we have already seen, there is at least the appearance of easily resolved conflicts between them and no explanation of why this appearance is misleading. Another possibility might be that values are so different if they are different in "type." This move may not seem to advance the issue, since now we need an account of what it is for values to be of different types. But we have an intuitive grasp of value types that may be illuminating. We can contrast two sorts of cases. The literary merit of a novel is a different type of value than the sculptural merit of a statue; however, literary and sculptural values can be put together by the more comprehensive value of artistic excellence. I can meaningfully say something about the relative importance of at least some instantiations of literary and sculptural merit with respect to artistic excellence; I can say that *Bride of the Wind* has less artistic excellence than a Henry Moore sculpture. In contrast, to take a nonevaluative case, color is a different type of consideration than mass, but there is no more comprehensive consideration that puts them together. If I am asked to give the relative "importance" of any instantiations of color and mass, I could not do it; I cannot meaningfully claim, for example, that a red stick is more ____ than a heavy stick, where the blank is to be filled in by some (nonstipulated, noninstrumental) more comprehensive nonevaluative consideration that combines color and mass. Now the question is, which type of type do moral and prudential values fall under? It seems that we can meaningfully say that, with respect to prumorality, a tiny bit of mundane prudential pleasure is less important than a significant moral value. Indeed, the appearance of such easy cases strongly suggests that moral and prudential values are more like literary and sculptural merit than like color and mass. An appeal to value types will not explain why the drowning case should be different from the philosophy case.

A different tack might be to urge that the *difficulty* of resolving certain conflicts shows that they cannot be likened to conflicts in which there is clearly a more comprehensive value at work. But the mere difficulty of a conflict does not provide a reason for thinking that the conflicting values cannot be put together by some more comprehensive value. Just as there are easy cases of conflict over philosophy appointments and also over morality and prudence, there are hard cases of conflict over philosophy appointments and also over morality and prudence. Indeed, the fact that some cases are easy and others are hard is very plausibly explained by the nature of the more comprehensive value that has the conflicting values as parts. A choice between Aye, who is quite original but historically insensitive, and Cee, who is less original but a crackerjack historian, might be difficult, not because there is no comprehensive value that puts those conflicting values together, but because the comprehensive value that does, namely, philosophical talent, is such that the normative relation between the values of originality and historical sensitivity borne by Aye and by Cee is difficult to ascertain.

Whether there is some convincing way in which the drowning and philosophy cases can be distinguished remains to be seen.[24] In short, the orthodox approach owes us an explanation of why some conflicts are handled by a more comprehensive value while others supposedly are not. In the absence of an explanation, we have a good prima facie case for the nameless value approach. Moreover, even if those who take the orthodox approach could explain why conflicts between morality and prudence are not handled by a more comprehensive value, they would be saddled with a fragmented account of conflict resolution, for on their view, some value conflicts, like the philosophy case, are resolved in virtue of a more comprehensive value, while other conflicts, like the drowning case, are not. The nameless value approach, in contrast, provides the basis for a unitary account of conflict resolution; what matters in choice is given by a more comprehensive value that has the values at stake as parts, and it is in virtue of this value that the conflict can be rationally resolved if at all.

The Orthodox Approach

The Simple Version. According to the simple version of the orthodox approach, the values at stake alone account for their relative weights regardless of the circumstances in which they figure.

On the face of it, this view seems mistaken, for sometimes the very same values have different relative weights in different circumstances. Suppose, for example, that a top philosophy department at a premier research university is faced with the choice of appointing Dee or Eee to a position in the department. The department takes two values to be at stake: philosophical talent and teaching ability. Dee, as it turns out, is a first-rate philosopher but a mediocre teacher, while Eee is merely okay as philosopher yet a first-rate teacher. Whom should the department appoint? Given that philosophical talent and teaching ability are the only values at stake, it seems that philosophical talent has greater normative weight than teaching ability, and the department would therefore be justified in appointing Dee over Eee. Suppose now we change the example so that the department making the appointment is at a teaching college whose focus is on teaching rather than research. Once again, the department takes it that the two values at stake are philosophical talent and teaching ability. In this case, it seems that teaching ability has greater normative weight than in the research university case. If these values alone determined their relative normative weights, then those weights should be the same in both cases. But in the first case, teaching ability counts less than it does in the second.

The same phenomenon holds in cases of conflict between moral and prudential values. Suppose I am sitting in my living room wondering what to do with fifty dollars my mother has just sent me. As I riffle through my mail, I see a postage-paid appeal from the Save the Children Fund. I could send my fifty dollars to save two children from starvation or I could buy myself an exquisite meal of duck confit, sweet corn, and truffle sauce. Suppose that at stake in the choice are the moral value of saving human life and the prudential value of gustatory pleasure. Whatever the normative weights of these values vis-à-vis one another, their weights are different in different circumstances. For suppose that, instead of sitting at home, I am lying in a hospital bed, recovering from a painful illness. Again, I am contemplating what to do with the fifty dollars my mother has just sent me. The envelope for the Save the Children fund lies next to my untouched hospital tray of red Jell-O, mashed peas, and a hockey-puck hamburger. Next to it lies a flyer advertising a service that delivers

exquisite meals prepared by Le Dernier Repas. Again, I could give my
fifty dollars to save two children from starvation or I could delight in
duck confit, sweet corn, and truffle sauce. In this case, it seems that the
relative normative weight of donating the money is different than it is in
the case in which I am sitting at home contemplating whether to mail a
check or make a reservation.

Note that in these examples, not only do the same generic values
figure in each pair of cases but so, too, do the same particular instantiations of them. It would be wholly unsurprising if the same generic
values instantiated differently had different normative weights in given
cases, for a generic value can be instantiated in a wide variety of ways
that will affect its normative weight in the given circumstances. In one
case, for instance, the value of saving a human life might be instantiated by an act that saves the life of Hitler, and in another it might be
instantiated by an act that saves the life of one's child. The claim that
the values at stake are the same, then, should be understood as entailing
that the particular instantiations of the generic values as borne by the
alternatives are the same. In this way, whatever is relevant about the alternatives to choice is built into the understanding of the particular values at
stake.

Our dismissal of the simple view is perhaps too hasty. For circumstances
might play a role in determining *which values are at stake in the first place*,
and thus a difference in circumstances may give rise to a value at stake
in the one case but not the other. In a choice between saving a dollar
and spending it on ice cream, for instance, which values are at stake
depends on features of the circumstances, such as whether I am down
to my last dollar or whether I am diabetic. If I am neither, then it is
plausible to suppose that the values of avoiding destitution or a diabetic
coma are not at stake in the choice. In the two above examples, the fact
that the appointment is to be made at a research institution may give rise
to different values than those in the case of the teaching college, and my
being in the hospital recovering from a painful illness may bring with it
values not present when I am deciding what to do while sitting in my living
room. If the circumstances in two cases are different, then the values at
stake in those cases might be different. The simple approach might yet
be correct, for once the identities of the values at stake are given, it may
seem that circumstances need play no role in determining the relative
normative weights of those values.

This move is sometimes made against arguments such as those of
Peter Singer and Peter Unger, who insist that if the value of human life

trumps the value of some portion of my wealth in one circumstance – for example, if the starving child is at my doorstep – then it should trump the same value in other circumstances – for example, when the starving child is halfway around the world. The argument of the Peters presupposes an "other things being equal" clause, and the objection is that other things are not equal: The difference in circumstances gives rise to a difference in which values are at stake in the two cases.[25] The fact that the child is on my doorstep gives rise to a new value of responding to an immediate moral demand physically present before one, which is at stake in that case but not in the other. And if there are different values at stake in the two cases, we have no grounds for thinking that just because the values common to both cases stand in a given normative relation in the one circumstance, they will stand in the same relation in the other.

It is relatively uncontroversial that circumstances can help frame a choice situation by determining which values are at stake. The debate over whether a *particular* difference in circumstance gives rise to a particular difference in values at stake in one case but not in another is, by contrast, often controversial. However, the correctness of the simple view need not depend on settling such controversial matters, for there are general grounds for thinking that it is mistaken.

Those who take the simple view must maintain that once a list of values at stake is given, the normative relations of those values hold *in abstracto*, apart from any circumstances in which the values might figure.[26] It makes no sense, however, to ask in the abstract which of two values gives rise to the greater reason. Suppose God is told in a circumstantial vacuum to choose between Eff and Gee with respect to philosophical talent and teaching ability. If there are no specified circumstances, even God cannot know whether Eff's technical prowess gives rise to a greater reason than Gee's easygoing teaching style because there is no fact about how those values normatively relate apart from circumstances. Without some specification of circumstances, the relative normative weights of philosophical talent and teaching ability, taken generically or in their particular instantiations, cannot be determined, and thus there is no truth about which alternative should rationally be chosen.[27] If values can account for their own normative relations, they can do so only with the help of the circumstances in which they figure.

The Sophisticated Version. The sophisticated version of the orthodox approach recognizes that values do not have relative normative weights *in abstracto* but that supplemental factors play a role in determining those relative weights. And we have just seen that whatever other supplemental factors may play a role, circumstances most certainly do.

Now if the simple version is mistaken because it fails to acknowledge that circumstances play a role in determining the relative weights of values, one might think that the sophisticated version, which acknowledges such a role, must be correct. But many approaches, including the nameless value one, can allow that circumstances help to determine the normative weights of values. Indeed, if the argument against the simple version is correct, then any plausible approach must give circumstances such a role. The question at issue, then, is whether a more comprehensive value is also needed. As I argue, the values at stake and the circumstances in which they figure underdetermine the way those circumstances affect the normative relations among those values; something with content beyond that given by the values and the circumstances in which they figure is needed to explain why the values at stake are normatively related as they are in those circumstances. And as I suggest, it is hard to see what could provide this content other than a more comprehensive value that gives what matters in the choice.

We start by distinguishing two roles circumstances might play in choice. Circumstances are "internal" when they are the circumstances *of* the choice situation; otherwise they are "external." External circumstances help to determine the identity of the choice situation, that is, *which* choice situation one is in, including which values are at stake and which circumstances are internal to the choice situation. They do not, as such, play a role in determining the relative weights of the values at stake once the choice situation has been identified; their role is to "set up" the choice situation as this one rather than that one. Internal circumstances, in contrast, help to determine the relative weights of the values at stake in a choice situation once it has been set up. For example, the fact that the dean has requested that we fill a position in ethics is an external circumstance: It gives rise to a decision-theoretic situation in which we seek to appoint a person who works in ethics, rather than in logic, or one in which we seek to have ourselves a fine meal. Once the identity of the choice situation has been determined, external circumstances leave the scene, and the internal circumstances, such as the fact that our department is part of a teaching college, may then affect the relative weights of the values at stake: It may give teaching ability greater relative normative weight vis-à-vis philosophical talent than it might have in different internal circumstances.

It will sometimes be difficult in practice to distinguish internal from external circumstances, for some nonevaluative facts that are relevant to determining the relative weights of values at stake might also help determine which choice situation one is in to begin with and vice versa. But this difficulty should not lead us to think that circumstances can play only one role and not two. It seems clear that circumstances that play an external role *need not* play an internal role, and vice versa. The fact that the dean instructs the philosophy department to hire someone in ethics is an external circumstance; it gives rise to a choice situation in which an ethics position is to be filled. But once that choice situation has been determined, the fact that the dean has instructed the department to hire someone does not play any internal role in affecting the relative normative weights of the values – say, philosophical talent and teaching ability – that are at stake. Similarly, the fact that my pension has been decimated by a downturn in the stock market may not be relevant to determining a choice situation in which I have a duty to give aid – such a choice situation might be determined by the fact that people are starving – but once the choice situation is determined as one in which a duty to give aid is at stake, the fact that I have suffered severe financial losses may be relevant to determining the relative normative weight of that duty against a competing prudential value.

Assuming this distinction in role is sound – an assumption to which we return in due course – the crucial question is, In virtue of what do the internal circumstances affect the relative weights of the values at stake in the way that they do? In virtue of what, for example, does the fact that I am a thousand miles from the victim make the relative weight of my duty to save lesser rather than greater than a competing value in a given choice situation?

Defenders of the sophisticated orthodoxy might appeal to one of two answers. They might claim that the way in which circumstances of a choice situation affect the normative relations among the values at stake is determined by the values at stake themselves or by some function of those values and those circumstances. In the alternative, they might allow that some further content beyond that given by the values at stake and the internal circumstances is needed to account for the way in which those circumstances affect the normative relations but insist that this further content is given by a purpose, principle, or a theory of value, not a more comprehensive value.

The first answer fails, however, because the values at stake and the circumstances in which they figure underdetermine the way in which those circumstances may affect the relative weights of those values. Imagine a choice situation in which one must choose between saving another from harm and avoiding some prudential cost. Now fix the circumstances of the choice situation, and include among them the fact that one is physically very distant from the victim. How does this circumstance affect the normative relations of the moral duty to save and the prudential cost of doing so? Other things being equal, it seems that the circumstance of being very far away from the victim diminishes the relative normative weight of one's duty to save vis-à-vis the competing prudential value.[28] But in virtue of what does this claim seem to be true?

The duty to save, the competing prudential value, and the internal circumstances, whatever they might be, cannot account for the truth of the claim, for *holding the values at stake and the circumstances in which they figure constant*, the values at stake could nevertheless have different relative weights in the very same internal circumstances. This is because circumstances *external* to a choice situation may determine that what matters in one situation is different from what matters in another, even though in both situations the same values are at stake in the same internal circumstances. Being physically distant from the victim diminishes the relative weight of one's duty to save vis-à-vis some competing value only if what matters in the choice is something that gives great weight to doing one's moral duty rather than, say, to doing what is supererogatory. If what matters instead is saintliness or doing the most supererogatory act possible, the circumstance of being physically distant would cut the other way – it would make one's duty to save have greater relative normative weight, not less, for, other things equal, helping a victim who is far away is more supererogatory than helping one who is nearby.[29] The values at stake and the internal circumstances of the choice situation cannot determine the normative relations among the values in those circumstances; something with further content is needed. Put another way, "what matters" in a choice cannot simply be given by the values at stake and the circumstances of the choice situation but must have some further content.

So now the question is, what is this further content? According to the second line of orthodox response, this further content is given by a purpose, principle, or theory of value, not by a more comprehensive nameless value.

But this answer, too, fails. To see why, we need to ask what it is about the content of a purpose, principle, or theory of value that *could* determine the normative relations among the values at stake. There are two possibilities. The relevant content might be thought to be given by a particular weighting of the values at stake. Or it might given by something else. Take each possibility in turn.

Suppose we must choose between candidates for a philosophy job, and the values at stake are philosophical talent and teaching ability. Now suppose that what matters in the choice is given by a purpose whose content is to choose in accordance with a particular weighting of philosophical talent and teaching ability (or a principle or theory of value with that content). In this case, once we have agreed on what choice situation we are in – and therefore on what matters in the choice – we have agreed on what the correct weighting of the values at stake is. There can be no genuine disagreement *within a given choice situation* about how the values at stake relate; you and I could not have a genuine disagreement about whether one candidate's philosophical talent provides more reason to choose her than another candidate's teaching ability. Since, however, there *can* be such disagreement, what matters in a choice cannot be understood in terms of a particular weighting of the values at stake. Indeed, genuine disagreement about how correctly to weight the values at stake presupposes a notion of what matters with content beyond a mere weighting of those values; it is that in virtue of which such disagreement is possible!

If purposes, principles, and a theory of value cannot be understood in terms of a particular weighting of the values at stake, then if they are to determine the relative weights of values in a choice situation, they must have some other content. What could this be? We have several clues that can be pieced together. We started with the stipulation that whatever else matters, the values at stake matter. We then saw that the values at stake cannot themselves account for their own normative relations; the circumstances of the choice situation in which they figure must also play a role. But it also turned out that the values and the circumstances in which they figure cannot account for the normative relations; keeping the values and internal circumstances constant, the relative weights of the values might differ in different cases since what matters in each case might be different. Thus, what matters must have content beyond the values and the circumstances in which they figure. We then explored a suggestion as to what this further content might be – a particular weighting of the values at stake. But we saw that this suggestion precludes the possibility of genuine disagreement within a choice situation about what the correct weighting of the values at stake is; indeed, the possibility of such disagreement presupposes some shared understanding of what matters with content beyond a particular weighting of the values at stake. In short, what matters must (1) include the values at stake, (2) have content beyond those values and the circumstances in which they figure, (3) have content beyond a particular weighting of those values in those circumstances, and (4) be that in virtue of which there can be genuine disagreement about what the correct weighting of the values is.

I cannot see what could fill this role other than a more comprehensive value that has the values at stake as parts. Values are just the sort of consideration that can fill this role; in particular, they have a "unity" in virtue of which their component values hang together in the way that they do. Take, for instance, philosophical talent. It is in virtue of this unity, for example, that, other things equal, a particular originality makes one more philosophically talented than does a particular historical sensitivity, that physical attractiveness is irrelevant to philosophical talent, and that you and I might have a genuine disagreement about whether technical prowess makes someone more or less philosophically talented than someone with a certain understanding of the historical sweep of philosophical ideas. I have a bit more to say about this unity below, but for now, I want to suggest that it is the unity of a more comprehensive value that accounts for the normative relations among its component values as they figure in practical conflict.

Indeed, it seems that a purpose, principle, or theory of value could determine the relative weights of values at stake only by presupposing a more comprehensive value with the values at stake as parts. Consider purposes. My purpose in choosing between two philosophy researchers might be to get the one with the most *philosophical talent.* Or in choosing between two actions that affect my family, it might be to be a *good daughter.* Or my purpose might be to lead a *certain kind of life* or to *be efficient.* Purposes involve some unified understanding of the competing values at stake in a choice, and it is in virtue of this unified understanding that purposes may determine what it is rational to do. Some purposes involve multiple criteria that do not appear to be part of any unified value. But how could motley criteria determine the normative relations of the values at stake? If a purpose presupposes a more comprehensive value, it would have the content required to provide a normative structure of the values at stake.

Similarly, if principles are to determine the correct weighting of the values at stake, they must presuppose a more comprehensive value. Consider the principle, "Other things equal, one ought to keep one's promises." How can a general slogan determine the relative weights of particular values in a given choice situation? Many principles have exceptions, and the relative weights a principle assigns to competing values may differ from one circumstance to another. In virtue of what does a principle operate in the way that it does? Those who appeal to principles allow that the operation or content of a principle depends on complex background claims as to when different circumstantial features affect the relative normative weights of the values at stake. So, for instance, Scanlon's contractualism holds that it is a background "structure of understanding" that determines when the cost of keeping a promise counts against keeping it, and Kamm's exploration of moral principles governing permissible harming relies on background fine-grained claims about when particular circumstances affect the moral strength of a duty not to harm.[30] If a principle is to be capable of accounting for the way particular circumstances affect the relative weights of the values at stake, it must do so by appeal to these background claims. The question then becomes, In virtue of what are these background claims as they are? Why, for example, do these background claims yield the determination that in a given choice situation in which the cost of keeping a promise is very high, the duty to keep a promise has less relative weight, rather than its opposite? Something is needed to account for the fact that the relative weights fall out in the way that they do. I have suggested that a more comprehensive value that gives structure to the component values at stake can do the required work.[31] It is hard to see what else could. The same line of reasoning holds against appeals to a theory of value.

Why a Value? Suppose it is conceded that purposes, principles, and a theory of value cannot account for the normative relations among values at stake in a choice without presupposing some further content that meets the four conditions already laid out. Why should we think that this further content is given by a *value?* Part of our answer to this question involves throwing down the gauntlet: What else could it be? What else could fit the bill besides a value that plays the same role that philosophical talent plays in certain conflicts between originality and historical sensitivity?

It might be suggested that a more comprehensive "category" concept, such as "value," "quality of life," "prudential value," "moral value," "political value," "aesthetic value," and so on, not itself a value, could, in conjunction with the values at stake, determine the normative relations among those values.[32] There are two ways this suggestion might be taken. First, it might be understood to claim that a formal category concept can itself determine the normative relations among the values that belong to that category. I do not see how a category concept, by hypothesis not itself a value, could determine the relative weights of values that fall under the category; a purely formal category concept simply offers a rubric under which values of a kind may be collected in an unstructured way. A value, in contrast, has a unity in virtue of which its components are structured, and thus may provide the normative relations among them. Second, it might be understood to claim that such category concepts help to determine which values are at stake in the first place. Their role, on this interpretation, would be to fix which evaluative features of the alternatives are relevant to the choice – for example, the particular prudential values instantiated by the alternatives or the particular moral ones. Once the values at stake are determined, they put themselves together, in good orthodox fashion. But on this interpretation, we are just led back to the beginning of our argument against the orthodox approach.

Another suggestion might be that *nothing* determines the normative relations among values; it is simply a "brute fact" that values are related as they are in the given circumstances. But the answer, "It's just a brute fact that the values are related as they are in circumstances in which they figure" will not do under the assumption that only internal circumstances can affect the normative relations of the values at stake. For, as we have already seen, there can be cases in which the values at stake are the same, the internal circumstances are the same, and yet the normative relations between the values is different. Something must explain this difference; it makes no sense to claim that it is just a brute fact that sometimes the values are related in one way and sometimes they are related in another when the putative resources for accounting for such a difference are identical. At the very least, there must be an appeal to external circumstances to account for this difference. This appeal, however, involves rejecting the claim that only internal circumstances can help to determine the relative weights of the values at stake and, as we see in the next section, leads to a problematic conception of choice.

I suspect that doubts about whether what matters in choice is given by a more comprehensive *value* have their source in the difficulty in explaining what it is about a value in virtue of which its component values are structured as they are – *what is* this unity in virtue of which its components hang together in the way that they do? Put another way, what makes a value different from a mere weighting of (component) values? This is a central question in axiology, though little philosophical progress has been made on the matter.

The difference between a mere weighting of values and a more comprehensive value that determines that weighting can, I believe, be illuminated metaphorically by a distinction between two kinds of jigsaw puzzle.

Some jigsaw puzzles are put together in virtue of a unifying picture; the puzzle, when completed, depicts a jungle scene, sleeping kittens, or an Oreo cookie. One piece goes next to another because according to the picture, the monkey is next to the elephant. Values are like this kind of jigsaw puzzle; there is a unifying "picture" that guides placement of its component parts, and it is in virtue of that picture that its parts are normatively related as they are. As we have already seen, a value, such as philosophical talent, has a unity in virtue of which disagreement about the correct weighting of its component values can proceed, and it is in virtue of this unity that, for example, a particular bundle of originality and historical sensitivity manifests more philosophical talent than another bundle. Other jigsaw puzzles are put together in some other way; there is no picture but perhaps only a depiction of something homogeneous like the color red or television static. The pieces then fit together simply by their shapes interlocking in the right way, or perhaps the pieces are all identical in shape and so the puzzle is put together by stipulation. Mere weightings of values are like this second kind of jigsaw puzzle; there is no picture in virtue of which the values are related in the way that they are. As we have argued, values cannot put themselves together simply by shape; something with further content – a picture – is needed. And as we have seen, a stipulated weighting of, for example, beauty, poise in a swimsuit, talent, and so on that gives what matters in a Miss America contest does not allow for the possibility of genuine disagreement over the correct weighting of those values. If someone were to insist that artistic talent was irrelevant or that poise in a swimsuit should count for twice as much, there would be no picture in virtue of which such claims could be correct or incorrect.

For present purposes, we need not attempt to explain just what is this picture that gives the unity of value. Instead, we need only point out that the problem of providing such an account raises no special difficulty for our approach. This problem of the unity of values is a problem even for ordinary values such as beauty and philosophical talent. We have no account of what it is about such values in virtue of which their components are weighted as they are. But this does not block the thought that they are values nonetheless and so should not ground skepticism about whether what we have identified as 'what matters' in choice is a value.

A recap of the argument is in order. We began by leaving open the possibility that what matters in a choice – prumorality in the case of conflicts between morality and prudence – is nothing more than a list of the values at stake. We then saw that there could be cases in which the values at stake are the same, the circumstances in which they figure are the same, and yet the values have different normative relations. This is possible because what matters in each case can be different. We then asked what the content of what matters could be. It cannot be given simply by the values and internal circumstances, for our question arose from seeing that the content could not be given in this way. We then examined the possibility that what matters is given by purposes, principles, or a theory of value. But each of these suggestions is subject to a dilemma. Either these considerations are understood in terms of a mere weighting of the values at stake or they have further content. If the former, they cannot account for disagreement over the correct relative weights of the values at stake in a given choice situation. If the latter, they very plausibly presuppose more comprehensive values that are at the heart of the nameless value approach. If the argument is right, the relative normative weights of values at stake in a given choice situation are determined by a more comprehensive value that includes those values as parts and gives what matters in the choice.

TWO CONCEPTIONS OF CHOICE

The above argument crucially relies on the assumption that there are two distinctive roles circumstances might play in choice, an "external" role in determining which choice situation one is in and an "internal" role in determining what one should do in a choice situation once one is in it. On this assumption, choice is a two-tier affair; first, there is the question of determining which choice situation to be in, and second, there is the question of determining what to do in that choice situation once one is in it. External circumstances play a role in the first and internal circumstances in the second.

This distinction between internal and external circumstances is crucial because the pivotal claim of the argument is that there can be two choice situations in which the values at stake are the same, the internal circumstances of the choice are the same, and yet the relative weights of the values differ because what matters in each choice is different. If there is no distinction between internal and external circumstances, however, it would be hard to see how it could be possible for two choice situations to be the same in *all* the circumstances and yet the relative weights of the values at stake be different. To think that it could would be to reject the supervenience of the normative on the nonnormative. It is only because the argument assumed that the external circumstances of two choice situations could be different that it made sense to suppose that what matters in the choice could be different, and thus that the relative weights of the values at stake could be different even though the internal circumstances of the choice situation were the same.

Proponents of the orthodox approach, however, might reject the distinction between internal and external circumstances and thus jump ship early in the argument. They might insist, for example, that what explains the appearance of there being two choice situations in which the internal circumstances are the same, the values at stake are the same, and yet their relative weights different is simply the fact that the external circumstances are different. There is no need to appeal to different more comprehensive values that give what matters in each choice situation, because the *totality* of circumstances explains the difference in the two cases. This move resuscitates the "brute fact" view of normative relations: Perhaps it is simply a brute fact that values are normatively related as they are in the totality of circumstances. But why should we, in seeking to answer the question of why values are normatively related as they are, settle with the answer, "That's just how it is," when there is in the offing a deeper explanation of why these putatively brute facts are as they are? The appeal to more comprehensive values provides such an explanation. In any case, as I now want to argue, the assumption on which the view is based – that there is no distinction between internal and external circumstances – leads to a fundamentally flawed conception of choice.

If there is no distinction between circumstances that determine a choice situation and circumstances that determine what one should do in a situation, choice is one-tier. On the one-tier conception, at any point in time for a given agent, there is a single choice situation defined by the circumstances that obtain in the universe at that time and all the values there are. What matters in the choice, then, is *every* value, and the circumstances of the choice situation are *all* the extant circumstances.[33] What one should do in a choice situation, then, is determined by the interaction of all the values there are with all the extant circumstances; values, in good orthodox fashion, put themselves together, with the help of the circumstances in which they figure, that is, every extant circumstance. This view takes its cue from theoretical explanation in science; explanation of the interaction of physical forces is not relativized to something specific that matters when the particular forces are in play; in physical explanation, what matters in principle is everything whatever.[34]

To take an example. As I finish typing this sentence, I am at a juncture of choice. What should I do next? The identity of the choice situation

I am in is given by the extant circumstances and every value. So, right now, certain circumstances obtain – millions of people are starving, my child wants me to read her a bedtime story, President Bush is gearing up for war with Iraq, I desire a cup of hot chocolate, this chapter is owed to the editors tomorrow, and so on. These circumstances come together with every value so that each value is assigned a relative weight in the circumstances. Perhaps in the circumstances that obtain now, the value of saving human lives has greater normative weight vis-à-vis the value of fulfilling my child's desire for a bedtime story, but if the circumstances were different, the relative weights might be different – if, for example, my child is on her deathbed and wants to hear *The Little Prince* one last time. And given the extant circumstances, perhaps many values will be assigned a zero relative weight; that is, they will not make any difference to how the other values relate in the extant circumstances and so in some sense drop away. How extant circumstances and values come together to yield relative normative weights is a complicated matter, but the key point, from the perspective of those who would defend the orthodox approach, is that the explanation of those weights need not appeal to anything beyond the values and the circumstances of the choice situation. What I should do, all things considered, is given by which of all the values there are have the greatest relative weight in the extant circumstances.

One difficulty with this conception is that it cannot recognize the intuitive distinction between cases in which a value does not matter and cases in which it matters but does not make a difference to how the other values at stake normatively relate. Suppose, for instance, that we are choosing between two philosophers to appoint to a chair in logic. The moral worthiness of the candidates does not matter in the choice. (If one finds that controversial, substitute physical attractiveness.) If, in contrast, we are choosing between two priests to appoint to a parish position, moral worthiness does matter. But perhaps with respect to moral worthiness, the priests are a wash; they are equally morally worthy and so their moral worthiness makes no difference as to how their instantiations of other values, such as pastoral ability and holiness, normatively relate. On the one-tier conception, both the philosophy and priest cases would have to be understood in the same way, namely, as cases in which moral worthiness matters but fails to affect the relative weights of the other values at stake. (Indeed, I suspect that the one-tier conception of choice may be partly responsible for the distorted importance that morality is often given in the practical realm. If moral values always matter in choice, and if, as it seems, moral values have special force, then choice situations become all too easily moralized. On the one-tier conception, it is easy to think of moral value as the dominant value, rather than as one value among many.)

This difficulty has its source in what I believe is a fundamental problem with the one-tier conception. Since what matters in every choice situation is the same, namely, every value, which choice situation one is in at any juncture is given by the circumstances that are extant at that juncture. The determination of *which* choice situation one is in, therefore, is not a *normative* matter. This means that there is no room for the normative question, Given the extant circumstances, what is an appropriate choice situation to be in?[35] There is only one normative question on the one-tier conception, namely, What should I do in the given choice situation? But it seems clear that the first question makes sense; people can disagree about which choice situation is appropriate in the extant circumstances. As I consider what to write in the next paragraph, I wonder, should I be in a choice situation in which morality matters, in which case perhaps I should stop typing and start writing a check to Oxfam, or is it appropriate for me to be in a choice situation in which prudence is what matters and thus finishing this paper is a priority? The marathon runner who happens on the drowning stranger makes a substantive mistake if she thinks what matters in the choice is simply her own well-being; it is inappropriate for her to be in *that* choice situation rather than in one that includes the morality of saving human life. Indeed, the complaint that someone is "insensitive" is best understood as pointing to a failure to see *which* choice situation is appropriate in the extant circumstances, not, as the one-tier conception would have it, as pointing to a failure to discern the correct normative relations between the values in the extant circumstances. Because it precludes normative inquiry into what choice situations are appropriate in given extant circumstances, the one-tier conception fails to carve choice at its joints.

On the two-tier conception, there are two normative questions. First, what is an appropriate choice situation to be in, given the extant circumstances? Second, what should one do in a choice situation once it is given? It is because there are two questions that there must be an "intermediary" between the determination of the choice situation and the determination of rational choice – something that answers the second question without also answering the first. As we have argued, this intermediary is a more comprehensive value. Disagreement over which choice situation is appropriate in the extant circumstances, then, is disagreement over which more comprehensive value should matter in the extant circumstances. Sometimes what matters in the extant circumstances is doing the moral thing; sometimes what matters is doing what makes one's life go best; and sometimes what matters is given by a more comprehensive nameless value that includes particular moral and prudential values as parts.

The argument for the nameless approach can thus be reframed as a dilemma: Either we must accept the one-tier conception of choice or we must accept the nameless value approach. This may be the deepest level at which the theoretical choice between the orthodoxy and the nameless value approach can be usefully understood. And as I have suggested, it is the one-tier conception that should be given up.

We can now see how the analogy between values and physical forces that was thought to support the orthodox approach breaks down. Indeed, the relation between values and physical forces is not one of analogy but the reverse. Physical explanation is not relativized to something specific that matters when certain physical forces are at work; "everything" matters in explaining physical reality. Sometimes, however, physicists offer "idealized" explanations; when explaining the interaction of the sun, moon, and earth, for instance, physicists may assume as an idealization that there are no other forces, such as those from distant stars, at work. Idealized physical explanation, then, may be relativized to a "closed system." But it is understood that idealized explanation of this sort gives only an approximation of physical reality; physical reality does not consist of closed systems. However, what physicists take to be an idealization, namely, relativization to a closed system, is the "reality" in the normative case. Values are different from physical forces because the normative relations of values are always relativized to a closed system, namely, something specific that matters in the choice between them. Failure to relativize the normative relations among values in this way will yield at best an idealized explanation that is only an approximate to normative reality.

Nameless Values

If the correct conception of choice is two-tier, something with content beyond the values at stake and the circumstances in which they figure is needed to explain the normative relations among the values in those circumstances. It is hard to see what this could be other than a more comprehensive value. By hypothesis, many of these values will be nameless.

The fact that many of these values are nameless might seem to provide evidence against their existence. Being nameless, however, cannot itself be grounds for thinking that there are no such values. Many ordinary named values of today were nameless not long ago. For example, a few decades ago, there was no name for sexual harassment, but there was a definite (dis)value that had as components ordinary named values such as sexual exploitation, condescension, and sexual domination. I believe that we are now in the same position with respect to many nameless values as we once were with respect to values such as sexual harassment.

Indeed, the idea that some values are nameless has a distinguished pedigree; it can be traced back to Aristotle, who thought that there were many nameless virtues and vices. In identifying the virtue and vice concerned with the pursuit of small honors, for example, Aristotle held that the mean between the extremes of ambitiousness and unambitiousness is nameless. Similarly, he thought that the regulation of feelings of anger involved a nameless virtue and vice; at one extreme is an excess of anger, which is nameless, and at the other extreme is a deficiency in anger, which is nameless, and the mean between these two extremes is also nameless.[36] I believe that Aristotle was right in pointing out that many perfectly ordinary virtues and vices have no names; my proposal takes Aristotle's insight and extends it to values generally.

A more serious doubt about nameless values might highlight the difficulty of latching onto them. But we must be careful to locate the difficulty. As we have already seen, there is no difficulty in *referring* to these values; they can be picked out by general descriptions, such as "what there is most reason to do, all things considered," and they can also be denoted by more specific descriptions, such as "what matters in this situation," "being the right person for this job," and "the relevant combination of cost, taste, and healthfulness."

Perhaps the difficulty in latching onto nameless values lies in our inability to reel off their contents. But the fact that we cannot explicitly articulate the content of a concept does not establish that there is no such concept or even that we do not possess it. Newton, for example, worked with the concept of the limit of series, which remained nameless for some two centuries, without being able explicitly to give its content.[37] And just as Newton possessed the concept of a limit, ordinary thinkers today may possess concepts associated with nameless values. When a philosophy department gets together to make an appointment, there is some or other concept combining into a unity the multiple criteria at stake in virtue of which there can be genuine disagreements about how they are to be correctly related. If members of the department pause to reflect on what this concept is, they may find it difficult to articulate. Nonetheless, it is in virtue of this concept that their decision of whom to appoint is rational (or not!).

Perhaps problems in latching onto nameless values lie in the fact that such values typically suffer from a high degree of epistemic or semantic indeterminacy, and this in turn raises doubts about whether they can be properly thought to exist as values. But many named values suffer from both kinds of indeterminacy, for example, "justice," and yet we have no doubt that those values exist. And although nameless values will typically be more indeterminate than named ones, it is not clear how this difference in degree can be parlayed into an argument that nameless values do not exist. After all, the determinateness of nameless values is not of degree zero; just as there are firmly determinate truths about justice – for example, that a tiny amount of efficiency is worse with respect to justice than a very great freedom – there are firmly determinate truths about prumorality – for example, that a small prudential pleasure is worse with respect to prumorality than a great moral duty. There could be some further difference in determinacy that might cast doubt on nameless values, but the challenge for our opponents is to articulate in what such a putative difference consists.

Another kind of doubt about nameless values might lie in the thought that such values are in some way fake – they are Frankenstein values, artificially stitched together to satisfy the mad cravings of those seeking unity where there is none.[38] Or to put the worry somewhat differently, once we allow nameless values, the floodgates are open for values to be put together any old way. But this worry overlooks the fact that values cannot be stipulated weightings of any values whatever. As we have seen, nameless values have content beyond a weighting of its component values, and it is in virtue of this content that its component values are weighted as they are. As we have suggested, this content is given by the unity of the value – the picture in virtue of which its components are put together as they are. Sometimes values come together to form a unity that is a more comprehensive value, and sometimes they do not. Why this is so remains a deep axiological mystery, but the fact that they sometimes do is not subject to doubt.[39] Unlike conflicts between beauty contestants, which are resolved by a stipulated weighting of talent, poise, beauty, and community spirit, conflicts between moral and prudential values are not resolved by stipulating some weighting of those conflicting values. Instead, there is a more comprehensive consideration that gives what matters in the choice and is that in virtue of which it is rational to choose one alternative over the other. Of course, this approach allows that there are many more values than we might have otherwise thought, but insofar as each has the requisite unity to distinguish itself from a stipulated patchwork of considerations, none can be distinguished as more monstrous than any other.

Although there are many more questions about the nameless values that need to be answered, I'll mention only one more.[40] If there are more comprehensive nameless values that put together named values, then are there more comprehensive nameless values that put together those nameless values, and so on up until we have a single super nameless value that includes all values as parts? If so, the nameless value approach might naturally dovetail with the one-tier conception of choice. I believe that there is no such supervalue, but a careful consideration of the question would take us too far astray. I doubt that any two values can be put together by some more comprehensive value because it seems that sometimes there is a picture in virtue of which two values hang together to form a unity, and sometimes there is not. A rough-and-ready test for whether two values come together to form a unity is to ask whether it makes sense to attempt to compare their intrinsic merits. Sometimes it makes no sense conceptually, as in the comparison between the abstract beauty of number theory and the utility of a corkscrew – which is better with respect to ____. Other times it makes no sense substantively, as in a comparison between the neatness with which someone can drink a glass of milk and the elegance with which she turns pages of a book. In these cases, even "nominal-notable" comparisons seem senseless – someone who drinks milk sloppily is not worse with respect to ____ than someone who flips the pages of a book with unparalleled elegance. This is not to say that a choice situation could not be jiggered so that there is some more comprehensive consideration that fills in the blanks and yields normative relations among the values at stake, but such a consideration would be gerrymandered and thus lack the unity of a genuine value.

CONCLUSION

This chapter presented two arguments for the nameless value approach to putting together morality and well-being. The first was an argument by analogy: Given that there are some practical conflicts that are rationally resolved in virtue of a more comprehensive value that includes the conflicting values as parts, why think that conflicts between moral and prudential considerations are any different? Various attempts to distinguish such conflicts were examined and found to be not up to the job. The second was an argument from circumstances. Insofar as circumstances can help determine the normative relations among values, what matters in a choice must have content beyond that given by the values at stake and the circumstances in which they figure, content that cannot be provided by a purpose, principle, or theory of value. It was suggested that the only thing that could provide this content is a more comprehensive value. The argument from circumstances, however, crucially relied on a distinction between two roles that circumstances might play in choice. An attack on this distinction was considered and found to lead to a fundamentally misguided conception of choice. Finally, possible sources of skepticism about the existence of more comprehensive nameless values were examined. It was argued that those doubts could be traced either to the mistaken assumption that the existence of a concept presupposes an ability among its would-be possessors to explicitly articulate its content or to a failure to recognize that nameless values have a unity beyond a stipulated weighting of their components.

The existence of nameless values that put together moral and prudential values helps to solve the two puzzles with which we began. If a moral value in conflict with a prudential one is a component of some more comprehensive nameless value, then the normativity of morality in the face of conflict with prudence derives from the normativity of that nameless value in just the way that the normativity of originality in the face of conflict with historical sensitivity derives from the normativity of the value of philosophical talent. It is in virtue of that nameless value that, in a particular case, a moral value has whatever normativity it does in the face of conflict with a prudential one. This, of course, is not to account for the phenomenon of normativity in general, but only to provide a structure for answering the question, Why should I be moral when my life will suffer as a result? The answer is, Because doing so is in accord with value X, which includes both the moral and prudential values at stake and gives what matters in the choice situation. If values in general are reason-giving, then we have the same kind of answer to the "why should I" question as we do when two moral values conflict or two prudential ones do. Even if moral and prudential values issue from fundamentally different points of view, conflicts between them are rationally resolved, if resolvable, just as conflicts between two moral values or two prudential ones are – in virtue of a more comprehensive value that has those conflicting values as parts.

Prumorality, and nameless values generally, also help to block the worry about the scope of practical reason. For if morality and prudence (or beauty and truth, or rights and utility, and so on) can be put together by more comprehensive nameless values, then conflicts between such different values can, like humdrum conflicts within morality or within prudence (or within beauty, truth, rights, and utility), be in principle rationally resolved. What looked like a possible gap in practical reason turns out not to be gap after all; nameless values rush in to show how there may be a justified choice in every case of value conflict.

Finally, the appeal to a more comprehensive value that gives what matters in a choice helps us to understand a long-standing puzzle about the demandingness of morality. Commonsense morality tells us that we are justified in failing to give some sizable portion of our income to help feed starving children halfway around the world. But it is also holds that if those starving children appeared on our doorstep, near death and in need of that same portion of our income, we are not justified – or are less justified – in turning our backs on them. How can commonsense morality account for the difference in these two cases? One way is to argue, as Frances Kamm does, that distance from a victim affects the *moral* weight of one's duty to save. But, as do many others, I have trouble believing that physical distance per se can make a moral difference in this way. The nameless value approach offers another way of explaining the difference in the two cases: What matters in each case is different. For even if the circumstances in the two cases are "equalized" and the values at stake are the same, it does not follow that their relative normative weights will be the same: The more comprehensive value that governs the relative normative weights of those values may be different. In the one case, it may make the choice a predominantly prudential one, and in the other a predominantly moral one. This difference in what matters explains why the seemingly same choice of refusing to give may be more or less justified in the one case than in the other.

If moral and prudential values are put together by more comprehensive nameless values, then we have the beginnings of a general model for explaining what determines the rational resolution of conflicts between any values whatever. Conflicts are resolvable, if at all, in virtue of a more comprehensive value that has the conflicting values as parts.

Notes

Many thanks are due to Kit Fine, James Griffin, Derek Parfit, and Joseph Raz for very helpful and detailed comments on or discussion of a near ancestor of this paper. The paper also benefited from discussion by audiences at Dartmouth College,

Bowling Green University, Swarthmore College, the Princeton Center for Human Values, and Philamore, among others. Members of those audiences or other commentators whose very useful and in many cases penetrating comments I remember are Peter Baumann, John Broome, David Copp, John Doris, Bernard Gert, Amy Gutmann, Olivia Harman, Ulrike Heuer, Bojun Hu, Shelly Kagan, Frances Kamm, Rahul Kumar, Sam Levey, Milton Meyer, Elijah Millgram, Liam Murphy, Josh Ober, Hans Oberdiek, Peter Railton, Henry Richardson, Scott Shapiro, Peter Singer, Walter Sinnott-Armstrong, Wayne Sumner, David Sussman, Sigrun Svavarsdottir, and Larry Temkin. Thanks also to David Sobel for inviting me to a conference on well-being that first provided the occasion for thinking about the ideas of this paper and to the editors of this anthology for prompting me to revisit them.

1. Thomas Nagel writes: "Conflicts between personal and impersonal claims...cannot, in my view, be resolved by subsuming either of the points of the view under the other, or both under a third. Nor can we simply abandon any of them" (Nagel 1979: 134; see also Nagel 1986: 197). For related discussion, see Baier 1958; Thomson 1992; Copp 1997; and Wolf 1997, 1999. See also Sidgwick 1981, who concluded that practical reason is hopelessly fragmented since there is no more comprehensive point of view from which to assess the justifiability of the egoistic and utilitarian points of view. It is perhaps worth pointing out that my understanding of "fundamentally different points of view," namely, as points of view that are not themselves subsumed under some common point of view, does not, unlike other understandings of the phrase, preclude *by definition* rational resolution of conflict between considerations issuing from such points of view.

2. By "rational choice" I primarily have in mind what one has most reason to choose "fullstop," although the argument applies also to what one has most reason to choose relative to one's own, perhaps faulty, mental states.

3. By "normative relations" I mean broadly "aggregative" relations – trumping, outweighing, overriding, being more stringent than, and so on – but not "canceling" relations – excluding, silencing, or bracketing as irrelevant. The relative weight of a value is greater or stronger than or outweighs another if it contributes more to the basis for rational choice in a given choice situation. See Raz 1975: 37–9 for a discussion of exclusionary relations and Scanlon 1998: 50–4 for a discussion of the "bracketing as irrelevant" relation.

4. I say "typically" because it might be argued that some named values, such as "supererogation," put together particular moral and prudential values. I say "at present" because their being nameless is a contingent matter.

5. As we see below, however, not any more comprehensive consideration will do. The consideration – whether or not a value – must have a "unity," that is, something in virtue of which its components hang together in the way that they do. Any deflationary or reductive account of values consistent with this requirement will be consistent with the favored approach. But see Scanlon 1998: ch. 1 for a powerful case, which generalized would show that an account in terms of desires will not work.

6. It might be objected that since some practical conflicts are resolved by some-thing like the Pareto rule, the nameless value approach cannot have universal application. The Pareto rule holds that one alternative is rationally preferred to another if it is at least as good with respect to every value at stake and bet-ter with respect to at least one. But it is far from clear that in cases in which the Pareto rule applies, the values *are* all at stake; perhaps the correct way to understand the application of the Pareto rule in such cases is that it is inde-terminate which of the various values is at stake. The Pareto rule would then tell us that whichever value is at stake, the Pareto superior alternative can be rationally chosen. Indeed, although my focus is on conflicts, the problem and, I believe, its solution extends to choice situations that do not involve conflict.

7. There are possible approaches that do not fit these categories. For instance, an "agent-based" approach might be worked up from what Amartya Sen has argued is a way of putting together consequentialist and deontological values, namely, by building into the badness of an outcome its badness as viewed by the agent who is responsible for it. See Sen 1982, 1983; cf. Regan 1983. Since my target is the third category of views, I do not discuss other possible approaches.

8. For the view that individual well-being or happiness is the basic notion from which all moral considerations are derived, see Aristotle 1985, Plato 1968, and Sumner 1996; for the view that moral considerations reduce to rational constraints on the pursuit of one's well-being, see Hobbes 1998 and Gauthier 1986; for the view that well-being is simply one aspect of morality, see Gewirth 1978. No one, as far as I am aware, has defended the idea that there is a third more comprehensive point of view that includes the moral and prudential points of view, though for a thoughtful rejection of this possibility, see Copp 1997. For discussion of the view from nowhere, see the locus classicus, Nagel 1986.

9. See, e.g., Brandt 1979; Williams 1981.

10. Thanks to Shelly Kagan for suggesting this analogy (to which I take exception later in the paper). For examples of the orthodox approach, see Griffin 1986, 1991, 1996; Kamm 1996; Nagel 1970: ch. 13; Parfit 1984; Raz 1975, 1999; Korsgaard 1996; and Scanlon 1998. The approach is implicitly endorsed in a wide range of writings in ethics. (Neo-Kantian constructivist accounts fall within the orthodoxy as described because "the values themselves" can be understood as constructions of practical reason.)

11. There is, in addition, the problem of showing how purely conative states can be normative states. See Quinn 1993: ch. 12; Raz 1999: ch. 3; Scanlon 1998: ch. 1.

12. It is perhaps worth noting that some proponents of the orthodoxy deny that moral and prudential values issue from fundamentally different points of view; the categories of "the moral" and "the prudential" do not mark any significant distinction but are just convenient ways of talking about values that share some feature such as impartiality or self-regardingness. See Griffin 1986: 161; Scanlon 1998, chs. 2–3; and Raz 1999: chs. 12–13. An extreme version of this denial – that there is no distinction whatever between moral

and prudential considerations – might be traced back to the Greeks. My discussion of the problem does not depend on insisting that moral and prudential values are significantly different in some way.

13. See Nagel 1986: 195–200, who thinks that when morality conflicts with prudence, morality "provides sufficient reason to sacrifice our own good." Compare Scheffler 1992, who argues that morality gives special weight to considerations having to do with individual well-being and that individual interests are already responsive to moral considerations, so that, in the end, morality and prudence are "potentially congruent." Thomas Scanlon employs a similar strategy in arguing that "contractualist morality makes room for projects and commitments" and that "other values have a built-in sensitivity to moral requirements," but concludes that moral considerations are "overriding." See Scanlon 1998, 2002: 514. For doubts about whether the Scheffler-Scanlon strategy will eradicate genuine conflicts between moral and prudential considerations, see Wallace 2002: 451–9. Of course, those who take this approach might hold that sometimes the values at stake give rise to reasons that are not on the same normative page, and in these cases there is no rational resolution of the conflict.

14. Specificationism is usually presented as a view about correct deliberation, not as a theory of the determination of rational choice, but I co-opt it for my own purposes. For versions of specificationism, see, e.g., Kolnai 2001; Wiggins 1976; Nussbaum 1990; and Richardson 1994.

15. For an example of coherentism, see Hurley 1989; for interpretivism, see Dworkin, forthcoming, and, in law, Dworkin 1986. It is not altogether clear how coherentists, interpretivists, specificationists, and their ilk should be interpreted. On the one hand, they might hold that circumstances play only an "external" role (see text below), that is, they help determine which values are at stake, but that once the values at stake are given, their relative normative weights can be determined in the abstract apart from the circumstances in which they might figure – in which case they would be proponents of the simple version. On the other hand, they might think that filling out the values is a matter of determining their relative normative weights. This would make them proponents of the sophisticated version. I believe the latter is the more sympathetic interpretation and treat them accordingly.

16. See Kamm 1996 for a deontological, Hurka 2001 for a virtue-theoretic, and Scanlon 1998 for a contractualist version of this view within the moral domain.

17. I set aside "particularism," the view that the identity of the values at stake is indexed to the particular circumstances in which they figure and that those very finely individuated values, perhaps in conjunction with Aristotelian practical wisdom, determine how those values normatively relate. Such a view, although orthodox in spirit, is not sufficiently general to be a challenge to my own approach. Note, too, that views about how one ought to go about choosing between alternatives when reasons run out are not relevant to our inquiry; we are searching for an account of how relative normative weights are determined *within* practical reason. Cf. Nagel 1979: 134–5.

18. This distinction between being the "primary determinant" and being a "supplementary factor" is not critical to my argument. While I assume that the determinant of normative relations is the *primary* determinant, one could instead take it to include everything that plays any role, even a background role, in determining the relative weights of values. In this case, the difference between the nameless value approach and the sophisticated version of the orthodoxy would appear less stark, for both would allow that something beyond the values themselves is required to put the values together; the difference would be that the nameless value approach insists, contra existing views of the orthodoxy, that this "something beyond" includes a more comprehensive nameless value.

19. Cf. Copp 1997, who assumes that if there is no more comprehensive point of view that includes the moral and prudential points of view, it follows that it makes no sense to ask in any particular conflict what we ought to do, taking into account both the moral and prudential values at stake. See also Foot 1978: 169–70.

20. I sometimes slide between generic and specific values for ease of presentation, but the slide is harmless.

21. Therefore, rational resolution of conflict is not a matter of doing what "one feels like" or "satisfying one's brute desires," since what matters must include all the conflicting desires. I believe that in some conflicts (e.g., choosing between desserts) what matters might be given simply by a brute preference, but such cases are rarer than one might think. In any case, I set aside such cases since they do not involve putting together conflicting considerations in the way of interest.

22. For simplicity, I ignore the possibility of organic interactions among originality, historical sensitivity, and the other respects in which they are equally matched. The examples used throughout the paper are purposefully schematic in form, and the reader should feel free to fill in or amend the details in a way that makes them seem as plausible as possible.

23. The details of the case can be jiggered to accommodate intuitions about when the prudential value is itself significant enough to be "at stake" in the choice. Note, too, that the case can be changed to involve someone whose well-being *is* affected by doing the moral thing, but such a case would have to be more complicated; for example, it might involve a strong supererogatory consideration against a weak prudential one.

24. Two other suggestions can be quickly dismissed. One is that easy cases involving morality and prudence follow as a *conceptual* matter from a proper understanding of the moral and prudential values at stake, and thus there is no more comprehensive value in virtue of which that resolution holds. But this thought quickly runs into the difficulty of explaining how grasp of a concept can yield substantive truths. Another is that that the difference between the drowning and philosophy cases *just is* that in the former there is no more comprehensive value and in the latter there is. This suggestion, while perhaps in the end correct, amounts to begging the question at the present juncture of argument: The challenge raised by the apparent parallel

between the two cases is to explain *why* there is a more comprehensive value in the one case but not, supposedly, in the other.

25. See Singer 1972 and Unger 1996. Cf. Kamm 1999b. More typically, attacks on Singer-Unger type arguments involve a related objection, namely, that a circumstantial feature that affects the relative weights of two values in one case may not affect the relative weights of the same two values in the same way, if at all, in another case. See Kamm's discussion of "the principle of contextual interaction" in Kamm 1996 and in Kamm 1983 and Shelly Kagan's (1988) discussion of "the additive fallacy." See also Temkin 1987. The argument of this paper can be seen as complementary to the Kamm-Kagan-Temkin argument that "transporting" normative weights from one case to another is illegitimate; the paper attempts to explain *why* it is illegitimate by appeal to the difference in the more comprehensive value that gives what matters in each choice.

26. Cf. Kamm 1996: 83, who thinks that ethical values have some kind of intrinsic "merit weight" independent of circumstances, but allows that those weights may be affected by different factors that obtain in different circumstances. The "weight" she has in mind seems distinctively *moral*, but her view about moral weight might be generalized to overall relative normative weight as a hybrid of the "simple" and "sophisticated" views.

27. Seeming counterexamples to this claim can be explained either by uncovering a surreptitious assumption that the circumstances are "ordinary" or by showing that as a substantive matter the one value has a certain normative weight vis-à-vis another in *every* circumstance. The possibility that two values have exactly the same relative normative weight in every circumstance seems unlikely: Even if, for example, the value of human life is always intrinsically weightier than the value of mild amusement in every circumstance, how much weightier it is will plausibly vary from circumstance to circumstance.

28. This claim should not be confused with Frances Kamm's claim that distance from the victim affects the *moral* strength of one's duty to save. Kamm is concerned with how circumstantial features can affect the *moral* weight of a consideration, not with how circumstantial features can affect the overall relative normative weight of a moral consideration – given its moral weight – and a prudential one – given its prudential weight. See Kamm 1999a and 1996: 233.

29. This is so under either an "objective" conception of what matters (what God would say should determine my rational choice) or a "subjective" one (what in fact determines my rational choice). Under an objective conception, saintliness could be what matters if, for instance, there has never been a supererogatory act previously performed and this will be the last act in the universe. Under a subjective conception, saintliness may in fact determine my rational choice without my having, paradoxically, to aim at it.

30. See Scanlon 1998: 197–201, 50–4; and Kamm 1996: 51–68.

31. For example, the background structure of understanding that fills out the content of Scanlon's contractualist principles appeals to "reasonableness." Scanlon allows that what counts as reasonable depends on values held by those party to the contract. If my argument is correct, some of those values

held will be more comprehensive nameless ones. My disagreement with Scanlon can be put in the terms of his framework as follows. Scanlon thinks that (as a description of how practical reasoning usually proceeds) an agent makes a normatively guided "decision" as to what is relevant to the choice. This decision amounts to take certain considerations as relevant to the choice, and these considerations, in conjunction with contractualist principles, determine their own relative weights (see Scanlon 1998: 47, 50–4). My suggestion is that an (ideal) agent makes a normatively guided decision as to what more comprehensive value is relevant to choice, and this more comprehensive value then determines the specific considerations relevant to the choice (i.e., its component values) *and* their normative relations. I believe that what the agent decides to take as relevant must be a more comprehensive value and not a list of considerations (or a particular weighting of them) because I cannot see how the considerations themselves, even in conjunction with principles supported by a complex and rich background structure of understanding, can put themselves together unless those principles presuppose a more comprehensive value.

32. In a forthcoming book on human rights, Griffin suggests that the rational resolution of conflicts between rights and the social good is determined by appeal to the more comprehensive concept of "quality of life." Griffin wants this notion to be a formal "category" concept rather than a value, because he is concerned to present a workable picture of how conflict is actually to be resolved, and he thinks the prospects for actually resolving such conflicts by appeal to a value would be dim. See Griffin, forthcoming. I do not see, however, how a category concept could do the normative work Griffin envisions. Thanks to Griffin for discussion on this point. Cf. Scanlon 1998: ch. 3 and Raz 1999: ch. 13, who argue that "prudence" and "individual well-being" are not more comprehensive concepts from which all prudential considerations derive their relative normative weights.

33. The one-tier conception discussed here is stripped of all bells and whistles. For instance, the extant circumstances that "obtain in the universe" might be restricted to include only those that are in some sense "agent-involving"; they are circumstances that could conceivably be relevant to what the agent might now do. And once the extant circumstances are restricted, only some values and not all will be relevant to the choice, and the relevance of certain values might make other values irrelevant, further narrowing the values and circumstances of the choice situation. Insofar as this "narrowing down" of the choice situation derives from a nonnormative restriction on circumstances, it does not affect my complaint against it. Once it is allowed that something normative, such as a commitment, plan, or intention, is what matters in the choice, the conception of choice is no longer one-tier. My claim is that any normative consideration that narrows down a choice situation must include a more comprehensive value if there is to be a rational choice in it.

34. Of course, "everything" is itself restricted to a domain – the domain of our natural world – and those who think that "every value" matters in every normative explanation would presumably restrict their domains to the normative world (or to the nonnormative world that subvenes it).

35. The only kind of normativity that the one-tier conception can make sense of in this question is epistemic; the agent may, for example, have overlooked an extant circumstance.

36. Aristotle, *Nicomachean Ethics*, Book IV, 1125b. Indeed, Aristotle repeatedly underscores the point that *many* virtues and vices have no names (1107b, 1108a, 1115b). Some examples: excessive fearlessness (1107b, 1115b), the mean between excessive fearlessness and rashness (1107b), excessive desire for pleasure (1107b), deficient desire for pleasure (1107b, 1119a), the virtue associated with pursuing honor and its corresponding state or condition (1107b), the condition corresponding to a deficiency in desire for honor (1107b), the vice of overstating the truth (1108a), the mean between overstating and understating the truth (1108a, 1127a), the virtue associated with seeking pleasure in everyday life (1126b, 1127a), the virtue associated with seeking pleasure in amusements (1108a), and, arguably, excessive and deficient desire for pleasure in daily life and in amusements (1108a).

   The question of why certain values are named and others are not admits of a variety of possible answers. I suspect that value-naming conventions depend on our evaluative practices, and that if we began to recognize that nameless values played a crucial role in determining rational resolution of conflict, we would begin to focus attention on their content and application in a way that would eventually result in our adopting shorthand expressions for them. Elijah Millgram suggested to me that Aristotle's explanation for why certain virtues and vices are nameless is that they rarely occur. (This reading of Aristotle is arguably implicit in Hardie 1968: 140.) I doubt that this is a correct interpretation; although Aristotle explicitly says that the particular vices of deficiency in desire for pleasure and of excessive fearlessness are unnamed "because [they] are not found much" (1119a, see also 1107b, 1115b), he does not seem to intend this to be more than a sufficient condition for namelessness. After all, he says that *all* the virtues and vices associated with feelings of anger are nameless (1125b), and surely the vice of excessive anger could hardly be thought to be rare, even in Aristotle's day. Moreover, he thinks the rare virtues and vices are rare because they go against human nature – the person who shuns pleasure or is unafraid of earthquakes is "a sort of madman" (115b, see also 1119a) – but many of the nameless virtues and vices he identifies are not rare in this way.

37. I take this example from Peacocke 1998a, 1998b, who argues that an inability to articulate explicitly the content of a concept does not show that one lacks the concept.

38. Thanks to Stephen Robert Grimm for pressing me to say more about this objection.

39. Although it is natural to think of the unity of values as something "out there," independent of us, the mystery of this unity may be a matter of the complexity of the social construction of value. After all, certain ordinary values are clearly the products of social invention, for example, goodness as a marriage. The line between socially constructed value and stipulated evaluative considerations is not an easy one to draw, but I believe there is such a line.

40. One particularly nettlesome problem I leave untouched is to explain how values, nameless or otherwise, are individuated, which has ramifications for how promiscuous our evaluative ontology is to be. Another is how these more comprehensive values work with the internal circumstances to determine the relative weights of the values at stake. Neither of these problems, however, is peculiar to the nameless value approach.

Bibliography

Aristotle. 1985. *Nicomachean Ethics*, tr. Terence Irwin. Indianapolis, Ind.: Hackett.

Baier, Kurt. 1958. *From the Moral Point of View*. Ithaca, N.Y.: Cornell University Press.

Brandt, Richard. 1979. *A Theory of the Good and the Right*. Oxford: Clarendon.

Copp, David. 1997. The Ring of Gyges: Overridingness and the Unity of Reason. *Social Philosophy and Policy* 14: 86–106.

Dworkin, Ronald. 1986. *Law's Empire*. Cambridge: Belknap Press.

Dworkin, Ronald. Forthcoming. *Justice for Hedgehogs*.

Foot, Philippa. 1978. Morality as a System of Hypothetical Imperatives. In Philippa Foot, *Virtues and Vices*. Oxford: Blackwell, 157–73.

Gauthier, David. 1986. *Morals by Agreement*. Oxford: Clarendon.

Gewirth, Alan. 1978. *Reason and Morality*. Chicago: University of Chicago Press.

Griffin, James. 1986. *Well-Being*. Oxford: Oxford University Press.

Griffin, James. 1991. Mixing Values. *Proceedings of the Aristotelian Society*, suppl. vol. 65: 101–18.

Griffin, James. 1996. *Value Judgement: Improving Our Ethical Beliefs*. Oxford: Oxford University Press.

Griffin, James. [no title]. Unpublished manuscript.

Hardie, W. F. R. 1968. *Aristotle's Ethical Theory*. Oxford: Clarendon.

Hobbes, Thomas. 1998. *Leviathan*. New York: Prometheus.

Hurka, Thomas. 2001. *Virtue, Vice, and Value*. Oxford: Oxford University Press.

Hurley, Susan. 1989. *Natural Reasons*. Oxford: Oxford University Press.

Kagan, Shelly. 1988. The Additive Fallacy. *Ethics* 99: 5–31.

Kamm, Frances. 1983. Killing and Letting Die: Methodology and Substance. *Pacific Philosophical Quarterly* 64: 297–312.

Kamm, Frances. 1996. *Morality, Mortality*. Oxford: Oxford University Press. Vol. II.

Kamm, Frances. 1999a. Faminine Ethics: The Problem of Distance in Morality and Singer's Ethical Theory. In Dale Jamieson (ed.), *Singer and His Critics*. Oxford: Blackwell, 162–208.

Kamm, Frances. 1999b. Rescue and Harm: Discussion of Peter Unger's Living High and Letting Die. *Legal Theory* 5: 1–44.

Kolnai, Aurel. 2001. Deliberation Is of Ends. In Elijah Millgram (ed.), *Varieties of Practical Reasoning*. Cambridge, Mass.: MIT Press, 259–78.

Korsgaard, Christine (with G. A. Cohen, Raymond Geuss, Thomas Nagel, and Bernard Williams). 1996. *The Sources of Normativity*, ed. Onora O'Neill. Cambridge: Cambridge University Press.

Nagel, Thomas. 1970. *The Possibility of Altruism*. Princeton, N.J.: Princeton University Press.

Nagel, Thomas. 1979. The Fragmentation of Value. In Thomas Nagel, *Mortal Questions*. Cambridge: Cambridge University Press, 128–41.

Nagel, Thomas. 1986. *The View from Nowhere*. New York: Oxford University Press.

Nussbaum, Martha. 1990. *Love's Knowledge*. New York: Oxford University Press.

Parfit, Derek. 1984. *Reasons and Persons*. Oxford: Oxford University Press.

Peacocke, Christopher. 1998a. Implicit Conceptions, Understanding and Rationality. *Philosophical Issues* 9: 43–88.

Peacocke, Christopher. 1998b. Implicit Conceptions, the *A Priori,* and the Identity of Concepts. *Philosophical Issues* 9: 121–48.

Plato. 1968. *The Republic,* tr. Allan Bloom. New York: Basic Books.

Quinn, Warren. 1993. *Morality and Action*. Cambridge: Cambridge University Press.

Raz, Joseph. 1975. *Practical Reason and Norms*. Princeton, N.J.: Princeton University Press.

Raz, Joseph. 1991. Mixing Values. *Proceedings of the Aristotelian Society,* suppl. vol. 65: 83–100.

Raz, Joseph. 1999. *Engaging Reason: On the Theory of Value and Action*. Oxford: Oxford University Press.

Regan, Donald. 1983. Against Evaluator Relativity. *Philosophy and Public Affairs* 12: 93–112.

Richardson, Henry. 1994. *Practical Reasoning about Final Ends*. Cambridge: Cambridge University Press.

Scanlon, Thomas. 1998. *What We Owe to Each Other*. Cambridge: Harvard University Press.

Scanlon, Thomas. 2002. Reasons, Responsibility, and Reliance: Replies to Wallace, Dworkin, and Deigh. *Ethics* 112: 507–28.

Scheffler, Samuel. 1992. *Human Morality*. New York: Oxford University Press.

Sen, Amartya. 1982. Rights and Agency. *Philosophy and Public Affairs* 11: 3–39.

Sen, Amartya. 1983. Evaluator Relativity and Consequential Evaluation. *Philosophy and Public Affairs* 12: 113–32.

Sidgwick, Henry. 1981. *The Methods of Ethics*. Indianapolis, Ind.: Hackett.

Singer, Peter. 1972. Famine, Affluence, and Morality. *Philosophy and Public Affairs* 1: 229–43.

Sumner, Wayne. 1996. *Welfare, Happiness, and Ethics*. Oxford: Clarendon.

Temkin, Larry. 1987. Intransitivity and the Mere Addition Paradox. *Philosophy and Public Affairs* 16: 138–87.

Thomson, Judith Jarvis. 1992. On Some Ways in Which a Thing Can Be Good. *Social Philosophy and Policy* 9: 96–117.

Unger, Peter. 1996. *Living High and Letting Die*. New York: Oxford University Press.

Wallace, Jay. 2002. Scanlon's Contractualism. *Ethics* 112: 429–70.

Wiggins, David. 1976. Deliberation and Practical Reason. *Proceedings of the Aristotelian Society* 76: 29–51.

Williams, Bernard. 1981. Internal and External Reasons. In Bernard Williams, *Moral Luck*. Cambridge: Cambridge University Press, 101–13.

Wolf, Susan. 1997. Meaning and Morality. *Proceedings of the Aristotelian Society* 97: 299–315.

Wolf, Susan. 1999. Morality and the View from Here. *Journal of Ethics* 3: 203–23.

6

The Second Worst in Practical Conflict

Isaac Levi

TIES FOR OPTIMALITY

Rational agents do the best they can. That is to say, they choose an option from those available to them that is the best, all things considered, among those available options. This maximizing recipe creates no difficulty in case there is exactly one option that is best among the options available to agent X. Agent X should choose the optimal option.

Suppose, however, that like Buridan's Ass, X faces a predicament where two or more options are optimal. Which option should X choose? It does no good to say that all optimal options are equally optimal. X knows that. But X may still want guidance as to what to do.

To insist that rational agents never face decision problems where more than one available option is optimal is to disallow the possibility that decision makers can judge distinct options to be equally valuable. If A and B are equally valuable, all things considered, and belong to set of feasible options S, then the subset of S consisting of the pair {A, B} could coherently be a set of available options. Both A and B are equally optimal relative to that set of available options.

Buridan's Ass X need not be frozen in indecision, leading to doom. X will choose for the best no matter which optimal option X chooses. X may not feel the need for guidance between equally optimal options.

To be sure, X's choice will not reveal a strict preference for the option chosen over the other optimal alternatives available. Choice behavior does not reveal all there is to know about preference. In some cases, there is a uniquely optimal option manifested by choice. In other cases, no option is uniquely optimal. In both cases, a rational agent will choose for the best, but only in the former case will the option chosen be uniquely for the best.

No dictate of reason requires that X justify choosing one optimal option over another when both are optimal. X might, nonetheless, seek some basis for discriminating among optimal options. X might wish to invoke some "tie breaking" consideration. If X is somehow committed to breaking ties for optimality, the presence of two or more optimal options presents itself as a sort of practical conflict. Such conflict is resolved by invoking some method of valuing the available options that would be totally ignored otherwise. Tie-breaking procedures arrange the options that are optimal according to the primary considerations in a weak ordering according to a secondary consideration. The circumstance that optimal option A is better than B according to the secondary criterion does not render A better or more valued than B according to the primary method of evaluation. A and B are still equal in value according to the primary criterion. And, by hypothesis, they are both optimal. B does not lose its optimality because it is inferior to A according to the secondary criterion.

Some think of affirmative action as a tie-breaker in employment policies in just this fashion. When several candidates for a job are equally qualified, various nonprofessional considerations (appearance, family connections, personality) often determine who gets the job. Advocates for affirmative action often suggest that in such cases one should favor the least advantaged rather than invoke one of these other devices. But one cannot claim that the least advantaged is more qualified than the other top candidates for the job.

Another example of this kind arises in expected utility theory when propositions countenanced as serious possibilities are allowed to carry 0 probability.

Unbiased coin a is to be tossed until the first time it switches from landing heads to landing tails or vice versa. There are three possibilities. The coin lands heads every time in an infinite sequence, lands tails every time in an infinite sequence, or is tossed only a finite number of times. X is offered a bet where X wins a million dollars if the coin lands heads every time, loses a half million dollars if it lands tails every time, and neither gains nor loses if it stops after a finite number of tosses. X can refuse the bet and receive nothing.

Table 6.1 gives the payoffs and probabilities.

The expected utilities of both options A and B are 0. In a pairwise choice, they are equipreferred if options are evaluated with respect to expected utility. Yet X might argue that X should choose option A. The choice between options A and B is "called off" when the tossing of the

TABLE 6.1

	Heads forever (o)	Tails forever (o)	Stops (1)
A	$1,000,000	–$500,000	$0
B	$0	$0	$0

coin is going to stop. There is no difference in value between the two options in that case. When this is so, the decision maker might consider the expectations of the two options *conditional on the tossing not stopping*. X might (though he need not do so) judge that the prospect of forever heads and the prospect of forever tails are equally probable conditional on one of them being the case. The conditional expectation of A is greater than that of B. The tie in unconditional expectation is broken by the conditional expectation.[1]

I have already suggested that when two or more options are tied for optimality it is not, in general, obligatory to choose an optimal option by invoking some reason. Those who think it rational to maximize expected utility might want to insist that the predicaments now under study are exceptional. Invoking conditional expectation to break ties is obligatory when unconditional expectation fails. How to do this does require great care (see Levi 1989).

Two contexts where a need to break ties by invoking secondary criteria is invoked have been identified. There are, of course, many others.

Some authors think that there should never be ties for optimality. In effect, all rational agents are required to have preferences imposing a strict total ordering of their options. The "secondary criteria" are no longer treated as tie-breaking standards that do not alter the judgment that the tie-breaking standard adjudicates between equally optimal options without ranking one as better than the other. Instead, the primary, secondary, tertiary, and so on preference rankings are amalgamated into a single evaluation yielding a lexicographical, nonarchimedean ordering as was suggested by I. M. D. Little for preferences for commodity bundles in the theory of consumer demand (see Little 1957).

Little insisted on this in order to ensure that strict preference could always be equated with what is chosen in pairwise choice. Two reasons for insisting that strict preference be equivalent to what is chosen in pairwise choice may be considered:

1. There is a widespread prejudice according to which rational agents always choose for the best, all things considered. Failure to optimize among the options available and relative to one's goals is irrational.

I return to this prejudice later, but even if it is endorsed, it surely does not entail hyperbolic maximization according to which rational agents never rate two options equally optimal.

2. The temptation to think of rationality as hyperbolic maximization may derive from an insistence that the preferences of rational agents ought to be revealed by their choices. To reveal that X strictly prefers A to B by X's choice of A over B, the possibility that A and B are equipreferred ought to be rejected.

Anyone who thinks that all rational agents are obliged to identify a uniquely optimal option among those available for reasons of the sort just described should find the existence of ties for optimality to be a kind of practical conflict from which the decision maker should extricate him- or herself on pain of irrationality.

In my judgment, requiring that rational agents choose for the uniquely best, all things considered, insists on an absurdly stringent constraint on rational choice. And the absurdity is not mitigated by noting that when the demand is satisfied, strict preference is revealed by choice. I myself do not appreciate the comfort being offered. But even those who do should not make the requirements of rationality hostage to the demands of the methodology of revealed preference. Detaching preference or valuing from choice behavior altogether would be silly. But insisting on the tight connection demanded by Little is a challenge to our credulity.

INCONSISTENT VALUE COMMITMENTS

X subscribes to the principle that everyone should keep their promises. Y subscribes to the principle that Y should keep Y's promises. Z subscribes to the principle that everyone should keep promises they make in a court of law. X, Y, and Z endorse value commitments. X's value commitment has a larger *scope* than Y's value commitment in the sense that it is applicable to all agents, whereas Y's value commitment is restricted to choices made by Y. The scope of X's commitment also comprehends the scope of Z's value commitment. X's value commitment covers all cases where the available options included opportunities to keep and to break promises. Z's value commitment covers cases where the available options include opportunities to keep and break promises made in a court of law. Nothing is said about other cases of promise keeping and breaking. Had Z's value commitment stipulated that in cases where there are opportunities to break promises not made in a court of law, the decision maker should rate the value of keeping and breaking the promise equally, the scope of the value commitment would be like X's but the *constraint* on X's value commitment would have been different from Z's.

Consider a decision problem where X faces a choice between keeping a promise made in court while breaking a promise not made in court and breaking the court-made promise while keeping the promise not made in court. The scope of X's commitment covers X's predicament. The constraint imposed by X's commitment mandates that neither promise be broken. X is not able to satisfy the constraint.

Value commitments as I conceive them have two components: a *scope* and a *constraint* (see Levi 1986). One can readily imagine confronting a decision problem falling within the scope of one or more value commitments that impose different constraints on the way options in the problem are to be evaluated. In some cases, all constraints imposed are satisfiable.

There are contexts where the decision maker is convinced that he or she can keep all the promises the decision maker has made. In other contexts, the decision maker is convinced that these obligations cannot all be met. In the latter situation, X cannot coherently subscribe to the value commitment endorsed by X and retain his or her beliefs. X's value commitments and beliefs are inconsistent.

I am assuming that a rational agent subscribing to a system of value commitments should take for granted that all of them are jointly satisfiable – on pain of inconsistency. Of course, the assumption of joint satisfiability is open to correction, as are all contingent beliefs. When the assumption of joint satisfiability conflicts with other beliefs, a new kind of practical conflict distinct from the kinds described in the previous section arises. This is practical conflict due to inconsistency.

Practical conflicts due to inconsistency in value commitments may be removed by taking two steps. X will need to give up his full belief that X's value commitments will always be jointly satisfiable. Such a change will not be sufficient.

This change in belief concerning what is true should be accompanied by a modification of X's value commitments as well. X will have to abandon the commitment to keeping all promises that are made.

CONFLICT DUE TO DOUBT

X need not give up the commitment to keeping all promises that are made altogether. X can restrict the scope of the commitment to cases where the commitment is satisfiable. But what about cases uncovered by the restricted commitment? One can endorse the view that court-made promises should be given precedence and thus take a leaf from Z's approach. Or one might give precedence to promises made outside the court of law. But unless X has good reason for taking one view rather than the other, wisdom suggests that X should suspend judgment and keep an open mind (see Levi 1986). That is to say, X should refuse to rule out either way of evaluating the options.

X should instead regard as "permissible" all ways of evaluating the options that are recognized as permissible according to the constraints imposed by the value commitments under consideration.

In addition, alternative ways of evaluation that may be regarded as "compromises" between ways of evaluation already recognized to be permissible should also be countenanced as permissible. According to X's original value commitment, ranking the keeping of the court-made promise over breaking it is mandatory. So is ranking the promise made outside the court. A fortiori, both rankings are permissible. In the new setting, keeping both rankings as mandatory is incoherent and, hence, should be abandoned. But abandoning this can be achieved while retaining the permissibility of both as well as all potential compromises. It is permissible to evaluate X's options so that the court-made option comes out optimal and also to regard it permissible to evaluate X's options so that the promise not made in court is optimal.

Observe, however, that neither keeping the court-made promise nor the other promise is optimal. These options are noncomparable. X cannot, from the open-minded point of view, choose for the best, all things considered.

Such open-mindedness is often condemned as incoherent if the decision maker X remains in such a state of doubt at the moment when a decision has to be made. Choice, we are reminded, is peremptory. Making up one's mind is inescapable, according to this objection.

Recall, however, that even if X recognizes only one way of evaluating options as permissible, X might recognize two or more options as optimal. Choice remains peremptory in that case as well, without precluding the possibility of two options being equally optimal.

In the case of open-mindedness, the set of options that are V-admissible (that is to say, not ruled out for choice) need not be tied for optimality. There need not be any optimal options. The *admissible* options might be noncomparable according to X's values. X is in doubt as to which of the admissible options are optimal.

A third kind of practical conflict is unresolved conflict with respect to the permissibility of the ways of evaluating options. Such conflict is not inconsistency. It is rather a kind of suspense. In a sense, the deliberating agent is in doubt as to what ought to be done. This kind of conflict comes in two interesting varieties.

MAXIMALITY AND ORDINAL-BASED VALUE STRUCTURES

Given a set of permissible ways of evaluating the options in set S (an *ordinal-based value structure* $V(S)$ for S), we can define the set of all preferences over S shared in common between the permissible ways in $V(S)$ to be a *categorical preference*. The ordinal-based value structure $V(S)$ could then be required to be the set of all weak orderings over S consistent with the categorical preference (which will, in general, yield a partial ordering).

If the set of permissible ways of evaluating options in S constitutes an ordinal-based value structure, then given any finite subset T of S taken as the options actually facing the decision maker X, the following two choice criteria are equivalent:

V-admissibility: Option x is *V-admissible* in T if and only if x comes out optimal according to at least one way of evaluation in the restriction $V(T)$ of $V(S)$.

V-maximality: Option x is *V*-maximal in T if and only if there is no y in T categorically strictly preferred to x according to the restriction $V(T)$ of $V(S)$.

V-maximality is the criterion favored by Herzberger (1973), Sen (1970), and Walley (1991). To formulate this criterion, one does not have to explicitly invoke a set of weak orderings that are permissible ways of evaluating the options in T. One can instead invoke the partial ordering of the options in T associated with $V(T)$. An option is maximal if there is no other available option better than it according to the partial ordering. If it were plausible to require that all value structures be ordinal-based value structures, no additional refinements needed to formulate *V*-admissibility would be necessary.

Even so, there is some advantage to invoking the criterion of *V*-admissibility. This criterion appeals to the set of permissible ways of evaluating all the available options. When two or more permissible ways of evaluation are recognized, the decision maker is in doubt as to which to use in seeking to choose an option that is best, all things considered. The decision maker is in suspense as to what to do. In suspense, the decision maker should recognize that each option that comes out best according to some permissible way of evaluation has not been prohibited for choice. All things considered, each such *V*-admissible option is admissible for choice.

When the value structure is ordinal-based, endorsing *V*-admissibility is equivalent to adopting *V*-maximality. However, the criterion of *V*-admissibility can be used when value structures are not ordinal, whereas *V*-maximality gives mistaken recommendations in such cases. This needs illustration and explanation.

SECOND WORST

X wants to give his parents a vacation in the Caribbean as an anniversary present, but he faces a quandary. X's father likes a good party and would prefer going to St. Martin where there is ample nightlife than to St. Bart's, which is far more sedate. X's mother would prefer the restful St. Bart's. Father and Mother are so much at loggerheads on this issue that Father would prefer staying at home to going to St. Bart's and Mother would prefer staying at home to going to St. Martin. X is then conflicted between these two ways of evaluating the available options (see Table 6.2).

The entries in the columns of Table 6.2 are ordinal numbers reflecting the preferences of father and mother. X's ordinal-based value structure consists of these two rankings and all other rankings that are consistent extensions of the set of binary comparisons that Father and Mother share in common. Father and Mother share no binary comparisons in common so that any ranking of the three options is permissible. If this ordinal value structure reflects X's values, then all three options are E-admissible. There are rankings that are consistent extensions of the set of common binary comparisons where each of the three options come out on top.

Each of the three options is maximal as well. No option is better than any other by universal consensus.

Let us now add some more structure to the evaluation of the options. Both Father and Mother agree that staying at home is to be rated second

TABLE 6.2

	Father	Mother
St. Martin	1	3
Stay at home	2	2
St. Bart's	3	1

among the three alternatives. Suppose now that both Father and Mother agree that staying at home is "second worse" in the sense that staying at home is slightly better than the worse option but much worse than the best option.

To capture this idea, we suppose that Father and Mother value the options in a manner that satisfies von Neumann-Morgenstern postulates for utility. Although the only options they face are the three listed, we suppose that both Mother's and Father's ways of evaluating their options are embedded in preference rankings over all roulette lotteries between these three options. These roulette options are not options available to Mother or Father (or to X, who is the decision maker in the given example). But they are potential options in a sense similar to that according to which commodity bundles above a consumer's "budget line" are potential options for the consumer even though the consumer cannot choose such commodity bundles owing to his lack of economic means. The consumer is supposed to have a preference over such potential options even though the commodity bundles are not economically accessible. The preference is characterized in terms of what the consumer *would* choose *were* his or her circumstances to change and the consumer could express preference by choice. In a similar sense, the roulette lotteries need not be available for choice to X. Even so, were any (finite) subset of these roulette lotteries to become the available set of options, X (Mother, Father) would have chosen the most preferred among these according to the way of evaluation weakly ordering the total set of roulette lotteries.

Thus, X, who is trying to please both parents, might consider what to do if, in addition to the options listed, X had available the option of choosing St. Martin with probability p and St. Bart's with probability $(1 - p)$ for some value between 0 and 1. Suppose staying at home were second worse according to both the rankings by Mother and by Father. No matter what value p takes, neither Mother nor Father would rank the lottery below staying at home. That is tantamount to saying that the utility difference between the best and staying at home (among the three options initially specified) is greater than the utility difference between staying at home and the worse). In this sense, staying at home is second worse.

In this case, staying at home remains maximal in a three-way choice. But it is no longer *E*-admissible. The value structure for the large set *S* of all roulette lotteries of these options is merely ordinal as before. The set of all consistent extensions of this set is representable by a convex set of utility functions over *S*. But the subset of three options faced by X is no longer ordinally based over the set of available options in the sense that all consistent extensions of the preferences over these three options are permissible.

It is true that the value structure over the set S of roulette lotteries is ordinally based. Because the permissible weak orderings of S each satisfy von Neumann-Morgenstern postulates, each such permissible way of evaluation is representable by a von Neumann-Morgenstern utility function unique up to a positive affine transformation. So the value structure over S may be said to be *utility-based* as well as ordinally based.

The relevant issue for decision making, however, is not the value structure for S but the value structure for the (finite) subset T of S that constitutes the set of available options for the decision maker. This should be a restriction of the value structure for S. However, the restriction should not be merely a restriction of the set of permissible weak orderings of S. That will yield an ordinally based value structure for T that ignores the information contained in the value structure of S indicating whether staying home is second worse or not.

If the information is not to be lost, the value structure for T should be the restriction of the set of permissible utility functions for S to T. The result will be *not* an ordinally based value structure but a utility-based value structure.

When the value structure for T is of the sort stipulated here where T contains three elements and one is second worse according to both of a permissible pair of desiderata, no other permissible way of evaluation can convert the second worse option into an optimal one. None of the permissible ways of evaluation rate staying at home as optimal. Yet staying at home is not considered inferior to the options according to all permissible ways of evaluation. It is therefore V-maximal as are the other two options. Consequently, the set of V-maximal options is a proper superset of V-admissible options (going to St. Martin or going to St. Bart's).

Thus, invoking the choice criterion of V-maximality as do Herzberger, Sen and Walley, among many others, rules out of consideration the relevance of the distinction between cases where one of three options is second worse and cases where this is not so.

Advocates of V-maximality rightly complain of the widespread neglect of the sorts of practical conflict that arise when several dimensions of value are of concern to the decision maker. They see quite clearly the fault in those who insist that rational agents should maximize according to a standard of value that weakly orders their options.

But they reject the assumptions needed to sever V-admissibility from V-maximality. One possibility is to deny that the weak orderings permissible in the set S (the set of roulette lotteries) ought to satisfy von Neumann-Morgenstern requirements according to which the weak orderings are expected utility orderings. Another possibility is that they insist that the value structure for T should be all weak orderings that are consistent extensions of the restrictions in T of the set of weak orderings in S. Both approaches preclude drawing a distinction between second best and second worse that can be of any use.

Those who advocate V-admissibility as a criterion of choice have an advantage in this controversy. They acknowledge the rational coherence of value structures for T that render V-admissibility and V-maximality equivalent and, hence, rationalize the use of V-maximality. But they also recognize cases where V-maximality cannot do justice as a criterion of choice to the practical conflicts deliberating agents can face. V-admissibility is more sensitive to the types of practical conflict than V-maximality is.

Second worse conflicts are not as arcane as some might think. A decision maker X concerned how to allocate benefits to members of a given community might face some variant of the predicament where there are three options: Option 1 allocates a very high benefit to members of group A and a miserable level of welfare to group B. Option 2 is the same allocation in reverse. Option 3 is an equal distribution where the welfare level for both groups is barely above the misery level for the worst off according to the other two options. The benevolent agent X is in conflict between two ways of evaluating the three options. One of them ranks the three options according to the welfare levels accruing to group A, and the other according to group B. Of course, other ways of evaluation are permissible as well. Any weighted average of the utility functions representing the welfare levels for A and for B is also permissible.

In a three-way choice, option 2 is not V-admissible on the assumptions I am taking for granted, but it is V-maximal. However, in a pairwise choice between 1 and 2 (2 and 3), both options are V-maximal as well as V-admissible.

I contend that following V-admissibility in these choices conforms well with presystematic judgment.

Presystematically we are more prone to favor "equal misery" when we have a choice between retaining the current privilege for the haves against the have-nots than we are when the competing groups are both candidates for becoming the haves. How do V-admissibility and V-maximality approach the problem?

In a three-way choice, the equal misery option is second worse when the interests of the As alone are taken into account. So, too, when the interests of the Bs alone are taken into account. No permissible way of evaluation that takes both interests into account rates equal misery better than the other two alternatives. That option fails to be *V*-admissible. The choice is restricted to the remaining options.

Consider, however, a choice between promoting the interests of the As alone and equal misery. Both options are *V*-admissible in the two-way choice. They are noncomparable rather than equipreferred. Yet we may seek to decide between them by a secondary criterion such as maximin. Protecting the least advantaged Bs argues for choosing equal misery.

By way of contrast, suppose that *V*-maximality is used. In the three-way choice, all three options are *V*-maximal. We might utilize maximin as a secondary criterion to decide in favor of equal misery.

In the two-way choice, equal misery will be favored as according to our previous analysis.

We find that starting with *V*-maximality leads to adopting equal misery regardless of which kind of choice we are addressing. This prescription seems insensitive to the differences between the two-way and three-way choice found in certain kinds of value conflicts where value structures are not purely ordinal-based.

Advocates of *V*-maximality such as Sen, Herzberger, and Walley have admirably called into question some of the shibboleths surrounding traditional views about rational choice demanding that rational agents at the moment of choice ought to choose for the best, all things considered. The criticisms of customary views are admirable for the discipline, good sense, and respect for generality they reflect.

My worry is that the principle of *V*-maximality is not comprehensive enough. There are forms of practical conflict that advocates of *V*-admissibility can countenance that are unrecognizable from the point of view of *V*-maximality. The admirable sensitivity that defenders of *V*-maximality display to forms of value conflict ought to be stretched further to accommodate the kinds of conflict that emerge when value structures are cardinal and not merely ordinal-based. In those settings, the possibility of value conflicts arising where there is consensus concerning options that are second worse invites us to take *V*-admissibility and not *V*-maximality to be the primary criterion of choice.

Note

1. When de Finetti understood conditional probabilities as expressing attitudes toward called-off bets, he was, so I surmise, implicitly taking conditional

expectation to be a secondary value to be used in breaking ties in unconditional expectation. To take his views literally condemns his position to inconsistency. De Finetti thought serious possibilities could be assigned zero unconditional credal probability and yet probabilities conditional on such propositions are well defined and are used to determine choices among called-off bets. This seems to mean that there are two ways to evaluate the options A and B: in terms of unconditional and conditional expectations. They deliver different verdicts and, hence, inconsistency in de Finetti's decision theory. Consistency is restored by taking conditional expectation to be a tie-breaking secondary consideration (see Levi 1989).

Bibliography

Herzberger, H. 1973. Ordinal Preference and Rational Choice. *Econometrica* 41: 187–237.

Levi, Isaac. 1986. *Hard Choices: Decision Making under Unresolved Conflict.* Cambridge: Cambridge University Press.

Levi, Isaac. 1989. Possibility and Probability. *Erkenntnis* 31: 365–86.

Little, I. M. D. 1957. *A Critique of Welfare Economics.* Oxford: Clarendon.

Sen, Amartya K. 1970. *Collective Choice and Social Welfare.* San Francisco, Calif.: Holden Day.

Walley, Peter. 1991. *Statistical Reasoning with Imprecise Probabilities.* London and New York: Chapman and Hall.

7

Personal Practical Conflicts

Joseph Raz

Neither in social order, nor in the experience of an individual, is a state of conflict the sign of a vice, or a defect, or a malfunctioning.

Stuart Hampshire[1]

This preliminary reflection about practical conflicts confronting single agents does little to solve the problems conflicts create. Rather, it attempts to explain what conflicts are and what questions they raise. I suggest that we have two distinct notions of single-agent conflicts reflecting two distinct theoretical questions. The first concerns the possibility of there being a right action in conflict situations. It is the question of whether and, if so, how reasons deriving from different concerns or affecting different people can be of comparable strengths. The second concerns a sense that there is something unfortunate about conflicts and that when facing conflicting options just taking the best or the right one is not sufficient. I offer (in outline) an answer to the second question but nothing about the first.

PRACTICAL CONFLICTS: INITIAL CHARACTERIZATION

What are practical conflicts? A fairly common way of characterizing them has it that

(*Initial 1st Definition*): Agents face a practical conflict when they are in a situation in which they have reasons to perform two acts (or more) such that they can perform either but not both.

A second, closely related characterization says that

(*Initial 2nd Definition*): Agents face a practical conflict in a situation where they have several reasons for action such that complying better with one makes it impossible to comply fully with another.[2]

The two definitions seem to be formally equivalent,[3] the first emphasizing the inability to perform all the actions for which one has reason, the second the inability to comply with all the reasons one has. One problem with the definitions is their vagueness. For example, the nature of impossibility remains obscure. And there are many other points to explore. The following clarifications will help, but will not eliminate the vagueness.

1. Conflict is relative to how things stand: that is, the same reasons may apply to an agent in situations where they do not conflict, but as things are, they do.
2. It does not matter whether the agent is aware of the reasons. But perhaps reasons apply to agents only if it is possible for them to find out what they are. This will not matter to our discussion.
3. The inability may be due to the limitations of the agents, their weakness of body, lack of skills, lack of imagination or knowledge, but not to absence of will or weakness of will or resolve.
4. We should understand the definitions to allow for conflict where one can comply partially with all the reasons that apply to one, so long as complying to a higher degree with one makes it impossible to comply with another to the degree that would have been possible had the first not applied to the agent.

I rely on our pretheoretical understanding of this idea. Yet a word of explanation may point toward a possible analysis: The proximate reasons for actions are evaluative properties of those actions, and they often "derive" from the relation of the action to some other evaluative fact, which is the "root reason." Thus, that an action is buying needed clothes for one's children or repaying a loan is a reason for it, and that is so because of one's duties toward one's children and their needs or one's promise to repay the loan. Where reasons for different actions derive from the same root reason, one of the actions may satisfy the root reason better than others, depending on the character of the root reason.[4]

Not intending to deal with all the technical emendations of these characterizations, let me mention but two of the more far-reaching objections to them. The first regrets their exclusive orientation toward action. Surely, we can be confronted, for example, with emotional conflicts, which themselves may be the product of reasons for different emotions such that one cannot have all of them in the purest and most appropriate (appropriate to the reasons, that is) form. As this remark shows, it is possible to extend the two definitions to the emotions and beyond. Conflicting emotions can be irrational, in not being adequately reason-sensitive. Fear often displays lack of sensitivity to reasons, as when we are afraid of a forthcoming journey or (different emotional color) of a job interview even while we know that the fear is without foundation. There could be more extreme cases, belonging to the pathology of the emotions. However, such pathological cases apart, even irrational emotions, such as "normal" irrational beliefs, are reason-related. They merely fail to be adequately sensitive to reasons. Hence, emotional conflicts have similarities to the conflicts as defined above.

In confining my attention to conflicts among reasons for action, I do not mean to suggest that they are more important or more fundamental. The limitation is made necessary by the differences between conflicts in different domains. For example, we can be subject to conflicting emotions, and having conflicting emotions need not be regrettable. It may be an essential part of a constructive experience; for example, experiencing conflicting emotions may be an appropriate reaction to a development in one's relationship with a friend. In contrast, one cannot perform both actions for which one has conflicting reasons. It is therefore necessary to confine the present discussion to conflicts regarding reasons for action.

The second objection is more troublesome. It can take various forms. One way of expressing its main point is this: Practical conflicts are conflicts between reason and the passions, desires, or inclinations. Conflicts internal to reason can occur, but far from being the essence of practical conflicts they are a special, and a less important, case of conflict. In overlooking this fact I succumb to an inappropriately rationalistic view of people.

The objection raises two issues: the role of reason in our life and the relation between practical conflict and personhood, especially its relation to the unity of the person. I say nothing of the second here. But consider for a moment the first: There are two familiar metaphors for the role of reason. It is sometimes regarded as a protagonist in (potential) conflicts, and sometimes as an adjudicator in conflicts among others. Both metaphors mislead, though that of reason as adjudicator less so than the other.

The facts that constitute reasons, the facts on which the so-called verdict of reason is based, are not themselves "facts of reason," whatever that may mean. They are not produced or generated by reason. They are merely recognized by it for what they are, that is, considerations favoring an action or against an action. Reasons for action are facts such as that some action will cause distress, or that an action will be fun, and so on. They are evaluative facts, that is, facts consisting in the possession of an evaluative property.[5] While facts that the action in question possesses an evaluative property are the primary reasons for or against that action, other facts, those in virtue of which the action has the reason-making evaluative property, are also reasons for and against it. These are facts such as that one has an illness that will be cured by a particular medicine, which is a reason for taking the medicine, for it shows that that action will restore one's health (the primary reason).

The facts that constitute reasons can be, and often are, facts about our emotions, feelings, passions, and desires, and about what arouses them or assuages them; alternatively, reasons often presuppose such facts. They may include facts such as that it is best to give vent to one's emotions, rather than bottle them up, or that humility in the existing circumstances marks lack of self-respect, that defiance is the appropriate reaction to the behavior one encountered, or that jealousy can be destructive of a healthy relationship. None of these facts (those constituting primary reasons or others, including facts about our emotions) is in any sense a "fact of reason." Some of them can be recognized only by rational creatures, meaning here those who possess the powers of reason, that is, the power to recognize reasons. But recognition is one thing, authorship is another. There are no conflicts between reason and the passions if that implies that reason is the source of, the author of reasons, rather than merely the power to recognize their existence.

Pascal's famous "*Le coeur a ses raisons que la raison ne connaît point.*"[6] is different. This resonant statement is not amenable to obvious philosophical analysis. I think that three points are relevant in this context. The first two are about two ways – one modest, one more radical – in which our responsiveness to reasons does not always involve the power of reasoning. The heart responds directly to reasons, some to do with our emotions or with other psychological conditions, and more. Its response need not always be mediated by reason. The first, modest point is that some reasons we can learn to detect and come to respond to, spontaneously, in a flash, or at any rate without deliberation. Typically, in these cases, reason is present but behind the scenes. Our responses are immediate and "intuitive," but they are typically monitored by our reason. That is, we are, typically, in a condition such that if our spontaneous response appears to us unreasonable, it will be checked. We start reflecting about it and deliberate its pros and cons.

We are often in such a state: We drive automatically without paying attention to what we do, but if something irregular happens, we as it were step in and take over from the autopilot. In all such cases, our actions are not a result of deliberation, but our reason is in the background monitoring what is going on and triggering our attention when things appear irregular. I described this condition metaphorically, personalizing reason, comparing it to an independent agent acting within us. Needless to say, that is not literally the case. It is just a handy way of saying that the process within us that triggers our attention when things appear irregular is to be regarded as an expression of the faculty of reason.

Pascal's statement, if it is to be understood in the most general way, embeds this point. It affirms the ability to know the right thing spontaneously and without deliberation. But it implies much more than that. It implies, second, a capacity to respond to reasons that altogether bypasses reason. It is a capacity to respond to facts that are reasons, in the way appropriate to their being reasons, without recognizing them or thinking of them as reasons (nor in analogous concepts).

That may be a more troubling thought for anyone who believes that reason is the capacity to recognize reasons. Would not that imply that any responsiveness to reasons is a manifestation of our faculty of reason? I do not think that it does. The power of reason is the power to identify reasons as reasons, that is, to identify both that some condition does, or would, or may, obtain and that that is a reason for a particular action (and thereby, the disposition to be motivated to act for reasons, or at least to be open to such motivation[7]). But our responsiveness to reasons need not depend and does not always depend on recognizing them as reasons. Most notably, we may be, as they say, hard-wired to respond to reasons of some kinds and culturally conditioned to respond to others. If something in the environment causes pain, we retreat from it. We need not think of the pain-causing feature nor of the fact that the action will avoid the pain as reasons for the action in order to respond to them as to a reason. Creatures who lack the power of reason or have it to a limited degree only can respond to such reasons. Moreover, given that the response is hard-wired, it is not accidental. It is fairly reliable and regular. More needs to be shown to establish that such regular responses are in some kinds of case the appropriate ones. But that cannot be done here.

Finally, this second point combines with the third,[8] namely, that various psychological states, especially the feeling of various emotions, are themselves reasons, that is, they are either welcome and desirable or unwelcome and undesirable ones. To that extent, that some emotional states or other psychological facts obtain or that they will obtain if some action is performed are reason-constituting facts, and they may conflict with other reasons.

That emotional states we do or may have can be reasons for us helps, of course, to explain how we can respond to some reasons (to such reasons) directly, without realizing their standing as reasons (though it is not the only case where we can do that: We are also hard-wired to respond to sudden movements, etc.). It also helps explain how the popular image of the conflict between reason and the emotions developed. It is natural that both on the personal level and on the cultural one, there will be people who respond more readily to reasons involving emotions than to others, and there are cultural periods when they are in tune with the dominant mood of the time.[9] It is also natural that when we are inclined, individually or culturally, to respond more to emotion-relating reasons we will more often be impatient with people who tend to rely, as we see it, "excessively" on reason in identifying the considerations to respond to and in deciding what to do.

The so-called conflict between reason and the passions is no such thing, at least not if it means that reason and the passions (or the emotions) are two sources of reasons that may conflict. Rather, talk of such conflict refers to the degree to which one is inclined to respond to emotion-related reasons and to the degree to which one relies on one's reason in deciding what to do, rather than responding to one's emotions directly.

PRACTICAL CONFLICTS AND PLURALISTIC CHOICE

Is it not clear that the definitions are too broad? They identify conflict situations with apparent choice. Whenever we have more than one option supported, as it appears to us, by reasons, we have to choose which one to take. That is the nature of choice. Some people omit the "supported by reasons" from their characterization of choice. This suggests that as I write I have a choice not only between carrying on with this chapter or taking a break to listen to the news, but also between either of these options and cutting off my finger or my ear, or taking my shoes out of the cupboard and putting them back in again, and so on. All these are options available to me, though I have not the slightest reason for any of them. But this is silly. Choice implies not a plurality of options but a plurality of options that are, as we believe,[10] supported by reasons.

Conflicts exist if things are a certain way, not if they appear to be that way. That marks a major difference between facing a conflict and facing a choice. But the relations between the two, according to the definitions, are too close. The definitions identify apparent conflict with choice. But not all choice implies apparent conflict. Suppose a good friend makes me two mutually exclusive gift offers (on an occasion when it would be proper to give friends such gifts): Either he will give me $10 or he will give me $15. I have to choose. There is no down side to either offer, and no other normatively relevant circumstance. It would be silly to say that I face a conflict. Of course I should choose the $15, and no conflict is involved. Or suppose that I go shopping for shoes. I find one pair that looks fine, and though not a perfect fit, it will be fine after the first painful week. Then I find another pair that looks even better and fits my feet perfectly. I have to choose. There are reasons for the first pair, but clearly the reasons for the second are better, and I should choose it. Equally clearly I did not face a conflict.

Why not? Perhaps because the choice was so easy. Does not "conflict" imply a difficulty in making up one's mind? Does it not imply a difficult choice? Perhaps it does, or rather, perhaps we would not describe a situation as one of conflict unless we were conflicted, unless we were torn both ways, finding it difficult to see which option is the better one or finding it difficult to decide for the option we take to be the better one. But I disregard this psychological dimension of conflict or of the use of "conflict." There is at least in the philosophical tradition, but beyond it as well, a familiar notion of conflict as a normative property of choice situations, rather than as a psychological property of the response to them. I concentrate exclusively on this normative, rather than psychological, notion of conflict.

Besides, even if we modify the shoes example so that the choice is no longer easy the situation will still not be one of conflict. Imagine, for example, that one criterion for the suitability of the shoes is whether I could wear them to work, and I am not sure what is the dress code in my new place of employment. Or imagine that though one pair is a much better fit, when I try it on that is not evident to me, and I hesitate. The case turns into one of difficulty and uncertainty, but not one of conflict. The difficulty is epistemic. The normative nature of the situation has not changed. It is still a case where one pair of shoes trumps the other by all the relevant criteria.

"Normative conflict," in one central understanding of the term, imports pluralism, that is, a plurality of irreducibly distinct concerns supporting various options, such that none of the options scores higher than all the others in all the concerns affecting the situation. Thus in having to choose between $10 and $15 we do not face a conflict, for only one concern is relevant to the choice, and the choice between the shoes is not a conflict because even though several concerns bear on it (suitability to wear for work, attractiveness, fitting one's feet), one option is superior to the other in every single one of them. Conflict exists where there is choice between different options supported by distinct concerns such that one option is better supported by some of them and another is better supported by the others. A choice between two jobs, say, involves conflict when one of them is a better job, while the other will enable one to live in a more interesting or agreeable city. To accommodate this point the definitions can be revised as follows.

Conflict as pluralistic choice, 1st definition: Agents face a practical conflict when they are in a situation in which they have reasons deriving from distinct values to perform two acts (or more) such that they can perform either but not both, and where each option is better supported by reasons deriving from a value different from those supporting some rival option.

The second definition can be more smoothly adapted:

Conflict as pluralistic choice, 2nd definition: Agents face a practical conflict when in a situation where they have several reasons for action deriving from distinct values such that complying better with one makes it impossible to comply fully with another.

CONFLICT AND IMPERFECT CONFORMITY WITH REASON

So understood, conflict is tied up with value pluralism, and the interest in conflicts is in the possibility that reasons deriving from different distinct values may be compared in strength, weight, or stringency. But there is another strand to our thinking about conflict. There is something unfortunate about conflicts. It is better not to have them. When in conflict we cannot do everything that it would be best for us to do. All these ideas are often associated with conflicts. They are not always clearly distinguished from the thought that conflict is an expression of pluralism. It is often, usually implicitly, assumed that the two strands of thought go hand in hand. It is assumed that the "unfortunate" aspect of conflict is an inevitable result of pluralism.

That assumption is mistaken. The "unfortunate" aspect of conflict is a common but not an inevitable result of pluralism. Nor is it always absent in single-value conflicts (though this depends on how we identify what is unfortunate in such situations). In the $15 versus $10 case it is unfortunate that I cannot have both. So having to choose is unfortunate, even though it is a single-value case. Similarly, imagine that I am interested in Dreier's films and that I have a chance to see two of them tonight (and am unlikely to have another chance to see either for the next year or so). I should clearly see one of them, which is one of his most important, rather than the other, which is one of the short documentaries he did during the lull years. Yet even though the decision is clear and easy and only one concern is involved, it is a case of conflict, for it is unfortunate that I have to choose between the two. The result of the choice leaves me with a reason to see the other, when I can.

The most striking examples of single-value choices that are cases of conflict, and are so because it is unfortunate that one has to choose, are cases affecting more than one person. If I have to choose between two courses of action, one that will benefit me and my oldest child but harm my youngest, and the other that will be beneficial to the youngest child, but will mean a loss of opportunity to me, I have a conflict on my hands. This is so regardless of degree of benefit and harm and regardless of whether there is one or more value or type of consideration involved. As in the Dreier example, I am left with an unrequited reason to do at some future time what I could not do (that is, should not have done) now. Many-person conflicts give rise to troubling special questions that will not be considered here.[11]

Just as choice can be unfortunate, in a yet to be explained sense, in cases of single-value choices, so it can lack that aspect when multiple values are present. The shoes example is one where various distinct considerations bear on the choice: esthetic considerations, convenience, and possibly others. Assuming that I have no reason to have a spare pair of shoes, once I have bought the better pair I have no reason left to have the other pair,[12] and being offered a choice has no down side.

Here and elsewhere, I disregard the possibility of the very need to make up one's mind (collect information needed to do so intelligently, etc.) being unfortunate. Since we are looking for conflict as a normative property of choice situations, I again disregard its psychological aspects, that is, I will not take difficulty or reluctance to choose, make up one's mind, or gather information necessary for decision as a mark of conflict.

Another example of a multiple-value choice not involving conflict is slightly more complicated. Suppose I have a reason to do something for another, but not to do too much. Doing too much will send the wrong signal, will put him in my debt, and in these and other ways will spoil things between us. If so, then I have reason to do this for that person and reason to do that, but if I do one of them the reason to do the other is cancelled. The choice between the different possible options may be a multivalue one, but once I make my choice I no longer have any reason to pursue the other option.[13] In such cases being faced with a multivalue choice does not seem unfortunate. Even though we have yet to identify the sense in which conflicts can be unfortunate, we have no reason to associate it with multivalue choices.

The examples just given suggest a way of understanding why conflicts are often thought to be unfortunate. They are when whatever the agents do there will be an unsatisfied reason left behind. This suggests the following notion of conflicting reasons.

Conflict as the impossibility of perfect conformity, 1st definition: Agents face a practical conflict when they are in a situation in which they have reasons to perform two (or more) acts such that they can perform either but not both, and where performing one does not cancel the reasons to perform the other nor make them inapplicable.[14]

Conflict as the impossibility of perfect conformity, 2nd definition: Agents face a practical conflict when in a situation where they have several reasons for action such that complying better with one makes it impossible to comply as fully with another as would be otherwise possible[15] and where compliance with one does not cancel the other nor make it inapplicable.

The impossibility of perfect conformity, naturally negating any thought that the agents are at fault, is what is unfortunate. However the agents choose, there will still be reasons that apply to them that they cannot follow or conform to. That does not mean that it is unfortunate for the agents to find themselves in such a situation or that it is against their interests. The conflict can be a moral conflict such that whichever way they choose, their choice will not bear at all on their self-interest or, alternatively, will be equally adverse to their self-interest. As noted, not all conflicts as imperfect conformity are conflicts as pluralistic choices, nor the other way round, though in most types of cases the two categories overlap.

CONDITIONAL AND INDEPENDENT REASONS

Arguably, this definition does not exhaust the sense in which conflict is understood to be an unfortunate situation. Think of all the things that I have reason to do tonight. I could go to a jazz concert, to a rock

concert, or to a good silent film from the 1920s. Or I could go for a
walk along the river or hear the Emersons live, playing the Razumovsky
quartets. Do I face a conflict of reasons? One doubt about a positive
answer is that I am fortunate in having so much to choose from, and yet the
case falls under the definition of conflict as the impossibility of complete
conformity.

One reaction to this objection is to doubt that I really have a reason to
do all those things. I am assuming that they are not, as I put it, "integrated"
into my goals, aspirations, and so on. That is, that I am not a music lover,
nor a jazz lover, nor a walker, nor a film buff, and so on. All the options I
mentioned are attractive ones – all have their value – but as none is part of
any goal, habit, and so on of mine, so this response to the objection goes,
I do not have a reason to pursue any of them. This response overlooks
the fact that if I chose one of these options I would be doing so for a
reason, and the reason would be (unless when choosing the option I act
out of some mistaken belief) that the option is desirable in the way the
objection concedes them to be desirable or attractive. It follows that I
have reason to follow each of them.

Another response claims that to succeed, the objection must show that
the reasons we face in *embarras de richesse* cases are independent of each
other. Otherwise, given our definition, the reasons do not conflict at all.
Perhaps while I have a reason to follow any of the options, once I do
follow one of them I no longer have a reason to follow any of the others.
Following one cancels the reason to follow the others. At first blush this is
unconvincing (I return to a variant of this response below). If I do one of
them, I still have reason to do the others, only I cannot. If I have reason
to see each of two films now, seeing one does not cancel the reason to
see the other. It only makes it impossible to do so.

Yet another response points out that I have only a conditional reason
to do any of these things. I have reason to do them only if I want to do
them. Some people think that desires are reasons or that reasons consist in
appropriate combinations of desires and beliefs. I do not share this view,[16]
and the thought that such reasons are conditional on the will is not meant
to reintroduce it. Rather, desires are part of the factual background that
conditions the application of reasons. Sometimes there is no point in
taking an action unless one does it in a spirit of willing engagement, or
at least the point is much reduced. Notice that the desires that condition
reasons in this way could be those of people other than the agent: There
can be no point in going to a party with X if X does not want to go there,
will do so unwillingly, and so on.

Reasons that are conditional on the will, the reply goes, do not conflict. In general, conditional reasons do not conflict. Perhaps they can conflict conditionally, that is, they can conflict once their condition is met, but not before.

This response is helpful in drawing attention to conditional reasons generally, and to will-dependent and goal-dependent reasons in particular. Will-dependent reasons are a special case of conditional reasons, when that last concept is broadly understood. They are reasons the application of which, or the strength or stringency of which are conditional on people's inclination, desire, or willingness at the time of action to engage in that particular action.[17] Another interesting case of conditional reasons is goal-dependent reasons, which are those the application or strength of which depends on the agents having a particular goal. Inasmuch as people's goals were willingly assumed by them or at least are willingly pursued by them (even though not all the time nor on all occasions), then goal-dependent reasons are reasons that depend on a desire. They depend on a desire to persevere with the goal, but not necessarily on a desire to perform the particular act for which the goal-dependent reason is a reason.[18] For example, Judith, a dancer, has a reason to rehearse today, a reason that is goal-dependent, because she would not have it unless she were a dancer, though it is not will-dependent, as she has it irrespective of whether she wants to rehearse today and independently of whether she would be doing it willingly.

Traditionally, categorical reasons, though said to be contrasted with conditional ones, are contrasted not with them but with will-dependent and with goal-dependent reasons. Categorical reasons are – as often defined – reasons the application and stringency of which do not depend on the agent's desires, inclinations, or goals at the time of action. Some reasons – we could call them "purely categorical" reasons – are independent of any desire of the agent at any time. Typical purely categorical reasons are reasons of respect. We have reason to respect other people, to respect works of art, and so on, regardless of our own goals, tastes, or preferences. Other categorical reasons depend on one's past will, as, for example, one's reason to keep one's promise depends on the voluntary making of a promise but is irrespective of a desire to perform the promised act.

With these points in mind, let us return to the objection. One response to it, I pointed out, was to agree that the examples it relies on, that is, cases in which we have many attractive options to choose from, are not cases of conflict as impossible complete conformity, but to deny that that is an objection. Because the reasons we face in them are will-dependent and therefore conditional, they do not conflict even by the definitions given at the outset.

In general it is true that conditional reasons do not conflict just because were their conditions to be met they would conflict. (Though where it is known that the conditions will be met, that is, that they will conflict at some future time, they can be treated as conflicting ahead of time.) But the same cannot be said of will-dependent reasons. Whatever we have reason to do if we want to we do also have reason to want (other things being equal). Our will as well as our actions are subject to reasons, and in general these are the same reasons; that is, with some exceptions, reasons for an action are also reasons for wanting to perform it, and the other way round. Hence will-dependent reasons that would conflict if the will were there already do conflict, for they are also conflicting reasons for wanting to perform those actions. So the objection is still with us.

To repeat, the objection says that situations in which one faces plenty of attractive options should be distinguished from cases of conflict, for there is nothing unfortunate in them as there is about being in a conflict situation. We must distinguish, it says, between conflict and an *embarras de richesse*.

I am, of course, exaggerating. The options may not be so many and so luxurious as to deserve that appellation. But the point is clear enough. Possibly, however, the notion of will-dependent reasons allows us to modify the definition of conflict to avoid the objection. Perhaps we should simply add to the definition the proviso that a conflict does not exist if one of the allegedly conflicting reasons is will-dependent.

Would that modification meet the objection? The thought behind the objection was that there is something unfortunate in being in a conflict, which is not captured by the original definition. Does the fact that some of the putatively conflicting reasons are will-dependent show that there is nothing unfortunate in the situation? Are there no other cases where the situation is not unfortunate? I think that the modification proves inadequate on both counts.

First, a distinction must be drawn between those cases in which we have a duty to meet the condition of a will-dependent reason, and to have a positive, willing attitude toward the action, and those were no such duty exists. The example of a teacher who has a reason to pay special attention to one of his students may illustrate the point. True, he should not attend to the student if he is reluctant and unwilling to do so. Or, at least, he has less reason to do so reluctantly, for his attention will be less effective.

However, he may well have a duty to have a willing attitude to spending more time with his students when his attention is needed.

In such cases the fact that the reason, or its stringency, depends on our will does not matter to the way we should think of conflict. Conflict is a conflict of reasons that apply to us, not of those we are minded to conform to. Extending this thought suggests that reasons that should apply to us, or should have certain weight (because we should be willing to perform the actions for which they are reasons) are, so far as identifying conflicts is concerned, to count as reasons that do apply to us. If conformity with them is incompatible with conformity with other reasons, we are in a conflict situation.[19]

Different considerations apply to will-dependent reasons where we have no independent reason to want to perform the act for which it is a reason (i.e., no reason other than the will-dependent reason itself).[20] In such cases, if we do not desire the action, the reason either does not apply or has a lesser weight. If it does not apply, it does not conflict with reasons that do. Does it follow that we can dissolve the objection by modifying the definitions in a more complicated way to exclude will-dependent reasons except when we have a special reason to make true their condition? I do not think that that gets to the root of the difficulty. It does not explain in what ways there is something unfortunate about facing a conflict.

What is the source of the problem? The definitions assume that the unfortunate aspect is the impossibility of complying with all the independent reasons that apply to the agent. The objection suggests that that is not necessarily true. According to it, inability to comply with all the reasons applying to the agent need not be unfortunate. When is it? Perhaps only when it means that the agent's compliance with reason on this occasion falls short of a required standard. To meet the objection by augmenting the definitions, we need to specify the relevant standard. That is not a straightforward task. Obviously, it is not the standard of blame or of doing one's best. Conflicts exist only where doing one's best is not good enough and where the agent is not to blame. What does that mean? What standard does one fall short of in cases of conflict?

Perhaps we should define it as follows: For all agents, two reasons conflict only if each of them is a reason such that, had the conflict not occurred and had the agents failed to conform with it, they would have been at fault. This will not do as it stands. The agents may be excusably unaware (i.e., their ignorance cannot count against them) of the existence of these reasons.[21] To meet the point, we may refer to a reason for the flouting of which they would be responsible, if the conditions of responsibility were met. The revised definitions may be the following.

Conflict as the impossibility of complete conformity, possible revision of 1st definition: Agents face a practical conflict when they are in a situation in which they have reasons to perform two acts (or more) such that they can perform either but not both, where performing one does not cancel the reasons to perform the other nor make them inapplicable, and where, had the conditions of responsibility obtained, they would have been at fault should they have failed to take either action, had the reason for the other not applied.

Conflict as the impossibility of complete conformity, possible revision of 2nd definition: Agents face a practical conflict when in a situation where they have several reasons for action such that complying better with one makes it impossible to comply as fully with another as would be otherwise possible, where compliance with one does not cancel the other nor make it inapplicable, and where had the conditions of responsibility obtained, they would have been at fault should they have failed to act for either reason, had the other reason not applied.

Do the revised definitions improve on the original ones? Three questions remain: If the definitions are good ones, do they vindicate the suggestion we started from, namely that situations of *embarras de richesse* are not situations of conflict? After all, the revised definitions in order to determine whether there is conflict where the options are plentiful look at what things would be like were all but one of them to be removed. Would it not follow that if we were at fault, then we are facing conflict even when there are plenty of options? Second, arguably the revised definitions are extensionally equivalent to the original one, for possibly failure to comply with any undefeated reasons is, if the conditions of responsibility obtain, a fault. Needless to say, this is not the place to settle this matter. Finally, and most important, even if the revised definitions are extensionally correct, they fail to explain what is unfortunate about being in a conflict situation. After all, that we would have been at fault had the situation been different does not show that there is anything unfortunate in the situation as it is. Perhaps it is rather the contrary. After all, it is a situation where we are not at fault, at least not for that reason.

Let me, therefore, return for the final time to the type of situations I used to raise the objection: They are situations relatively isolated from one's major concerns or from possible major consequences to the world in general: "What shall I do tonight?" or "How shall I spend the weekend?" sort of questions asked on an ordinary day. What characterizes the sort of reasons that apply (to play chess, go for a walk, see a film, etc.) is not that in the context there would be no fault in not choosing them (had the other reasons not applied). There may be such fault (the failure may be irrational, show one to be lazy, etc). Rather, it is that they are what I will call opportunity reasons: reasons one has because one's background reason is to do something worth doing on a relatively isolated occasion. The reasons for each of the specific options are dependent on their background reason. Once one course of action, no worse than its alternatives, is undertaken, the background reason is satisfied, and one has no uncomplied-with reason. Hence the case is not one of conflict given the definition above.

This makes the identification of conflict sensitive to background reasons. Take, for example, a choice of career. We may say that the core reason is to have a worthwhile career, and again the existence of multiple worthy options fails to establish a conflict. But this time the situation is different, since there may be background reasons to have a career with various aspects, satisfying various needs, and so on, such that none satisfies all of them. A choice of any career leaves some of them unsatisfied, and that makes the situation one of conflict.

CONFLICT AND COMPLIANCE

The distinctive feature of conflicts is the impossibility of complete conformity with reason, or, to be precise, the fact that conflict makes it impossible to conform to reason as well as but for it one would have been able to do. In conflict situations our best efforts still leave us short. Even when we do our best, even when we act effectively and without fail, the conflict either makes it impossible to conform completely to reason or it reduces the possible degree of conformity. Whatever we do, some of the reasons remain unmet (i.e., they are fault-establishing reasons and are not cancelled nor made inapplicable by our actions). This is why conflict situations are unfortunate, or rather this is what is unfortunate about them. This is the standard we fall short of; a personal standard not of knowledge, will, or competence (for one may be in an unfortunate situation even when faultless so far as these factors go) but of reason: Conflicts generate ways in which one is unable to conform to reason in full.

How unique are conflict situations in this regard? There are cases in which it is impossible for us to follow all the reasons that apply to us (or to follow them to the highest degree) due to our blameless ignorance of what they are. Perhaps these should be set aside on the ground that what we have reason to do is limited to those reasons of whose existence we can be aware.[22] I think that the concept of a reason is vague on this point, and theorists may refine it for various theoretical purposes. However, the point reminds us that the boundary between failure due to our shortcomings (incompetence, weak will, ignorance, carelessness, etc.) and impossibility of full conformity with reason due to the way the world is is not a sharp one. The inability of the blind due to their blindness counts, normally, as an aspect of the world constraining their options, while inability due to forgetfulness is put down to us. When we fail fully to comply with reason due to forgetfulness, it is we who fall short of the mark. And there are many other cases in which the distinction is vague, and the rationale for applying it one way or the other is not all that firm.

Leaving ignorance aside, there are many other factors that reduce the possible degree of conformity with reasons. One typical type of case is where the impossibility of complete conformity results from a past failure. Assume that, modifying the shoes example, I choose the wrong pair. I still have a reason to buy the better pair, since the one I did buy is not entirely satisfactory. But I can no longer do so. It has gone, or I lack the money, and so on. I made a bad decision and bought the wrong shoes. As a result, the reason I failed to act for is not cancelled. But I can no longer follow it. Now I face no conflict, but just as in the case of conflicts I cannot fully conform to reason.

Needless to say, that latter situation where I have reason to get a pair of shoes or to take any other action, but am unable to do so, can arise not only through a previous bad decision but in a whole range of other circumstances, that will often, but need not, involve conflict. Such cases resemble conflict in being situations where awareness of our inability to conform to reason may burden us. They lack the feature that makes conflict distinctive, namely that we can choose which reason to conform to and which to neglect. The "burden of choice" when without conflict (or when the conflict is that of pluralistic choice only) has a different aspect: It is the burden of having to choose what is the right thing to do. In situations of conflict we have that burden, but also the burden of choosing which good to sacrifice. When the reason for one option is taken to be better than the reason for the other, that burden merges with the burden of establishing which is the better reason. Often enough, however, there are several incommensurable best options (i.e., ones better than when there are none in the situation). In such cases the burden of deciding which reason to let go unfulfilled or, as is sometimes the case, the interests of which person to sacrifice, where the sacrificing is justified, but regrettable, is distinct and particularly irksome. It forces us to be involved in certain events in ways in which we may well not wish to be involved. This is an important difference between such conflicts and other cases of inescapable incomplete conformity with reason. But it is not one affecting practical reasons or practical rationality. Given that in such conflict situations reason gives us no guidance in the choice, the fact of the burden of choice has no bearing on the rest of this discussion, which revolves on the consequences of conflicts to the reasons that apply to agents facing them.

CONSEQUENCES OF CONFLICT AND INCOMPLETE CONFORMITY

My claim is that conflicts of incomplete conformity are not normatively distinctive. There are, as we saw, other cases where incomplete conformity is inevitable. Beyond that, cases of (not necessarily inevitable) incomplete conformity are very common. They include all occasions in which agents fail to conform to reasons that they could conform to, through their mistakes, irrational motivations, weakness, incompetence, bad luck, or other factors. In discussing many of these cases the question of whether agents are to blame often occupies center stage. Agents who face conflicts are clearly not to blame (except where they are to blame for being in the conflict situation[23]). Incomplete conformity, however, whether or not in situations of conflict, has consequences important in practice and challenging in theory.

In principle these results are simple and straightforward:
The conformity principle: One should conform to reason completely, insofar as one can. If one cannot, one should come as close to complete conformity as possible.

The two most common and important implications are:[24]

1. There may be "a next best possibility": I should (meaning I have reason to) send my child to the best school, but I cannot. So I should (i.e., I have reason to) send him to the next best school.
2. Not being able to conform with reason completely is a matter of regret, which it may be appropriate to share with another if the reason is a relational reason addressed toward that person.

The conformity principle is not an "independent" principle. It is not as if one has a reason to do something, and because of the conformity principle one should conform to that reason. Rather that one should conform to it is what we say when we say that it is a reason. And if we have two reasons, which do not cancel each other, then we should conform to both. That, too, is what we say when we say of each of them that it is a reason. The conformity principle merely repeats this. Nor does the second part of the principle, about coming as close as possible to complete conformity, state anything other than is stated by a statement of reasons for action. If I have reason to give you $10 and I can only give you $8, then that same reason is a reason to give you the $8.

The second part of the conformity principle is spelled out in the first implication above. The second implication is merely an expression of the fact that reasons can be known and appreciated. Knowing that they require conformity means that inability to conform is a source of regret. I do not elaborate on the tail end of that implication here. It applies to relational reasons, that is, reasons we have toward some people. Reasons are relational in that way if they arise out of a relationship (e.g., reasons that are constitutive of friendship or of the parent-child relationship) or are justified out of concern for the other (e.g., reasons not to assault a person). In most cases it is appropriate to regard relational reasons as owed to the person to whom they relate. It is part of what makes relational reasons what they are that (other things being equal) it is appropriate to make the regret known to those to whom the reason is owed. Elaborating that aspect of the principle will have to involve an account of relational reasons, and thus of the character of certain relationships and transactions. Conformity with such reasons is, by the nature of these reasons, a matter of concern for those others, too. They are not strangers to our reasons; they have a standing regarding them and our conformity or non-conformity with them. But elaborating on the nature of such relational reasons will take us too far from the concerns of this article.

I hope that the conclusions so far seem uncontroversial, for they have far-reaching and often-neglected consequences. They show that both some reasons to compensate and some reasons to apologize are implications of incomplete conformity. This means that

a. They do not require independent principles of compensation.
b. They do not presuppose responsibility.
c. Finally, they do not presuppose conflict. Some reasons of compensation and apology are consequences of incomplete conformity, of which conflict situations are but one special case. When I cannot send my child to the best school, does it matter whether this is because I do not have the money for it, or because though I have the

money I have a conflicting reason to feed my child? Probably not. Either way, I should simply look for the next best school.

In one of its senses, compensation is a reaction to failure fully to conform to reason, when the failure compromised the rights or interests of another person, a reaction aimed at mitigating the consequences of that failure. But one can compensate oneself as well, as when I go to the cinema today to compensate myself for missing an opportunity to have an enjoyable evening yesterday.[25] The principle of conformity points out that when we fail to conform fully to a reason, we have reason to come as close to full compliance as we can, call it reason to do the next best act. It is the very same reason that we did not conform to which is, or becomes, reason for the next best thing. The first point above claims that in some cases compensation to others for harm inflicted or for rights violated is just a special case of the conformity principle or a natural extension of the reason to take the second best course of action, having failed fully to conform to reason. So if I have reason not to damage your property, and I do damage your fence, I have reason to compensate you, that is, to mitigate the consequences of failure, and this reason is the very same reason I had initially (the reason not to trespass or not to disturb your peace). There is no need for an independent principle of compensation to establish the case for it.

Determining to which cases of compensation the conformity principle applies and establishing that it does is not a task for this chapter. Perhaps the reason for its application can be partly surmised by listing some of the implications it does not have. Most important, it does not claim that one has a conclusive reason to compensate whenever one fails to conform to reason. The strength of the reason is its original strength. It may be defeated by conflicting reasons when it comes to the second best just as it was, assuming that compensation is a result of acting correctly in a case of conflict, defeated when the question was whether to take the action needed for full conformity with that reason. Of course, by the same token, if it is so defeated, it does not disappear. It merely becomes a reason for the third best course of action. This qualification has important practical consequences. For example, many reasons to refrain from certain actions are, in normal circumstances, easy to comply with, as conformity does not reduce one's options and has virtually no cost. Compensating for violation of the reason to refrain will typically be a much more burdensome and costly action, which may therefore be more frequently defeated in normal circumstances.

Furthermore, the claim is not that compensation should be required by law or obtainable through some other enforcement mechanism. Normally, there are numerous adverse effects to any legal intervention and that would undercut the argument for legal enforcement in many cases. However, it has to be borne in mind that the claim is a relevant consideration in the argument for legal enforcement.

Third, either by law or by custom different societies can accept regimes in which compensation is subject to conditions inconsistent with the conformity principle and that constitute a societal decision to relocate rights and duties, increasing (let us say) people's liberty of action by releasing them from the need to bear the cost of their nonconformity in some circumstances, in exchange for increasing their security in some respects. Many such regimes are sensible and can override and displace the reasons that obtain in their absence.

Finally, while the conformity principle itself points to the existence of reasons to compensate that do not derive from independent moral duty to compensate or from independent duty of compensation, it does not negate the possibility that such independent duties may exist to supplement it in certain circumstances. Indeed, if common legal duties of compensation reflect moral duties, then there are such additional moral duties to compensate. Not only can punitive and exemplary damages not be justified by the conformity principle, but neither can many cases of damages for suffering, among others, be justified. If we define "compensable harm" to mean harm that can be remedied at least in part, then we can say that the conformity principle explains compensation for compensable harms only, and only to the extent that they mitigate the harm.

Many cases of legal liability to damages as well as common beliefs about what compensation is morally required are unjustified by the principle of conformity. To give but one example: Suppose I undertook to make it possible for you to get to Australia for your mother's wedding (I may be your employer, and I promised timely leave and the cost of the ticket). Having failed to do that, I offer you a week's holiday in Brighton as compensation. This may be a sensible way to mollify hurt feelings, but it does nothing to bring you closer to sharing in your mother's great day, and therefore nothing to get me closer to fulfilling my undertaking. It may be justified, and something like it may be required, but it is not required or justified by the conformity principle.

Probably the most controversial implication of the conformity principle is that the reason to compensate that it points to does not depend on the agent being responsible or at fault for the failure to achieve full conformity with reason. If compensation is nothing but acting to get as close as possible to complete compliance, then the reason one has to compensate is the reason one had in the first place. That reason does not (special cases apart) presuppose fault and nor does the reason to compensate. I ought to send my child to the best school, to avoid damaging my neighbor's tree, to avoid polluting the river, and to acquire full command of Brandom's theory, and none of them arise out of any fault of mine. Therefore, if I cannot achieve them, I should come as near as possible, which may involve sending my child to the next best school, paying to cure the damage to my neighbor's tree, to clean up the river, and for any interim damage caused until the harm is undone, and learning as much as I can of Brandom's theory (say, reading *Articulating Reasons*, because I cannot manage in time to read *Making It Explicit*). This suggests there is strict liability to compensate, liability regardless of the fact that the harm we caused was not our fault.

The strict liability implication is avoided where the reason, failure to conform with which is the ground of liability, is a reason intentionally (or with knowledge) to refrain from some action. If I do not have a reason not to kill others, but only a reason not to murder them, then I do not fail to conform with reason if I kill others, so long as I do not do so intentionally. Hence the principle of conformity does not lead to strict liability in such cases.[26] There are cases where the reasons we have are reasons for intentional omissions. But most common cases are not like that. This is clear in the case of reasons for positive action: I have reason to repay my debt, not to repay it intentionally. If it were the latter, I would not be failing to comply with reason so long as I merely forget to pay my debt. Hence, no one could reproach me for being forgetful or for failing to repay my debt. There is nothing I have reason to do that I failed to do. Similarly, I have reason not to humiliate other people, not merely a reason not to do so intentionally.

In some ways this implication appeals. It confirms the view that what matters is what we do, how we live, and whether we respond to reason, and not what we intend or want as various Kantians would have it. But it may be premature to claim the conformity principle in support of this way of thinking. There is more work to be done before we get there.[27] The conclusion argued for so far is merely that we think of conflicts either as cases of pluralistic choices or as a special class of cases of inevitable failure of complete conformity, and that as such conflicts are not normatively distinct but are subject to the very general conformity principle.

Notes

I am grateful to Ulrike Heuer, Véronique Munoz-Dardé, Stephen Everson, Jonathan Wolff, Cristina Redondo, John Finnis, Leslie Green, and Timothy Macklem for helpful comments and suggestions.

1. Hampshire 2000: 33.
2. The conflicts here discussed are complete conflicts, to be distinguished from partial conflicts, in which some, but not all, ways of conforming to one reason are inconsistent with conformity with another reason.
3. This is a conclusion depending on the characterization of reasons given below.
4. Neither this remark nor anything else in this chapter denies that the individuation of reasons is often underdetermined.
5. We take both the fact that a particular action has an appropriate evaluative property and the fact that actions of a type have such a property as a reason.
6. *Pensées* (1670), sect. 4, no. 277. The full remark reads: "The heart has its reasons, which reason does not know. We feel it in a thousand things. I say that the heart naturally loves the Universal Being, and also itself naturally, according as it gives itself to them; and it hardens itself against one or the other at its will. You have rejected the one and kept the other. Is it by reason that you love yourself?"
7. On the relation between reason and motivation, see Raz 1999; ch. 5.
8. The interrelation of the two points misleads Pascal in no. 276: "M. de Roannez said: 'Reasons come to me afterwards, but at first a thing pleases or shocks me without my knowing the reason, and yet it shocks me for that reason which I only discover afterwards.' But I believe, not that it shocked him for the reasons which were found afterwards, but that these reasons were only found because it shocked him." Pascal's remark does not conflict with M. de Roannez's. My points two and three above echo M. de Roannez's view.
9. In saying this, I am assuming that commonly we are confronted with many incommensurate reasons. Which ones we respond to is a matter of personal inclination, since responding to any of them would be rational.
10. Though sometimes this qualification is out of place. There is a use of "choice" where if I had no reasons for an alternative course of action, then I had no choice, however matters appeared to me.
11. I discuss them in Raz, forthcoming.
12. And having chosen the better pair, I have no reason to have the other unless I fear that I will not be able to get my chosen pair. I disregard such complications.
13. I am assuming that my sole reason for giving him, for example, the book and the CD is that these will be ways of "doing something for him," which is the only thing I have reason to do (i.e., I assume that I do not have an independent reason to give them to him. I have only a reason to do something for him).
14. To be more accurate, the definition should meet an additional complexity. Sometimes an action cancels a reason or makes it inapplicable by being the

wrong action the performance of which makes the right course of action no longer possible, thereby making certain reasons inapplicable. The definition should therefore read: "does not cancel those reasons nor make them inapplicable, and where if they are cancelled or rendered inapplicable, this is not due to the fact that the wrong action was chosen or taken." For the sake of brevity I do not include this qualification when repeating the definitions or modifying them.

15. I rely on this condition, rather than on the simpler "makes it impossible to comply fully with another" so that we need not worry that there are cases where the underlying reason does not admit of complete and exhaustive compliance, for there is always something more one can do for that reason (say, the reason parents have to look after their children).

16. See Raz 1999: ch. 4.

17. I use "will-dependent" to refer only to reasons where the dependence is positive, that is, where one has the reason or it is stronger if one desires the act or would do it willingly. Sometimes the connection is reversed: You have reason or more reason to do something if you do not want to do it. These are not will-dependent in the sense here meant. A similar qualification applies to "goal-dependent" reasons, which are discussed below.

18. Sometimes one is caught up in a goal, which one may have assumed willingly in the past but has to carry on with now even though one no longer wants to at all. Reasons one has because one has such a (currently) unwilled goal are not goal-dependent in the sense here defined.

19. This assumes the other conditions for conflict are met.

20. As noted above, in general reasons for action are also reasons to want to do the act for which they are reasons. The fact that with (some) will-dependent reasons the stringency of the reason depends on one's willingness to perform the action makes them no exception. Assume, however, that the very applicability of the reason is conditional on the will. In such cases the reason can be said to be an invitation to want to perform the action. It shows that should we want it, the action would have merits, that it is desirable if wanted.

21. According to some views of "acting wrongly," agents act wrongly, though they are not blameworthy, even when their action is due to excusable ignorance. If that is so, then the emendation built into the modified definition to meet the point can be dispensed with.

22. We are aware of them as reasons, but not necessarily through the possession or application of the concept of a reason. The remarks regarding the second objection above are relevant here, though they do not exhaust the point.

23. This point is important to the argument of Marcus 1980.

24. It may be worth mentioning that partial conflicts (see note 2 above) allow complete conformity and that agents facing them should perfectly conform by avoiding the ways of conforming one reason that would constitute or lead to nonconformity with the conflicting one.

25. Most generally, compensation is just rendering an equivalence or as near an equivalence as can be or is thought appropriate. For example, a salary is compensation for work done.

26. This conclusion does not apply where I have a reason to act, rather than to refrain from action. I have a reason to feed my child. Suppose it is a reason to feed intentionally. My unintentional failure intentionally to feed my child does give rise, by the conformity principle, to the strict liability standard.
27. Much of the work was done by Tony Honoré and John Gardner.

Bibliography

Hampshire, Stuart. 2000. *Justice Is Conflict*. Princeton, N.J.: Princeton University Press.

Marcus, Ruth Barcan. 1980. Moral Dilemmas and Consistency. *Journal of Philosophy* 77: 121–36.

Pascal, Blaise. 1943. *Pensées*, tr. W. F. Trotter. London and New York: Dent/Dutton.

Raz, Joseph. 1999. *Engaging Reason: On the Theory of Value and Action*. Oxford: Oxford University Press.

Raz, Joseph. 2003. Numbers, with and without Contractualism. *Ratio* 16, no. 4 (December 2003).

8

Sources of Practical Conflicts and Reasons for Regret

Monika Betzler

It is a widespread phenomenon that we often experience regret after having resolved a practical conflict: In such a case, we had a reason (or reasons) to do A, and we had a reason (or reasons) to do B, but we could not do both A and B. Given that we could act on only one option,[1] we seem to have a reason (or reasons) to regret not having acted on the forgone option after the resolution of the conflict. Consider the following examples:

(a) John wants to spend his vacation in the mountains, and he also wishes to spend his vacation on the seaside. Since he cannot travel to both locations given his one-week time constraint, he is in a conflict over where to spend his vacation. When he finally opts for mountain climbing and consequently travels to the Alps, he regrets that he is not taking a sunbath on the beach.

(b) Or think of the question we all had to confront at a certain age, namely, which career to pursue. Given the uncertainties about how various professions really turn out and in light of the difficulty in assessing what we really value, such a choice can be traumatic. But even if we opt for a career path that seems justified by virtue of the information available at the time of the choice – let's say we opt for philosophy – we might have to put up with regret. We might regret that we had to reject another highly valued option, for example, the career as a successful businessperson.

What appears to be especially striking is that we react emotionally, even if the resolution of the practical conflict appears to be well justified. For example, even if John values the mountains somewhat more than the beach, or even if we opt for philosophy because we prefer it to

197

the business career (that is, even if we have stronger reasons for A than for B, and consequently rationally resolve the conflict between them such that we opt for A), more often than not we regret that we had to forsake B.

Regret is thereby thought to be an emotional state with a distinct propositional content.[2] It involves the experience of some greater or lesser degree of sorrow or psychic distress, and it is connected with the evaluative judgment that something has gone wrong. Regret that we experience after having resolved a practical conflict expresses a retrospective evaluation of what one did and/or what one failed to do.[3] It is associated with counterfactual reasoning or imagination about what might have been if the regretted matter had not occurred, and it is frequently accompanied by the wish that one had not had to act as one did.[4]

Obviously, regret is not only occasioned in connection with practical conflicts, and various degrees of an agent's intentional involvement in his action and choice can be distinguished with regard to it. Before I put the regret that ensues after a seemingly well-justified choice between conflicting options under closer scrutiny, let me set it aside from two other kinds of regret. This will help to clarify what is distinctive about the regret I focus on. For example, we may regret that our neighbor had an accident from which he is still traumatized. Spectator regret due to harm occurring to others differs from agent regret[5] in that only the latter kind is connected with actions and choices of one's own that can be regretted for having been either committed or omitted. But there is agent regret of various kinds, even though they may all arise in connection with practical conflicts. We may regret that we acted wrongly either because we should have known at the time of action that another course of action was called for or because later, unpredictable consequences undermined the initial justification of the action. In both of these cases we regret not having acted for the best reason.[6]

The kind of agent regret that arises after the rational resolution of a practical conflict, however, differs from these cases in that it is connected with actions and choices of one's own that are well justified. In regretting after having rationally resolved a conflict, the agent does not deplore having acted for less good or even bad reasons, nor is the harm or wrong that occurred due to something he did not know and could not have known at the time of action. What seems special about this last variety of agent regret is that the agent chose between conflicting options with good reasons and that the harm occurred as a foreseeable, but unintended, by-product of that well-justified choice. Yet circumstances are such that the agent cannot do all the things for which he has a reason. The agent thus regrets in spite of his having rationally resolved the conflict. What distinguishes this kind of regret[7] from other reactive emotions such as guilt, resentment, remorse, or indignation[8] is that the agent did not commit any moral or deliberative mistakes at the time of acting. This is what makes regret after rationally resolved practical conflicts a peculiar reactive emotion.[9]

What gives it a special status is that it is taken to indicate that there is something worrisome about such choices between conflicting options despite their appearing to be rational. According to the argument from regret, the reactive emotion we are susceptible to after a practical conflict has been resolved raises concerns about the scope of practical reason. After all, how rational could the resolution of a conflict be if we react to it with painful feelings?

The argument from regret maintains that if a person feels regret, there is a reason not acted on that still obtains, and therefore continues to call for action. The reason or reasons that support the option not acted on simply cannot be undone. Since many conflicts give rise to regret, and reactive emotions of that kind are "intelligent dispositions,"[10] it is concluded that conflicts that engender regret cannot be eliminated and therefore turn out to be genuine. This view stems partly from a certain picture of practical reason. It is thought to be a capacity that allows us to resolve practical conflicts without "remainder."

That there are practical conflicts, however, whose supposedly rational resolution cannot do away with a remainder in the guise of regret, has hitherto lent support to critics of the rationalist framework. Standard theories of practical reason seem unable to explain why we are liable to regret in situations where the agent has rationally resolved the conflict.[11] After all, if we correctly balanced the reasons at stake, if we consequently did not violate any requirement of rational deliberation, and if we finally acted for the best reasons, a painful reactive emotion, such as regret, simply does not seem to be justified. Confronted with the argument from regret, rationalists, who – despite their differences – share the view that we can rationally resolve conflicts without remainder, resort to two different strategies. They are either hostile to the idea of taking regret seriously right from the start or they deny that it responds to reasons for actions that continue to obtain. They try to accommodate it as spectator regret, that is, as an attitude that responds to the loss of value more generally. Adherents of the first view consider regret not only to be irrational given the rational resolution of the conflict. They also take it to lack any motivational import, since it is supposed neither to prevent conflicts in the future[12] nor to undo the harm that had occurred.[13] This leads them to the conclusion that we should rather rid ourselves of the "unreason" of an emotion such as regret.[14] However, the fact that we acted for the best reasons and yet experience painful feelings does not show that regret is not justified. Our reactive emotions could very well challenge the reach of standard conceptions of practical reasons and practical rationality more generally.

According to the second explanation offered by rationalists, regret is qualified as rational in a looser sense. It is considered to be an appropriate attitude in that it reacts to the harm that occurred.[15] Even though regret is thereby conceived as an intelligible response – after all, we have to deal with losses of value – it is not taken to reveal that there are reasons for action that continue to stay in force. On this account, regret is explained at the cost of divorcing if entirely from our own practical reasons. Agent regret is thought to boil down to spectator regret.

Contrary to these claims, two explanations have been offered so far as to the rationality of regret that supposedly reveal that a practical conflict has only "imperfectly"[16] been resolved. They differ, however, with regard to the reasons to which regret is taken to respond.

According to one view, regret after a rationally resolved conflict indicates that practical reasons share the feature with desires more generally in that they continue to stay in force and press for their satisfaction, even if they are rejected for good reasons. Despite the fact that we can balance the reasons and arrive at an all-things-considered judgment about which of the conflicting options to pursue, the practical reason not acted on preserves its normative grip like an unfulfilled desire and survives in the guise of regret.[17]

According to another view, regret reveals that values are incommensurable. Inasmuch as practical reasons are derived from values, we are confronted with incommensurable guidelines as to how we should act. Consequently, we cannot rationally resolve the conflict for all-things-considered reasons, but only for "undefeated"[18] reasons. This does not make our choice irrational. Practical reason just cannot do more than let us choose one of the options supported by reasons, however incommensurable with other reasons supporting other options. Consequently, regret shows that we could not comply with the reason not acted on that is generated from a value that remains incommensurable with the value we did act on.

Given the rationalist picture and the arguments provided by its critics, we are confronted with the following puzzle: Either the distinct kind of agent regret that reveals one's own practical reasons not acted on as binding is irrational right from the start (as rationalists maintain) or the resolution of a practical conflict that engenders agent regret is rationally underdetermined (as critics of the rationalist model maintain).

My aim in this article is to propose a solution to this puzzle. Hence, my question is neither why supposedly irrational regret survives nor how to disconnect it entirely from our reasons for action in order to render it generally intelligible. Rather, it is this: What kind of justification is there for holding that emotional stance[19] that is compatible with the rational resolution of a practical conflict? After all, and as I try to show below, there are cases in which there is something to agent regret that goes beyond the deplorable general fact that harm or loss of value has occurred. In its painful phenomenal quality, it appears – at least in some cases – to be more closely connected with what we as agents did or failed to do. If we want to take our practice of emotionally reacting to our rationally justified resolution of a conflict seriously, and if *ceteris paribus* nothing speaks against it, we should consider further what bolsters it. After all, there is a compelling explanation provided by evolutionary psychology that our emotional responses have important adaptive functions. Creatures without such an emotional repertoire are ill-equipped to stay loyal to their own goals, pursue stable plans, and remain trustworthy in the eyes of others affected by their goals.[20] In the following, I examine more closely how regret fulfills that function.

Two objections, however, could be raised against the general thrust of this endeavor. Those who harbor suspicion about the rationality of emotions could resort to the following two kinds of claims. First, it may be argued that regret simply is not reason-*responsive*. The fact that we can regret too much and for too long such that we are no longer capable of going on with our life is thought to be enough to indicate that regret is insensitive to reasons. In such a case, one is stuck with ruminating about what would and could have been had there simply been no conflict. But this pertains to the question of how much regret is rational and does not render it irrational *tout court*. If we want to make sense of our emotional practice after the resolution of a practical conflict, we just have to be wary that regret can fail to respond adequately to reasons. This does not, however, entail that it does not respond to reasons at all, and I content myself in the following with specifying those reasons it responds to.

But one could also object that regret cannot be rationally justified in a further sense. Not only does it not have the reason-responsive capacity, but one could argue that reasons cannot call for regret. After all, emotions are attitudes we cannot choose to feel, and therefore they cannot be rationally required. If we happen not to feel such reactive emotions after the rational resolution of a practical conflict, we cannot be blamed. The resolution of the conflict seems equally rational whether we are liable to regret or not. Since regret cannot be rationally called for, it cannot reveal anything about our reasons.[21] This perspective, however, is unduly voluntaristic. Even though it is true that emotions cannot be chosen and therefore cannot be required, this does not entail that once we experience them – and in the case of regret that just seems a widespread empirical fact – there is no reason to which our emotions are responding. Given that regret could be connected with a belief about the object of regret, and given that this belief could be true, there may very well be something about its object that justifies it. Moreover, I show, as I go along, that in some cases regret has a distinct motivational import.

Since critics of the rationalist picture draw our attention to the reason-responsiveness of regret, I first focus on their suggestions and investigate whether they succeed in adequately explaining regret. This leads me in a second step to examine more thoroughly what it could be about the intentional objects a person's regret is directed to that would give her a reason (or reasons) for holding that stance.

My contention is that regret is reason-responsive in a sense that has been overlooked. It is rational to feel regret after certain types of conflicts are rationally resolved, even if we made no deliberative mistakes about the options. I argue that this is due to the distinct character of the objects regret is typically directed to. More precisely, substantive regret[22] responds to valuable pursuits and relationships that are rationally generated by our evaluative or moral commitments and that greatly affect how we lead our life. Forgoing one of our commitments – even if it is done for better reasons, all things considered – can leave intact what we came to consider and experience as valuable. What we come to consider and experience as valuable gives us reasons to value it and thus to entertain appropriate attitudes with regard to it and to pursue actions expressive of our evaluation. It is a condition of valuing some pursuits or relationships that we respond as well as possible to what we consider and experience as valuable. Regret is an evaluative attitude responsive to what we still have reason to value in light of the fact that we cannot appropriately act on it any longer. In fact, having reasons to value pursuits and relationships gives us reason to regret if we are not able under the circumstances to realize further these pursuits and to entertain these relationships.

If we get clearer on what the proper intentional objects of regret are, it will also become apparent that regret is a more varied phenomenon than has hitherto been acknowledged. My account of regret will help to show that there are sources of practical conflicts that do not prevent their rational resolution and yet leave room for regret. Moreover, we will discover what the actual motivational impact of regret is such that creatures without reactive emotions of that kind would be at a loss to pursue stable goals.

According to the first suggestion as to the rationality of regret, the fact that we experience regret after the rational resolution of a conflict reveals an important characteristic of practical reasons.[23] Contrary to theoretical reasons, like beliefs, practical reasons, such as desires, are characterized by their distinct "direction of fit" between mind and world. Whereas beliefs are states that entail our regarding them as made true by the world, desires entail our regarding them to be brought about or to be satisfied. If two beliefs conflict, one of them must be false and will usually be given up. The state of believing can be characterized by the fact that the belief that is logically inconsistent and therefore conflicts with a true belief vanishes.

If two desires conflict, however, their inconsistency is merely practical.[24] The fact that a desire's propositional content is false is not a flaw in the desire. Such a desire should not therefore be abandoned simply because it cannot be satisfied.[25] It is not our reasoning that is at fault, but the world which does not make it possible to satisfy both desires. One could say that the actions motivated by these desires are merely incompatible under the circumstances. Thus, the source of practical conflicts is taken to be circumstance, given that practical reasons are desires that require satisfaction.

According to Bernard Williams, we are susceptible to regret in the case of conflict, just because the practical reason not acted on remains to exert its normative grip on us. It still applies to the situation and does not cease to be a reason for action. This is a feature that moral obligations share with desires. The ensuing emotional reaction expresses the unsatisfied desire in another guise, that is, as regret "for what was missed."[26]

But do we really have a good reason to regret because one of the options not acted on continues to make demands on us like unsatisfied desires? To answer this question, let me consider the example of conflicting desires as described above in (a). John is in a conflict between wanting to spend his vacation in the mountains and wanting to go to the seaside. After deliberating about the two alternatives, he finally opts for the mountains. Is he justified in regretting not being at the seaside, given that he opted for the best reasons and that no unforeseen consequences call his decision into question? After all, John still values the sea, and he really likes lying on the beach, too. However, there does not seem to be much room for regret, even if his desire to spend holidays on the beach still lingers. Even if his desire to be on the beach initially generates a reason for him actually to go there, it does not necessarily continue to be a reason for action surviving in the guise of regret, once he opts for climbing the mountains with good reasons. We may advance various reasons to bolster this claim.

On the one hand, his desire to be on the beach is not sufficient to justify regret. The significance of enjoying the seaside, given that John likes the mountains at least equally well, is simply not great enough to call for regret. After all, John can easily spend his vacation next year at the seaside. Moreover, even if his desire to go to the seaside is now frustrated, his overarching desire to spend his vacation in a pleasurable place is not. Since spending one's vacation is a goal that is constituted by various activities, pursuing one rather than another does not undermine the overarching goal. Hence, the fact that John desires to spend his vacation at the seaside is not sufficient for him to have a reason to regret not actually going there, once he opts for another location with good reasons. Furthermore, if John's skin is, for example, very susceptible to the sun, he may not even have a good reason to go to the beach despite his desire for it. In this case, his desire cannot generate a reason to act on it at all.

He may at best mildly regret that one of his desires could not be satisfied. Such mild regret on the frustration of a desire will quickly fade once John enjoys his vacation in the mountains. It does not amount to the kind of agent regret according to which a reason not acted on remains binding. The frustration of his desire can either be sufficiently compensated, or his desire leads him astray. One might object, however, that this does not show that desires in general do not yield practical reasons we come to rationally regret if we cannot satisfy and thus act on them.[27] It simply shows that John's desire to spend his vacation on the beach is not a reason that stays in force.

After all, we could have desires we make no mistake in having, and which are directed at long-term projects that cannot be compensated. But even the frustration of such desires does not affect one's life to an extent that justifies regret. Therefore, they do not carry in themselves any demand to act on them if we choose to satisfy another desire instead.

The discussion so far lends itself to the conclusion that regret is not justified simply because one of our conflicting desires remains unsatisfied. Either desires do not express what is really valuable for us or what they are directed to does not affect us enough to render regret justified on their frustration. Interpreting our emotional reactions and their intentional objects more carefully elucidates that regret does not rationally respond to unfulfilled desires that continue to stay in force. Instead, it seems that we have to value an option in a more committed way and that not acting on it must incur far-reaching consequences on how we understand ourselves in leading our life.[28] Only such pursuits could capture the significance necessary for reactive regret to be justified if they remain not acted on. I therefore now turn to consider in what way more comprehensive goals could yield reasons for regret if not acted on.

COMPREHENSIVE GOALS AND INCOMMENSURABLE VALUES

The conflict over which career to choose seems to represent precisely such a conflict between two comprehensive goals with far-reaching and thus significant consequences. Let me consider example (b) and turn to the second suggestion as to the rationality of regret. Are comprehensive goals supported by stronger or more important reasons, such that if I fail to act on them they will continue to make demands on me and justify regret, even if I choose another option with good reasons? To make sense of this idea, however, it does not seem to be enough to simply assume that comprehensive goals are supported by stronger or more important reasons. According to one suggestion, their very importance is due to the fact that they are generated by incommensurable values.[29] Given that the value borne by the comprehensive goal not acted on is incommensurable with the value borne by the comprehensive goal we come to choose, we finally seem to face a reason for regret derived from the value of the unchosen goal that remains binding. So far, while locating the reason-responsiveness of regret in the reason deriving from the option finally not acted on, I have tacitly assumed that we can, in fact, balance the reasons that support conflicting options and that we are therefore able rationally to resolve a conflict all things considered. Since I did not come up with a reason-providing feature that justifies regret, let me now examine in more detail whether the claim of value incommensurability could give us such an explanation. What exactly does it entail?

Conflicting options are taken to be incommensurable if neither of them is better than the other with respect to a common evaluative standard that allows us to compare them.[30] Moreover, incommensurable values are not considered to be of equal or even "roughly equal"[31] value, either. Instead, there could be a third option that is better than the first but not better than the second option.[32]

The claim of value incommensurability is based on the assumption that there would be no reason to regret an option and its forgone valuable property or properties if they could be compared with the valuable properties for the sake of which we choose the other option. If the forgone valuable properties, however, cannot be compared with the valuable properties we opted for, we face different reasons for different, that is, incommensurable, valuable goals. Hence, the reasons deriving from the valuable option not acted on still prevail, thus justifying regret. The valuable properties are simply not included in the valuable properties that we took as reason-giving and that propelled us to action, since it is impossible to compensate for the loss of one value by the gain of the other.[33] Consequently, it seems plain that we divide our attitudes in proportion to the options' relative, but incommensurable values: One is forgone and therefore regretted, the other one is promoted or appreciated and therefore enjoyed.[34] We thereby take an evaluative stand to the value or to the evaluative properties that are left outside the resolution of the conflict and that supposedly continue to give us reasons to value and thereby act on them.

But is value incommensurability a sufficient condition of rational regret? Is our reactive emotion justified because the value or valuable goal not acted on yields reasons that are incommensurable with the reasons that support the value or valuable goal we choose – a claim that seems particularly suggestive when it comes to comprehensive goals?

To pursue this question further, let me examine what regret is directed to if we consider the valuable options at stake as incommensurable. In the case of different valuable careers, we are taken to face incommensurable evaluative properties such as – if you think of the choice between a business career and philosophy – financial security versus intellectual fulfillment, or social recognition versus freedom.[35]

Several attempts have been made to show that there is more to comparability than meets the eye,[36] but I do not want to delve here into the question of how valuable properties, appearances to the contrary notwithstanding, can be compared. Instead, I want to consider whether value incommensurability could justify reactive regret. Let me therefore assume for the sake of argument that we really cannot come up with an evaluative standard that covers both careers. Let's say I opt for philosophy because of its intellectual fulfillment – a standard that allows me to recognize reasons and that makes that career "eligible"[37] for me without defeating the evaluative standard provided by financial security that speaks for the career as a businessperson. Does the financial security associated with the business career (and, let's assume, absent from the career as a philosopher) give me reasons to regret in the sense that I should still act on them, once I opt for the career in philosophy because of its intellectual fulfillment?

I believe we can answer this question in the negative. Provided that I am still happy with my choice for philosophy and, in fact, find the intellectual fulfillment I was seeking, it does not seem rational to painfully regret what might have been. The more I pursue my career in philosophy, and the more I thus come to value it for its intellectual fulfillment (and possibly for other properties, too), the less justified it seems to regret another career for the evaluative properties I initially considered worthwhile. It did not sufficiently enter my "affective reach."[38] Once I opt for a career even with undefeated good reasons, the choice is rationally reinforced by experience, whereas the other option not acted on stays in the abstract, and thus eventually loses its force. Consequently, the initially undefeated reasons supporting the goal of being a financially secure businessperson are gradually overruled the more I actually pursue the other career. No matter whether the career as a philosopher is initially incommensurable with the career as a businessperson, it is the fact that I only evaluatively experienced the career as a philosopher and shaped my life accordingly that provides me with further reasons to pursue it. Since I did not choose to become a businessperson, I do not face further reasons resulting from its pursuit which I could come to regret.

In such a case, regret seems to make sense only to the extent that I deplore not having certain valued experiences I would have had if I had led the life of a businessperson. I thus come to regret that choices – as autonomous as they might be – still constrain the range of opportunities I can have in a life. But clearly, this does not amount to saying that the reason – that is, "financial security" – for which I would have chosen the option not acted on continues to call for action. I just engage in counterfactual reasoning, imagining what another life would have been like, and I think about the discrepancy between the path not chosen and the actual path taken. Such a stance may help me to stay content with, and thus reinforce the reasons for, my initial choice or at least to realize its advantages and down sides in an imagined comparison. But it does not at all amount to saying that this is the kind of regret that responds to reasons that I should still act on, provided my initial choice for philosophy is not rationally overruled.

The only kinds of regret we have encountered so far are two versions of mild regret connected with frustrated desires and abstract evaluative properties we did not come to value experientially ourselves. The latter kind seems to come close to some kind of spectator regret. Inasmuch as mild regret results from frustrated desires we made no mistake in having, it may be as intelligible as spectator regret. Both kinds of regret derive from valuable properties that we do not experience but generally deem valuable. However, I could not show that we are justified in feeling regret after having resolved a practical conflict with the best reasons in the sense that there are reasons unacted on that remain binding. When we examine more closely what we come to regret after having chosen one of two conflicting options, neither bare desires nor incommensurable values prove to be conditions that can account for agent regret. Consequently, the task is still with us to identify the reason that justifies regret after the rational resolution of a practical conflict. What we have learned so far is not only that we have to value an option in a more committed way, but also that we have to have evaluative experiences with it such that we could react to the option with regret once we cannot act on it.

COMMITMENTS, THE TWO-TIER MODEL OF REASONS, AND SURROGATE VALUING

The discussion so far suggests that the agent needs to have an even closer connection to the valued option not acted on such that forsaking it might produce regret. Let me move on to investigate what such a connection could look like. I reconsider for this purpose the career example and slightly change it into (b*): Suppose that you already committed yourself to a career as philosopher. It is just the kind of profession you find most important. After having settled on this path for yourself and after having engaged in this commitment for a while, your father finally discourages you from pursuing it. He highlights the job insecurities connected with it and advises you to pursue a business career, which he finds you most talented for. Since your father's reasons are important to you, and considering all the other reasons he brings into play and that favor the career as a businessperson, you reconsider your career, and you rationally choose to go to business school. In this case, your regret about not pursuing the career of a philosopher is much stronger and seems more appropriate than in the initial example (b).

Let me therefore examine how commitments of this kind differ from mere desires and incommensurable values such that stronger, and possibly rationally justified, regret ensues if we do not act on them. Contrary to mere desires, commitments are based on reasons.[39] An agent is committed as long as he has decisively made up his mind and, furthermore, has taken overt steps to implement his decision. He thereby provides himself with a stable and reasoned evaluative outlook. Subscribing to such a commitment entails considering the reasons speaking for it as binding.[40]

A commitment differs from comprehensive goals based on incommensurable values in that it creates new reasons that transcend the reasons for undertaking the commitment in the first place.[41] It can be characterized by what I call a "two-tier model of reasons." Considering the reasons speaking for a commitment as binding entails having reasons generated by that commitment for arranging many of one's pursuits according to it. Having already embarked on that career path for a while created new reasons you did not have before and hence transformed your previous reasons. For example, it made you select a certain graduate school suitable for your commitment to philosophy. It made you gather friends with whom you discussed philosophical problems, it made you identify yourself more strongly with a contemplative lifestyle, and it motivated you to rearrange many of your other goals and pursuits. It made you govern yourself by that commitment, and it made you invested in that commitment and therefore vulnerable to losses connected with it.[42]

The more you had already committed yourself to philosophy and the more you shaped your life accordingly, the more would the reconsideration of reasons that now favor the career in business have painful effects on you, to which your regret would be a response. More specifically, there are two scenarios that account for regret, and which we have to carefully distinguish. Regarding the first, your change of reasons that now favors a commitment to a different career turns your pursuit of the original career path into failure[43] and wasted effort that you strongly come to regret.[44] After all, in being committed you expect from yourself that you can rely on the stability and success of that very commitment.[45] Your own expectations associated with leading a life of successful pursuits derived from your initial commitment are thereby breached. Your emotional reaction will be particularly strong if the reasons pertaining to the new career do not yet positively affect and shape your ongoing life and thereby make up for your wasted efforts. What you have now rationally decided to commit yourself to is not yet valuable for you as a protagonist of an ongoing life. As long as you do not manage to rearrange your pursuits – and that will take time and experience[46] – you will continue to regret strongly. In such a case you regret ever having committed yourself to philosophy. Your new set of reasons reveals that you lived the wrong kind of life. But this is certainly not the kind of regret pointing to reasons that remain binding. By contrast, it reveals that you originally committed yourself to a career for the wrong reasons. Given that the effects are greater the more you shaped your life accordingly, your regret is simply stronger. But this does not turn it into regret that points to reasons that continue to call for action. By contrast, it is regret resulting from having acted for bad reasons.

Let me assume in a second scenario that you already had very good reasons to commit yourself to philosophy. The reasons supporting the business career just prove on balance even better in the circumstances. After considering further aspects provided to you by your father, you simply discover that your talents make you more apt for a business career, that your prospects will be much better, or that you want to comply with your father's values.

In such a case, you come to regret losing what you came to value, and that was rationally generated from your original commitment. To be sure, this does not apply to all pursuits derived from your initial commitment. But there will be some you continue to regard as worthwhile. Even if it now turns out that a business career is on balance preferable, the reasons resulting from your initial commitment to philosophy engender various valuable pursuits and relationships you came to value and that continue to yield reasons to respond to them. For example, you may continue to consider gatherings with your philosopher friends as worthwhile. After all, these meetings meant a lot to you. Judging your friendships as valuable involves, at least in part, valuing particular friends by developing appropriate attitudes and pursuing actions that express that friendship. Since you are unable to entertain those attitudes and pursue those actions expressive of your friendship any longer, given your new commitment to a business career, you are unable to appropriately respond to what your philosophy friends mean to you.

Consequently, you regret not being able to continue to appreciate adequately what you have come to consider and experience as valuable. You regret not responding to the reasons that your valuable pursuits and relationships continue to generate. This kind of regret differs from spectator regret. You do not regret some general loss of value. Instead, you regret not being able to respond to reasons that your own reason-based commitments engendered. What is distinctive about this kind of regret is that it does not directly respond to lingering reasons requiring us to act on them. Instead, it responds to what we came to consider and experience as valuable but are unable to value actively any more. To the extent that what we came to consider and experience as valuable[47] gives us reasons to value it, we have a reason to regret if we cannot value and thus act on it any longer. Part of what it is to consider something valuable is to show proper appreciation for the fact that we cannot act, and therefore adequately value, what we still consider to be valuable. Regret is an attitude that is expressive of that fact.[48] It responds to the reasons engendered by what we have come to consider and experience as worthwhile in light of the fact that we cannot act on them. It is thus a form of *surrogate valuing.*

MORAL CONFLICTS, NORMATIVE EXPECTATIONS, AND SACRIFICE

So far, commitments not acted on provide the key to understanding regret. This is so because commitments – even if they are rationally overruled – create reasons for certain valuable pursuits and relationships. Once we come to hold some of these pursuits and relationships valuable, and shape our life accordingly, they continue to give us reasons to evaluatively respond to them. They give us reasons for regret if we cannot adequately value and act on them any longer. Regret is thus an evaluative attitude. It responds to reasons, but it does not entail that we should act on them.

Let me now turn to moral commitments. Maybe there is something to moral commitments not acted on that warrants justified regret in the sense that there are reasons that require us to act on them. Consider the following examples:

(c) A friend of mine promised to comment on the paper I plan to deliver at a conference and to help me with the final revisions. On her way to my house, however, she witnesses a car accident. She faces a conflict between breaking her promise and rescuing the victim. When she opts for the latter, she regrets having made me wait in vain for her to come and help.

(d) A parent is able to rescue only one of his two children out of a burning house. He is confronted with the terrible choice between his children. When he picks one child, the parent feels deep regret.[49]

Given the special authority attributed to moral reasons, they may continue to be normative and thus require action even if they were overruled in a given conflict. What does my friend in example (c) regret when she assists the victim instead of keeping her promise to help me revise my paper? Williams describes the constitutive thought of regret as "how much better if it had been otherwise."[50] But the moral importance of saving someone's life is undoubtedly so much greater than that of helping someone to revise a paper, even if promised long before. So what reason is there for her to regret at all? Clearly, my friend will not deplore that she acted as she did, since she acted for reasons that outweighed the reasons for keeping the promise. She should not have acted differently. But is the normative grip still there, even if it is weaker than the one she acted on? Is this finally a case in which her promise still waits to be fulfilled such that she should still act accordingly?

Promises are commitments of a moral kind that typically involve having made up one's mind to keep them and take steps to fulfill them. Since my friend made this promise to me, she is bound to fulfill that promise. In fact, making a promise entails accepting such a binding commitment. The person the promises are made to relies on that commitment and develops expectations accordingly. In that sense, promises, like other moral commitments, are connected with two kinds of reasons. There are reasons that speak for making a promise, and there are reasons deriving from having once made that promise. For example, my friend's reason for promising to help me with the final revisions of my paper is that she is my friend, or that she wants to offer help. Since she commits herself to helping me by making a promise, she has reasons to arrange her goals such that she can keep the promise, and I have reasons to rely on her promised help and develop trust in our friendship. The reasons for keeping the promise, however, are clearly overruled given the emergency of the accident. They are silenced by the moral urgency that the victim represents.

The moral case, however, differs from the nonmoral case of commitments in that the binding force of moral reasons extends to other persons. What is special in this case is that as long as I do not learn about her reasons for not keeping her promise to me, I seem justified in trusting my friend to come and help me. What my friend will come to regret is not only that I still sit at home waiting for her and that my paper will be less well revised due to her not helping me. In addition to this kind of spectator regret that responds to the harm that occurred, she may respond to my normative expectations[51] as to her fulfillment of her promise. But does this kind of regret about having breached my normative expectations really respond to reasons that continue to remain binding? Is this finally the kind of agent regret we are looking for?

Her reactive painful feeling responds to the reasons resulting from having made the promise. She may thus regret that I still expect her to come and/or that I develop distrust in our friendship. Consequently, she will feel strongly inclined to inform me about her justified change of reasons. Her regret thus motivates her to make excuses and/or to compensate. This does not imply, however, that there is a reason for her to act according to the promise she once made.

Regret that ensues from moral commitments not acted on again turns out to be justified regret of a slightly different type than we were looking for. It is not that the original reasons for keeping the promise to her friend still require her to act on them. Instead, what remains binding, and thus justifies regret, is to live up as well as possible to her friendship and to the normative expectations engendered by her promise once made to her friend. This includes informing me about her change of reasons, expressing her proper acknowledgment of my feelings and her evaluation of our relationship by offering compensation if possible. In that sense her regret responds to reasons ensuing from moral commitments once made for a reason.

Let us now turn to the tragic case (d). Maybe this represents, finally, a case of pure agent regret. After all, the case differs from the last one in that the reason that speaks for rescuing the one child does not outweigh the reason that favors rescuing the other child. Given what is at stake in his choice between conflicting options, the parent is in a real moral quandary. It therefore seems suggestive that he is not only liable to regret because something very harmful happened. Instead, he responds to something stronger that makes his regret seem justified.

However, the tragic case is not all that different from other cases of practical conflict with regard to its rational resolvability. Given the dilemma, the parent does not have an obligation, all things considered, to rescue his first child, and an obligation, all things considered, to rescue his second child. He simply has an obligation to rescue one of his children.[52] Given that the parent can rescue only one of his children, there is no reason that requires him to act on it even though he cannot. What makes this case tragic, however, is that the life of a person is lost, and that this loss is even something the parent has to choose. In fact, he has to choose which of his own children he will sacrifice. The loss connected with the death of the child is so great that it cannot be compensated. Given the tragic case, the parent is deprived of perfectly fulfilling his obligations to his second child. He cannot even fulfill them second best.

This case differs from regret in (b*) (that is, from regret expressive of not being able to appropriately respond to something we still consider and experience as valuable) and from regret that is connected with breached normative expectations in (c) in that the value attributed to persons, and to those with whom we entertain close relationships, in particular, is itself destroyed. In fact, even contrary to (b*), we regret not that we have to cease adequately valuing the person we deem valuable and love but that the person herself is lost. There is nothing left we could adequately or inadequately respond to. Valuing that very person is entirely undermined by having to sacrifice her. In such a case, regret comes down to grief about the loss of a person one has close relationships with and despair about having had to sacrifice that person through one's own choice. The parent thus becomes an agent with regard to the death of his own child.

Once again, there is no reason that continues to call for action once the parent acts on his obligation to save one of his children. Given the loss of his beloved child, however, he has a reason to express his love and hence his evaluation of his child in the guise of grief.

RESPONDING TO REASONS IN REGRET

The question I pursued in this article was whether and, if so, what kind of reasons regret responds to after we have rationally resolved a practical conflict. It was fueled by the concern that regret could reveal either that practical reason is imperfect or that our reactive emotions are irrational.

The reasons regret responds to, however, prove to be neither the reasons that linger like unsatisfied desires nor the reasons that are generated from incommensurable values and that we therefore are still called on to comply with. In fact, in cases of conflicting desires or conflicting goals, regret does not reveal any strong connection to reasons that require us to act on them.

A more thorough analysis of the objects to which regret is directed reveals that nonmoral and moral commitments not acted on provide the key to understanding rational regret. As the discussion of various examples shows, commitments are characterized by two tiers of reasons. There are reasons that favor the commitment as such (R_1) and reasons created by these commitments once made for a reason (R_1^*) that give rise to valuable pursuits and relationships. When we can balance R_1s, we rationally resolve a conflict.[53] R_1^*s are the reasons for action derived from commitments we cease to have if the reasons speaking for that commitment are overruled. However, R_1^*s let us continue to hold certain pursuits and relationships as valuable. Holding something valuable and deeming it worthwhile itself gives us reasons to respond to it as appropriately as possible. Even if we have lost the reason to act on what we have come to hold valuable, we have a reason to respond to that loss with regret. This is the case because it is the very condition of our holding something valuable that makes its loss matter to us.

What makes us react more strongly in such cases is that commitments are connected with how we shape our life according to what we come to value. Our rationally overruled commitments engender various kinds of regret, depending on the kind of loss of what we come to value. Regret thus encompasses a family of emotions. These emotions, however, are united as a class in their connection to commitments (moral or evaluative).

Depending on the kind of loss of value involved in a forgone commitment, there is (i) regret for having acted for bad reasons that made our life less valuable, (ii) regret connected with the loss of valuable pursuits we continue to consider and experience as valuable but cannot act on, (iii) regret responding to breached normative expectations, particularly in light of an ongoing appreciation of a close relationship, and (iv) regret about the loss of a beloved person as a result of our well-justified choice.

The result is that regret does not respond to reasons that remain binding in that we are still required to act on them. Agent regret in that sense does not exist. Regret in cases (ii), (iii), and (iv), however, differs from mere spectator regret and other forms of mild regret, and it is phenomenologically varied. It amounts to sadness, feelings of disloyalty, and at times even anger about not being able to continue one's valuation of certain pursuits in (ii). It comes down to guilt feelings vis-à-vis other persons affected by one's resolution of a conflict in (iii). In the last case, regret amounts to grief and despair. Consequently, regret after the rational resolution of a practical conflict turns out to be a more varied phenomenon than has hitherto been acknowledged.

These forms of regret that are connected with commitments are reason-responsive in a hybrid way. The fact that we once had a reason to act on certain pursuits and experiences that we have now lost does not mean that we cease to consider them valuable. Regret is a response to what we consider valuable but are unable to value actively any longer.

Regret thus reveals an important source of practical conflicts. It is not the fact that we cannot balance the reasons for conflicting commitments that explains why conflicts appear to be so challenging. It is rather that the commitments once embarked on yield reasons that engender valuable pursuits and relationships that, more often than not, continue to be valuable to us even after the reasons for the commitments that gave rise to them are overruled.

Regret proves to be an important practical competence, inasmuch as it motivates us to express our evaluation of those pursuits and experiences that arise from commitments we have to give up and provides evidence of our evaluation to others. For example, regret motivates us to make excuses, to provide compensation, and to express our continuing evaluation. It enhances the agent's trustworthiness and his self-trust in light of his not having lived up to what he really has come to value. It thus serves the function of reassuring us of the stability of our moral and evaluative commitments even in cases where our rational choice for one of them to the detriment of the other seems to undermine that stability.

A more thorough analysis of the intentional objects of our reactive attitudes thus alleviates the worry either that our reactive attitudes must be irrational in light of the rational resolution of the conflict they respond to or that the rational resolution of a practical conflict is necessarily imperfect or underdetermined.

It is the reasons that are created by the moral or evaluative commitments we once made for a reason that engender our valuable pursuits and experiences. These reasons do not continue to remain binding such that we should act on them. What continues to stay in force is that we continue to value those pursuits and experiences. To that extent we also have a reason to respond to any threat to what we value and to realize what we value, if possible. This does not affect the resolution between reasons supporting conflicting commitments, yet it does leave room for rational regret.

Notes

For extensive comments on various previous drafts of this paper I am grateful to Carla Bagnoli, Luz Marina Barreto, Peter Baumann, Rüdiger Bittner, Michael Bratman, Donata Conrad, Julien Deonna, Ronald deSousa, Jodi Halpern, Agnieszka Jaworska, Niko Kolodny, Elijah Millgram, Connie S. Rosati, Samuel Scheffler, Sally Sedgwick, J. David Velleman, and R. Jay Wallace. I am indebted to the audience of the 2003 conference of the British Society for Ethical Theory in Belfast for a stimulating discussion of the penultimate version of this paper, and to an anonymous referee of the British Society for Ethical Theory for helpful suggestions. I am also thankful that this paper was accepted for presentation at the 2003 Congress of the German Society for Analytical Philosophy in Bielefeld.

Work on this article was supported by a Feodor-Lynen Research Fellowship from the Humboldt Foundation at the University of California at Berkeley.

1. In the following, I use the terms "options," "valuable goals," "pursuits," or "commitments" interchangeably as alternatives of choice.

2. Since there is much to be done with regard to an adequate theory of emotions, I remain neutral as to how this connection between feelings and cognitive states, such as beliefs or judgments, can be exactly conceived. In any case, I am inclined to believe that regret has a cognitive basis.

3. I take reactive emotions, such as regret, guilt, or remorse, to be essentially backward-looking. In experiencing regret we react and thus look back to what we did or failed to do. But it can also be anticipated as future regret, that is, as a later evaluative attitude that concerns courses of action that are now available to the agent at the time of the anticipation. This perspective is entertained mostly by decision theorists. But more recently, it has also attracted the attention of those more generally interested in an adequate conception of our temporal extended agency. Anticipatory regret is especially relevant to the question of when it is reasonable to reconsider a plan and when not. However, it is taken to be an attitude that involves the thought that one has not acted for the best reason. I therefore disregard this kind of regret, which is different from regret after having rationally resolved a practical conflict. Moreover, anticipating regret is not regret we are experiencing now. See Sugden 1985: 77–99. See also Bratman 1999: 79–90.

4. See Landman 1993: 36 and 254–61; see also Rorty 1980: 496, who characterizes regret as "a particular sort of painful feeling, a pang, a stab, waves of stabs, relatively low keyed in comparison with remorse and guilt." See Baron 1988: 261–3.

5. This term goes back to Williams 1981a: 27. Williams was the first to point to the importance of agent regret and initiated the discussion on its role. See Williams 1973a: 166–86; Williams 1985: 123–6. Taylor 1985: 98–9, in her analysis of emotions of "self-assessment," focuses instead on spectator regret.

6. We may also have acted for bad reasons. For example, we may have acted negligently outright. In cases in which we acted for bad reasons and the regretted outcome has moral implications, we feel remorse. Oftentimes, regret is only associated with not having acted for the best reasons. See, for example, Burks 1946: 170–2. However, in this chapter I am exclusively interested in regret after having rationally resolved a conflict for the best reasons available. For a critical discussion of regret occasioned with bad luck, see Betzler 1999: 640–52.

7. In the following, I exclusively concentrate on agent regret as reason-responsive regret, even if I sometimes just stick to the term "regret" for reasons of simplicity.

8. Contrary to regret and despite its variants, I take guilt, resentment, remorse, and indignation to express that normative expectations have been breached without having any justification for breaching them. In that respect, guilt can also differ from feeling guilty.

9. Even though this kind of regret has received quite a bit of attention in the debate about the status of moral dilemmas, it has, so far, received little attention in the discussion on reactive attitudes.

10. This term was coined by Williams 1985: 36. Dispositions are "intelligent" to the extent that they involve the agent's exercise of judgment. They structure our reactions to others, but also – as the case of regret suggests – to ourselves. The argument from regret goes back to Williams 1973a: 166–86.

11. These theories include Kantianism or consequentialist theories such as rational choice theory and utilitarianism.

12. Marcus 1987: 197, for example, believes that it prevents conflicts in the future. Since conflicts are highly contingent, however, they cannot be foreseen and thereby prevented.

13. Bittner 1992: 267–8 is the most ardent contemporary defender of this view, which can be traced back to Spinoza. I need to emphasize, though, that Bittner develops his argument against the kind of regret connected with actions done for bad reasons or with bad luck. The reasons he mentions against it, however, should also hold against regret connected with the rational resolution of conflicts. He takes regret to be irrational in any kind of case.

14. See Bittner 1992: 262–73.

15. See Foot 1987: 258, who calls it "regret for a consequence." See Hurley 1989: 171–4; Scheffler 1992: 44–5; Hill 1996: 170; and Bagnoli 2000: 177–82.

16. See Williams 1981b: 81. See also Dancy 1993: 120ff.

17. See Williams 1973a: 166ff.

18. See Raz 1986: chs. 12–13. Cf. Raz 1999: ch. 5. See Levi 1986: 80, who refers to the "admissibility" of various options. See also Levi's contribution to this volume.

19. I share this perspective with Bagnoli 2000: 172.

20. I am grateful to Elijah Millgram for pressing me on this point.

21. I owe this objection to Connie Rosati.

22. That is, regret that responds to reasons, and therefore is justified.

23. See Williams 1981c: 101–13.

24. See Williams 1973b: 204–5.

25. See Williams 1973a: 166–86.

26. Williams 1973a: 170.

27. I am grateful to Niko Kolodny and Samuel Scheffler for prompting me to elaborate on this point.

28. Millgram 2002: 218 refers to such cases as "the process of constructing a self." Not acting on more comprehensive pursuits thus has effects on the core components of one's personality.

29. Kekes 1993: 54–8 deems regret to be outright "unreasonable" if the conflicting values that gave rise to it were not incompatible and incommensurable.

30. For Raz, the idea of incommensurability entails the idea of incomparability. Accordingly, incommensurable options cannot be compared using a single measure. Others maintain, however, that there are ways of comparing, even if there is no single measure that allows quantitative comparison. In that sense incomparability is an even stronger claim. I use the term "incommensurability" in the following as "incomparability." See Raz 1986: 322–4; Lukes

1990: 34; Broome 1991: 70–75; Seung and Bonevac 1992: 800–2; Chang 1997: 4ff.

31. Rough equality implies that we could be indifferent between two options, even if they are supported by weighty but totally different reasons. See Raz 1986: 331–2. Cf. Griffin 1986: 96–7 and Broome 1999: 152–3 for different conceptions of rough equality.

32. Incommensurability can thus be explained as a failure of transitivity. See Raz 1986: 324.

33. I am grateful to David Velleman for helping me to clarify this point.

34. See Hurka 1996: 558. Hurka, however, thinks that a modest pluralism can account for regret. See Stocker 1990: 241–77; Anderson 1993: ch. 1.

35. Even conflicting moral commitments can be traced back to incommensurable moral values such as obligations, rights, utility, perfectionist goals, and other personal commitments. See van Fraassen 1987: 138–9; Lemmon 1987: 101–14; Nagel 1987: 174–87; Railton 1992: 720–42.

36. See Chang 2002 for the most recent attempt.

37. See Raz 1986: 338–9.

38. Rosati 1995: 316–24 argues convincingly that a person's good must be within her "affective reach" to qualify as a "good" for that person. Given that our motivational and cognitive features affect how we experience comprehensive goals, there is no neutral standpoint that allows us to independently evaluate goals such as careers.

39. At least, such reasons could be provided on reflection.

40. See Bratman 2001: 320, who emphasizes this fact: "We can normally expect general policies to be, other things equal, subject to stronger demands for stability than are temporally specific intentions. This is at least in part because their generality is normally the result of prior reflection."

41. I owe this distinction between reasons speaking for a commitment and reasons created by such a commitment to Raz 1986: 386–9.

42. This is how Frankfurt's notion of "caring" could be interpreted: We continue to care about our commitment to philosophy even though we believe that there are better reasons to pursue a business career. This is so because we are vulnerable to losses connected with that commitment. Contrary to Frankfurt, however, I do not subscribe to his noncognitive conception of caring. See Frankfurt 1997: 155–80. For my critique, see Betzler 2001: 159–77.

43. According to Velleman, our self-trust is undermined in such cases. I have benefited from his discussion of guilt. See Velleman 2003: 235–48.

44. See Raz 1986: 385–7; cf. Velleman 1991: 48–77.

45. See Bratman 1987: ch. 5.

46. See Millgram 1997: 161, who emphasizes that experience and inductive deliberation may supply the information necessary to resolve conflicts.

47. This may be captured by natural properties that give us reasons to value friendship, such as enjoying the company of your friends or being intellectually inspired by them. See Scanlon 1998: 95ff.

48. See Anderson 1993: chs. 1–2 for her expressive theory of rational attitudes.

49. It may sound particularly weak in this case that the parent feels regret given the tremendous harm that occurred. However, this merely underlines the

fact that regret encompasses a family of emotions that unite as a class under the rather technical term "regret." I elaborate on this as I go along.

50. Williams 1981a: 27.

51. I am indebted to Wallace's conception of normative expectations, which he develops with regard to reactive emotions, especially with regard to guilt, resentment, and indignation. See Wallace 1994: chs. 2–3. I believe that regret is a further distinct reactive emotion that can be connected with normative expectations.

52. I cannot argue for this thesis here. For a more detailed defense, see, for example, Brink 1996: 115ff.

53. I cannot offer an argument here for the comparability of conflicting commitments. I have argued in unpublished work how, appearances to the contrary notwithstanding, such comparisons are possible. See Betzler n.d.

Bibliography

Anderson, Elizabeth. 1993. *Value in Ethics and Economics.* Cambridge, Mass.: Harvard University Press.

Bagnoli, Carla. 2000. Value in the Guise of Regret. *Philosophical Explorations* 3: 169–87.

Baron, Marcia. 1988. Remorse and Agent-Regret. *Midwest Studies in Philosophy* 8: 259–82.

Betzler, Monika. 1999. Warum wir bedauern. Zu Bernard Williams' moralischer Auszeichnung eines Gefühls. Eine Reinterpretation. In Julian Nida-Rümelin (ed.), *Rationality, Realism, Revisions: Proceedings of the Third Congress of the German Society for Analytical Philosophy.* Berlin: de Gruyter, 640–52.

Betzler, Monika. 2001. How Can an Agent Rationally Guide His Actions? *Grazer Philosophische Studien* 61: 159–77.

Betzler, Monika. N.d. Qual der Wahl – Überlegungen zur Vergleichbarkeit wertvoller Ziele. Unpublished manuscript.

Bittner, Rüdiger. 1992. Is It Reasonable to Regret Things One Did? *Journal of Philosophy* 89: 262–73.

Bratman, Michael. 1987. *Intention, Plans, and Practical Reason.* Cambridge, Mass.: Harvard University Press.

Bratman, Michael. 1999. Toxin, Temptation, and the Stability of Intention. In Michael Bratman, *Faces of Intention: Selected Essays on Intention and Agency.* Cambridge: Cambridge University Press, 58–90.

Bratman, Michael. 2001. Two Problems about Human Agency. *Proceedings of the Aristotelian Society* 101: 309–26.

Brink, David O. 1996. Moral Conflict and Its Structure. In Homer E. Mason (ed.), *Moral Dilemmas and Moral Theory.* New York and Oxford: Oxford University Press, 102–26.

Broome, John. 1991. *Weighing Goods: Equality, Uncertainty and Time.* Oxford: Basil Blackwell.

Broome, John. 1999. Incommensurable Values. In John Broome, *Ethics Out of Economics.* Cambridge: Cambridge University Press, 145–61.

Burks, Arthur W. 1946. Laws of Nature and Reasonableness of Regret. *Mind* 55: 170–2.

Chang, Ruth. 1997. Introduction. In Ruth Chang (ed.), *Incommensurability, Incomparability, and Practical Reason*. Cambridge, Mass.: Harvard University Press, 1–34.

Chang, Ruth. 2002. *Making Comparisons Count*. New York and London: Routledge.

Dancy, Jonathan. 1993. *Moral Reasons*. Oxford: Blackwell.

Foot, Philippa. 1987. Moral Realism and Moral Dilemma. In Christopher W. Gowans (ed.), *Moral Dilemmas*. New York and Oxford: Oxford University Press, 250–70.

Fraassen, Bas C. v. 1987. Values and the Heart's Command. In Christopher W. Gowans (ed.), *Moral Dilemmas*. New York and Oxford: Oxford University Press, 138–53.

Frankfurt, Harry G. 1997. On Caring. In Harry G. Frankfurt, *Necessity, Volition, and Love*. Cambridge: Cambridge University Press, 155–80.

Griffin, James. 1986. *Well-Being: Its Meaning and Measurement*. Oxford: Oxford University Press.

Hill, Thomas E. 1996. Moral Dilemmas, Gaps, and Residues: A Kantian Perspective. In Homer E. Mason (ed.), *Moral Dilemmas and Moral Theory*. New York and Oxford: Oxford University Press, 167–98.

Hurka, Thomas. 1996. Monism, Pluralism, and Rational Regret. *Ethics* 106: 555–75.

Hurley, Susan. 1989. *Natural Reasons*. Oxford: Oxford University Press.

Kekes, John. 1993. *The Morality of Pluralism*. Princeton, N.J.: Princeton University Press.

Landman, Janet. 1993. *Regret: The Persistence of the Possible*. New York and Oxford: Oxford University Press.

Lemmon, E. J. 1987. Moral Dilemmas. In Christopher W. Gowans (ed.), *Moral Dilemmas*. New York and Oxford: Oxford University Press, 101–14.

Levi, Isaac. 1986. *Hard Choices: Decision Making under Unresolved Conflict*. Cambridge: Cambridge University Press.

Lukes, Steven. 1990. Incommensurability in Science and Ethics. In Steven Lukes, *Moral Conflict and Politics*. Oxford: Clarendon, 33–49.

Marcus, Ruth B. 1987. Moral Dilemmas and Consistency. In Christopher W. Gowans (ed.), *Moral Dilemmas*. New York and Oxford: Oxford University Press, 188–204.

Millgram, Elijah. 1997. Incommensurability and Practical Reasoning. In Ruth Chang (ed.), *Incommensurability, Incomparability, and Practical Reason*. Cambridge: Harvard University Press, 151–69.

Millgram, Elijah. 2002. Commensurability in Perspective. *Topoi* 21: 217–26.

Nagel, Thomas. 1987. The Fragmentation of Value. In Christopher W. Gowans (ed.), *Moral Dilemmas*. New York and Oxford: Oxford University Press, 174–87.

Railton, Peter. 1992. Pluralism, Determinacy, and Dilemma. *Ethics* 102: 720–42.

Raz, Joseph. 1986. *The Morality of Freedom*. Oxford: Clarendon.

Raz, Joseph. 1999. *Engaging Reason: On the Theory of Value and Action*. Oxford: Oxford University Press.

Rorty, Amélie. 1980. Agent-Regret. In Amélie Rorty (ed.), *Explaining Emotions*. Berkeley: University of California Press, 489–506.

Rosati, Connie S. 1995. Persons, Perspectives, and Full Information Accounts of the Good. *Ethics* 105: 296–325.

Scanlon, Thomas. 1998. *What We Owe to Each Other*. Cambridge and London: Harvard Belknap.

Scheffler, Samuel. 1992. *Human Morality*. New York: Oxford University Press.

Seung, T. K., and Daniel Bonevac. 1992. Plural Values and Indeterminate Rankings. *Ethics* 102: 799–813.

Stocker, Michael. 1990. *Plural and Conflicting Values*. Oxford: Clarendon.

Sugden, Robert. 1985. Regret, Recrimination and Rationality. *Theory and Decision* 19: 77–99.

Taylor, Gabriele. 1985. *Pride, Shame, and Guilt: Emotions of Self-Assessment*. New York: Oxford University Press.

Velleman, David. 1991. Well-Being and Time. *Pacific Philosophical Quarterly* 72: 48–77.

Velleman, David. 2003. Don't Worry, Feel Guilty. In Anthony Hatzimoysis (ed.), *Philosophy and the Emotions*. Royal Institute of Philosophy Supplement 52. Cambridge: Cambridge University Press, 235–48.

Wallace, R. Jay. 1994. *Responsibility and the Moral Sentiments*. Cambridge, Mass.: Harvard University Press.

Williams, Bernard. 1973a. Ethical Consistency. In Bernard Williams, *Problems of the Self*. Cambridge: Cambridge University Press, 166–86.

Williams, Bernard. 1973b. Consistency and Realism. In Bernard Williams, *Problems of the Self*. Cambridge: Cambridge University Press, 187–206.

Williams, Bernard. 1981a. Moral Luck. In Bernard Williams, *Moral Luck*. Cambridge: Cambridge University Press, 20–39.

Williams, Bernard. 1981b. Conflicts of Value. In Bernard Williams, *Moral Luck*. Cambridge: Cambridge University Press, 71–82.

Williams, Bernard. 1981c. Internal and External Reasons. In Bernard Williams, *Moral Luck*. Cambridge: Cambridge University Press, 101–13.

Williams, Bernard. 1985. *Ethics and the Limits of Philosophy*. Cambridge: Harvard University Press.

9

Conflicting Values and Conflicting Virtues

Nicholas White

Some philosophers say that goods can "conflict." Others deny this. What are they disagreeing about? The issue might appear simple, but it turns out to be complex. Among various conflicts generated by our thoughts about what is good, one conflict arises concerning whether to call conflicting things good or to avoid doing so.

Isaiah Berlin cites "freedom and equality" as an example of a conflict between goods. He also says that happiness can conflict with knowledge, mercy with justice, and liberty with fraternity.[1] We may start by making a few remarks about such cases.

It seems utterly implausible to deny that sometimes particular things that we are strongly inclined to insist are good come into conflict, in the sense that gaining more of one can lead to having less of the other. At first sight it seems obvious that both freedom and equality can be called good, and that at least sometimes an increase in one leads to less of the other. True, there might be a case for saying that in the long run, an increase in equality might lead to greater freedom for all. That might happen, for instance, to the extent that restrictions on freedom are generated by resentments caused by inequalities. It seems flatly unbelievable, however, that all conflicts of things that we actually call goods can be so neatly explained. When Berlin asserted that goods can conflict, then, did he really exert himself on behalf of a blandly obvious claim, and can anyone nowadays mean to deny such a thing?

If anything substantial is at issue here at all, then there must be more to the dispute than meets the eye. Probably it would lie in questions about either the ascription of goodness to freedom and equality or the designations of the terms "freedom" and "equality," or what a conflict is. For example, perhaps the disagreement concerns whether freedom is really good when it conflicts with equality. Or perhaps it concerns whether something really is "freedom" when it conflicts with equality. Or whether something is "freedom" when it is not good. Or perhaps it is whether the relation that holds between freedom and equality is really conflict after all. At any rate, something has to be said to show how, if at all, this dispute can have any noteworthy content.

It does not help matters that this issue should be tangled up with a number of other difficult problems. Current philosophical discussions link the question of conflict of goods closely with issues about, for example, whether values are "plural," "comparable," or "commensurable" – as well as problems about "dilemmas," "conflicts of obligations," and relations between values and obligations, not to mention controversies over the respective roles within ethics of evaluation, deliberation, and the guidance of action.[2] In addition, there are numerous questions about what "conflict" amounts to. Moreover, questions about conflicts of goods are also intertwined with questions about whether the same thing may properly be said to be both good and bad, and in what sense or senses.

Within this constellation of problems the question of whether goods can conflict has recently been assigned a subordinate place. Berlin paid special attention to the question largely because he thought that denying the possibility of the conflict of goods is apt to lead to serious political and ideological disasters. For various reasons, however, most subsequent discussions have focused on other matters, usually treating the question of whether goods can conflict as ancillary to such questions as whether goods are all comparable or commensurable.[3] Berlin, however, asserted emphatically that the mistake of believing that goods cannot conflict can and does lead to political disaster. It seems worthwhile, accordingly, to attend to some extent to this question itself, to see whether it has the significance that Berlin thought it did.

The best way to start, it seems to me, is to point out a difference between two ways of attacking the issue. One is more or less straightforwardly factual, whereas the other has more to do with the way in which we propose to treat certain kinds of evaluations.

A person who claims that goods can conflict may attempt to support the claim in two distinguishable ways. One is to cite particular things that he supposes we take to be good, G_1 and G_2, and maintain that they conflict. To the extent that we understand what G_1 and G_2 are, then we can see what might be meant by claiming that they conflict, and we can accordingly determine whether the claim is true or false or for that matter whether it is a matter of degree. In favorable circumstances we can assess such claims when no issue of value is involved. For example, we can try to determine whether in a certain locale hot summers work against early fall foliage, quite apart from whether we regard either hot summers or early fall foliage as good, bad, or neutral.

The other approach can be illustrated by thinking of someone who maintains as a general matter that goods cannot conflict. He might do this without citing any particular things that he thinks are good. Rather, he might simply urge that *whatever* things are called good, it holds true that they may not conflict. Calling something good, he might maintain, implies that it does not work significantly against anything else that is good. Thus to hold that G_1 and G_2 are both good, he might conclude, is to hold that they do not work significantly against each other. On the other side of the debate we would place someone who contends that calling something good has no such implication, and thus that we can perfectly well call two things good even when we know that they may or do clash.

It is worth pointing out that the former way of thinking has substantial implications for the way in which evaluation is to be carried out. If we really think that goods cannot conflict with other goods, and that that implies that we should not call something good except to the extent that it will not turn out to conflict with anything else that we shall call good, then we are committed to a "global" as opposed to a "pointwise" style of evaluation insofar as goodness is concerned. We must then regard the project of evaluating as one of determining globally what a good overall state of affairs is, and then assign goodness to the parts of it on the basis of a determination that they "fit together within" it or "contribute to" its overall goodness. Some philosophers – the Stoics, for instance – have carried precisely this sort of scheme of evaluation a long way, insisting that ascriptions of goodness proceed against a background assumption of the goodness of the whole universe. Various theological theories proceed similarly.

When I say that this way of thinking involves thinking "globally" about goods, I do not mean to suggest that the resulting ascription of goodness is either unique or all-inclusive. It could be that there are many sets of mutually compatible goods (even given, e.g., all of the "facts" that there are). Moreover, when one evaluates a set of things globally and finds that it is internally consistent, one need not think that it includes everything that could be positively evaluated. In the present sense, "global" evaluation merely indicates that one of a group of things is not deemed finally to be good unless it is determined to be consistent with the other things that are so deemed.

In fact I believe that our ordinary thinking about evaluation, and also much philosophical thinking, involve a mixture of the two attitudes that I have sketched. Sometimes we concentrate on particular things that we have decided (whether in a fixed way or with some flexibility) are good and ask ourselves whether they might clash with each other, and sometimes we withhold attributions of goodness until such time as we receive more information about potentially conflicting factors. The interplay between these two attitudes has repercussions for our evaluative activities.

When one reads Berlin's remarks, one comes away with the impression that in his view, the belief that goods do not conflict normally arises from a fanatical devotion to one particular thing that is identified as good and a feeling that given that *it* is good, nothing that conflicts with it could possibly have any value. Such an outlook might be associated, for instance, with a fanatical devotion to equality, to freedom, or to some other value (let us assume that such terms are clear enough to use in this way). But it seems that this outlook does not necessarily derive merely from the belief that equality is good, for example, but in addition from an assumption that licenses an inference to the conclusion that the goodness of that thing excludes things that conflict with it from being good. This assumption seems to be or to be based on the general belief that goods may not conflict.

It accordingly seems plausible to say that both of the approaches that I have mentioned play a role in the debates in which Berlin sees himself as participating. We see further reasons below for thinking that both approaches often figure in people's thinking and that they interact in interesting and problematic ways.

Though the fact seems to have gone unnoticed in recent times, the early history of philosophy offers us a laboratory, so to speak, for working on this type of problem. Socrates' and Plato's reflections on the so-called unity of virtue have directly to do with conflicts of goods. We can therefore hope to turn to account, in our treatment of conflicts of goods, some of the considerations about virtues that they raised.

What is important in these ancient reflections is fortunately not the obscure issue of the "unity" of virtues, but rather the related but somewhat more tractable matter of the compatibility of the virtues. Whereas Socrates apparently wished to advocate a fairly strong thesis to the effect that the virtues "are one" – whatever exactly he meant by that – he was also thereby entangled in a dispute with thinkers who believed that there are distinct virtues and that they can conflict. (Also in play was a thesis, which Socrates accepted but which is weaker than his thesis of the unity of the virtues, to the effect that virtues mutually imply each other.[4])

Given that virtues are traits that are good, the thesis that virtues can conflict implies that goods can conflict – or at least that goods of a particular kind can do so.[5] Moreover, many of the considerations supporting the idea that virtues do not conflict are analogous to the considerations that weigh in favor of saying that goods do not conflict. That is one reason why ancient treatments of the unity of the virtues are pertinent to discussions of conflicts of goods. Another reason why the two discussions are connected is that when one examines Berlin's proposed examples of conflicting goods, one notices that some of them, too, are virtues. Some are or can be taken as virtues of individuals, such as justice and mercy, and others are virtues of political institutions or societies, such as freedom and equality. Thus, even if there has been little or no common discussion of Socrates' and Berlin's issues, they clearly are related.

Moreover, I think it clear that Socrates was trying to make two points, which respectively illustrate the two approaches to conflicts of goods that I just described.

(A) On the one hand Socrates thought quite generally that whichever two traits you pick, there must be something wrong with calling them both virtues and nevertheless saying that they conflict. This is not a point about particular traits already identified, but rather a point about how we should think about virtues in general. (B) In addition, however, Socrates also advanced another claim or a set of claims about particular traits that he, in common with many (though not all) of his fellow Athenians, thought were, or probably were, virtues. One such claim would be that, say, the virtues justice and temperance are compatible, and another, that the virtues wisdom and piety are compatible. And so on for the other traits (the list is not quite fully fixed, but it is almost so) that were taken to be virtues. Here one is not merely saying something about virtues in general; one is saying both that certain particular traits are virtues and that they are compatible with each other.

In the discussions of virtue in Plato's dialogues, one sees both of these approaches at work together. Sometimes Socrates is presented as believing that, even if we have not yet fully determined which traits are virtues, or exactly which, we can already know that *if* a given trait is a virtue, then by that very fact it *must be* compatible with all other virtues. At other points he seems to be proceeding on different grounds, related to facts about particular virtues. Nevertheless on the whole I think it can be said that a belief in the general thesis (A) influences most of his discussion. That is, Socrates seems to be guided largely by the general thesis that it makes sense to think of the virtues as all compatible, rather than primarily by a simple curiosity about whether, when the standardly acknowledged virtues are investigated one by one, they turn out to go together.

In the *Republic*, Plato seems to be guided by the same thought. His procedure in Book IV is to sketch in a general way a kind of personality or "soul," which he then labels "perfectly good."[6] Next he examines that personality in order to determine which of its features are responsible for its goodness, and simultaneously which of them can be labeled with the terms designating the virtues "wisdom," "temperance," "courage," and "justice." Whatever else one may say about this procedure for identifying virtues, it is certainly designed to ensure that the four standard words for those virtues will be assigned to traits that are compatible with each other (and indeed will even in a sense support each other).

Moreover, Plato's procedure illustrates the idea of treating the ascription of virtues as a global rather than a pointwise matter. Plato first evaluates a personality as a whole, and then he assigns virtues roles within that overall economy. He thus treats the value of each virtue as consisting essentially in its contribution, in some sense, to the overall goodness of the personality. (As is noted again below, this notion of "contributing" is not unproblematic.)

In addition to the connections that I have already mentioned between the Socratic and Platonic thoughts about virtue and Berlin's animadversions about goods, I should mention another link as well. It appears quite clear that in the *Republic*, at least, Plato takes the compatibility of virtues not merely to be a special case of the compatibility of goods, but also to presuppose that compatibility of goods quite generally. It is a special case of the general thesis insofar as, as noted, virtues are traits that are good. But Plato also understands the virtues to include a knowledge of what is good in general, which makes up most of wisdom, and he takes this knowledge to be brought to bear in the organization of the personality so as to exhibit all of the virtues. It thus appears that if Plato thought that goods could conflict at all, he would have found it very difficult to maintain, at least in the way he did, that the virtues could be consistent, let alone (as he also probably thinks) mutually supporting or even entailing.[7]

In this connection it is advisable to return to the point noted earlier, that a proviso that all virtues be compatible does not imply a unique list of virtues. One of the deficiencies in Plato's argument in the *Republic* lies in the fact that he holds a very restricted view of what the virtues – of an individual or for that matter of a political society – might be. When he says that the person whom he has described (and who will turn out to be wise, courageous, temperate, and just) is "completely good," he has not come close to canvassing all of the traits that a "completely good" individual might plausibly be claimed to possess, though perhaps in his time and place his list seemed more plausible than it does now. Obviously, a more extensive canvassing might generate other lists of compatible virtues besides the one that he arrives at.

The most important insights into Berlin's issue of conflicts of goods that can be gained from thinking about the Socratic question about the compatibility of the virtues seem to me to arise from the interplay between the two approaches, (A) and (B), that I have mentioned. We need to ask ourselves both whether there is reason to believe in general that a virtue can or cannot conflict with other virtues and whether there is reason to believe that the particular traits that we in fact identify as virtues do or do not conflict with each other. And likewise we need to ask the two corresponding questions more generally about goods. Moreover, we need to see how the members of each pair of questions bear on each other.

I suspect that many people consider the tendency to believe that virtues or goods do not conflict to be mainly the product of an obsession with artificial systematic theory building to which philosophers are often said to be subject. Certainly, some philosophers have urged that attention to the realities of our lives shows us that conflicts of goods are real and that this in turn (among other things) shows also that there are plural values.[8]

Perhaps this diagnosis is true to an extent, but whether it is true or not there is still good reason to believe that ordinary thinking, quite apart from active engagement with philosophy, shows its own ambivalence over whether goods can conflict or not. This ambivalence comes to light when we reflect on the respective pressures that we feel to say, and to deny, that a virtue may conflict with another virtue.

In passing I should remark that just as it is in many ways unclear what it means to say that two goods "conflict," this is definitely so in the case of virtues. Conflicts of virtues could at least in theory take various forms. For one thing, given that a virtue can properly be said to "require" or "forbid" a particular action in particular circumstances, as for instance Philippa Foot sometimes puts it,[9] then perhaps one virtue might require an action that another virtue forbids. For another thing, whether or not that sort of conflict arises, the training required for inculcating one virtue might work against the inculcation of another. Third, what is required in order to maintain one virtue might work against maintaining, exhibiting, or acquiring another. I leave these refinements aside.

The view that virtues cannot conflict might be based on the following argument, which exemplifies the former of the two approaches that I have introduced – namely, the general one, (A). This argument certainly plays a role in Socrates' thinking.

It seems extremely plausible to assert that a tendency to interfere with a virtue – with its possession or its manifestation – is pro tanto a bad thing. Certainly, the so-called auxiliary virtues and vices are called virtues and vices at all because they support or interfere with traits that have an independent title to be called virtues. To the extent that diligence is a virtue at all, for instance, it is so because it furthers other virtues. An ability to teach people to be just also seems to be itself a good trait and in some manner a virtue, and correspondingly a tendency to make the people around one intemperate is also for the same reason a vice or defect.

This way of thinking seems to be based on the assumption that part of what makes a trait good, in such a way that it is a virtue, arises from its consequences. We may take "consequences" here in a broad sense, so that the word covers not only the causal results of a trait, but also things that it "contributes" to in other ways, such as the value of the wholes of which it is a part or constituent. It seems quite plain to me, indeed, that even if we consider causal results alone, having good results is highly relevant to whether or not a trait is a virtue. But it seems even more certain that the consequences of a trait in the broader sense are germane to its being a virtue. (This natural thought grounds Aristotle's claim at *Nicomachean Ethics* I.5 that virtue cannot be the good.) It may be, to be sure, that a trait can have purely intrinsic value. Moreover, as will emerge, the evaluation of traits is not merely a matter of what they cause. Nevertheless, as will also emerge further, much of our thinking is based on the view that both the value of a trait and its status as a virtue are derived substantially from the value of its results and in particular of its causal results.

One of Socrates' grounds for thinking that virtues cannot conflict runs very much along these lines. A virtue must be good, he reasons. Insofar as it has bad effects, it is not good. To the extent that it is not good, it is not a virtue. By interfering with a virtue, a putative virtue is the less a virtue. If we reserve the title "virtue" for those traits that are *wholly* good, then we must say that virtues are traits that do not interfere with other virtues at all. It would then follow that virtues properly so called cannot conflict. (By supposing furthermore that insofar as a trait fails to support another virtue, it is thereby not good, we can strengthen the foregoing argument to reach the conclusion that virtues properly so called must support each other; further strengthening may also be feasible.)

These considerations seem to show that if a trait has a tendency to interfere with an acknowledged virtue, then to that extent it loses its entitlement to be thought of as a virtue itself. But if the trait in question is itself one that we are inclined to call a virtue, then we must say that if it interferes with another virtue, the entitlement of the former to be thought a virtue is diminished. This is so because the putative virtue is, insofar as it interferes with another virtue, by that very fact *less good* than it would be otherwise. This way of thinking does not seem to be artificially systematic, but rather reflects the quite ordinary idea that it is bad to interfere with a virtue.

Nevertheless, even if we take it to be mere common sense to think that a trait is the less a virtue for interfering with a virtue, the forgoing argument for complete compatibility of virtues might seem to depend on imposing excessively high standards on what it is to be good, and hence on what it is to be a virtue. The argument involves reserving the term "virtue" for traits that are flawless at least in a certain respect. The flaw of interfering with a virtue at all is assumed to be enough to keep a trait from being a virtue. Socrates' insistence that a virtue is "good" seems to embody such standards of unqualified goodness. But we need not talk in this way. We can think of a trait as *good enough* to be a virtue even if it does not have this defect or at least does not have it to a significant degree.

We do not, however, want to carry this thought too far. If we did, then we could call a trait a virtue even if it thwarted other traits that we called virtues. Thus if we keep our standards low enough, we can allow a trait to be called a virtue even if the level of conflict between it and other virtues is not negligible. Nevertheless, we plainly feel uncomfortable about doing this. Similarly, Socrates expects no demurral to his view that a virtue should not have bad effects.[10]

One way to avoid the discomfort of saying that a virtue can have bad features is to qualify our ascriptions of goodness to traits, even to traits that are standardly called virtues, and thus to say that a certain trait is a virtue in some situations but not in others. We can say, for example, that a certain kind of courage is a virtue in wartime, but in peacetime is not a virtue or may even be a vice. We thus relativize the term "virtue" through a relativization of the goodness ascribed to a trait, in order to avoid calling something good simpliciter if it contributes to something bad.

The same effect, however, can be achieved by a different strategy. This is to claim a difference in etiology between actions that we consider good and those that we take to be bad. Being a virtue or a vice, as I have said, is not simply a causal matter – that is, simply a matter of *causing* good or bad actions. Nevertheless, the causal role of a trait must obviously have something to do with its being a virtue. Sometimes one is inclined to say that a person's bravery leads him to do certain good actions that involve facing danger. On the other hand, when he does something very unwise through facing dangers that a sensible person would avoid, we may well say that what made him do it is not bravery but rashness. Bravery is good; rashness is bad. We thus find a bad cause for a bad thing, reserving the good cause to bring about good things. I have more to say below about this matter, because it seems to me symptomatic of a problem in our thinking. At the moment, I simply point out that this strategy is designed to avoid saying that something that is recognized to be in some way bad is nevertheless comfortably to be called a virtue.

For the moment, however, we can say that these reflections show how in determining which traits are virtues, we tend in ordinary thinking to effect a compromise between insisting that virtues never conflict and disregarding conflict entirely. But certainly we feel pressure to avoid such conflicts. The idea that there is absolutely nothing wrong with conflicts of virtues seems quite out of kilter with the obvious fact that interfering with a virtue seems like a bad thing.

I now offer some points about conflicts of virtues that make further use of the idea that virtues and vices play a role in the causing of actions and more generally figure in the whole network of causes and effects. First, however, some explanation is in order.

What a virtue causes, as I have said, is an important part of it – that is, both of its being the trait that it is and of its having the value that it has, which is essential to its being a virtue. This is true even though there is certainly more to virtues than causing actions and more, indeed, than causing emotions, thoughts, susceptibilities, and other things. What a trait causes cannot be ignored in assessing its claim to be considered a virtue.

This is so even though various causal results of virtues are not *merely* their effects – that is, they bear more than a merely cause-effect relation to them. The effects must also usually "make sense in the light of" them, for instance, and "manifest," "express," or "exhibit" them. Moreover actions, emotions, and thoughts are not merely coordinate effects of virtues. Bravery has both actions and emotions and thoughts among its characteristic effects, but these must be related to each other in various ways. For instance, the emotions must play certain roles in causing the actions, and the contents of the thoughts must be grounds of the actions. There are additional complexities as well.

Nevertheless, it remains true that virtues cause actions, emotions, thoughts, and more.[11] For instance, being brave must (normally) cause certain kinds of actions, which we tend (given further conditions) to call "brave actions." It is not enough, for instance, that the actions merely be "rational in light of" bravery. Otherwise, there would be nothing to explain either the fact that when facing of danger is required, you should prefer to have a courageous person around rather than a cowardly one, or the fact that an action done by A can manifest or express the courage of A rather than the courage of B even when it makes sense in the light of both. It is all right to say, if you like, that the actions "express" bravery and are not merely its causal consequences. Nevertheless, a cause-effect relation must certainly be in the works, and moreover must even be a part of what is involved in that kind of "expression" itself.

Accordingly, we may take it that virtues (and vices) are, inter alia, causes of actions and that these facts bear on their goodness and badness and hence on their status as virtues or vices. It is obvious, furthermore, that actions are causes of other things. Indeed, it is hard to see how something that was not a cause of further things could be an action at all. So traits cause quite a lot of things. This means that traits and the possession of them are firmly planted within the causal structure of the world. And this point applies to virtues and vices. Indeed, as I have said, part of what constitutes a particular trait as a virtue is that it plays a role in causing actions of certain kinds and does not cause actions of certain other kinds.

If we recognize that having bad consequences endangers the eligibility of a trait to be a virtue, then as I have noted we can regard Socrates as having carried this idea to the strict extreme of believing, first and quite generally, that a virtue cannot have any bad consequences at all and, second, that particular traits that Greeks of his day called virtues are in fact such. He was thus committed to holding, and did hold, that *those* particular traits do not have bad consequences. Furthermore, he thought that if a virtue has no bad consequences and if the blocking of the good consequences of a virtue is a bad consequence, then those virtues cannot clash.

The entanglement of virtues, as virtues, within the causal order is obviously relevant to conflicts among them, in a way that can be extended to conflicts of goods, and also has repercussions for other philosophical issues. Let us see how.

Many concepts of causal connections have no substantial connection with evaluation. We grasp the concept of solubility in water, for instance, without thinking about whether anything is good or bad or right or wrong. Normally, our determinations of which things are soluble in water are not subjected to any evaluative constraints. The same holds for very many concepts. Nevertheless, these concepts also are bound up with the causal order as we take it to be (quite apart from any particular analysis of what causation is). Being soluble is causally linked in some way to particular events of dissolving, and having weight is causally linked to particular events of falling. We can take note of these facts, too, without evaluating anything or being concerned with evaluations.

Concepts of virtues, on the other hand, offer interesting examples of concepts that are simultaneously linked both to evaluation and to causation. Moreover, the very use of them for evaluation depends on their being linked to certain kinds of causal transactions. A trait that is a vice, for instance, cannot too consistently cause good actions or else it will lose its title to being a vice and may even have to be considered a virtue instead. Moreover, this line of thought, as we have seen, can lead us to think that virtues must be compatible or perhaps must even support each other. This conclusion may be extreme. As noted, perhaps we should say that a trait can be "good enough" to be a virtue even if it causes some bad things or interferes with other virtues to some extent. Nevertheless, when not carried to an extreme, the kind of reasoning that leads us to deny that a virtue can be a crippling impediment to other virtues seems to be impeccable.

Problems can arise, however, when we try to coordinate the further causal and the evaluative aspects of virtues and vices. Recall the example of courage and rashness mentioned earlier. If we classify actions and their outcomes in accordance with whether they are good or bad, we may well say that a certain action was brought about not by courage but by rashness, and that a certain omission was brought about not by temperance but by priggishness. Here we take what seem salient features of the effects and draw conclusions about their causal antecedents. This way of thinking, as we saw, went along with certain tendencies that lead us to say that virtues cannot conflict.

Nevertheless, this way of thinking also raises problems when we adopt another viewpoint. If we examine the states of a person that lead to courageous and to rash actions, but do so without any attention at all to whether the actions are good or bad, we may well conclude, it seems, that these states are not distinguishable. One common thing to say would be that the conditions are not distinguishable in straightforwardly *physical* or *empirical* terms. But whether we invoke the notions of the "physical" or the "empirical" or not, it seems clear that when we consider the whole matter in this way, we shall have no ground for classifying the actions as arising from different sorts of causal antecedents. Courageous and rash actions will then seem to be classifiable together indiscriminately and to arise from the same cause, namely (in rough terms), a tendency not to be affected by danger or the thought of it. On this basis, then, we shall not be able to distinguish between the virtue of courage and the defect of rashness, nor the actions (or for that matter the emotions, etc.) to which they respectively give rise.[12]

Someone might object that the distinction between brave and rash actions was never intended to be a causal issue in the first place but is simply a matter of evaluating the actions without attention to causal connections. Thus, someone might say that brave actions are the good actions that are caused by a certain good degree of insusceptibility to danger, and correspondingly for rash actions. If that were so, then we would always try to determine the causes of actions without any attention to our evaluations of them or, for that matter, our evaluation of their causes.[13]

It would be quite wrong, however, to hold that we actually do think in this way. Quite the contrary, our evaluations of actions, as of other things, sometimes do lead us, for better or worse, to adjust our judgments about their etiology. A good example of this can be found, once again, in Socrates and Plato. Crudely described, Plato's tendency is to think that a consistently good series of actions results from "knowledge," whereas only an inconsistently good series of actions results from "(true) opinion" and a consistently bad series of actions results from badness or ignorance. Knowledge was not just taken as a good capacity for judgment and opinion as a bad one. Rather, all of these conditions were thought of as associated with various different kinds of causes and effect – for instance, knowledge would have been brought about in particular ways and have particular collateral effects, and so on.[14]

One way to think about Socrates and Plato is accordingly this. By holding that virtues are kinds of knowledge or are closely associated therewith, they tried to ensure that virtues would "track" good actions and the occasions for them. Courage would thus lead to good actions rather than bad ones because it would include, so to speak, an evaluative pilot that would steer it aright. It would thus not be regarded as a tendency to do the actions of some neutrally described type. This was a way of trying to keep a trait that one labels a virtue from undermining that label by leading to bad results.[15]

Some philosophers might hold that Plato's way of thinking, with its separate etiologies for good and bad actions, reflects a primitive state of scientific and philosophical thought and can therefore be ignored or discounted. Possibly, it does represent primitive explanatory thought, but if that is so, it is thought that is very deeply planted in our ordinary ways of looking at things. In setting up a rough network of causes and effects among our actions and traits and in labeling both causes and effects, ordinary thinking is influenced by nonevaluative causal judgments and by evaluative judgments simultaneously.[16] This tendency on our part is inseparable from our usual way of thinking about virtues.

It seems to be held, sometimes, that the existence of conflicts of goods shows straightforwardly that goods are "plural" or "incomparable." The matter is a good deal more complicated than that.

First, as is often observed, there can be conflicts between good *things* that are all good in the same sense and way. The fact that one cannot eat both pieces of cake does not show that they are good in different, let alone incomparable, ways. Moreover, the thesis that one should not call a thing "good" if it conflicts with anything else that is good does not show that we ever have cases of plural or incomparable goods. For there can be conflict between different incompatible *bearers* of one and the same value, without there being different or incomparable values. What is intended by "plural" or "incomparable" values is rather, so to speak, "plural" or "incomparable" *goodnesses* or "good-making properties".

Plainly, the thesis that goods in *this* sense can conflict, even if it is true, is not a premise apt for demonstrating that goods are plural. The reason is that the thesis that, in these words, "goods conflict" *presupposes* their plurality rather than serving as a ground for accepting it. If one wishes to be justified in saying, using the plural, that *goods* conflict, one should already have established that they are plural. Putative cases of mere conflict are not enough, because one needs some basis for supposing that the plural label is justified, that is, that the putative conflict is not a conflict of bearers of one and the same value.

What arguments such as Plato's try to do is to show that – the phenomenology of our experience of evaluative conflict notwithstanding – there cannot really be conflict at all. And if there *cannot* be conflict, then it seems fairly plain that there cannot be plural or incomparable values.[17]

This is why Plato's discussion in the *Republic* does not directly confront the question of whether values are plural. He does indeed examine something that looks like evaluative conflict, when he argues in Book IV for the partition of the soul. However, he does not take those conflicts to be conflicts of values, but only (at best) conflicts between evaluations made by, on the one hand, reason and, on the other, desires that are seated in other parts of the personality and that thus do not rise to the level of evaluative judgments. He does not examine the phenomenology of conflict with the serious aim of determining whether it forces us to acknowledge plural values. Rather, he adopts a different approach.

In effect he assumes from the start, as a working hypothesis, that there is but one kind of goodness. Then, after that hypothesis has yielded what seem to him adequate results, he takes it as thereby shown that there is only one kind of goodness. The hypothesis is expressed in his claim, noted earlier, that the ruler and the society that he describes are "perfectly good."[18] When he then discovers, within the ruler's soul and the society, what he thinks is an adequate way of identifying each of the traditionally acknowledged virtues, he takes it as sufficiently demonstrated that the hypothesis was correct. He then tells us that the rulers will come to understand what the good is (so as to be able to distinguish it from everything else) and will organize their city according to it. He does not, however, tell *us* what it is.[19]

Other philosophers have followed Plato in claiming that there is an all-embracing structure – individual, society, or the whole universe – possessing an overall goodness or perfection and that the evaluation of anything else is a matter of its contributing to that order by in some sense fitting into it. One thinks here of the Stoics, Hegel, and various theological views. The phenomenology of our experience of conflicts is discounted on the ground that it represents a merely partial outlook.

Such suggestions are in one way, of course, merely promissory notes, since as noted the account of all-embracing goodness actually does not come to light. Those who believe in plural or incomparable values are understandably skeptical about such promises and maintain that our actual experience is more powerfully on the side of saying that not all values are comparable.[20]

The current state of the discussion has something of the look of a stalemate. To put it roughly, the evidence of phenomenal experience is on the side of pluralism and considerations of system are on the other side. As I have said, however, we cannot settle the question by favoring the solidity of common sense over the artificial systematizations of philosophy, since, as I have noted, common sense, too, exhibits some inclination to avoid calling things good if they conflict with other things that are good.

I want to conclude by pointing out one lesson that seems to me to emerge from Socratic and Platonic reflections on the matter. I do not propose to side with them in hypothesizing away the possibility of conflict. That seems unpromising. However, I do think that they focus on something that we need to attend to, because it helps show why conflicts can sometimes seem so hard to settle or even to imagine settling.

The idea that things often need to be evaluated within broader contexts is not, I think, generally a good way to rule out the possibility of evaluative conflict. However, the existence and importance of such cases makes us aware of one significant reason why it is often so difficult to see how conflicts could be resolved. The aim of these last remarks is to begin to work toward an understanding of that difficulty itself.

What Plato saw is that many important evaluations are made globally rather than pointwise. What looks at first like a question about the intrinsic value of a thing taken by itself really involves evaluating that thing in a network of many other things. The problem is that even though we often sense clearly that such complex evaluations are called for, we recognize that we are very poorly equipped or positioned to carry them out. This fact is often the source of our befuddlement when we are faced with a need for difficult comparative evaluations.

Start with a datum on which everyone seems to agree. Sometimes it strikes us as impossible to compare two things clearheadedly. "Freedom or equality?" "Mozart of Michelangelo?" "Chalk or cheese?" "A career as a clarinetist or as a mathematician?" These are some examples. At first sight, the one seems neither better or nor worse than the other nor equally good, and it is not easy to think of a fourth possible relation.[21] It is difficult even to say what makes for the difficulty of comparing goods.[22] One tends in such cases simply to draw a blank when asked to compare values or to choose.

Some (I do not say all) of the difficulty arises from the fact that choices are almost always made within contexts, which are often quite large and complex or, on the other hand, may simply not be at all well defined. The pervasive difficulty is one of seeing what the context is to be taken to be, especially if it has ramifications for something as big as one's life or a society, let alone the history of the world or anything larger! Even one's own life is certainly not surveyable in more than a few respects. Still, one needs such surveyability if one is to take account of the fact that not a few choices not only have far-reaching consequences for it but – what is signally relevant here – fit into it in ways that one is aware exist but that one can scarcely identify clearly.

When one is confronted by an artificial philosophical example, such as a choice between "liberty and fraternity" or "Mozart and Michelangelo," it is utterly unclear what the context of the ranking is supposed to be. The problem may be one of covering value,[23] but there are also questions about what the situation within which the evaluation fits might possibly be. This can be partly an issue about causal interaction with other evaluations (What will happen if I say, "Mozart"?). However, it can also concern how the choice will fit into other parts of one's context and how the evaluation fits into some extensive or overall whole (how is account to be taken of the fact that I might come to live in a community for the deaf?).

The same is true of many less outlandish but more complex comparisons, such as one between "a career as a clarinetist" and "a career as a mathematician." Not only are "careers" complicated things; they are also embedded in complicated ways within even more complicated things, namely, lives. Asked to make the comparison, one is not too clear about how to fill out the two proposed pictures. The difficulty seems not so much to be to give the result of the comparative evaluation as to say what the comparison is.

These points are obvious, of course, but I think that even so, it is fair to say that they are not sufficiently attended to in the current discussion of incomparability. When they receive attention, we notice that one of the important factors that makes for difficulty or impossibility of comparison is the indefiniteness of the conditions under which contributive goodness is to be assigned.[24] It is hard to be clear about what the larger whole is to which contributions of value are pertinent, and also, once that be fixed, how contributive values can be assigned to components. Thus, the difficulty of making comparisons may be not that the proffered options are themselves intrinsically incomparable but that the comparative evaluation of them must – by the standards of evaluation that we normally try to employ – take into account contributive values that we cannot even begin to think about clearly.

The importance of contributive considerations dawns on us most vividly when we attend to such philosophical projects as Plato's attempt to think about how virtues are to be coordinated. If we ask how we might deal with trade-offs between virtues, we see that Plato was right to treat that issue as one of how traits fit together into a personality, even if the particular answer that he arrived at was mistaken. His discussion focuses on the fact that the fitting together of goods is often an inescapable problem. That realization, however, also makes us see how difficult and even impossible the question may be to answer clearly, even when it is inescapable, because the parameters of "fitting together" are so hard to be clear about.[25]

In addition, our evaluations of traits and other things involve a tricky interplay of evaluations and judgments about what causes or leads to what. Sometimes we find that our etiologies affect our evaluations, and sometimes vice versa. These combined issues of causation and evaluation are compounded when the relevant evaluations are made not pointwise of things singly but globally of things in groups. Then matters can become too complex for us to have a clear idea of what the evaluative comparison is that we are being asked to carry out. When complex options face us, this complexity can be a factor generating tensions in our evaluations that we simply do not know how to resolve.

Notes

Thanks to Christine Chwaszcza and Cynthia Freeland for helpful comments on previous drafts.

1. See Berlin 1969: xlix–l, liii–liv, and "The Pursuit of the Ideal," in Berlin 1991: 1–19.
2. See, e.g., Williams 1979; Sinnott-Armstrong 1988; and the essays in Chang 1997b. There exist also various older discussions, including, e.g., Ross 1930.
3. See, e.g., Griffin 1997. Chang 1997a argues convincingly that the important issue is comparability, not "commensurability."
4. The attitudes of Plato and Aristotle toward this thesis are a complicated matter; for some issues relevant to the present discussion, see White 2002: chs. 5 and 6.
5. I here swerve around issues concerning the fact that some uses of "good" are "attributive" and others are not. That matter can certainly complicate the discussion of Berlin's thesis.
6. See *Rep.* IV, 427e.
7. We thus see exhibited here one reason why in Plato's view, the discussions of the unity of virtue in which Socrates had engaged required an expanded treatment of the question of what the good is and in particular whether or not *it* "is one" – which the *Republic* certainly holds it is (504, 534, 541).
8. See Wiggins 1997 and Stocker 1997. Below I discuss the question of whether the "plurality" or the "incomparability" of goods can be inferred from the existence of conflicts.
9. See Foot 1978.
10. One illustration of tendencies in this direction is provided by Thrasymachus in *Rep.* I, 343a–344c, 348c–d, who will not call justice a virtue because he thinks it harms the relevant person, namely, the person who has it. The general claim is relied on in the *Meno*, e.g., at 96e–97a.

11. What causation is I do not attempt to say. I am not committed to any particular account of it. Nor do I say that a virtue must be "the" cause, though it must seemingly be more than just one among an undifferentiated set of causal factors.

12. Harman 2000 discusses some other ways in which talk of virtues arguably can diverge from what a more neutrally experimental approach might yield.

13. The tendency to think in this way is obviously stronger when one tries to think about the physical states on which some such traits might be thought to supervene, because talk of "physical states" is normally carried out with much less evaluative focus.

14. Consider the difference between a cocktail lounge and a dive. One might take the view that they are the same places, but simply labeled differently in accordance with whether one thinks them good or bad. But someone might think that they are two different kinds of places, each with its characteristic causes and effects. Cocktail lounges would be elegant, established by and for tasteful people with lots of money, whereas dives would be produced by poverty and undesirable social conditions and would lead to more of the same. Here, too, ordinary language allows a kind of interplay between evaluative and causal judgments.

15. See in this connection McDowell 1998: 51–3.

16. I find it unclear just how to take this point as relevant to Davidson's (1980) arguments for "anomalous monism," but there is pretty plainly a connection.

17. The merely actual absence of conflict could be accidental, and thus not sufficient to guarantee the conclusion.

18. See *Rep.* 427e. We may think of this as a hypothesis in this way, even if Plato did not regard himself here as employing his "method of hypothesis" (though I think that he probably did).

19. See *Rep.* 534b–c, 541a–b.

20. A different monist strategy is to argue that our notion of goodness somehow compels an evaluative ordering that covers all evaluated things, but without Platonic or similar structures to whose overall value other things allegedly contribute. Moore and Regan adopt this approach; pluralists such as Stocker and Wiggins are unconvinced here, too.

21. See esp. Chang 1997a: 26–7 for a suggestion.

22. Frequently, people say that the problem arises when the options are "very different" (see, e.g., Regan 1997: 131; Taylor 1997: 170). This seems to me mistaken. It is often very, very easy to choose between "very different" options, so degree of difference – whatever that is – cannot itself be what makes for difficulty of comparison.

23. See esp. Chang 1997a: 27–34.

24. See Gibbard 1973. Another problem is how to relate intrinsic goodness and contributive goodness. This is closely related to the problem of double bookkeeping that is discussed by Stocker 1990.

25. Taylor 1997 optimistically holds that seeing how goods are "integrated" into "our lives as a whole" (p. 183) will help us see how comparisons can be made between them. That seems to me to be the good news. The bad news is

that it will also help us see how difficult or even impossible the comparisons may be.

Bibliography

Aristotle 1984. *Nicomachean Ethics*, tr. W. D. Ross; rev. J. O. Urmson. In *The Complete Works of Aristotle: The Revised Oxford Translation*, ed. Jonathan Barnes. Princeton, N. J.: Princeton University Press.

Berlin, Isaiah. 1969. *Four Essays on Liberty*. Oxford: Oxford University Press.

Berlin, Isaiah. 1991. *The Crooked Timber of Humanity*. New York: Random House.

Chang, Ruth 1997a. Introduction. In Ruth Chang (ed.), *Incommensurability, Incomparability, and Practical Reason*. Cambridge, Mass.: Harvard University Press, 1–34.

Chang, Ruth (ed.). 1997b. *Incommensurability, Incomparability, and Practical Reason*. Cambridge, Mass.: Harvard University Press.

Davidson, Donald. 1980. Mental Events. In Donald Davidson, *Essays on Actions and Events*. Oxford: Oxford University Press, 207–25.

Foot, Philippa. 1978. Euthanasia. In Philippa Foot, *Virtues and Vices*. Oxford: Blackwell, 33–61.

Gibbard, Allan. 1973. Doing No More Harm Than Good. *Philosophical Studies* 24: 158–73.

Griffin, James. 1997. Incommensurability: What's the Problem?. In Ruth Chang (ed.), *Incommensurability, Incomparability, and Practical Reason*. Cambridge, Mass.: Harvard University Press, 35–51.

Harman, Gilbert. 2000. Moral Philosophy Meets Psychology. In Gilbert Harman, *Explaining Value and Other Essays*. Oxford: Oxford University Press, 165–78.

McDowell, John. 1998. Virtue and Reason. In John McDowell, *Mind, Value, and Reality*. Cambridge, Mass.: Harvard University Press, 50–73.

Moore, G. E. 1922. *Principia Ethica*, 1st ed. Cambridge: Cambridge University Press.

Plato. 1946. *The Republic*, tr. Paul Shorey. Cambridge, Mass., and London: Harvard University Press and Heinemann.

Plato. 1980. *Meno*, tr. G. M. A. Grube. Indianapolis, Ind.: Hackett.

Regan, Donald. 1997. Value, Comparability, and Choice. In Ruth Chang (ed.), *Incommensurability, Incomparability, and Practical Reason*. Cambridge, Mass.: Harvard University Press, 129–50.

Ross, W. D. 1930. *The Right and the Good*. Oxford: Oxford University Press.

Sinnott-Armstrong, Walter. 1988. *Moral Dilemmas*. Oxford: Oxford University Press.

Stocker, Michael. 1990. *Plural and Conflicting Values*. Oxford: Oxford University Press.

Stocker, Michael. 1997. Abstract and Concrete Value: Plurality, Conflict, and Maximization. In Ruth Chang (ed.), *Incommensurability, Incomparability, and Practical Reason*. Cambridge, Mass.: Harvard University Press, 196–214.

Taylor, Charles. 1997. Leading a Life. In Ruth Chang (ed.), *Incommensurability, Incomparability, and Practical Reason*. Cambridge, Mass.: Harvard University Press, 170–83.

White, Nicholas. 2002. *Individual and Conflict in Greek Ethics.* Oxford: Oxford University Press.

Wiggins, David. 1997. Incommensurability: Four Proposals. In Ruth Chang (ed.), *Incommensurability, Incomparability, and Practical Reason.* Cambridge, Mass.: Harvard University Press, 52–66.

Williams, Bernard. 1979. Conflict of Values. In A. Ryan (ed.), *The Idea of Freedom.* Oxford: Oxford University Press, 221–32.

10

Involvement and Detachment:

A Paradox of Practical Reason

Peter Baumann

If the world were perfect, it wouldn't be.

Yogi Berra

I am going to present what I think is an interesting paradox. I will first give an exposition of the paradox (which could be called a "preface paradox for goals" – for reasons that will become obvious soon). I will then deal with some objections and finally discuss a proposed solution to the paradox.

THE PARADOX

A good starting point is, as always, a triviality: Agents want their goals to be realized. More precisely:

(1) If an agent A has a goal G, then A wants that G will be realized (by A or somebody or something else).

This has to be taken in the *de dicto*-sense – hence not in the *de re*-sense of "something would constitute the goal's realization, and A wants it."[1] I use "A wants that p" in the strong sense of "All things considered, A prefers the truth of 'p' to the truth of 'not-p.'"[2]

Having a particular *desire* is, of course, compatible with not wanting its realization. Goals, however, are different: They imply the desiredness of their realization. It is simply incoherent to say something like, "I have this goal but I do not want to realize it."[3]

The following thing seems trivial also:

(2) Agents have many goals (at any particular time as well as throughout their lives).

As does this:

> (3) If an agent A has a finite number of goals $G_1, G_2, \ldots, G_n$, then A wants that G_1 will be realized, A wants that G_2 will be realized, $\ldots$, A wants that G_n will be realized.[4]

Can we infer the following (from (1) and (2) or from (2) and (3))?

> (4) Agents want that all their goals will be realized.[5]

No. If A has n goals $G_1, G_2, \ldots, G_n$, then it does not follow that A also has the conjunction of all these particular goals as a goal. A might just not "construct" the conjunction of all his particular goals. However, it would be irrational to have all those particular goals and still not accept their conjunction as a goal if one were asked, "Do you want all your goals realized?" Hence, the following seems also true:

> (5) If an agent has n different goals, then he has an indefeasible reason to accept the conjunction of his n different goals as a goal.

An indefeasible reason is a reason that is not "trumped" by another reason. More precisely, an indefeasible reason to x is a reason such that there is neither another, better reason not to x nor another equally strong reason not to x.[6] Two reasons are equally strong iff neither reason is better than the other reason and both reasons are commensurable with each other. Two reasons are commensurable iff either one of them is better than the other or this is not true but an additional amount of what makes one of these reasons a good reason (i.e., an additional amount of evidence, etc.) would (ceteris paribus) make this reason better as well as better than the other reason.[7] One could also call the case of equally strong reasons "indifference" of reasons. For example, I might have both a good reason to go to the movies tonight and a good reason not to go to the movies tonight (but rather to stay home). Nothing might speak against accepting both reasons as good reasons; none of the reasons might be better than the other one and both might be equally strong. In such cases, there is nothing wrong with throwing a coin or just picking one option.[8] And if additional evidence would make my reason to go to the movies a better reason, it would (ceteris paribus) also make it better than my reason not to go to the movies.

To be sure: When I say that a person has an indefeasible reason to accept something as a goal, I do not mean to imply that the person is aware of this reason. The person is not necessarily irrational if she does not see that there is an indefeasible reason to accept something as a goal. Other things might be on her mind. A fortiori, the person is not necessarily irrational if she does not make this goal her own. However, the person is irrational if she would not accept the reason or the goal in case she came to think about it and could, in principle, notice that it is a good reason. Hence, "having an indefeasible reason to accept something as a goal" has a counterfactual aspect.[9]

Now, (5) does not seem quite right as it stands. A's goals might be mutually incompatible. For logical, analytical, nomological, or particular contingent reasons it might be impossible to realize all of the goals from a given set of goals.[10] This seems to suggest the following thesis: If an agent has n different and mutually incompatible goals, then he has no indefeasible reason to accept the conjunction of his n different goals as a goal. Hence, (5) seems false. Is this true? Let us distinguish between two types of incompatibility between goals: incompatibilities that a rational agent can detect (by logical thinking, noticing of empirical data, etc.) and incompatibilities that a rational agent cannot detect. Since we are talking about human agents here, and since humans are even in the best case only nonideally rational agents,[11] it is really non-ideal, "human" rationality that matters here. Now consider an incompatibility of goals that a human agent could detect (let us call such an incompatibility "detectable").[12] A rational (human) agent would detect the incompatibility and change his system of goals in such a way that the incompatibility would disappear. Hence, since the problem I am talking about here is one about rational agency, the existence of detectable incompatibilities does not threaten (5).

What about incompatibilities of goals that a rational human agent cannot – given his limitations – detect ("undetectable" incompatibilities)? For instance, it might be beyond the grasp of even the best mathematicians that one cannot prove a particular theorem and at the same time stick with a certain mathematical theory.[13] Given the plausible principle that "ought" implies "can" and "cannot" implies "not ought," there is no basis for saying that an agent ought to do what he cannot do. Similarly, what we have reason to do is constrained by what we can do. It is not irrational not to do what we cannot do. Some incompatibilities are undetectable, and thus the agent is not irrational if he does not detect and remove such incompatibilities. But does he also have an indefeasible reason to accept the conjunction of his (undetectably) incompatible goals as a goal? I think he does, and here is why. The following general principle seems very plausible: If in cases of type C the agent has an (indefeasible) reason to X and if the agent cannot see a relevant difference between cases of type C and cases of type I, then he also has an (indefeasible) reason to X in cases of type I.[14] Hence, if (5) is true in the case of compatible goals, then it is also true in the case of undetectably incompatible goals.

The upshot of all this is that neither the existence of detectable nor the existence of undetectable incompatibilities between goals threatens (5). The reason mentioned in (5) is indefeasible because there is no better or equally good reason contrary to it. The topic of incompatibility can easily become a red herring; hence, it is a good idea to continue with the main line of the argument.

Now, (2) and (5) lead to

(6) An agent has an indefeasible reason to accept the conjunction of his n different goals as a goal.

(6) together with the rather trivial

(7) If an agent has an indefeasible reason to accept something as a goal, then he has an indefeasible reason to want that that goal will be realized

leads to

(8) An agent has an indefeasible reason to want that all his goals will be realized.[15]

What I said above about indefeasible reasons suggests

(9) If an agent has an indefeasible reason to x, then he does not have an indefeasible reason not to x.

(9) presupposes that reasons are commensurable in the sense that for every pair of reasons R_1 and R_2 it is true that either one of them is better than the other or they are equally good.[16] Hence, if R_1 and R_2 are commensurable and if R_1 is indefeasible, then there is no other reason (different from R_1) that is indefeasible. If R_1 is A's indefeasible reason to x, then there is – a fortiori – no indefeasible reason for A not to x. I come back to this point below and discuss an objection related to it.

(8) and (9) imply

(10) An agent does not have an indefeasible reason not to want that all his goals will be realized.

A fortiori, it is also true that

(10*) An agent does not have an indefeasible reason to want that not all his goals will be realized.

Now, my main problem here – which generates the paradox – is that the following seems also true:

(11) An agent has an indefeasible reason not to want that all his goals will be realized.

(11) is true because something stronger is true:

(11*) An agent has an indefeasible reason to want that not all his goals will be realized.[17]

Why (11) or (11*)? Well, if a person could (and would) realize all of her goals,[18] her life would not only be extremely successful but also extremely boring. This seems true even if we take into account that many bad things that happen are completely beyond our control and have nothing whatsoever to do with the goals we have. Even given that, most human beings would not consider a completely successful life worth living (for them). It is not that we just want to always have goals to pursue (which is also true). Rather, the point is that, in addition, we would not want to always succeed in realizing our goals. In other words, failure, too, is important to us (not only success). Not that anybody would like to have a life full of failures.[19] We do not value failure as such and we have no reason to do so. But if we had the choice (suppose this scenario makes sense) between (a) a life without any failure and (b) a life with some (but not too much) failure, we would rather choose (b). We would even be suspicious of (a). And rationally so. Even though human persons are goal pursuers, they want more: They *want* to be goal-pursuers[20] *and* they want to be goal-pursuers such that not all of their goals are realized. Happiness and the satisfaction of (first-order) preferences is important for us, but it is not everything that matters to us; we also have second-order goals such as the one just described. If all that is true, a person has a very good reason to want that not all of her goals will be realized.[21]

The upshot of all this is that (11*) and (11) are true, too. The reason mentioned in (11) or in (11*) is indefeasible because there is no better or equally good reason contrary to it.

Games offer a good analogy here. For each individual game of, say, Tetris we play, it is true that we want to win it. On the other hand, we do not want to win all of the individual Tetris-games we play. What is the point of playing a game you always win? Such games are boring. Sure, we also do not want to always or often lose. But some failure seems to be part of the attraction of a game. Life is like a game in this respect.[22] Goethe might have been up to something like this when he remarked that we can put up with everything but a couple of nice days. And Yogi Berra later added that if the world were perfect, it wouldn't be.

Now, given all that, the whole problem is this: (11) clearly contradicts (10), and (11*) contradicts (10*). And we seem to have very good arguments for both (10) (or (10*)) and (11) (or (11*)). Both arguments seem valid and use plausible premises. In other words: We have a paradox here – a paradox of practical rationality.

To put it differently: What we have here is both a reason to x and a reason not to x (cf. (8) and (11)). Neither of these reasons is better than the other. How could they be? Are they "equally strong"? In that case, none of these reasons would be indefeasible and the contradiction would disappear. One can have a reason to x and a reason not to x and both reasons might be equally strong reasons and good reasons (the case of "indifference"). One reason might tell me to go to the movies and the other might tell me not to go. There is nothing paradoxical about this. Does our case here differ significantly from cases of indifference? Yes! In the case of indifference, there is no problem at all with accepting both reasons at the same time. One can imagine how additional evidence could make one of the reasons a bit better and thus better than the other reason. And one can, for example, throw a coin to solve the practical problem of what to do. In our case, however, there is no such "peaceful coexistence." We must decide between both reasons. It would be inappropriate to throw a coin in order to settle the problem. In our case, we cannot imagine how additional evidence could make one of the reasons better. And even if there were such evidence, it would not make one reason better than the other. We cannot accept both reasons as equally strong reasons. Since neither one is better than the other, both reasons are indefeasible. Hence, we have a paradox here. What can we do about it? Since it is a paradox, something must be done about it.

Even if we have a hard time solving the paradox, we can already learn an interesting lesson from it. The contradiction between (10) and (11) or between (10*) and (11*) is based on a conflict between two perspectives that we take on our actions: the "involved" perspective of the agent who finds himself in a particular situation and tries to reach his particular goals and the "detached" perspective of the reflective person who takes a step back and looks beyond the limits of particular situations and goals. Both perspectives are important and irreducible; there does not seem to be any good reason to give up one of the perspectives for the sake of the other. In addition, it seems that we just cannot do that. That there is not only a tension between perspectives but a paradox about practical reason makes this duality of perspectives even more interesting.[23]

All this could also have interesting implications for our thinking about moral responsibility. I can give only a very rough hint here. Consider the example of a doctor who performs a lot of operations throughout her life. Since "nobody is perfect," she will make terrible mistakes from time to time ("terrible" because of the consequences). Let us assume that our doctor is excellent and makes very few terrible mistakes. If we think of these individual mistakes, we would tend to blame her and hold her morally responsible. However, if we think of all the operations she was doing and of the fact that she is such an excellent doctor, and if we add that nobody is perfect and that nobody can be blamed for not being perfect, then we would rather tend not to blame her and not to hold her morally responsible. In other words, it seems that we have both an indefeasible reason to hold her responsible for her mistakes as well as an indefeasible reason not to do so. If that is true, then it is not clear what consequences we should draw with respect to our thinking about moral responsibility.

SOME OBJECTIONS

I discuss three objections now that seem quite strong and suggest that nothing needs to be done here because there really is no paradox.

Working Hard for Success

One possible objection attacks the reasoning behind (11) and (11*). One could argue that a person might realize all her goals but not be bored at all because she often has to put a lot of effort into it. The realization of her goals might very often be hard work. Can't we like games we always win but only with much effort? Can't we enjoy the fact that the realization of our goals is not a trivial task? There is a lot of truth in this objection. However, it is doubtful whether this is a good objection against the ideas behind (11) and (11*). A lot depends on what exactly is meant by "realizing a goal with much effort." Consider the example of somebody who tries to write a good paper. If this is hard for the person, then she will typically need to write several different versions until she can come up with an acceptable (for her) final version. Consider the nonfinal versions. For at least some of these versions it is true that the person had the goal to make it a good version (and thus the final version). Sure, one can write a version of a paper (especially an early one) knowing that it probably will not be the final version and thus without having the goal to make it the final, acceptable version. But if it is really hard for the person to write a good paper, then there will be versions she wrote with the goal in mind to make them good versions but that she could not turn into good versions. In other words: If a person succeeds in realizing a goal but only with much effort, then at least in many cases she will need several attempts to realize her goal. But this, of course, implies that she was not always successful and did not manage to realize all of her goals (e.g., the goal to make the version that later turned out to be the second-last version the last version). Hence, the above objection does not show what it is supposed to show: namely, that a completely successful life could be interesting. It just is not about a completely successful life.

In addition to this "trial and error" aspect of goal pursuing, there is also very often a "goal/subgoal" structure.[24] To write a good paper, our person has to make a good argument. Suppose her conclusion follows from a set of three premises. To come up with a good argument, she has to make each of these premises plausible. Her overall goal to make a good argument thus consists in a series of (three) subgoals (to make each of the three premises plausible). If it is hard for the author to make the argument, then it is hard for her to reach the subgoals. That is, she will – in some cases at least – have to undergo the pain of trial and error with respect to her subgoals. This gives additional support to the above conclusion that nontrivial success at least often implies some failure.

But are there not cases in which the person does not have to try again and still has to put in a lot of effort? Are there such cases of "hard success without failure"? Consider Mike, who is very strong. He set himself the goal to lift his piano and hold it in the air for thirty seconds. He tries, puts a lot of effort into it, sweats, and screams – and succeeds. It seems that there is no failure involved here. He did not aim to lift the piano without any effort. On the contrary, the whole point was that it would not be easy. It seems that there really are cases such as this one. However, many cases are not like this. In such cases – which are usually also the more important ones – we do not have hard success without any failure. So, the upshot of all this is that we have good reason to stick with (11) and (11*). The paradox does not go away.

Future Goals

So far I have not said anything about the temporal aspect of having goals. One might suspect that this could lead to another objection. Let us start with some relatively unproblematic remarks about goals and time. Some goals are "time-specific" in the sense that their content indicates a time within which or at which the relevant event is supposed to happen. I might have the goal to reach you on the phone between now and midnight or at midnight. Some goals are very vague with respect to the relevant time, such as the goal of somebody who has never been to Mexico to go there some day. In this case, the relevant time might be any time during the person's life. Apparently, there are also goals that are not time-specific at all. A poet might have the goal that some day somebody will appreciate his poems. Goals can be realized a long time (even an indefinitely long time) after the death of the person who has this goal. Whether goals are time-specific or not, they are always held by a person at a certain time or during a certain time. And our goals change over time, perhaps not all of them (such as the goal to stay out of trouble) but many of them. Some goals disappear because they have been realized and others disappear because we could not realize them. We often give up goals because we decide they are not worth it or because we just forget them (which is an unconscious way of giving up a goal). In addition to that, we continue to develop new goals as we go along. We usually do so until the end of our life. This also explains why there are in almost everybody's life some goals that remain unfulfilled: We die before they could be realized. This fact, however, is much less interesting than an objection lurking behind it in the background.

Let us assume that a person has a set of goals S_1 between t_1 and t_2 and a set of goals S_2 at some later time, between t_3 and t_4.[25] Let us further assume – for the sake of simplicity – that no goal is a member of both S_1 and S_2. Let "P_1" refer to the person between t_1 and t_2 and "P_2" to the person between t_3 and t_4. Couldn't P_1 say "I want all the goals I now have realized but not all of the goals that I will have in the future [P_2's goals]"? P_1 has the set of goals S_1 but not the set of goals S_2. Hence, it is only true that

(12) P_1 has an indefeasible reason to want that S_1 will be realized (cf. (8))

and

(13) P_1 does not have an indefeasible reason not to want that S_1 will be realized (cf. (10)).

It is, however, also true that

(14) P_1 does not have an indefeasible reason to want that S_2 will be realized.

The reason is simply that P_1 does not have these goals (S_2). P_1 can coherently allow for the nonrealization of S_2. We can generalize this:

(15) P_1 does not have an indefeasible reason to want that all the goals she will ever have in life ($S_1, S_2, \ldots, S_n$) will be realized.

The argument behind (11) and (11*) also shows that

(16) P_1 has an indefeasible reason not to want that all the goals she will ever have in her life ($S_1, S_2, \ldots, S_n$) will be realized.

The whole point of the objection is that (13) (as well as (12)) does not contradict (16). Hence, there is no paradox. A person has an indefeasible reason to want the realization of her present goals. She can – without contradiction – at the same time have an indefeasible reason not to want the realization of all her present as well as future goals. The paradox is an apparent one and exploits an ambiguity of the phrase "all the goals": "all the present goals" versus "all the present as well as future goals."

I can think of two replies to this objection. First, one can argue that even with respect to the present goals of a person, the paradox arises because the person has an indefeasible reason not to want all of her present goals realized:

(17) P_1 has an indefeasible reason not to want that S_1 will be realized.

And (17) contradicts (13). Hence, our paradox does not go away.

There is another reply. It denies (14) and (15). P_1 does indeed have an indefeasible reason to want S_2 realized even though P_1 does not (yet) have the set of goals S_2.[26] S_2 is not just any set of goals. It is not like another person's goals. It is a set of some of P_1's future goals. P_1 is the same person as P_2. Hence, P_1 has a good reason to be interested in P_2's well-being, that is, in his own future well-being.[27] He has good reason to "identify" himself with his future self. We can say that

(18) P_1 has an indefeasible reason to want that S_2 will be realized

and

(19) P_1 does not have an indefeasible reason not to want that S_2 will be realized.

We can generalize this:

(20) P_1 has an indefeasible reason to want that all the goals she will ever have in life $(S_1, S_2, \ldots, S_n)$ will be realized

and

(21) P_1 does not have an indefeasible reason not to want that all the goals she will ever have in life $(S_1, S_2, \ldots, S_n)$ will be realized.

(21), of course, contradicts (16). Hence, the paradox is still with us.

Conditional Goals

Here is still another major objection. Don't we have conditional goals? More precisely: Couldn't it be true that some of our goals have the following logical form (with parantheses indicating scope):

A has the goal that (p, but if and only if not all other goals are going to be realized).[28]

We need to assume not that all our goals are conditional but only that some of them are (we can leave open how many would be enough). Conditionality of this sort implies some kind of holism. One cannot understand and pursue one (conditional) goal without having other goals in mind. To be sure: Having the goal that (p, but if and only if not all other goals are going to be realized) does not imply that one has a certain other particular goal. But it requires that one keeps one's other goals in mind, whatever they are. Conditionality also implies a certain kind of indeterminacy. If A has just two different goals, namely,

the goal that (p, but if and only if not all other goals are going to be realized)

and

the goal that (q, but if and only if not all other goals are going to be realized),

then we can neither infer that A will try to bring it about that p nor that A will try to bring it about that q. What we can say is that A will try to bring it about that either p or q. This again shows the nonatomistic nature of conditional goals: The person who pursues them has complex sets of goals in mind and not just lots of isolated individual goals.

How does conditionality bear on our thesis that there is a paradox about goals? Well, it seems possible that all the goals (conditional and unconditional) of a person are being realized without any threat of boredom or life losing its point. Let us (for the sake of simplicity) assume that a person has just two goals, both of them conditional:

the goal that (p, but if and only if not all other goals are going to be realized)

and

the goal that (q, but if and only if not all other goals are going to be realized).

Let us further assume that she brings it about that p but not q. This means that all her goals are realized even though she did not bring it about that both p and q. The latter seems to guarantee that life will not be boring or lose its point. Hence, there is no way to get to (11) or (11*) and the paradox is gone. By the way, one might reply that this objection also cuts the other way: Isn't it really *p and q* that matters here? Shouldn't we say that there still is an important sense in which the person has not realized all her goals? I do not think so: These really are conditional goals.

The problem with this conditionality objection is that it is hard to see why one should think that we have such conditional goals. The main motivation to assume this seems to be that it would avoid the paradox. This, however, is an ad hoc argument and thus not a good one. Moreover, it seems more psychologically realistic to assume that people do not have these kinds of goals; at least, it seems that many of us do not and for those of us who do, it seems to be an exception rather than the rule. Even if some of us sometimes have such conditional goals, this would not make a difference big enough to threaten the ideas behind (11) or (11*).

To avoid a possible misunderstanding, I am not saying that we do not have goals such as this one:

Ann has the goal that (she makes it to the movies tonight if and only if she does not reach her goal to convince Jack to prepare dinner for her).

But is this not a perfect example of a conditional goal? No, not in the above sense. For conditional goals in that sense, the nonattainment of other goals as such is an essential part of the content of the goal, no matter what these other goals are. Not so in the example just given. Here the individuality of the other goals matters but not their realization as such and independently from their content. We can reformulate the description of Ann's goal without loss of something essential in the following way:

Ann has the goal that (she makes it to the movies tonight if and only if she does not convince Jack to prepare dinner for her).

Here, mention of "goal attainment" is not an essential part of a description of the content of the goal. However, it is essential in the case of conditional goals. Hence, we cannot reformulate the description of conditional goals in the same way in which we can reformulate a description of Ann's goal. This shows that Ann's goal is not a conditional goal in the sense that is relevant here. Furthermore, Ann's goal presupposes that she has two individual goals (make it to the movies; convince Jack to cook) such that success with respect to one of them is linked with failure with respect to the other one. There will thus be some failure. However, the idea of conditional goals is introduced here as a way to circumvent the possibility of failure.

I want to end this section with three shorter objections. The first has to do with (9) above. I said that (9) presupposes the commensurability of reasons. But couldn't one deny the commensurability of reasons, let (9) collapse, and say that the reasons behind (10) and (11) (and (10*) and (11*)) are incommensurable? If yes, then the paradox disappears and an incommensurability between the reasons mentioned in (8) and (11) would take its place:

(8) An agent has an indefeasible reason to want that all his goals will be realized

and

(11) An agent has an indefeasible reason not to want that all his goals will be realized

would both be true.

This would certainly be an interesting alternative and perhaps even still another argument for the possible incommensurability of reasons for action.[29]

However, it would, I think, not be very convincing. Why should one assume that there is an incommensurability here – just because this would avoid the contradiction? There might even be incommensurabilities somewhere else (we can leave that open), but why here? To assume incommensurability between the reasons mentioned in (8) and (11) would seem ad hoc and perhaps even question begging (against the paradox). I can see no independent argument that would show that we face incommensurable reasons here. One certainly cannot avoid a contradiction just by assuming that it really is a case of incommensurability.

It also does not help at all to take the contradiction as evidence against the idea that our two reasons are both indefeasible reasons. This would, again, beg the question against the argument that there is a paradox here. Similar problems arise if one considers the above contradiction as a reductio of the assumptions behind (11) or (11*) or, alternatively, of the assumptions behind (10) or (10*). This would be ad hoc, motivated only by the fact that rejecting those assumptions avoids the contradiction. One would need independent reasons showing that the arguments leading to (11) and (11*) – or to (10) and (10*) – are not acceptable. It is hard to see any reasons such as that. It seems that there really is a paradox. So what can we do?

WHAT IS TO BE DONE?

First, this paradox resembles the well-known preface paradox for beliefs.[30] It is quite reasonable for an author of a book to assume (in the preface) that not everything she says in the book is true. We know we are not infallible, and it is only rational to assume that we make mistakes from time to time. On the other hand, it can be perfectly rational for an author to sincerely believe every single thing she says in the book; in this case it is also rational to believe that everything said in the book is true. This, of course, leads to a contradiction; the same contradiction arises for everybody who holds a plurality of beliefs. You cannot escape the preface paradox by writing no books or only books without prefaces.

There is a convincing solution to the preface paradox for beliefs that goes back to Frank Ramsey.[31] Beliefs are no yes/no matter but rather allow for different degrees. This allows us to assign subjective probabilities close to 1 (but below 1) to belief contents such that (according to the probability calculus) the conjunction of many of those contents is assigned a very low probability (especially if they are probabilistically independent from each other). The person can thus hold each and every particular belief (even assigning a very high subjective probability to it) and still not bet much on the conjunction of those contents.

One might expect or hope that there is an analogous solution to our ("preface") paradox for goals. Unfortunately, however, nothing like that will do, even if we assume degrees of desiredness (rational or not) similar to degrees of belief. The attempted analogy breaks down because there is no way to compute the degree of desiredness of a conjunction exclusively on the basis of the degree of desiredness of the conjuncts. To have a coffee now might have a desiredness of .9, and to read a novel now one of .5. It simply does not follow that, for example, the desiredness (rational or not) of reading a novel and at the same time having a coffee is below each single desiredness (say, .45). There are no implications whatsoever as to the desiredness (rational or not) of the conjunction. The combination of coffee and novels might have any possible degree of desiredness without rendering the person irrational. Hence, the strategy to solve our problem by exploiting the analogy to the preface paradox for beliefs and to a Ramseyan solution of it will not work. The question remains an open one: What can we do?

Notes

I would like to thank Monika Betzler, Luc Bovens, Jon Cameron, Ruth Chang, Michael Clarke, Gisela Cramer, Christoph Fehige, Jörg Fehige, Harry Frankfurt, Ulrike Heuer, Luis Eduardo Hoyos Jaramillo, Keya Maitra, Bob Plant, Wlodek Rabinowicz, Abdul Raffert, Neil Roughley, Thomas Schmidt, Jörg Schroth, and an audience at the University of Memphis for discussions and for comments on earlier versions of this paper.

1. Sentences such as (1) could raise the question of whether we are allowed to quantify into intensional contexts and what the exact logical analysis of such sentences is. However, we do not have to deal with this question here since nothing essential hinges on it and the crucial point is pretty clear.
2. Some goals are recurrent: At t_1, I want to eat; after eating, at t_2, I do not want to eat any more; some time later, at t_3, I regain the goal to eat something. Has my goal to eat been realized or not? The situation at t_2 seems to suggest a positive answer, whereas the situation at t_3 seems to suggest a negative answer. If one looks more closely at the situation, one realizes that the answer must be positive: At t_1, my goal was, more precisely, to eat something *soon*. At t_2 this goal has been realized. My goal at t_3 was to eat something soon. This goal is of

the same type as the former one (eating soon, whenever that might turn out to be). However, it is a different particular goal because t_1 is different from t_3 and the identification of the time belongs to the full description of the respective goal. Hence, it is important to distinguish between the realization of a particular token of a goal (eating at t_2, etc.) and the realization of a type of goal (eating soon, whenever that might turn out to be). The former sense of "goal" is the relevant one here. One other point to be mentioned is that goals differ with respect to their importance for the person. For the sake of simplicity, I disregard this complication here; it would only make the argument more complicated than necessary.

3. This reminds one of Moorean sentences, such as, "It's raining but I don't believe it" (see Moore 1952: 542f.). The incoherence above differs from Moore's paradox insofar as it is not tied to the first person or the present tense.

4. The case of infinitely many goals is more tricky but also much less realistic; hence, we do not have to deal with it here. The attributions of wants above are *de dicto*, again, and not *de re*.

5. This is taken in the *de dicto*-sense.

6. The word "indefeasible" could create the impression that indefeasible reasons *cannot* be overriden by other reasons. However, given the explanations above, it only follows that indefeasible reasons *are in fact* not defeated by other reasons. One could alternatively say: *Given* the reasons the person has, an indefeasible reason cannot be defeated. Indefeasible reasons are not overriding reasons (see Raz 1986: 339). Somebody has an overriding reason to x iff he has a better reason to x than not to x and if this reason is a good reason to x (rather than no or no good reason to x). To put it differently: A reason to x is an overriding reason to x iff it is stronger than any reasons not to x. I confine myself here to indefeasible reasons, but one could, perhaps, make a similar argument in terms of overriding reasons.

7. See Raz 1986: 325 (who does not accept this as a definition, though). According to the completeness axiom of classical decision theory, either two options are equally good or one is better than the other (see, e.g., Luce and Raiffa 1957: 223, 25).

8. See Ullmann-Margalit and Morgenbesser 1977 for the idea of "picking" rather than "choosing" an option.

9. One could call this use of "reason" an "objective" use and contrast it with a "subjective" use that implies that the person is in fact aware of the reason. (5) is much less convincing if one takes "reason" in the subjective sense.

10. Two goals are logically incompatible if their contents contradict each other; two goals are analytically incompatible if their contents "analytically contain" a contradiction (let us not worry about analyticity here); two goals are nomologically incompatible if there is a law of nature excluding the realization of both goals; two goals are incompatible for particular contingent reasons if they cannot both be realized because of contingent singular circumstances. By the way: Neither does incompatibility imply incommensurablity nor does the latter imply the former.

11. See, e.g., Simon 1983: 3ff.

12. The distinction between what we can and what we cannot detect is, of course, very vague; in many cases it is not clear at all whether the agent could or could not do it.

13. I owe this point and example to Ruth Chang.

14. In this sense of "subjective" (not to be confused with the one mentioned above), rationality is subjective.

15. This is taken in the *de dicto*-sense and collectively, not distributively.

16. See, however, Chang 1997a: 25–7.

17. This is taken in the *de dicto*-sense and collectively, not distributively.

18. To avoid possible misunderstandings: I do not have the case in mind in which a person can realize a goal immediately or without any effort (see the first objection below on the aspect of effort).

19. For an argument on why an agent cannot always or very often fail to reach his goals, see Baumann 1996: 50–7.

20. See, e.g., Frankfurt 1992: 13ff. and Ullmann-Margalit 1992: 73ff.

21. For the sake of simplicity, I am assuming here that the person is never ignorant or in error about the sucesses and failures of the actions she has performed. Nothing essential changes (it only gets more complicated) if we make the more realistic assumption that people are sometimes ignorant (we forget things) or in error about their past failures and successes. A lot would change if we would assume that people are often or always ignorant or in error about the outcome of their past actions. This, however, is not a realistic assumption at all and we can disregard it for this reason. To be sure, very often an agent cannot know in advance whether he will succeed or fail to reach the goal he is just trying to realize. However, past experiences gives him a lot of evidence about what can be expected for the future. So, the element of ignorance about some future outcomes does not make an extremely successful life substantially less boring.

22. This also tells us something about the idea of omnipotence. To be sure, the completely successful agent as such is not necessarily omnipotent: He can realize all the goals he in fact has, but not necessarily all possible goals. However, a completely successful agent would probably develop more and more goals and thus "converge" toward omnipotence. My argument suggests that omnipotence is not a good ideal for human beings.

23. See, of course, Nagel 1986.

24. See Bratman 1987 for the importance and complex structure of plans.

25. One could be tempted to think that in the last analysis persons have goals at points of time rather than during time intervals. This, however, is highly unrealistic. No human being can have a goal just for a millisecond. If an extremely short time interval is too short, then a fortiori an extensionless point of time is much too short.

26. That I want that my future goal F (that p) will be realized does not imply that I already have goal F. Suppose that I do not want that p now (or even want that not-p); suppose further that I know that I will want that p in the future. Hence, we can say that I have a want of the following form:

    (a) I now want that (p, if/ as soon as I have the goal that p).

We also assumed that

    (b) I will have the goal that p.

  (a) and (b) do, of course, not imply

    (c) I now want that p.

Hence, we can also avoid the conclusion that I both do want that p and do not want that p. Analoguously, I might want that you reach your goals without sharing your goals.

27. Some philosophers – such as Parfit 1984 – deny both this view of personal identity and its implications for practical rationality. I cannot go into these discussions here. It is clear that there is a certain (rational) bias toward the present; this, however, does not effect my reply to the objection above.

28. Goals can be "conditional" in still another sense: "If and only if not all other goals are going to be realized, then A has the goal that p." It is, of course, impossible that all our goals are like that. Everything would "hang in the air." It would be completely indeterminate what the person would be trying to do. So, let us assume that only some of our goals are like that. Does this case show anything interesting about our paradox? I do not think so. It tells us only that there are certain conditions under which persons develop certain goals.

29. See the contributions in Chang 1997b. Chang 1997a prefers the expression "incomparability" to "incommensurability"; nothing substantial depends on it and I use the latter expression because talk about "incomparable" goals or reasons sounds a bit odd. I would, of course, be pleased if friends of incommensurability would find my argument useful for their own purposes.

30. See Makinson 1965: 205ff.

31. See Ramsey 1990: 111.

Bibliography

Baumann, Peter. 1996. Mephistos Problem: Über den Zusammenhang von Absichten und Handlungserfolgen. In Christoph Hubig and Hans Poser (eds.), *Cognitio Humana – Dynamik des Wissens und der Werte. XVII Deutscher Kongress für Philosophie (Leipzig 1996)*. Leipzig: Institut für Philosophie, vol. 1, 50–7.

Bratman, Michael. 1987. *Intention, Plans, and Practical Reason*. Cambridge, Mass.: Harvard University Press.

Chang, Ruth. 1997a. Introduction. In Ruth Chang (ed.), *Incommensurability, Incomparability, and Practical Reason*. Cambridge, Mass.: Harvard University Press, 1–34.

Chang, Ruth (ed.). 1997b *Incommensurability, Incomparability, and Practical Reason*. Cambridge, Mass.: Harvard University Press.

Frankfurt, Harry. 1992. On the Usefulness of Final Ends. *Iyyun: The Jerusalem Philosophical Quarterly* 41: 3–19.

Luce, R. Duncan, and Howard Raiffa. 1957. *Games and Decisions: Introduction and Critical Survey*. New York: Wiley.

Makinson, D.C. 1965. The Paradox of the Preface. *Analysis* 25: 205–7.

Moore, George Edward. 1952. A Reply to My Critics. In Paul Arthur Schilpp (ed.), *The Philosophy of G. E. Moore* (The Library of Living Philosophers, vol. IV, 2nd ed.). New York: Tudor, 533–677.

Nagel, Thomas. 1986. *The View from Nowhere*. Oxford: Oxford University Press

Parfit, Derek. 1984. *Reasons and Persons*. Oxford: Clarendon.

Ramsey, Frank P. 1990. Knowledge. In Frank P. Ramsey, *Philosophical Papers*, ed. David Hugh Mellor. Cambridge: Cambridge University Press, 110f.

Raz, Joseph. 1986. *The Morality of Freedom*. Oxford: Clarendon.

Simon, Herbert A. 1983. *Reason in Human Affairs*. Stanford, Calif.: Stanford University Press.

Ullmann-Margalit, Edna. 1992. Final Ends and Meaningful Lives. *Iyyun: The Jerusalem Philosophical Quarterly* 41: 73–82.

Ullmann-Margalit, Edna, and Sidney Morgenbesser. 1977. Picking and Choosing. *Social Research* 44: 757–85.

11

Outcomes of Internal Conflicts in the Sphere of *Akrasia* and Self-Control

Alfred R. Mele

Practical conflicts include conflicts in agents who judge, from the perspective of their own values, desires, beliefs, and the like, that one prospective course of action is superior to another but are tempted by what they judge to be the inferior course of action. A man who wants a late-night snack, even though he judges it best, from the identified perspective, to abide by his recent New Year's resolution against eating such snacks until he has lost ten pounds, is the locus of a practical conflict. So is a woman who judges it best (in the same way) to run a mile this morning but is tempted to spend the entire morning working in her office instead. The topic of this essay is practical outcomes of conflicts of this kind. My concern, more specifically, is with outcomes of two general kinds: akratic (from the classical Greek term *akrasia*: want of self-control) and enkratic (from *enkrateia*: self-control) actions.

Strict akratic action may be defined as free, sane, intentional action that the agent consciously believes at the time of action to be inferior to another course of action that is open to her then, inferior from the perspective of her own values, desires, beliefs, and the like.[1] The belief against which an agent acts in strict akratic action may be termed a *decisive* belief. An agent's belief that *A* is the best of his envisioned options at a given time is a decisive belief, in my sense, if and only if it *settles* in the agent's mind the question which member of the set is best (from the perspective of his own desires, beliefs, etc.) and best not just in some respect or other (e.g., financially) but without qualification.[2] Ann believes that *A*-ing would be morally (or aesthetically, or economically) better than *B*-ing, and yet, in the absence of compulsion, she intentionally *B*-s rather than *A*-s. In *B*-ing, Ann need not be acting akratically; for she may also believe, for example, that on the whole, *B*-ing would be better than *A*-ing.

Elsewhere, I have argued that strict akratic action is possible (see Mele 1987). I take that possibility for granted here. I also have argued for the possibility of a derivative kind of akratic action in scenarios featuring a last-minute change of decisive belief or judgment (see Mele 1996b). I discuss such action below in the section titled "Socratic Akratic Actions and Enkratic Counterparts."

Akratic action is one possible outcome of a practical conflict of the kind at issue here, and enkratic action is another. Aristotle examines akratic action in connection with the trait of character *akrasia* (see, e.g., *Nicomachean Ethics*, bk. 7, chs. 1–10). The contrary of this trait is *enkrateia*, or self-control (*Nicomachean Ethics* 1145a15–18).[3] Faced with practical conflicts of the kind that concern me here, agents seemingly may either succumb to temptation or master it.[4] My question is how these outcomes come to be.

GARDEN-VARIETY AKRATIC AND ENKRATIC ACTIONS

In some cases of akratic action, agents intend in accordance with a decisive belief that favors *A*-ing and then backslide (see Mele 1987). In others, they do not make the transition from decisive belief to intention (see Audi 1979; Davidson 1980, 1985: 205–6; Rorty 1980; Mele 1987: 34–5, 52–4). Elsewhere, I have argued that akratic actions of both kinds are possible (see Mele 1987). In the present section, I first discuss akratic actions of the second kind and enkratic counterpart actions and then turn to akratic actions of the first kind and their enkratic counterparts.

Many decisive beliefs favoring specific courses of action are arrived at on the basis of practical reasoning. It is a truism that practical reasoning is reasoning about what to do. One might say that it is reasoning conducted with a view to answering the question "What shall I do?" (That question must be distinguished from "What will I do?" The former calls for a decision or at least the acquisition of an intention. The latter calls for a prediction.) Sometimes people faced with this practical question reason about what it would be best to do. A natural hypothesis about this fact is that they do this because they are concerned to *do* what it would be best to do and have not yet identified what that would be. (At other times, agents may settle – and rationally so – on the first alternative that strikes them as good enough: for example, when they take little to be at stake and believe that the cost required to identify the best alternative would probably outweigh the benefits.) In such cases, if things go smoothly, decisive best judgments issue in corresponding intentions. This is no accident, given what motivates the reasoning that issues in the judgments. Elsewhere, I have defended the idea that practical reasoning is an inferential process, involving evaluative premises, driven at least partly by motivation to settle on what to do (see Mele 2003: ch. 4; 1992: ch. 12; 1995: ch. 2). This settling motivation naturally disposes agents to intend in accordance with the reasoning's evaluative conclusion, since agents become settled on a course of action in forming or acquiring an intention. Their being so disposed supports the primary point of practical reasoning, which is to lead to a satisfactory *resolution* of one's practical problem. An agent who decisively judges it best to *A* but is still unsettled about whether to *A* has not resolved his practical problem.

If common sense can be trusted, things do not *always* go smoothly: People can identify the better and – owing partly to the influence of recalcitrant desires – intend the worse. This shows not that decisive beliefs have no role to play in the etiology of intentions and intentional behavior, but rather that the formation or acquisition of a decisive belief in favor of a prospective course of action does not ensure the formation or acquisition of a corresponding intention. In Mele 1987, I attempted to explain *how* this can be true, how decisive beliefs may be rendered ineffective by competing motivation. Here I am concerned both with how this can happen and with how decisive beliefs can be rendered effective by means of exercises of self-control.

In Mele 1992 (ch. 12), I argued that a common route from decisive beliefs that it is best to *A* to intentions to *A* is a default route. Consider *default* procedures in computing, for example, a standard procedure in common word-processing programs for the spacing of text. When authors create new documents, any text they type will be displayed single-spaced, unless they preempt this default condition of creating a document by entering a command for an alternative form of spacing. When authors do not issue a preemptive command and their software and machines are working properly, starting a new document systematically has the identified result. Similarly, in the absence of preemptive conditions (e.g., recalcitrant desires) in normally functioning human beings, their decisively judging it best to *A* might systematically issue in an intention to *A*. Forming a decisive judgment in favor of *A*-ing might figure importantly, by default, in the production of an intention to *A* in particular cases, even if the transition from such judgments to such intentions is blocked in other cases – even if the disposition to make that transition is defeasible.

The basic idea is that "normal human agents are so constituted that, in the absence of preemption, [decisively] judging it best . . . to *A* issues directly in the acquisition of an intention to *A*" (Mele 1992: 231). In simple cases involving little or no motivational opposition, the transition from judgment to intention is smooth and easy. In such cases, having reached a decisive best judgment in favor of *A*-ing, we have no need to reason or even think about whether to intend to *A*; nor, given our motivational condition, do we need to exercise self-control to bring it about that we intend to *A*. No special intervening effort of any sort is required. The existence in normal human agents of a default procedure of the sort described would help to account for the smoothness and ease of the transition. Indeed, we should expect an efficient action-directed system in beings who are capable both of making deliberative judgments and of performing akratic actions to encompass such a procedure. Special energy should be exerted in this connection only when one's decisive beliefs or judgments encounter significant opposition. When one akratically fails to intend in accordance with one's decisive judgments, opposition is encountered: Something blocks a default transition.

Three kinds of case in which one's decisive judgment in favor of *A*-ing is opposed by competing motivation are distinguishable: (1) a default process unproblematically generates an intention to *A* even in the face of the opposition; (2) the agent forms an intention to *A* even though the default route to intention is blocked by the opposition; and (3) the motivational opposition blocks the default route to intention and figures in the production of an akratic intention. What is needed is a principled way of carving up the territory. In Mele 1992, I suggested that a continent intention is produced (in the normal way) by default, as opposed to being produced via a distinct causal route, when and only when (barring causal overdetermination, the assistance of other agents, science fiction, and the like) no intervening exercise of *self-control* contributes to the production of the intention (233). (Sometimes opposing motivation is sufficiently weak that no attempt at self-control is called for.) If the move from best judgment to intention does not involve a special intervening effort on the agent's part, the intention's presence typically may safely be attributed to the operation of a default procedure.

Self-control also plays an important role in explaining why, when a default route from best judgment to intention *is* blocked, we sometimes do, and sometimes do not, intend on the basis of our decisive judgments. Barring the operation of higher-order default processes, overdetermination, interference by intention-producing neurosurgeons, and so on, whether agents intend in accordance with their decisive judgments in such cases depends on their own efforts at self-control. In simple cases of self-indulgence, agents make no effort at all to perform the action judged best or to form the appropriate intention. In other cases, having decisively judged it best to A, agents might attempt in any number of ways to get themselves to A or to get themselves to intend to A. They might try focusing their attention on the desirable consequences of A-ing or on the unattractive aspects of not A-ing. They might generate vivid images of both. If all else fails, they might seek help from a behavioral therapist. Whether their strategies work will depend on the details of the case, but strategies such as these *can* have a salutary effect, as empirical research on delay of gratification and behavior control indicates.[5]

Now, even agents who, in accordance with a decisive judgment, intend to A straightaway may backslide. There is time for their intentions to A to be replaced by competing intentions. So at least I have argued elsewhere (see Mele 1987: 42–8, 19–21). Successfully exercising self-control in bringing it about that one intends in accordance with a decisive judgment favoring one's A-ing straightaway does not ensure that one will even try to A. What is an agent to do?

The move from a decisive A-favoring judgment to an intention to A is progress toward A-ing (see Mele 1992: 72–7). In the face of strong competing motivation, further progress can be made by means of techniques of the sort already mentioned. I illustrate this point with a three-part story.

Part I is from Mele 1987 (34–5). John's Biology 100 lab assignment is to ascertain his blood type by pricking his left index finger with a needle and examining a sample of his blood under a microscope. John, who is averse to drawing blood from himself, weighs his reasons in favor of executing the assignment against his contrary reasons and decisively judges that it would be best to prick his finger straightaway with sufficient force to release a suitable amount of blood for the experiment. He intends to act accordingly, and he moves the needle toward his finger with the intention of drawing blood. However, executing his intention is more difficult than he thought it would be. When John sees the needle come very close to his skin, he stops. His intention to prick his finger is replaced by an intention to halt the process. John retains his decisive belief in favor of pricking his finger straightaway, but he has lost his matching intention. (I argue for the coherence of this case in Mele 1987: ch. 3. See Mele 2002a for a critique of arguments for the thesis that agents in such cases do not act freely and therefore do not perform strict akratic actions.)

Part II of the story picks up a few seconds later. John is disappointed with himself for chickening out. He still believes that it would be best to prick his finger, and he tries to talk himself into doing so. John reflects on two things: how to make it easier for himself to prick his finger and how to motivate himself to do so. He judges that if he did not look at the needle, it would be easier to execute his assignment. Emboldened by this thought and spurred on by motivation intentionally primed by reflection on how silly he would look to his friends if they were to discover that he chickened out on this modest assignment, John decides to prick his finger straightaway. He tries again, this time without looking. But when he feels the needle touch his finger, he stops. He backslides again.

Now for part III. In part II, John tried to exercise self-control in support of his decisive judgment and failed to prick his finger even so. Are things hopeless for him? John thinks not. He is angry with himself for chickening out again. John wants to prove to himself that he is not a chicken, and he consciously lumps this consideration together with all the others that speak in favor of executing the assignment. He also concentrates on thinking clearly about the intensity of the pain that he expects to experience: He suspects that he must somehow be unconsciously overestimating how much it will hurt. Having done all this, John is again confident about his prospects of success. He decides again to prick his finger. This time he succeeds, flinching just a little.

On my view (see Mele 1987: chs. 1–7; 1995: chs. 3 and 4; 2003: chs. 7 and 8), the trick to successful self-control in cases of the kind at issue is bringing it about that the course of action favored by one's strongest motivation is the course of action already favored by one's decisive belief or judgment.[6] Other things being equal, if it is within one's power to do this, it is within one's power to act enkratically in accordance with one's better judgment. In practical conflicts of the kind I have been discussing, the outcome turns on whether or not the agent successfully exercises self-control. The etiology of successes and failures in this area is a difficult and fascinating topic. My fullest treatments of it are in Mele 1987: chs. 1–7, 1995: chs. 3 and 4; and 2003: ch. 8.

SOCRATIC AKRATIC ACTIONS AND ENKRATIC COUNTERPARTS

I mentioned a derivative kind of akratic action in scenarios featuring a last-minute change of decisive belief or judgment. This section explores akratic actions of this kind and enkratic counterparts.

Elsewhere (see Mele 1996b), I dubbed akratic action of the type at issue in this section "Socratic akratic action" (without meaning to suggest that Socrates himself regarded these actions as akratic). In defending the thesis that no one *knowingly* does wrong, Socrates argued that what actually happens in apparent instances of strict akratic action is that, owing to the increased proximity of the anticipated pleasures, agents change their minds about what it would be best to do (*Protagoras* 355d-357d). Even if Socrates is mistaken in denying the reality of strict akratic action, he has identified an important phenomenon. In some such cases of changing one's mind, as I explain below, the agent acts akratically.

In instances of Socratic akratic action, the change in decisive belief is a product of a *motivationally biased* process.[7] When we are tempted to do things that are at odds with our decisive beliefs, we have motivation to believe that the tempting option would be best. After all, acquiring that belief would diminish our resistance to acting as we are tempted to act (see Pears 1984: 12–13). In Socratic akratic action, the agent's new belief is not produced by an impartial reassessment of the pertinent data; rather, it issues from a process biased by the agent's desire for the tempting course of action. Now, biased processes are biased relative to some standards or other. In the present context, the most relevant standards are the agent's own. Perhaps the agent accepts a principle about judgments or beliefs that is violated by her present change of mind, for example, the principle that it is best not to allow what one wants to be the case to determine what one believes is the case.[8] And if a motivationally biased change of mind of this kind is avoidable by the agent by means of an exercise of self-control, it is itself an *akratic* episode, an episode manifesting *akrasia* or an associated imperfection. Surely, a perfectly self-controlled person would not make motivated judgments that are biased relative to her own standards, if she could avoid doing so by exercising self-control? Furthermore, an intentional action that accords with the new judgment would be derivatively akratic (see Mele 1987: 6–7; Pears 1984: 12–13; Rorty 1980). A perfectly self-controlled agent would avoid the avoidable, motivationally biased judgment to which our imagined agent's action conforms.

If we want to know whether what Socrates substitutes for strict akratic action is itself, in some cases, akratic conduct of another kind, we should answer the following two questions. (1) Is it possible for people to make motivationally biased reversals of their decisive judgments about what it is best to do, reversals that are biased given their own standards? (2) Are such reversals of judgment ever avoidable by exercising self-control?

If both questions are properly answered affirmatively, Socratic akratic action is a genuine possibility.[9]

The extent to which motivational, or "hot," factors are involved in the production and sustaining of biased beliefs continues to be a source of controversy in social psychology, but even influential proponents of the "colder" views have admitted that "many inferential errors... can be traced to motivational or emotional causes" (Nisbett and Ross 1980: 228).[10] A host of studies have produced results that are utterly unsurprising on the hypothesis that motivation sometimes biases beliefs. Psychologist Thomas Gilovich reports:

A survey of one million high school seniors found that 70% thought they were above average in leadership ability, and only 2% thought they were below average. In terms of ability to get along with others, *all* students thought they were above average, 60% thought they were in the top 10%, and 25% thought they were in the top 1%!... A survey of university professors found that 94% thought they were better at their jobs than their average colleague. (1991: 77)

Apparently, we have a tendency to believe propositions we want to be true even when an impartial investigation of readily available data would indicate that they probably are false. A plausible hypothesis about that tendency is that our *wanting* something to be true sometimes exerts a biasing influence on what we believe. Sometimes the pertinent beliefs may be about what it would be best to do.

Psychologist Ziva Kunda ably defends the view that motivation can influence "the generation and evaluation of hypotheses, of inference rules, and of evidence" and that motivationally "biased memory search will result in the formation of additional biased beliefs and theories that are constructed so as to justify desired conclusions" (1990: 483). In a particularly persuasive study, undergraduate subjects (75 women and 86 men) read an article alleging that "women were endangered by caffeine and were strongly advised to avoid caffeine in any form"; that the major danger was fibrocystic disease, "associated in its advanced stages with breast cancer"; and that "caffeine induced the disease by increasing the concentration of a substance called cAMP in the breast" (Kunda 1987: 642). (Since the article did not personally threaten men, they were used as a control group.) Subjects were then asked to indicate, among other things, "how convinced they were of the connection between caffeine and fibrocystic disease and of the connection between caffeine and... cAMP on a 6-point scale" (643–44). In the female group, "heavy consumers" of caffeine were significantly less convinced of the connections than were "low consumers." The males were considerably more convinced than the female "heavy consumers," and there was a much smaller difference in conviction between "heavy" and "low" male caffeine consumers (the heavy consumers were slightly *more* convinced of the connections).

Given that all subjects were exposed to the same information and assuming that only the female "heavy consumers" were threatened by it, a plausible hypothesis is that their lower level of conviction is due to "motivational processes designed to preserve optimism about their future health" (Kunda 1987: 644). Indeed, in a study in which the reported hazards of caffeine use were relatively modest, "female heavy consumers were no less convinced by the evidence than were female low consumers" (ibid.). Along with the lesser threat, there is less motivation for skepticism about the evidence.

Since motivation can bias our beliefs, there might be a place for motivationally biased belief in the etiology of an important species of akratic action. Some akratic actions may be accounted for, in part, by a motivationally biased change in decisive judgment. That change itself may manifest *akrasia*.

Socratic akratic action must be distinguished from another kind of akratic action involving a significant cognitive change. Suppose that Al has come to believe that he should do something about his weight and has judged, decisively, that it would be best to avoid eating between meals until he has lost ten pounds.[11] He has abided by this judgment for two weeks and has lost three pounds. Al particularly enjoys snacking while watching sporting events on television, and tonight he is tempted to eat a piece of the pizza that his children just brought home. Although he believes that he can work off the calories in one piece by exercising longer than usual tomorrow, he also believes, on the basis of his knowledge of his track record, that his succumbing to temptation tonight would significantly weaken his resolve to resist temptation on subsequent occasions.[12] And he judges both that the pleasure he would find in indulging his appetite tonight is far outweighed by the cost and that it would be best to resist the temptation. But now Al's children join him in the den to watch the game, and the pizza – smothered in his favorite toppings – looks and smells delicious. He finds himself thinking that he can make an exception tonight without weakening his resolve about future occasions all that much, and, still judging that it would be best not to eat, he believes that refraining from eating tonight would be only *slightly* better than eating. Having made it this far, Al decides to eat a piece.

In this case, there is a significant change in Al's assessment of the situation, a change that seemingly makes it easier for him to succumb to temptation. But this is not an instance of Socratic akratic action; for, when Al decides to eat, he still decisively believes that it would be best not to do so. A Socratic akratic agent would have abandoned this belief. In a Socratic version of the case, perhaps Al seriously underestimates the effect that a present lapse is likely to have on future dieting before decisively judging that it really would be best to make an exception in this case.

To see how this can happen, a brief, preparatory look at some mechanisms of "cold" or unmotivated biased belief will prove useful. Here are three, gleaned from the psychological literature.

1. *Vividness of information.* A datum's vividness for an individual often is a function of the concreteness of the datum, its "imagery-provoking" power, or its sensory, temporal, or spatial proximity (see Nisbett and Ross 1980: 45). Vivid data are more likely to be recognized, attended to, and recalled than pallid data. Consequently, vivid data tend to have a disproportional influence on the formation and retention of beliefs.[13]

2. *The availability heuristic.* When we form beliefs about the frequency, likelihood, or causes of an event, we "often may be influenced by the relative availability of the objects or events, that is, their accessibility in the processes of perception, memory, or construction from imagination" (Nisbett and Ross 1980: 18). For example, we may mistakenly believe that the number of English words beginning with "r" greatly outstrips the number having "r" in the third position, because we find it much easier to produce words on the basis of a search for their first letter (see Tversky and Kahneman 1973). Similarly, attempts to locate the cause(s) of an event are significantly influenced by manipulations that focus one's attention on a specific potential cause (see Taylor and Fiske 1975, 1978; Nisbett and Ross 1980: 22).

3. *The confirmation bias.* People testing a hypothesis tend to search (in memory and the world) more often for confirming than for disconfirming instances and to recognize the former more readily (see Nisbett and Ross 1980: 181–2; Klayman and Ha 1987; Baron 1988: 259–65). This is true even when the hypothesis is only a tentative one (as opposed, e.g., to a belief one has). The phenomenon has even been observed in the interpretation of relatively neutral data. For example, "subjects who tested the hypothesis that a person was angry interpreted that person's facial expression as conveying anger, whereas subjects who tested the hypothesis that

the person was happy interpreted the same facial expression as conveying happiness" (Trope, Gervey, and Liberman 1997: 115).

Obviously, the most vivid or available data sometimes have the greatest evidential value; the influence of such data is not *always* a biasing influence. The main point to be made is that although sources of biased belief can function independently of motivation, they may also be triggered and sustained by motivation in the production of particular *motivationally* biased beliefs.[14] For example, motivation can increase the vividness or salience of certain data. Data that count in favor of the truth of a hypothesis that one would like to be true might be rendered more vivid or salient given one's recognition that they so count, and vivid or salient data, given that they are more likely to be recognized and recalled, tend to be more "available" than pallid counterparts. Similarly, motivation can influence which hypotheses occur to one and affect the salience of available hypotheses, thereby setting the stage for the confirmation bias.[15] Since favorable hypotheses are more pleasant to contemplate than unfavorable ones and tend to come more readily to mind, desiring that *p* increases the probability that one's hypothesis testing will be focused on *p* rather than ~*p* (see Trope and Liberman 1996: 258; Trope et al. 1997: 113).

Consider a Socratic version of the pizza example. Given Al's desire for pizza, he has some motivation to believe that eating some would be permissible. Suppose he does come to believe this and that is explained partly by his underestimating the effect that a present lapse is likely to have on future dieting. A predictable effect of Al's motivation to believe that it would be permissible to eat the pizza is the enhanced salience of data that apparently support that proposition, including data that do so by supporting favorable estimations on the score just mentioned. For example, Al's recollections of having resisted temptation during the past two weeks may become salient and boost his estimation of his powers of self-control, thus supporting the hypothesis that there is little danger that eating tonight would promote backsliding in the future. Furthermore, his motivation may make salient for him the hypothesis that he has sufficient willpower consistently to honor his resolution in the future even if he makes an exception now, thus preparing the way for the confirmation bias. With the hypothesis in place, Al will tend to notice and to attend to confirming data more readily than disconfirming data.

Now, I am not suggesting that any time we make exceptions to our resolutions or bend our personal rules, we are behaving akratically. Sometimes our resolutions or rules are excessively rigid or exacting, and we may come to recognize that. Also, there may be cases in which motivationally biased reversals of judgment are simply inevitable. But when an appropriately avoidable judgment that an exception is warranted or permissible is a motivationally biased one, and biased relative to the agent's own relevant standards or principles, the judgment itself is due, in part, to *akrasia* or an associated imperfection and so, derivatively, is the corresponding action. Perfectly self-controlled agents would not make such avoidable, motivationally biased revisions of their judgments. They would retain the judgments at issue in the face of motivation to revise them.

One might suppose that when mechanisms of "cold" irrational belief work in conjunction with motivational elements, people are at the mercy of forces beyond their control and therefore do not behave akratically. However, as I pointed out in another connection in Mele 1987, "this is to take the image of combined forces too seriously. Indeed, I suspect that when motivation activates a cold mechanism, the ordinary agent is more likely to detect bias in his thinking than he would be if motivation were not involved; and detection facilitates control. The popular psychology of the industrialized Western world certainly owes a great deal more to Freud than to the attribution theorists; and for members of that world, a thought-biasing 'wish' is likely to be more salient than, for example, a 'cold' failure to attend to base-rate information" (147–8). There is a lively debate in social psychology about the extent to which sources of biased belief are subject to our control (see Kunda 1999). And there is evidence that some prominent sources of bias are to some degree controllable. For example, subjects instructed to conduct "symmetrical memory searches" are less likely than others to fall prey to the confirmation bias, and subjects' confidence in their responses to "knowledge questions" is reduced when they are invited to provide grounds for doubting the correctness of those responses (see Kunda 1990: 494–5). Presumably, people aware of the confirmation bias may reduce biased thinking in themselves by *giving themselves* the former instruction, and, fortunately, we do sometimes remind ourselves to consider both the pros *and* the cons before making up our minds about the truth of important propositions – even when we are tempted to do otherwise.

It is not difficult to see how salutary exercises of self-control might be open to Al or another agent in his shoes. Sometimes, not long after the fact, we recognize that our reversals of judgment about what we should do were biased and unwarranted, and we feel some guilt, or at least sheepishness, about having changed our minds. And sometimes, to qualify the proverb, to be forewarned is to be in a position to be forearmed. An agent's recollection that he has reversed his judgments in situations like the present one only to recognize later that the reversals were unwarranted and harmful gives him some basis to suspect that a reversal of judgment in the present situation would be unwise. And assuming that the agent has some motivation to promote his longer term interests, he has motivation as well to see to it that he does not err again now. But what can he do to keep on the right path? In addition to the strategies already mentioned, he can think about how he would be likely to feel tomorrow about a reversal of judgment today and vividly imagine the feeling, or he can announce his present judgment to a friend or relative who would think less of him if he were not to abide by it. Often, agents are not helpless victims of strong temptations, including the temptation to reverse their assessment of what it would be best to do.

It is an interesting question whether strict or Socratic akratic action is more common. This is an empirical question, of course, but it is worth pointing out that a moderately reflective agent's performing Socratic akratic actions in a given sphere should, before long, decrease the probability of further actions of that type in the same sphere. The Socratic akratic agent changes her mind, in the face of temptation, about what it is best to do. For this to happen again in the same sphere (e.g., about eating between meals), she must first revert to her original judgment (or form a similar one), and this normally would involve her seeing her earlier akratic action as a departure from a proper policy. The more frequently this happens, the harder it should become for her to judge again, in the same sphere and under similar circumstances, that it would be best to bend her personal rules or to make an exception to her resolutions. Remembering that, in the past, she consistently came to view these changes of mind as unwarranted, it will be difficult for her to view a change of mind of the same kind as warranted in very similar circumstances. After a time, believing yet another violation of her resolution against eating between meals to be warranted would be rather like knowing that a certain person regularly lies about his exploits and yet believing a tale of his that has all the marks of his other fabricated stories.[16]

CONCLUSION

I have sketched a partial account of important possible outcomes of personal practical conflicts featuring a clash of practical evaluative judgment or belief and temptation. In the process, I have ducked some hard questions. For example, there is an intriguing puzzle about the very possibility of exercising self-control in a certain garden-variety kind of personal practical conflict. In cases raising a strong version of what I have dubbed "the paradox of uphill self-control" (Mele 1987: 64), the basic worry is whether agents who have stronger motivation at a time to A at that time than not to A then can have enough motivation at the time to exercise self-control in support of their not A-ing then, even if they decisively believe A to be an inferior option.[17] There are also the usual questions about whether akratic action is possible, including the challenge to explain how one can *freely* act contrary to one's better judgment and how the desires on which agents of alleged akratic actions act differ from irresistible desires.[18] I am pleased to say that I did not akratically duck these questions. Rather, owing to space constraints and to my having devoted considerable attention to them elsewhere, I judged it best to duck them here.[19]

Notes

1. Compare this with my characterization of strict akratic action in Mele 1987: 7. The mention of sanity is an addition. That addition is motivated in Mele 2002b: sec. 2. I leave it open that an agent may freely A without sanely A-ing.

2. An agent who makes such a judgment may or may not proceed to search for additional options. He may regard the best member of his currently envisioned options as "good enough."

3. On a standard conception of akratic action, assuming that there is a middle ground between *akrasia* and self-control, some akratic actions might not manifest *akrasia*. An agent who is more self-controlled than most people in a certain sphere of her life may, in a particularly trying situation, succumb to temptation in that sphere against her better judgment. If her pertinent intentional action is free and sane, she has acted akratically, even if her action manifests not *akrasia* itself but an associated imperfection.

4. Cf. Aristotle, *Nicomachean Ethics* 1150a11–13. The akratic person, he writes, "is in such a state as to be defeated even by those [pleasures] which most people master," while the person who has the trait of self-control (*enkrateia*) is in such a state as "to master even those by which most people are defeated."

5. For discussion of the practical potential of strategies such as these in effective self-control and some empirical literature on the topic, see Mele 1987: 23–4 and chs. 4–6 and 1995: ch. 3. For more on intentions by default, see Mele 1992: ch. 12.

6. In other cases, the trick is to keep one's motivation in line with one's decisive judgment or to ensure that one will be unable to act on preponderant contrary motivation that one expects to emerge (as in the case of Odysseus and the Sirens). See Mele 1996a.

7. Motivationally biased belief is a central topic of Mele 2001.

8. On "accepting a principle" about beliefs or judgments, see Mele 1995: 92–4.

9. Owing to the possibility of Frankfurt-style cases (Frankfurt 1969) – in which if an agent who A-ed had not decided on her own to A, she would have been compelled by a potential intervener to decide to A and to A – I do not make an agent's being able to avoid A-ing a necessary condition of her akratically A-ing (Mele 1995: 94–5; 2002a). Analogous cases can be generated for reversals of decisive judgments. Hence, I am not suggesting that the avoidability of a change of mind is required for its being an akratic episode. (For a defense of the coherence of Frankfurt-style cases, see Mele and Robb 1998.)

10. See Kunda 1990 for a review of the controversy.

11. Notice how natural it is to interpret "best" here as "better than the relevant alternative" (as opposed, e.g., to "the best of all possible actions open to him"). The natural interpretation is the intended one. Obviously, Al may give collecting his monthly paychecks a higher evaluative rating than refraining from eating between meals until he loses ten pounds.

12. On the practical importance of this effect of succumbing to temptation, see Ainslie 1992 and Mele 1996a.

13. For a challenge to studies of the vividness effect, see Taylor and Thompson 1982. They contend that research on the issue has been flawed in various ways, but that studies conducted in "situations that reflect the informational competition found in everyday life" might "show the existence of a strong vividness effect" (178–9).

14. This theme is developed in Mele 1987: ch. 10 and 2001 in explaining the occurrence of self-deception. Kunda 1990 (see Kunda 1999: ch. 6) develops the same theme, paying particular attention to evidence that motivation sometimes triggers the confirmation bias.

15. For motivational interpretations of the confirmation bias, see Frey 1986: 70–4; Friedrich 1993; and Trope and Liberman 1996: 252–65.

16. There also are "unorthodox" instances of akratic action, in which agents act *in accordance with* their decisive judgments, and, similarly, unorthodox exercises of self-control in support of conduct that conflicts with the agents' decisive judgments (Mele 1987: 7–8; 1995, 60–76; Bigelow, Dodds, and Pargetter 1990, 46). Here is an illustration of unorthodox akratic action from Mele 1995: "Young Bruce has decided to join some wayward Cub Scouts in breaking into a neighbor's house, even though he decisively judges it best not to do so. . . . At the last minute, Bruce refuses to enter the house and leaves the scene of the crime. His doing so because his decisive judgment has prevailed is one thing; his refusing to break in owing simply to a failure of nerve is another. In the latter event, Bruce arguably has exhibited weakness of will: he 'chickened out'" (60). If, instead, Bruce had mastered his fear and participated in the crime, we would have an unorthodox exercise of self-control. Bigelow et al. 1990 regard unorthodox episodes of these kinds as support for the idea that what is essential to akratic action is the presence of a second-order desire that either loses or wins against a first-order desire in the determination of action, independently of what (if anything) the agent judges it best to do. For argumentation to the contrary, see Mele 1995: ch. 4.

17. I tackle this puzzle in Mele 1987: ch. 5 and again in 1995: ch. 3.

18. I defend answers to these questions in Mele 1987; 1992: ch. 5; and 2002a.
19. Parts of this essay derive from Mele 1987, 1992, 1995, 1996b, and 2001.

Bibliography

Ainslie, George. 1992. *Picoeconomics.* Cambridge: Cambridge University Press.

Aristotle. 1984. *Nicomachean Ethics,* tr. W. D. Ross, rev. J. O. Urmson. In *The Complete Works of Aristotle: The Revised Oxford Translation,* ed. Jonathan Barnes. Princeton, N.J.: Princeton University Press.

Audi, Robert. 1979. Weakness of Will and Practical Judgment. *Noûs* 13: 173–96.

Baron, Jonathan. 1988. *Thinking and Deciding.* Cambridge: Cambridge University Press.

Bigelow, John, S. Dodds, and R. Pargetter, 1990. Temptation and the Will. *American Philosophical Quarterly* 27: 39–49.

Davidson, Donald. 1980. How Is Weakness of the Will Possible? In *Essays on Actions and Events.* Oxford: Clarendon, 21–42.

Davidson, Donald. 1985. Replies to Essays I–IX. In B. Vermazen and M. Hintikka (eds.), *Essays on Davidson.* Oxford: Clarendon Press, 159–229.

Frankfurt, Harry. 1969. Alternate Possibilities and Moral Responsibility. *Journal of Philosophy* 66: 829–39.

Frey, Dieter. 1986. Recent Research on Selective Exposure to Information. In L. Berkowitz (ed.), *Advances in Experimental Social Psychology,* vol. 19. New York: Academic Press.

Friedrich, James. 1993. Primary Error Detection and Minimization PEDMIN Strategies in Social Cognition: A Reinterpretation of Confirmation Bias Phenomena. *Psychological Review* 100: 298–319.

Gilovich, Thomas. 1991. *How We Know What Isn't So.* New York: Macmillan.

Klayman, Joshua, and Y.-W. Ha. 1987. Confirmation, Disconfirmation, and Information in Hypothesis Testing. *Psychological Review* 94: 211–28.

Kunda, Ziva. 1987. Motivated Inference: Self-Serving Generation and Evaluation of Causal Theories. *Journal of Personality and Social Psychology* 53: 636–47.

Kunda, Ziva. 1990. The Case for Motivated Reasoning. *Psychological Bulletin* 108: 480–98.

Kunda, Ziva. 1999. *Social Cognition.* Cambridge, Mass.: MIT Press.

Mele, Alfred. 1987. *Irrationality.* New York: Oxford University Press.

Mele, Alfred. 1992. *Springs of Action.* New York: Oxford University Press.

Mele, Alfred. 1995. *Autonomous Agents.* New York: Oxford University Press.

Mele, Alfred. 1996a. Addiction and Self-Control. *Behavior and Philosophy* 24: 99–117.

Mele, Alfred. 1996b. Socratic Akratic Action. *Philosophical Papers* 25: 149–59.

Mele, Alfred. 2001. *Self-Deception Unmasked.* Princeton, N.J.: Princeton University Press.

Mele, Alfred. 2002a. Akratics and Addicts. *American Philosophical Quarterly* 39: 153–67.

Mele, Alfred. 2002b. Autonomy and Akrasia. *Philosophical Explorations* 5: 207–16.

Mele, Alfred. 2003. *Motivation and Agency.* New York: Oxford University Press.

Mele, Alfred, and D. Robb. 1998. Rescuing Frankfurt-Style Cases. *Philosophical Review* 107: 97–112.

Nisbett, Richard, and L. Ross. 1980. *Human Inference: Strategies and Shortcomings of Social Judgment*. Englewood Cliffs, N.J.: Prentice-Hall.

Pears, David. 1984. *Motivated Irrationality*. Oxford: Oxford University Press.

Rorty, Amelie. 1980. Where Does the Akratic Break Take Place? *Australasian Journal of Philosophy* 58: 333–46.

Taylor, Shelley, and S. Fiske. 1975. Point of View and Perceptions of Causality. *Journal of Personality and Social Psychology* 32: 439–45.

Taylor, Shelley, and S. Fiske. 1978. Salience, Attention and Attribution: Top of the Head Phenomena. In L. Berkowitz (ed.), *Advances in Experimental Social Psychology*, vol. 11. New York: Academic Press.

Taylor, Shelley, and S. Thompson. 1982. Stalking the Elusive "Vividness" Effect. *Psychological Review* 89: 155–81.

Trope, Yaacov, and A. Liberman. 1996. Social Hypothesis Testing: Cognitive and Motivational Mechanisms. In E. T. Higgins and A. Kruglanski (eds.), *Social Psychology: Handbook of Basic Principles*. New York: Guilford Press.

Trope, Yaacov, B. Gervey, and N. Liberman. 1997. Wishful Thinking from a Pragmatic Hypothesis-Testing Perspective. In M. Myslobodsky (ed.), *The Mythomanias: The Nature of Deception and Self-Deception*. Mahwah, N.J.: Lawrence Erlbaum.

Tversky, Amos, and D. Kahneman. 1973. Availability: A Heuristic for Judging Frequency and Probability. *Cognitive Psychology* 5: 207–32.

12

Are There Insolvable Moral Conflicts?

Peter Schaber

Is there a solution to Bernard Williams's famous Jim/Pedro example?[1] Jim is on a tour through South America and finds himself one day confronted with Pedro, an Army officer, who is about to kill twenty rebellious Indians. Jim cannot prevent Pedro from doing so. But Pedro offers Jim the "privilege" of killing one of the Indians, in return letting the others off. Should Jim accept Pedro's offer? Is there an answer to this question? Is Jim faced with a conflict, but one that can be resolved? Or is this a situation in which we are faced with an insolvable moral conflict, in which different moral demands draw us in different and incompatible directions without an ought being available, that is, a situation where it is even in principle impossible to say what Jim ought to do, all things considered?[2] It is not that we are not able to determine what we ought to do; it is rather that there is nothing that could be discovered as something that ought to be done.

According to what Alan Donagan calls moral rationalism, this cannot be the case. Moral theories cannot allow for moral dilemmas. A moral theory that would do so would have to be revised. As Donagan puts it: "The generation of moral dilemmas is to moral rationalism what the generation of self-contradictions is to theories generally: an indispensable sign that a particular theory is defective."[3] Thus, insolvable moral conflicts are excluded for conceptual reasons: Insolvable moral conflicts imply contradictions no moral theory can allow for without being in need of revision.

Which view should we accept? Are there insolvable moral conflicts? This is the question I deal with in this chapter. I first clarify how insolvable moral conflicts should be conceived of. I then discuss the difficulties we face if we conceive of insolvable moral conflicts as conflicts of oughts. I then argue that insolvable moral conflicts should be taken as conflicts of moral reasons. But not any conflict of moral reasons is an insolvable moral conflict. Most conflicts of moral reasons can be solved. They are only insolvable, as I finally argue, if they are practically incommensurable and at the same time symmetrical.

EQUALLY GOOD OPTIONS

Moral conflicts are conflicts of oughts or of moral reasons. They have the form: I ought to do A and I ought to B or I have reasons for doing A as well as for doing B, but I cannot do both A and B. Such conflicts are resolved if it turns out that I ought to do, say, A rather than B or that the reasons that speak in favor of doing A are stronger than the reasons for doing B. But what is actually meant by "insolvable moral conflict"? What does it mean for a moral conflict to have no solution? Let us take the following case: I have a choice between helping John to write a paper and helping Lisa to write a paper. Suppose that from a moral point of view the two options are of equal value or importance. Thus, one could not say that helping John would be better than helping Lisa and vice versa. Would I then face an insolvable moral conflict? Somehow, of course, yes. There would be no correct solution in such a situation in the sense that one option should be preferred over the other one. If it is the case that I ought to help John, then I also ought to help Lisa. The weighing of these oughts would not yield a result of the kind that would say that I ought to help John and I ought not to help Lisa. In this sense I would be faced with an insolvable conflict. But then, of course, there would be an answer to the question of what I ought to do in the given situation, namely, I ought to help either John or Lisa.

Compare this with a situation where I have to choose the best candidate for a job. As it turns out, Anna and Jim are equally good candidates. What should I do? It would be wrong to say that I ought to prefer Anna to Jim in the same way as it would be wrong to say that I ought to prefer Jim to Anna. But it would certainly not be wrong to say that I ought to choose either Anna or Jim. Thus, there is something that ought to be done. There is no particular action that ought to be preferred. Still, there is something I ought to do: I ought to choose either Anna or Jim, all things considered.[4]

One could consider such conflicts of equally good options to be insolvable moral conflicts, because they are indeed in a sense insolvable. But if we took choices between equally good options to be insolvable conflicts, it would be very difficult to deny the existence of insolvable moral conflicts. To do so, one would have to deny that different options are ever equally good. But this would certainly be a very difficult position to defend. And even if options were never equally good, one could nevertheless think of situations where we were confronted with equally good options. If so, insolvable moral conflicts would at least be possible. And the rationalist picture of morality would thus be refuted.

But the kind of insolvability that is linked to equally good options is in any event not at stake in the debate about insolvable moral conflicts. The question is not whether there can be equally good options between which we have to choose. The question in this debate is rather whether there are moral conflicts where no ought, *all things considered*, is even in principle available. This is exactly what moral rationalists, such as Alan Donagan, deny: According to them, there are no situations where there are moral considerations speaking in favor and against different courses of action without there being any actions that ought to be done. Thus, we are faced with insolvable moral conflicts in situations where no ought, all things considered, is in principle available. If so, equally good options do not confront us with insolvable moral conflicts, because in a situation where we have to choose between equally good options, there is something that ought to be done, all things considered. Where I have to choose between, say, the lives of two children, a solution is available in terms of an ought, all things considered. "I take it that . . . most rationalists would object that the question which child is to be saved is no moral question at all. . . . Where the lives of identical twins are in jeopardy and I can save one but only one, every serious rationalist moral system lays down that, whatever I do, I must save one of them."[5] The question then is: Are there situations where no ought, all things considered, can even in principle be found?

CONFLICTS OF OUGHTS?

No ought might be available where we were faced with a conflict of oughts. The oughts I have in mind here are *conclusive* oughts. If an ought is a conclusive ought, it is not outweighed by another ought. An ought could be outweighed by another ought. This is certainly the case where the ought is used in the sense of "having reasons." "I ought to be nice to my neighbor" might just mean "I have reasons to be nice to my neighbor." There is, in other words, something that speaks in favor of being nice to him. But unlike a conclusive ought, this ought does not make a strict demand on me.[6] It could well be the case that there are other reasons that outweigh the reasons I have to be nice to my neighbor.

An insolvable moral conflict could be seen as a conflict of conclusive oughts: It is impossible to follow both oughts and it would at the same time be in principle impossible to tell which ought one should follow; that is, which ought proves to be stronger. This would be a situation where I ought to do A and at the same time I ought not to do A. And it would at the same time also not be correct to say that I ought to do either. It would just hold that I ought to do A and that I ought not to do A. Thus, there were two oughts, all things considered.

Are there such insolvable conflicts of oughts? There are insolvable conflicts of oughts only if there are conflicts of conclusive oughts in the first place, which is as a matter of fact far from clear. Let us take Williams's Jim/Pedro example. Jim is faced with an insolvable conflict of oughts only if it is correct to say that

(i) He ought to accept Pedro's offer,

and

(ii) He ought not to accept Pedro's offer.

But is this the case? I think there are two reasons for doubting that (i) and (ii) hold at the same time: (a) If Jim were confronted with two conclusive oughts, it would not be clear what he ought to do. The problem is not – as some think[7] – that he would be faced with a contradiction. This is not the case. He would be faced with a contradiction if one said that

(iii) It is the case that Jim ought to accept Pedro's offer,

and

(iv) It is not the case that Jim ought to accept Pedro's offer.

If (iii) and (iv) held, then we would have: $O(a) \ \& \ \neg\, O(a)$, which is definitely a contradiction; but if (i) and (ii) obtained, we would have $O(a) \ \& \ O(\neg a)$, which is at least not a contradiction. The latter could be true in the same way as "Paul believes that p" and "Paul believes that non-p" can actually be true. If it were true, Paul would have to change his beliefs, but this does not impinge on the fact that it could be true. The propositions "Paul believes p" and "Paul does not believe p" cannot both be true, nor can they both be false. And in the same way (iii) and (iv) cannot both be true nor both be false.

The problem here is less one of the *logical form* of conflicts of oughts but rather that it is far from clear whether Jim is faced with demands that make sense. That is to say, it would be unclear what the demand on Jim would be. Moral demands have an action-guiding force: We normally demand of someone that she perform a particular course of action (or omit a particular course of action). But what would be demanded of Jim if we demanded that he accept and not accept Pedro's offer? What would be the thing he ought to do? No answer could be given to this question. Thus, conflicts of oughts seem just incompatible with the action-guiding force that oughts in general are supposed to have.

(b) The second problem with conflicts of conclusive oughts is that they are incompatible with the principle "ought implies can." If we demand that Jim accept Pedro's offer and at the same time that he not do so, we demand of him something he is not able to do. Conflicts of oughts therefore violate the principle "ought implies can."

Of course, this principle should not be regarded as an analytic truth. It should rather be seen as a necessary condition of reasonable moral demands. That is to say, it would not be reasonable to demand of someone things he or she cannot do. I think that the principle "ought implies can" should be respected for exactly this reason: Conflicts of conclusive oughts should not be allowed for by any moral theory that aims at formulating reasonable moral demands.

I do not mean to say that these two reasons prove conclusively that there are no conflicts of oughts. But they at least make clear why there might be something wrong with a moral theory that does not exclude conflicts of conclusive oughts.

CONFLICTS OF MORAL REASONS

The fact that there are no conflicts of conclusive oughts might lead one to the conclusion that there are no insolvable moral conflicts. But I think it is more sensible to say that insolvable moral conflicts should be conceived of in a different way, not as conflicts of oughts. My suggestion is that insolvable moral conflicts should be conceived of as conflicts of moral reasons. So it might be – to take our example – that Jim has moral reasons to accept Pedro's offer and at the same time moral reasons not to do so. And it would not be correct to say that he ought to do either the latter or the former. It is just that he has moral reasons to choose one course of action as well as moral reasons to choose the other one. There is no contradiction in such a case.

There are often reasons for and against the very same action. There is no difficulty with this as long as the reasons speaking in favor of a particular action are not based on the same considerations as the reasons speaking against it.

As I said, insolvable moral conflicts should be conceived of as conflicts of moral reasons. But conflicts of reasons are not necessarily insolvable. Reasons in general can be weighed against each other. And some reasons prove without any doubt to be stronger or weightier than other reasons. Let us take the following example: If the reasons I have to help a friend write a paper are in conflict with the reasons I have to stay with my son, who has suddenly fallen ill, then no one would doubt the latter reasons are stronger than the former. And as a consequence it would be clear what I ought to do in a situation where I have to choose between these two actions. Such conflicts of reasons are easily solvable. Other conflicts might be more difficult to solve, but they are still not insolvable. Conflicts of reasons are insolvable only if the weighing of reasons yields no result and as a consequence no ought; that is to say, where the weighing of reasons cannot even in principle deliver an ought, because there is simply no ought available. The question is: Are there such insolvable conflicts of moral reasons?

INCOMMENSURABLE REASONS

Say I have a choice between two options, x and y. Both options are supported by moral reasons. If option x is supported by stronger moral reasons, then I ought to choose x (and of course vice versa). If they are of equal strength, then I ought to choose either option x or option y. Of course, it would not be right to say that I ought to prefer x to y (and vice versa), rather, the right thing to say is that I ought to choose just one of them (provided the reasons supporting these options are not outweighed by reasons speaking in favor of a third option available in this situation).

How then could a conflict of moral reasons be insolvable? One could say it is insolvable if the reasons are *incommensurable*. And the reasons are incommensurable, for instance, if the options at stake are incommensurable in value.[8] One option would then be neither better than nor equal in value to the other one.[9] Thus, I might have reasons to do A and reasons to do B, but the reasons for A are neither stronger nor weaker than nor equally strong as the reasons for B. This is not meant as epistemic indeterminacy, where we are not able to determine the relative strength of the reasons. It is rather meant as a case where the reasons for A are neither stronger nor weaker than nor equally strong as the reasons for B. Would we then have a conflict of reasons that could not be solved in the sense that no ought would be available? That is, would it then be wrong to say that I ought to do either A or B?

The question here is: Does the incommensurability case differ from the equality case? Ruth Chang believes that it does.[10] According to Chang, it is right to say in the equality case that I ought to do either A or B. She thinks that this is the case because of the specific positive value relation that holds between the two options ("you ought to do either A or B, because A is as good as B"). But it would be wrong to say the same thing in the incommensurability case, simply because there is no positive value relation that obtains between the two options.

Thus, as Chang thinks, we are not justified in choosing to do A and we are at the same time not justified in choosing to do B, provided A and B are incommensurable in value. In the equality case we are justified in doing A as well as B, because A is as good as B.[11] If so, conflicts of reasons are insolvable, if the reasons are incommensurable.

Should we accept this account of insolvable moral conflicts? I do not think so. Say the reasons for A are neither stronger nor equally strong as nor weaker than the reasons for B. Would there be nothing in such a case that you ought to do? I think there is indeed an ought available, namely, that you ought to do either A or B. There is no practical difference between the incommensurability and the equality case, because there is in both cases an optimal solution available: If the reasons for A and B are incommensurable, it is false to say that the reasons for A are stronger than the reasons for B (and of course vice versa). Interestingly enough, the same applies to the equality case: If the reasons for A and B are of equal strength, then it would be false to say that the reasons for A are weaker than the reasons for B. Thus, if I decide to choose A, I am not open to rational criticism either in the equality or in the incommensurability case: It would be wrong to say that I could have done better. As a matter of fact, I could not have done better in either case. If that were so, how could one not be justified in choosing A or B, provided there is no option available that is better (that has stronger reasons on its side)? As in the equality case, one is not justified in preferring A to B; no reasons could be given for preferring A to B or B to A. But one is – again as in the equality case – justified in doing either, because there is no better option available. There is therefore no practical difference between the equality and the incommensurability case:[12] Doing A or B would in both cases be the optimal choice; no better option could be chosen. If so, conflicts of reasons are not insolvable even if the relevant reasons are incommensurable.

PRACTICAL INCOMMENSURABILITY

Yet the insolvability of conflicts of moral reasons depends on a certain kind of incommensurability. The kind of incommensurability that is important here is not to be taken as the fact that reasons cannot be compared, but rather as the fact that they *should not be compared*. Let us call this *practical incommensurability*. Reasons that are theoretically incommensurable cannot be compared, but it would not be wrong if one compared them. In the case of practical incommensurability, it would be wrong to do so. It is not – as in the case of theoretical incommensurability – that neither reason is stronger nor equally strong as the other. It is rather the normative fact that it would be wrong to compare them in the first place.

Joseph Raz thinks that, for instance, friendship provides us with reasons of this kind. It would be inappropriate to compare the reasons you have to care about your friend with the reasons to accept money in exchange for friendship. This is – as Raz rightly thinks – just implied by what it means to have friends. "Only those who hold the view that friendship is neither better nor worse than money, but is simply not comparable to money or other commodities are *capable* of having friends. Similarly only those who would not even consider exchanges of money for friendship are capable of having friends."[13] It is not the case that having tried to compare the two options we reach the conclusion that friendship is neither better nor equally good as a given amount of money. It is rather the case that it would be inappropriate to compare them in the first place.

The fact that reasons are practically incommensurable is itself based on practical reasons. There is a reason why friendship should not be compared with money or other similar goods. The reasons that are conducive to practical incommensurability are provided by the inherent norms of goods, such as friendship. These norms tell us how we should engage with values such as friendship, and what it means to value friendship. To value friendship, such a norm tells us, would be incompatible with calculating its value in monetary terms. Practical incommensurability is thus unlike theoretical incommensurability based on practial reasons that are provided by the inherent norms of certain goods.

I think that such goods are also at stake in the Jim/Pedro example: The reasons to accept Pedro's offer should not be compared with the reasons not to accept Pedro's offer. It would not be appropriate for Jim to weigh his killing of a person with his allowing twenty persons to die. This fits well with a widespread intuition. It explains why most of us consider the Jim/Pedro example a difficult decision. This would not be the case for someone who saw no problem in comparing the two items that are at stake in this example.

It is not that the options of killing someone yourself and of letting twenty die are equally bad. There is rather something wrong with asking how many persons it would take to justify the killing of one yourself. In any case, the difficulty most people have with Jim's situation is not due to the fact that they consider letting twenty persons die to be as equally bad as your killing one yourself. We do not even think about how many people are enough to outweigh the killing of a person.[14] Where should the limit be drawn? With two hundred people? Would the killing of a person still be equally bad? Or do we need, say, a thousand people? These questions are odd. The difficulty we have in answering them is due – I think – to the fact that there are no answers to be found here. Neither is it the case that the value of one option is infinitely higher than the value of the other one: There is no lexical ordering between the options. That is to say, it is not the case that, for instance, friendship is so valuable that no amount of money, however large, could ever outweigh the value of friendship.[15] And it is also not the case that, say, killing someone oneself is infinitely worse than allowing twenty people to die. If it was the case that the value of friendship (or the disvalue of killing someone) could not be outweighed by any amount of money, however large (or the saving of lives, regardless of how many persons are concerned), then they would of course be comparable. To say that A is infinitely more valuable than B amounts to a comparison of these two items. Moreover, it is not what we mean by saying that two items should not be compared. It is not that the weighing of reasons is senseless, because the result is already clear. It is rather that we think it would be wrong to weigh the relevant reasons, for instance, the reasons for killing someone with the reasons for letting twenty people die.

INSOLVABLE MORAL CONFLICTS

Let us come back to the insolvability of conflicts of moral reasons. Of course, conflicts of reasons that are practically incommensurable in the sense just described are not necessarily insolvable. The reasons friendship and money provide us with are practically incommensurable, but there is no doubt what ought to be done in cases where we are asked to exchange friendship for money. The reasons of friendship dominate in such cases the reasons money provides us with. This does not mean that they are much stronger than these other reasons. There is rather an inherent norm of friendship according to which not only an exchange of a friendship for money would be inappropriate, but also even seriously considering such an exchange would be so. Thus, there is only an apparent conflict of reasons. Someone who values friendship properly would not consider trading friendship for money. There is no weighing needed to reach this result.

Thus, in the friendship/money exchange case we are not really faced with an insolvable moral conflict, because the reasons in play are *asymmetrical*. Conflicts of reason are insolvable only if the reasons are – besides being practically incommensurable – *symmetrical*. This is the case when neither of the conflicting reasons is dominated by the other. I think that this is the case in the Jim/Pedro example. The reasons for accepting Pedro's offer do not dominate the reasons for not accepting it. If this was not so, we would not have any difficulty deciding what ought to be done in such a case. In the friendship/money case it is clear what ought to be done, if we were asked to exchange friendship for money. It is obvious what has to be done because the reasons are asymmetrical; the reasons provided by the norms of friendship silence the reasons in favor of accepting the money. This is not so in the Jim/Pedro example, because there is no silencing of reasons in this case.

This is confirmed by the fact that most of us would hesitate to demand of Jim any particular course of action. The situation that Jim is in is such that it would be inadequate either to say that he *ought* to accept or that he *ought* not to accept Pedro's offer. Of course, there are moral reasons in favor of either course of action. And Jim would therefore be justified in accepting Pedro's offer as well as in not accepting it.[16]

Most of us would think that the decision is ultimately up to him; that Jim has to decide according to what he thinks he could live with,[17] but that there is nothing he ought to do.

And because there is no ought in play here, it would also not be wrong to perform either course of action. If Jim accepts Pedro's offer, he will not do something he ought not to do. He will rather do something he has moral reasons to do, reasons that are practically incommensurable with the competing reasons and that at the same time neither dominate nor are dominated by them. Thus, when we are faced with insolvable moral conflicts there is – contrary to what Gowans believes – no inescapable wrongdoing.[18] If one is faced with an insolvable moral conflict, one is forced to perform an action that has moral reasons speaking against it, but that is not one that is wrong. Yet that does not mean that it ought not be performed. It is bad at least in some respect to do it,[19] which is not to say that it is wrong to do it. This again fits well with an idea that many of us share, namely, the idea that Jim could not be blamed for whatever he chooses to do.[20] Blame would be appropriate only if he did something wrong. But neither accepting nor not accepting Pedro's offer would be wrong.

Thus conflicts of moral reasons are insolvable if and only if they are practically incommensurable and at the same time symmetrical. If these conditions obtain, there is nothing an agent ought to do. There are just different options supported by different moral reasons. Whatever the agent does, it is in some respect bad without being wrong.

OBJECTIONS

Let us turn finally to three objections.

(1) One could of course object that there are no reasons that should not be compared with certain other reasons, either in the Jim/Pedro case or in any other case. Let us take again the Jim/Pedro case: What if he could save not just nineteen people but rather a whole nation? It seems to be sensible to say that in such a situation, he ought to accept Pedro's offer. If so, the reasons for killing someone are comparable with the reasons for saving a whole nation. But why should it then be inappropriate to compare the relevant reasons in the original Jim/Pedro case? This is of course a substantial moral issue. One could hold the view that Jim ought not to accept Pedro's offer even if he could thereby save a whole nation. We cannot deal with this issue here.

But suppose now for argument's sake that he indeed ought to do so. I think that even if that were the case, it would not follow that a weighing of the relevant reasons is appropriate. An ought could come into play in a situation where a whole nation would be in danger due to an obligation Jim is under that is not necessarily based on a weighing of reasons that are relevant here. "One ought to save a nation" might be the moral norm that becomes important here. This norm might dominate the reasons that speak against killing someone. That is to say: Jim might be under the obligation to save a whole nation not because we have now reached the number of people we need to outweigh the badness of killing a person. The badness is not outweighed by the goodness brought about by the saving of a whole nation. It is just that the norm holds that one ought to save a nation. This does not imply that the reasons speaking for and against the particular courses of action are comparable.

(2) One might also object[21] that regardless of whether reason A is practically incommensurable with reason B, reason A must be either stronger, equally strong, weaker, or theoretically incommensurable with reason B.

One of those four relations obtains. There can be no negation of all four predicates. Of course, one might think that this could be true in cases where the items to be compared are *noncomparable*.[22] Two items are noncomparable in cases where the question of whether one of them is better than the other is meaningless. The question "Is Plato better than water?" is such a case. There is no anwer to this question as long as we do not have – as Chang puts it – a "covering value"[23] that allows for comparison. One can assume that covering values can always be found, for instance: "Does reading Plato provide you with more pleasure than drinking a glass of water?" But even if that were not so, where we have a covering value, a negation of the four predicates mentioned above is impossible. If so, the claim that reasons are practically incommensurable amounts in such cases to nothing but the claim that one should not find out which reasons relation actually obtains. That is to say, there is a solution that should not be found out. If the reasons A and B are theoretically incommensurable, it would be right to do either A or B; but then, due to the fact that they are at the same time practically incommensurable, it would be wrong to find that out. But of course this is not what we mean when we talk about insolvable moral conflicts.

Is this a fatal objection to our proposal? I do not think so. If the question "Is it better to accept Pedro's offer than to refuse it?" is meaningful, which it certainly is, the reasons for accepting it stand in one of the four relations to the reasons against doing so.

Say now that they are incommensurable. Would this fact yield an ought in Jim's case, an ought that he is not supposed to find out? I think it would yield an ought if they were merely theoretically incommensurable. The reasons I have for choosing a career as a philosopher might be incommensurable with the reasons I have to become a journalist. It would at the same time definitely be permissible to compare the relevant reasons. Thus I ought to choose just one of these careers. But I think that this does not hold if the reasons are at the same time practically incommensurable. The objection presupposes that theoretical incommensurability yields an ought, independently of whether or not there is at the same time practical incommensurability. But I think that one should accept the following constraint on the practical importance of theoretical incommensurability: Theoretical incommensurability brings about an ought, provided there is no practical incommensurability. This holds simply because practical incommensurability is normatively more important than theoretical incommensurability. The former trumps the latter. Thus, if there is theoretical as well as practical incommensurability, there is no "you ought to do either," but rather "you ought not to compare the relevant reasons for doing either A or B." This does not mean that you cannot compare them. Of course, you can, but you will not come up with something that is in a normative sense important. This is implied by the fact that different reasons are practically incommensurable.

(3) Let us turn to the third objection: Why should the Jim/Pedro example be an example of an insolvable moral conflict? Is it not the case that one ought outweighs the other one? One can hold the view that the negative ought outweighs the positive ought. That one ought not to kill is weightier than that one ought to save nineteen persons. This corresponds well to the widely shared idea that there are constraints on what we may do to others or how we may treat them.[24] Thus, Jim ought to refuse Pedro's offer, period. Due to the limits that exist in promoting goodness, it cannot be demanded of him to save nineteen persons.

I do not think that this is the case. If he ought to refuse Pedro's offer, we were justified in demanding that he do so. And we could at the same time blame him if he did not do it. But I think that most of us would not make such a demand on Jim nor would we blame him if he did accept Pedro's offer. It is not that we would not want to be too demanding (he should refuse, but it might too hard for him if we told him this); we did not blame him and not because we wanted to spare Jim criticism due to the difficult time he went through. We do not make a demand nor do we blame him if he accepts, simply because there is nothing to be demanded and, as a consequence, nothing Jim could be blamed for. And this is I think due to the fact that the reasons that are in play are practically incommensurable and at the same time symmetrical.

CONCLUSION

Insolvable moral conflicts should be conceived of not as conflicts of conclusive oughts, but rather as conflicts of moral reasons. Conflicts of moral reasons are insolvable, if the following conditions obtain:

1. The conflicting reasons are not just theoretically but also *practically incommensurable,* and
2. They are symmetrical, that is, none of them dominate the others.

If so, there is no ought. There are just moral reasons speaking for and against particular courses of action. I think that this holds for Jim's situation. There is no solution to his predicament. This fits well with the fact that most of us would not demand anything of him and would not blame him for whatever choice he made. Morality just draws Jim in two different and incompatible directions without providing us with a conclusive ought. This is what it means to be confronted with an insolvable moral conflict.

Notes

I am very grateful to Norbert Anwander, Peter Baumann, Monika Betzler, Thomas Schmidt, and Jörg Schroth for their helpful comments.

1. Cf. Williams 1973: 98f.
2. This would be a situation where we had what Nagel calls a "true practical dilemma"; cf. 1979: 135: "[T]here are true practical dilemmas that have no solution, and there are also conflicts that judgement cannot operate confidently."
3. Donagan 1996: 15.
4. One could argue that this is no practical solution. I still would not know what I ought to do. This presupposes that reasoned choice is always choosing for better reasons. But I cannot see why one should think so. Reasoned choice is acting for undefeated reasons.
5. Donagan 1987: 286.
6. Cf. Broome 2000: 81: "The difference between the oughts relation ... and the reasons relation might be put like this: the former makes a strict demand on you; the latter a slack one."
7. Cf. Conee 1987: 240; cf. also Brink 1996: 113.
8. I do not mean that the incommensurability of reasons is necessarily based on the incommensurability of the underlying values. There might be an incommensurability of reasons that has nothing to do with the way the values of the relevant options are related to each other.
9. This is what Joseph Raz has in mind when he talks about incommensurability; cf. Raz 1986: 322: "A and B are incommensurate if it is neither true that one is better than the other nor true that they are of equal value." For a slightly modified version of this definition of incommensurability, cf. Broome 1999: 150: "[L]et us define one option A to be 'incommensurate' with another B if and only if it is not the case that A is better than B, and not the case that B is better than A, and not the case that A and B are equally good."
10. Cf. Chang 1998: 1572: "[T]he comparability of alternatives is necessary to the possibility of justified choice."
11. In other words, there is a positive value relation that obtains in the equality case.
12. John Broome comes to the same conclusion; cf. 1999: 155: "I conclude that, when we think about an isolated choice between two options there is nothing in practical decision making that is different between the incommensurate case and the equality case."
13. Raz 1986: 352.

14. This is not to say that it might never be right to sacrifice someone in order to save other persons. As I argue in the next section, if this could be right it would not be due to the weighing up of the goodness the options at stake would bring about.
15. This is how Chang sees the value relation between friendship and money; cf. Chang 1997: 21.
16. Utilitarians would of course deny this. According to them, Jim should accept Pedro's offer. But then, on the other hand, utilitarians cannot account for the difficulty we have with Jim/Pedro cases.
17. Cf. Williams 1973: 103: "[O]ur moral relation is partly given ... by a sense of what we can 'live with.' ... "
18. Cf. Gowans 1994: 117–54.
19. Or as Dancy 1993: 123 puts it: "In tragic dilemmas ... whichever choice one makes one does a wrong." Doing a wrong is not the same as doing something that is wrong.
20. We hold this view also for other reasons. We think that we cannot be blamed for things we are not responsible for. Thus, if Jim cannot avoid doing something that is bad, he should not be blamed for doing so.
21. I owe this objection to Norbert Anwander.
22. Cf. Chang 1997: 28.
23. 1997: 5.
24. Cf., for instance, Nagel 1986: 176.

Bibliography

Brink, David O. 1996. Moral Conflict and Its Structure. In Homer E. Mason (ed.), *Moral Dilemmas and Moral Theory.* Oxford: Oxford University Press, 102–26.

Broome, John. 1999. Incommensurable Values. In John Broome, *Ethics Out of Economics.* Cambridge: Cambridge University Press, 145–61.

Broome, John. 2000. Normative Requirements. In Jonathan Dancy (ed.), *Normativity,* Oxford: Blackwell, 78–99.

Chang, Ruth. 1997. Introduction. In Ruth Chang (ed.), *Incommensurability, Incomparability, and Practical Reason.* Cambridge, Mass.: Harvard University Press, 1–34.

Chang, Ruth. 1998. Comparison and the Justification of Choice. *University of Pennsylvania Law Review* 146: 1569–98.

Conee, Earl. 1987. Against Moral Dilemmas. In Christopher W. Gowans (ed.), *Moral Dilemmas.* Oxford: Oxford University Press, 239–49.

Dancy, Jonathan. 1993. *Moral Reasons.* Oxford: Blackwell.

Donagan, Alan. 1987. Consistency in Rationalist Moral Systems. In Christopher W. Gowans, *Moral Dilemmas.* Oxford: Oxford University Press, 271–90.

Donagan, Alan. 1996. Moral Dilemmas, Genuine and Spurious: A Comparative Anatomy. In Homer E. Mason (ed.), *Moral Dilemmas and Moral Theory.* Oxford: Oxford University Press, 11–22.

Gowans, Christopher W. 1994. *Innocence Lost: An Examination of Inescapable Moral Wrongdoing.* Oxford: Oxford University Press.

Nagel, Thomas. 1979. The Fragmentation of Value. In Thomas Nagel, *Mortal Questions.* Cambridge: Cambridge University Press, 128–41.

Nagel, Thomas. 1986. *The View from Nowhere.* Oxford: Oxford University Press.

Raz, Joseph. 1986. *The Morality of Freedom.* Oxford: Clarendon.

Williams, Bernard. 1973. A Critique of Utilitarianism. In J. J. C. Smart and Bernard Williams, *Utilitarianism: For and Against.* Cambridge: Cambridge University Press, 73–150.

13

Moral Dilemmas of Transitional Justice

Jon Elster

"Transitional justice" refers to the process of coming to terms with the past in the transition to democracy. It includes, notably, *trials*, administrative and professional *purges*, *restitution* of property, and *compensation* for suffering. Notable examples of transitions to democracy that had some measure of transitional justice include

- the demise of the Athenian oligarchs in 411 and then again in 403 B.C.;
- the restoration of democracy after 1945 in countries that had been occupied by the Germans during World War II;
- the return to or introduction of democracy after 1945 in the main Axis countries: Germany, Japan, Italy;
- the fall of military dictatorships in Southern Europe in the mid-1970s;
- the return to or introduction of democracy after 1989 in numerous countries in Eastern Europe;
- the recent fall of the dictatorships in many Latin American countries, notably, Argentina, Chile, and Bolivia; and
- the transition to democracy in South Africa.

These cases pose some extraordinary hard and sometimes unusual moral questions, for which we often lack firm intuitions. Here is a preliminary example: Among the agents of the Nazi or Communist regime, should the fanatic or the opportunist be punished more severely? In other words, is the personal commitment to an inhumane ideology an aggravating or an extenuating circumstance? In the fourth *Provinciale*, Pascal heaps scorn on the Jesuits, who teach that one cannot sin if one does not know that what one is doing is wrong. Yet the Jesuits were writing for hardened sinners who wanted to be able to enjoy the pleasures of the flesh without paying the price of damnation, not for dedicated ideologues who were willing to risk their lives for the perverse causes they believed in. Could not an argument be made that those who join the same evil causes and perform the same evil acts merely for their career advantage are even more debased?

I proceed as follows. In the first section, I raise what is perhaps the core dilemma in transitional justice: the dilemma, roughly speaking, between procedural and substantive justice. In the second section, I consider the tension between consequentialist and nonconsequentialist arguments in transitional justice. In the third section, I discuss some of the complexities of the notions of suffering and victimhood. In the fourth section, I consider some of the excuses that perpetrators and wrongdoers have offered for their actions. The last section offers a brief conclusion.

"WE ARE NOT LIKE THEM"

The former Czech dissident Jachym Topol recounts the following:

In 1994, I came across the address of one of the communist secret police (StB) agents who tortured me at a police station during an interrogation. He allegedly killed one of my friends and raped others who were in jail. Together with two mates with whom I was in prison, we decided to punish him. We managed to kidnap this former StB agent and to transport him to a hidden place; we were thinking of killing him. Then I stayed alone with him for a while, and he was so scared and hopeless that I could not do anything else but to release him. When my friends returned, I was afraid to say what I had done. When they found out the truth they sighed with relief. We were not able to kill him, because we are not like them. We are not animals. (http://www.dfn.org/voices/czech/topol.htm.)

The phrase "We are not like them" originated with Vaclav Havel and became a mantra of the Czech dissident movement. The thought behind it is a bit more complex than the cited passage would suggest. It can be amplified by citing another famous phrase, uttered by a former East German dissident, Bärbel Bohley, "We expected justice, but we got the *Rechtsstaat* instead."[1]

There are in fact three motivations that can be at work in these situations: the desire for revenge, the desire for substantive retributive justice, and the desire to follow procedurally correct principles in implementing substantive justice.[2] Topol's story illustrates the temptation of revenge. Bohley's remark expresses the frustrated desire for substantive justice. In practice, the desire for revenge and the desire for substantive justice often fuse. Although those who demand severe punishment for leaders and agents of the predemocratic regime may believe themselves to be motivated by concerns of justice, the demand loses its force with time. In trials in German-occupied countries after World War II, sentencing was almost invariably more severe in the initial stages than after two or three years.[3] This is a typical pattern of emotional reactions, whereas standards of justice presumably do not decay with time.[4]

The desire to perceive oneself as motivated by concerns of impersonal justice rather than by revenge is by no means universal. In feuding societies, the idea would appear farfetched. Yet in the specific circumstances of the transition to democracy, there is often a strong normative pressure to differentiate oneself from the predemocratic regime by insisting on justice rather than revenge. "Victors' justice" is an oxymoron. One sign of the new regime's sincerity in its demand for justice rather than revenge is its willingness to punish those who take justice into their own hands or to compensate their victims. In 1945, de Gaulle's government showed that it was willing to draw the line.

The government, by a symbolic act, made it clear that it would tolerate no yielding before the threat of violence. The previous October, in Maubeuge, an angry mob had stormed the local prison, demanding the execution of two collaborators whose death sentences had been commuted by General de Gaulle. The mob threatened to massacre all the other inmates of the jail if it did not receive satisfaction; the three Forces Françaises de l'Intérieur officers in charge did as the mob demanded. Brought to trial in Paris, the three officers were sentenced to prison terms of five to seven years. Numerous other arrests of *résistants* for unauthorized executions took place during early 1945.[5]

By contrast, in 1945 the Belgian government suspended the application of a law from 1795 that would have enabled the collaborators to obtain compensation for violence against themselves or their property.[6]

In democracies that emerge from lawless regimes, whether authoritarian or totalitarian, the new leaders often want to show their adherence to the rule of law and the *Rechtsstaat*. The post-1945 trials in Western Europe were shaped by this consideration. In Norway, the use of summary trials was dismissed as an expression of an unacceptable Nazi mentality.[7] In Belgium, internment practices were severely criticized for resembling how things were done "on the other side of the Rhine."[8] In France, retroactive legislation was condemned as a Vichy practice.[9] Anonymous denunciations – another Vichy custom – were not accepted.[10]

The desire for legality often goes together with a strong desire for a large fraction of the collaborators to be convicted. As Peter Novick remarks about France, "side by side with this *passionate* longing [for retribution] was the attachment of *résistants* to those principles of justice and equity which distinguished them from the rulers of Nazi Germany and Vichy France."[11] Istvan Deák notes that in post-1945 Hungary, the Minister of Justice insisted "both on the need to observe strict legal procedures and on the need to exercise revolutionary political justice."[12] In many cases, however, there is a conflict between the desire for procedural justice and the desire for substantive justice, between the desire to demarcate oneself from the earlier regime and the desire to punish the regime as severely as it deserves. As Bohley noted, strict adherence to the *Rechtsstaat* may stand in the way of substantive justice.

New democracies can resolve the dilemma in one of three ways. First, one can insist on respect for basic legal principles such as a ban on retroactive legislation or an extension of the statute of limitations. This has, for instance, consistently been the approach of the Hungarian Constitutional Court after 1989.[13] Second, one can frankly and openly accept the need to violate these principles in an unprecedented situation. After 1945, Denmark and Holland adopted explicit retroactive legislation, a procedure that was probably facilitated by the fact that neither country has a ban on retroactivity in the constitution. Third – and this is the most common procedure – one can use subterfuge to try and have it both ways. In 1948, a Belgian commentator wrote, "The Dutch system [of specifically permitting retroactivity] is more sincere than ours. The Belgian legislator pretended to adhere to the principle of non-retroactivity in criminal law. In reality [the Penal Code] . . . was made increasingly severe by so-called interpretative laws."[14] In the same year, a Dutch law professor criticized the French who – in order to avoid retroactive penalties – called the often severe sanctions of the new "national indignity" crime "losses of rights" instead of penalties. "This seems to me a mere playing with words; a confiscation of one's entire property, or even a loss of certain rights, is as much a . . . [penalty] as say a fine or the deprivation of liberty."[15]

The trials of the border guards in the former German Democratic Republic arguably rested on legal subterfuge. To comply with the clause in the unification treaty that prosecution could target only acts that were crimes under East German as well as West German law, the Federal Supreme Court of Germany reconstructed an "ideal" law of the GDR from supralegal principles of natural law. Commenting on the decision, Peter Quint writes:

For all their earnestness and complexity, opinions of this sort seem to be lacking in candor. The court creates an ideal law of the GDR, through the use of techniques and principles resembling those current in the Federal Republic, solely for the purpose of saying that this hypothetical construct was "really" the law of the GDR and therefore its application today is not retroactive.... It would seem much more direct and honest to say: The law of the GDR as it actually existed was unacceptable and therefore we are applying a new law to these cases. Perhaps under prevailing interpretations of the Unification Treaty... that acknowledgment could mean the end of these cases, but these issues nonetheless deserve a more general consideration.[16]

From the moral point of view, the only unambiguous statement one can make about such cases is that subterfuge is to be avoided. Either of the two nonhypocritical positions seems defensible. To say "equally defensible" would presuppose a metric, which I do not have.

A final issue deserves to be mentioned. Many transitions to democracy are negotiated between leaders of the outgoing regime and the new democratic forces. Typically, the negotiated deal guarantees immunity for prosecution for the new leaders. After the transition the question may arise of why the promise of immunity should be respected. Why keep a pact with the devil? One answer may be: Because we are not like him.[17] That the devil does not keep his promises does not imply we should not keep our promise to him. To explain why he did not want to prosecute the Communist leaders in Poland after Solidarity – to universal surprise – won the elections in June 1989, the first post-Communist Prime Minister Tadeusz Mazowiecki said simply, *"Pacta sunt servanda."* [18] Adam Michnik is quoted as making an even stronger statement: "If I didn't tell [General Czeslaw] Kiszczak at the Roundtable that he would be judged if I came to power, it would be deeply wrong of me to demand it now."[19]

FORWARD-LOOKING OR BACKWARD-LOOKING?

The contrast between consequentialist and nonconsequentialist (or deontological) principles of justice is a familiar one. In some cases they can converge on the same recommendation, notably, when rule-utilitarian and rights-based arguments point in the same direction. The principle of "finders keepers" is an example. In other cases they can diverge dramatically. Acting on (something like) the categorical imperative, that is, doing what would have the best outcome if everyone did the same, may in fact make the situation worse if others do not follow suit. Unilateral disarmament is an example. In transitional justice, as we see below, we find instances of both convergence and divergence.

Writers who advocate severe punishment of agents and leaders of the former regime on consequentialist grounds typically rest their argument on a deterrent effect. Severe punishment of dictators and their collaborators is supposed to act as a precedent that will deter would-be dictators from taking power, in part presumably because others will be deterred from assisting them. This was, for instance, Justice Robert Jackson's position during the Nuremberg trials: They were needed "to make war less attractive to those who have the governments and the destinies of peoples in their power."[20] A French member of the International Military Tribunal, Donnedieu de Vabres, stressed the function of the Nuremberg judgment as an "incomparable precedent." Otto Kirchheimer, who cites this phrase, goes on to comment, "The incomparable precedent would backfire, however, if it induced the leaders of a future war to fight to the bitter end rather than surrender and face the possible future of war criminals."[21]

The precedent argument does, in fact, have a number of flaws. Suppose (implausibly) that severe punishments in the present will indeed install the appropriate belief in potential coup makers that they will be harshly punished if they take power illegally and then are deposed. It is extremely unlikely that the deterrence effect of this belief will reduce the chance of an illegal seizure of power to *zero*. In a given case, a rational would-be dictator might find that the expected benefits from taking power exceed the costs, even when the latter are inflated by the prospect of severe punishment. Some aspiring dictators may be fanatics rather than opportunists and care little about their personal fate. Given that some illegal seizures of power are likely to occur, Kirchheimer's observation applies forcefully. In this perspective, the net effect of severe penalties in the present on human-rights violations in the future is essentially indeterminate.[22] On the one hand, some rational would-be dictators will be deterred from taking power. On the other hand, the dictators who actually do take power will hang on to it for longer and apply more violent means to retain it, reasoning that they might as well be hanged for a sheep as for a lamb.[23]

By assumption, the nonconsequentialist argument favors severe punishment, whereas the consequentialist argument is indeterminate in its implications. There is no moral dilemma, only an epistemic one. If the democratic leaders impose severe punishment on their predecessors, they (or their successors) might come to regret it when the incentive effects work themselves out, but that is the case also of a probabilistic argument that assigns greater expected utility to one outcome than to another.

Let me now contrast the deontological argument for severe punishment with consequentialist arguments for leniency. Among the several consequentialist arguments that are relevant here, I focus only on one.[24] Often, transitional justice takes place in societies that have been ravaged by war (as after 1945) or by a massively inefficient economic system (as after 1989). In Western Europe, there was a need for large-scale economic reconstruction; in Eastern Europe, for transition to a market economy. In both cases, it was widely believed that the unfettered pursuit of retributive justice might interfere with these tasks. In Western Europe, this belief justified a low rate of prosecutions for economic collaborations with the Germans, as well as a generally modest level of purges in the administration. In Germany itself, de-Nazification was initially envisaged at a large scale. To take an extreme example: To address the particularly delicate problem of the severely tainted judiciary, it was at one point envisaged "closing all German courts for ten years and replacing them with a 'colonial' system, so that a new generation of judges could be educated in the meantime."[25] Needless to say, this impracticable proposal was not implemented nor were other proposals that would have been more feasible but still very costly for the reconstruction effort.

In the former GDR, the impact of these pragmatic considerations is clear if one compares the rate of purges in different Länder. "Among the state governments, a rift soon appeared between Saxony and the four other new Länder on the definition of criteria [for dismissal from public service of those who had worked for the state security]. The Saxons argued for the application of the strict criteria in use in Berlin, where intransigence was facilitated by the on-site availability of alternative (western) officials. Officials from the four other Länder argued for more flexibility."[26] In Poland, it has been argued that decommunization was frustrated by the fact that the new leaders "had no choice but to rely on the experience and cooperation of many former nomenklatura members."[27]

In Eastern Europe and the former GDR, similar issues arise with respect to restitution and compensation. Although restitution of property to former owners does not involve direct expenses for the government, it can interfere with economic efficiency. Thus, the German "Unification treaty provided that a former owner can be denied a return of expropriated property if the property is needed for urgent investment uses that would yield general economic benefits in Eastern Germany."[28] In the region, the Czech government has most consistently favored restitution in kind of expropriated property. Several reasons are involved: a philosophically based respect for the rights of the original owners (a backward-looking argument), a desire to send a signal to foreign investors that property rights will be protected (a forward-looking argument), and a desire to reduce the chances that the property would end up in the hands of the former nomenklatura.[29]

As for compensation for suffering (see also the third section below), the obvious backward-looking arguments have to be balanced against the fact that compensation is expensive and never more so than in times of scarcity and reconstruction. Thus, "according to some reports, the value of the assets confiscated from Hungary's Jews during the war, allowing for unpaid interest, was equivalent to the total national wealth of Hungary."[30] Similarly, full compensation to the three million Sudeten Germans expelled from Czechoslovakia after World War II would have bankrupted the country. In the typical case, however, full compensation is not literally unfeasible. Rather, given the feasible combinations of funds allocated to compensation and funds allocated to reconstruction, the authorities choose a combination that involves less than full – sometimes, much less than full – compensation. The cost of justice itself may absorb much of what is to be restituted. In one Norwegian case, the cost of settling a Jewish estate worth 1.8 million Crowns (about $3 million today) was 1.5 million Crowns, which was deducted from the estate before restitution.[31] In another post-1945 decision, the Norwegian Directorate for Compensation took account of whether a claimant could reasonably have *expected* to receive the full amount to which he would have been entitled under normal rules of inheritance. Since Jews whose families had died in the extermination camps could not have expected to inherit from all their relatives, the amount they received was correspondingly curtailed, thus liberating funds for reconstruction.[32]

These decisions can be challenged. In Poland after 1989, there was initially an arbitrary limitation of compensation to suffering of Poles within Polish borders, thus excluding those handed over to Soviet secret police. When the latter turned out to be the majority, the law was changed. In the Czech Republic, the original stipulation that restitution may be made only to the citizens of the Czech and Slovak Republic who have their permanent place of residence in the country was declared unconstitutional by the Czech Constitutional Court. In Norway, fifty years after Liberation, recalculation of the value of property expropriated from Jews during the war led Parliament to award a large compensation payment to the Jewish community. In the meantime, it should be said, Norway had become one of the richest countries in the world.

There is no general formula for balancing consequentialist and de-ontological principles against one another when they point in different directions. Either kind of principle, if taken to the extreme, becomes absurd. Either, up to a point, is defensible. Yet once again, there is no metric.

SUFFERING AND COMPENSATION

Acts of wrongdoing that cause suffering can elicit two reactions in the victim (or in third parties). First, there may be a desire to impose a cor-responding suffering on the wrongdoer: an eye for an eye. Second, there may be a desire to undo, at least to some extent or as far as possible, the harm that was done.[33] As shown by the institution of Wergeld, these can serve as substitutes for each other. In ancient Teutonic and Old English law, this was "the price set upon a man according to his rank, paid by way of compensation or fine in cases of homicide and certain other crimes to free the offender from further obligation or punishment" (Oxford English Dictionary). Conversely, one might think of punishment as a sub-stitute for compensation if the wrongdoer is unable to pay the Wergeld. Yet in modern legal systems, punishment is not justified by the needs of the victims. Compensation for victims of wrongdoing is uncoupled from punishment of the wrongdoer.[34]

To determine the just compensation for suffering, we must first deter-mine what shall count as suffering and how to measure it. The conceptu-ally simplest form of suffering is loss of tangible (movable or immovable) property. The principle for compensation is also simple: If the piece of property and the original owner still exist, he or she should get it back. Yet even this simple case raises many issues. If property has been confis-cated by the predemocratic authorities and then sold to particulars, the latter may claim to have acted in good faith, with the result that the prop-erty may seem to have two legitimate owners. This problem arose in the very first recorded instance of compensation following the restoration of democracy. As part of the reconciliation treaty in Athens in 403 B.C., it was stipulated that

[i]ndividuals who had purchased confiscated goods will retain possession of them, and any property which had not been auctioned off will revert to the original owner.... This provision only involves movable property. Not all confiscated prop-erty remained in the hands of the purchasers. The reconciliation treaty ordains

that immovable property, such as land and houses, will be returned to their former owners ... on the condition that they paid.[35]

The problem arose again in the recent East European transitions, much exacerbated by the long interval between confiscation of property and demands for its return. Those who bought apartments or houses that the state had confiscated might have lived in them for several generations. The German reunification treaty stipulated that an "exception to the principle of return of expropriated property is made when individuals or certain institutional owners have acquired property 'in an honest manner.' ... In these cases the rights of the innocent party purchaser are protected, and the purchaser can keep the property."[36] The original owner receives equivalent property or, if that is not possible, monetary compensation. In other East European countries, the solution chosen was that housing property was returned to the original owner while the secondary owner obtained a life tenancy.

In other property issues, counterfactual speculations are involved. If the value of the property has been enhanced through improvements, should the original owner compensate the interim owner before getting the property back?[37] Although the interim owner would seem to have a right to be compensated for his investment, the original owner might respond that he would have made similar improvements had he retained possession. In the Czech Republic, a compromise was reached that gives the original owner the right to pay the difference in value or take a share of the business.

All of these dilemmas become more acute if the original owner is no longer alive. Although the legal issues may be straightforward, the moral (and political) ones are not. Consider, for instance, affluent citizens of the former West Germany whose parents fled the GDR, leaving behind them property that was either appropriated by the state or allocated to private individuals. The moral claims of the generally deprived citizens of the GDR to retain what little they have come into conflict with the legal (*and* moral) claims of the West German heirs. "For to those who have more shall be given; and from those who have nothing, even what they have will be taken away."

A second form of suffering involves damage to body and health as the result of imprisonment, torture, or persecution. Barring special cases, this leaves no room for restitution: Only compensation is feasible. To decide whether a person shall be compensated for suffering incurred during the predemocratic regime, one has to establish a causal link between acts of wrongdoing and the suffering. This innocent idea, "to establish a causal link," is fraught with difficulties. During the medical examinations of victims of persecution in Nazi Germany, "people were forced to recall their experiences, with destructive consequences for many."[38] Thus, according to the New York psychoanalyst Kurt Eissler, "The patient should actually receive compensation for the agitation and degradation suffered in the course of the reparations procedure."[39] This is iatrogenic medicine: exacerbating the problems it is supposed to help resolve.[40] Such cases pose a genuine dilemma. On the one hand, one cannot simply grant compensation to all who claim to have suffered as a result of persecution. On the other hand, the process of establishing a causal link with sufficient high degree of probability can cause genuine, additional damage to the claimant.[41]

Apart from this question, what *is* a "sufficient high degree of probability"? Although the (mostly ex-Nazi) doctors who examined Jewish claimants for compensation usually had no difficulty in establishing or denying causality, their basis for doing so was flimsy. The case of Herr W. is typical.[42] He was eleven years old in 1933, popular with everyone at school. Then "everything changed overnight," and in October 1934, W. and his parents emigrated to Palestine. After many problems, he emigrated to the United States in 1957, where he had more problems. One doctor found that

"Herr W. had been traumatized not by mistreatment as about of ten to twelve years of age, but as a small child, due to the separation of his parents, the loss of his biological father, and a troubled relationship with his father." The doctor concluded that "if W.'s childhood had been happy, the discrimination at age ten should not have made any difference. On the contrary it should have toughened him. Such social discrimination "does not lead to psychological harm; it is more likely to strengthen the ability to cope with life."

In citing this piece of Nietzschean psychotherapy I want to argue not that it is wrong, only that it is manifestly unproven. As scientific disciplines, psychology and psychiatry are so undeveloped that it is morally irresponsible to rely on them for important decisions of this kind. Yet what shall we *do* in face of a claim whose causal foundations we are unable to evaluate? How are we to weigh the avoidance of false positives against the avoidance of false negatives? By giving the claimant the benefit of the doubt, one might open the floodgates for spurious claims. By shifting the burden of proof to the claimant, one might add to the injustice for which reparation is sought.

I have discussed two forms of suffering: tangible and material (loss of property) and tangible but nonmaterial (damage to body). There is also a third category: the intangible and nonmaterial suffering that takes the form either of loss of opportunities or of opportunities forgone. During Communism, almost everybody suffered in these ways. People were prevented by law from selling their labor power. Unless they were willing to engage in deeply compromising behavior, they could not travel abroad or ensure access for their children to higher education. In the Nazi regimes of Germany and countries allied with or occupied by Germany, Jews were prevented from exercising a number of professions, with substantial loss of income as the result.

Different compensatory regimes have addressed this class of sufferings in different ways. In Hungary, the Second Compensation Law passed in 1992 addressed (among other issues) the question of compensation for harm done to Jews during the war. As Istvan Pogany writes,

the law provides compensation only for interferences with *property* rights after 1 May 1939. It applies to government takings authorised by the Second Jewish Law but does not extend to other and far-reaching interferences with the economic life of the Jewish community.... However, the economic consequences of expelling Jews from certain sectors of employment... was at least as severe, for the individuals concerned and for their families, as the confiscation of property proved for others.[43]

Note that Pogany does not address the losses suffered by those in the younger generation who were prevented from *entering* these sectors of employment. The same focus on actual losses is found in the Federal Restitution law passed by the West German Parliament in 1956. The law included, among its eight categories of grounds for compensation, both harm to career advancement and harm to economic advancement. Yet with the exception that I italicize below, the harms are actual losses (compared with a preexisting baseline) rather than opportunities forgone (compared with a counterfactual baseline). The harms include "revocation of admission to legal practice, layoffs from the civil service... or a private business, reduced income, *prevention* or interruption of education or training, and loss of contributions to life insurance."[44] A similar bias or rather ambiguity is found in Peter Quint's comments on a 1991 decision by the German Constitutional Court in which it argued that

compensation [to former owners of GDR property] need not be made at full market value: lesser payments might be reasonable in light of the government's other obligations incurred upon unification, such as the cost of economic renewal in the former GDR, and in light of the fact that during the same period of history many people had undergone serious *deprivations* without compensation. Perhaps the Court was suggesting that if the former . . . owners received too much, that would create a new inequality by virtue of the disparity with those who *lost* life, health or freedom without compensation during the same period.[45]

The two words that I have italicized point in different directions. Whereas "deprivation" may refer both to actual losses and to opportunities forgone, "loss" is unambiguous. Elsewhere Quint cites both *"dismissal* from employment in retaliation for filing an application to leave the GDR" and *"exclusion* from an advanced high school on political grounds" as typical cases of political discrimination for which compensation might be claimed.[46]

There are several reasons why the focus tends to be on lost opportunities rather than on opportunities forgone. For one thing, the general phenomenon of loss aversion implies that losses loom larger than forgone gains.[47] For another, "the problems of proof, as well as the difficulties of measuring the ultimate consequences of the claimed discrimination, [are] daunting."[48] A bureaucracy does not deal easily with counterfactual claims of this nature. Damage to property and body can be measured and quantified in a natural way. The likelihood that I would have taken up an opportunity that was blocked to me, and my likely degree of success in that career, do not lend themselves to objective quantification. The loss of preexisting options that the agent had in fact already chosen falls somewhere in between. Although he might later have gone on to do something else or become a failure in his chosen profession, there is a presumption in his favor that does not exist in the purely counterfactual case.

But there may be a deeper reason as well. It can be brought out by citing an article by Ernst Ehrmann in *Die Zeit* from 1964. In the summary of Christian Pross, the author

felt that the demands of the persecutee organizations would lead to an enormous number of new trials and proceedings: "In the still-closed world of the persecuted, especially the emigrants, it's buzzing like a beehive. New desires are being awakened." Increasing the sum, for example, for interference with education for "the peculiar people, the Gypsies" was completely out of place, as Gypsies placed no value on education and thus did not need to be compensated for lost educational opportunities.[49]

The argument, for all its unpleasant overtones, is related to recent debates over the relative importance of desires and opportunities in ranking social states.[50] There are strong reasons against ranking states merely on the basis of preference satisfaction and against basing compensation merely on the basis of unfulfilled desires. There might be too much compensation if people report desires they do not really have. There might be too little if they adjust their desires to their opportunities. Yet the proposal to rank states merely on the basis of the opportunities they offer and to base compensation merely on blocked opportunities is also problematic. Is state A really better than state B if the two are identical except that in A one individual has an opportunity that he does not want to take up? *Couldn't state A in fact be worse,* if it involves the wasteful provision of a costly opportunity? And if that individual is deprived of that opportunity, ought he to be compensated for the loss? Should a Jewish-Hungarian man who was eighteen years old in 1939 be compensated for the lack of opportunity to become a lawyer if his overwhelming desire was to become a violinist? More generally, if a very small proportion of a given segment of the population have a desire to enter a certain profession, ought all members of that population to be compensated if the opportunity to do so is taken away from them?

EXCUSES AND COUNTERFACTUALS

The moral dilemmas can be approached through the lens of *excuses.* What counts as a valid excuse? I focus on those that take the form of counterfactual statements, that is, statements about what would have happened if the agent had abstained from committing the acts he is accused of. Consider, for instance, the role of the judge who implements and legitimates the inhumane policies of the predemocratic regime. In France during the German occupation, only one judge refused to take the oath to Pétain. Many argued that it should be taken, "since the alternative was to see captured *résistants* come before a judiciary even more Pétainized than it already was. . . . Frequently it had been a question of passing an unjust sentence short of death lest the case – or future cases – be taken out of the judge's hand and put in those of a Vichy fanatic."[51] In Denmark, too, judges collaborated with the Germans to prevent the occupying power from simply taking the judicial system into their own hands, which would have had predictably worse outcomes for the population.[52] Along similar lines, during the apartheid era a South African human rights lawyer asserted, "If we . . . argue that moral judges should resign, we can no longer pray, when we go into court as defense counsel, or even as the accused, that we find a moral judge on the Bench."[53]

Are theses excuses too comfortable? Do judges embrace them because they enable them to reconcile their personal or professional interest with their self-image as being moved not merely by interest? Do they *know* or merely *assume*, self-servingly, that if they resigned or refused a more zealous collaborator would take their place? When we are in doubt, doesn't what one might call "self-critical morality" tell us to do what would harm us most rather than what we think would most benefit others? Isn't there a larger duty to the cause of resistance to oppression that trumps the duty to minimize the impact of oppression? I leave these questions on the table.

Economic collaborators also justify themselves with counterfactual statements about how refusals to collaborate would have made things worse. In Norway, owners of newspapers that had adapted to the occupation defended themselves by saying that a completely German-dominated press would have had a negative impact on public opinion.[54] An enterprise that produced for the Germans might claim that more harm to the country would have been done had the factories been dismantled, machinery shipped to Germany, and workers conscripted into German labor service. Alternatively, if laying idle the machines would have deteriorated and not been available for postwar reconstruction; also, there would have been no occasions for sabotage and slow-down actions.[55] Self-serving as these arguments sound and often were, they cannot be dismissed out of hand.

A different kind of counterfactual excuse refers to what would have happened to oneself, rather than to others, in the case of refusal to carry out inhumane orders. "If I hadn't shot, I would have been shot." This was the defense routinely offered by those who carried out Nazi or Communist atrocities. Objectively, it may have been groundless. In the 1963–5 trials of the Auschwitz guards, one defendant, Mulka, said that he would have been signing his own death warranted if he had refused to obey. "The court took care to explore the plausibility of Mulka's fear: the evidence suggested that camp officers who refused orders could expect to be transferred to the front and/or to a punishment battalion, but no other penalties were likely."[56] Yet can we be sure that, subjectively, the guards did not believe that they would be shot if they refused to obey? If they believed, nonself-servingly, that to be the case, they might claim that they were "forced" to kill. Whatever the legal response might be to that claim, a moral response might be that it is better to be killed for refusing to kill an innocent person than to kill that person. But what if that person would be killed by somebody else in any case? There is a double counterfactual:

If A had refused to kill B, C would have killed A and D would have killed B. By killing B, A saved one life: his own.

CONCLUSION

In this chapter I have tried to offer some empirical material that might be useful for students of practical conflicts. I have not addressed the philosophical issues head-on or even obliquely. Moral dilemmas present "hard cases" about which intuition is mute or torn. If they can be decided at all, it will have to be in the light of a comprehensive moral theory for which firm intuitions about simple cases serve as constraints.[57] I can propose no such theory, and I do not know whether any is likely to be forthcoming.

I have been concerned with distinguishing moral dilemmas from epistemic dilemmas. The distinction is not always clear-cut. Consider the question, which has come up in South Africa and in several East European countries, of whether victims benefit from learning the identity of those who persecuted them, tortured them, or informed on them (and their relatives). This might seem to be pose a purely epistemic dilemma: Will knowledge induce catharsis and healing or, on the contrary, increase resentment and bitterness? Although the former view is the more common, the latter also has some claims to truth. When wrongdoers are exposed without being punished, victims may feel as if they are being "forced to forgive."[58] Be this as it may, there is also a moral dilemma. Isn't it *better* to know than to live in a fool's paradise?

There are many kinds of moral dilemmas. Suppose A and B are evils. A dilemma can arise for the agent if he is forced by circumstances to do either A or B. A dilemma can arise for an observer if he has to decide whether someone who does A (without being forced to) is to judged more severely than someone who does B (without being forced to). In the Introduction, I used the example of opportunism versus fanaticism as an example. Another example is when we have to decide whether people should be judged more severely for pretransitional acts of wrongdoing or for posttransitional lying about these acts. Should people be excluded from public office on the basis of past collaboration with the secret police (as in Germany) or on the basis of lying about their collaboration (as in Poland)? Or suppose that A and B are two evil regimes, for example, Nazi Germany and Communist GDR. Should the lenient treatment of Nazi officials induce severe or lenient treatment of their Communist counterparts? Many Germans after 1989 said to themselves, "This time we are going to get it right." Others said that it would be absurd to impose much more severe punishments for what were, after all, much less serious crimes. Both views seem defensible.

Other dilemmas arise when we ask what *is* evil. What is, for instance, the proper role of counterfactual reasoning in imputing moral responsibility? Also, how do we *respond* to evil (and to suffering)? How much importance should we accord to procedural versus substantive concerns and to forward-looking versus backward-looking concerns? And again, what is the proper role of counterfactual reasoning? In particular, how much weight should we give to the thought, "There but for the grace of God go I"? Isn't it unfair to hold to account the citizens of the former East Germany, when most of them had never in their adult lives known anything but a totalitarian regime? Should not the West German prosecutor or judge recognize that it is a mere accident of geography that he did not end up on the other side of the border and thus on the side of the accused?

Notes

1. Cited in McAdams 1997: 240.
2. See notably Sa'adah 1998: 145ff.
3. For Norway, see Andenæs 1980: 229; for Denmark, Tamm 1984: ch.7; for Holland, Mason 1952: 187n36; for Italy, Domenico 1991: 178; for Belgium, Huyse and Dhondt 1993: 231. The last authors consider and reject the objection that the trend could be an artifact of the most serious crimes having been tried first. The only exception is France, for which Novick 1968: 164n12 finds no evidence for the hypothesis of progressive leniency of sentencing, without, however, being able to rule it out.
4. The passage of time may, to be sure, be taken as an extenuating circumstance: "It was so long ago that I am no longer the same person."
5. See Novick 1968: 77.
6. See Huyse and Dhondt 1993: 50–1.
7. See Andenæs 1980: 62.
8. Huyse and Dhondt 1993: 100.
9. See Lottman 1986: 50. François Mauriac saw in the willingness of Albert Camus to adopt retroactive laws "the corrosive effect of four years of fascist rule" (Sa'adah 1998: 54).
10. See Lottman 1986: 186.
11. Novick 1968: 141.
12. Deák n.d.
13. See Halmai and Scheppele 1997; see also Schwartz 2000: ch. 4.
14. Mason 1952: 130. For arguments about the de facto retroactivity of much Belgian legislation, see also Huyse and Dhondt 1993: 28–9, 64–5.
15. Ibid. For arguments about the de facto retroactivity of this French legislation, see also Novick 1968: 146 and Lottman 1986: 51–2.

16. See Quint 1997: 203.
17. There are at least two other answers. In some countries, notably, Latin American ones, the outgoing dictators can enforce the promise through their control over the military, security, and police forces. In the South African transition, the new democratic regime is essentially constrained by the international capital market. There is a widely held belief that if there were to be either large-scale redistribution of land or retribution beyond the narrow limits of the Truth and Reconciliation Commission, both capital and capitalists would flee the country.
18. See Walicki 1997: 205–6.
19. Halmai and Scheppele 1997: 179.
20. Cited in Taylor 1992: 55.
21. Kirchheimer 1961: 325n29.
22. See also Elster 1999: ch. 1.
23. Thus, "the early actions of the Alfonsín regime in prosecuting the former military rulers stimulated some Uruguayan military to back away from their commitment to relinquish power" (Huntington 1991: 103). The same argument is stated in an editorial in *The Economist* of August 31, 1996: "It is probably true that neither the generals who run Myanmar, nor President Suharto in Indonesia, nor the Communist Party in China, will be encouraged to move towards democracy by the fate of Messrs Chun and Roh. After all, Mr Roh ceded power as gracefully as any military man can. Now he has fallen victim to the process of democratisation that he helped to foster. The moral drawn by Asia's nervous dictators may well be that, when democrats are at the door, lock them up rather than usher them in."
24. Among other consequentialist arguments in favor of leniency, the most important relies on the need for national reconciliation and healing. As noted by Sa'adah 1998, however, this need can also be used as an argument for severity. "We can't move forward unless we forget the past" has to contend with "We can't move forward unless we first address the past." Note that this is an epistemic dilemma, not a moral one.
25. Müller 1991: 201.
26. Sa'adah 1998: 218. For the special case of dismissal vs retention of judges, see the similar observation by Quint 1997: 187.
27. Walicki 1997, 195. Tucker 1999 argues, however, that the nomenklatura did not in fact have much useful expertise.
28. Quint 1997: 129.
29. See Cepl 1991.
30. Pogany 1997: 177.
31. See Norges Offentlige Utredninger 1997: 110.
32. See ibid.: 98–102.
33. Acts of wrongdoing can elicit similar reactions in the wrongdoer. First, he may try to undo the harm he did; second, he may try to impose a similar harm on himself. The first is an expression of rational guilt, the second of irrational guilt.
34. Yet in transitional justice, there may sometimes appear to be a coupling. According to McAdams 2001: 138, "By emphasizing restitutions and

reparations, [Adenauer] may have hoped to deflect attention from his government's decision to refrain from making criminal trials or purges of former Nazi officials a central feature of its Vergangenheitsbewältigung." (For an objection to this argument, see Herf 1997: 7.) It has also been argued that the Chilean reparations have served as a substitute for retribution.

35. Loening 1987: 51–2. The last clause ("on the condition that they paid") is somewhat conjectural.

36. Quint 1997: 131.

37. See ibid.: 133, 146.

38. Pross 1998: 141. He also quotes (96) the following statement: "We must not forget the constant rousing of memories, aggressions, and resentments caused by the restitution process – the endless difficulties of producing witness statements and documents on damage to property and education, proof of persecution as such, the dealing with medical disagreements on the backs of the persecutees, the slowness of the process and the sometimes insistent narrowmindedness of the restitution bureaucracy that led to new illnesses."

39. Ibid.: 106.

40. For some related issues, see Elster 1989: ch. 3.

41. The related issue of "pension neurosis" is also worth mentioning. In the wake of World War II, psychiatrists in Great Britain, France, and Germany developed a theory to the effect that the payment of pensions for war neuroses tended to perpetuate the symptoms. The effect of pensions and allowances on war neurotics had already been noticed during the war. "The whole therapy was so vitiated by the pension system," the respected British psychotherapist T. A. Ross wrote of his work between 1917 and 1921, "that it was impossible to gauge the value of any form of treatment." Ross found that "as men got better, the thought of losing their allowance (and with it a guaranteed livelihood) would cause their hysterical symptoms to return or new symptoms to appear. . . . Other liberal-minded doctors agreed. Bernard Hart warned that it was very dangerous for there to be a relationship between symptoms and pensions. Consciously or not, as long as a pension depended on the existence of symptoms, recovery would be impeded" (Sheppard 2000: 151). After 1945, German doctors continued to rely on this theory to deny compensation to victims of Nazi persecution (see Pross 1998: 84–5).

42. See Pross 1998: 122ff.

43. See Pogany 1997: 171.

44. Pross 1998: 51.

45. Quint 1997: 138.

46. See ibid.: 224; emphasis added. On 225 he refers to "the interruption or denial of a chosen career," without noting that some careers (such as setting up a small privately owned and run factory) were not opportunities that could be granted to some but withheld to others as a form of political discrimination, but were simply not available at all.

47. Thaler 1980 offers the following example. When credit cards were first introduced, the credit card lobby preferred that any difference between cash and credit card customers take the form of a cash discount rather than a credit

card surcharge. Although the two descriptions are logically equivalent, consumers were less likely to use the cards if the difference was described as a cash discount. In general, a loss seems to be given twice as much weight (in absolute terms) as an equal-sized gain and, therefore, twice as much weight as forgoing an equal-sized gain.

48. Quint 1997: 224.
49. See Pross 1998: 63.
50. See, notably, Le Grand 1992 for an example-studded exposition.
51. Novick 1968: 85–6.
52. See Tamm 1984: 36. Here even more than elsewhere, I simplify what was a much more complicated situation.
53. Dyzenhaus 1998: 57.
54. See Hjeltnes 1990: 105. The investigative commission reached the opposite conclusion: The German propaganda would have been less harmful if it had been exposed openly as such.
55. See Mason 1952: 103; Tamm 1984: 486; Andenæs 1980: 134–42; Rochebrune and Hachera 1995: 320–8.
56. Sa'adah 1998: 169.
57. This is the method of reflective equilibrium.
58. Hamber 1998: 66.

Bibliography

Andenæs, J. 1980. *Det Vanskelige Oppgjøret.* Oslo: Tanum-Norli.

Cepl, V. 1991. A Note on the Restitution of Property in Post-Communist Czechoslovakia. *Journal of Communist Studies* 7: 368–75.

Deák, I. N.d. Political Justice in Austria and Hungary after World War II. Unpublished manuscript.

Domenico, R. P. 1991. *Italian Fascists on Trial.* Chapel Hill: University of North Carolina Press.

Dyzenhaus, D. 1998. *Judging the Judges, Judging Ourselves: Truth, Reconciliation and the Apartheid Legal Order.* Oxford: Hart Publishing.

Elster, J. 1989. *Solomonic Judgments.* Cambridge: Cambridge University Press.

Elster, J. 1999. *Alchemies of the Mind.* Cambridge: Cambridge University Press.

Halmai, G., and K. Scheppele. 1997. Living Well Is the Best Revenge: The Hungarian Approach to Judging the Past. In A. J. McAdams (ed.), *Transitional Justice and the Rule of Law in New Democracies.* Notre Dame, Ind.: University of Notre Dame Press, 155–84.

Hamber, B. 1998. *Past Imperfect.* Derry/Londonderry: INCORE.

Herf, J. 1997. *Divided Memory: The Nazi Past in Two Germanies.* Cambridge, Mass.: Harvard University Press.

Hjeltnes, G. 1990. *Avisoppgjøret etter 1945.* Oslo: Aschehoug.

Huntington, S. P. 1991. *The Third Wave: Democratization in the Late Twentieth Century.* Norman: University of Oklahoma Press.

Huyse, L., and S. Dhondt. 1993. *La Répression des collaborations.* Bruxelles: CRISP.

Kirchheimer, O. 1961. *Political Justice.* Princeton, N.J.: Princeton University Press.

Le Grand, J. 1992. *Equity and Justice.* London: Routledge.

Loening, T. C. 1987. *The Reconciliation Agreement of 403/402 B.C. in Athens.* Stuttgart: Franz Steiner Verlag.

Lottman, H. 1986. *L'Épuration.* Paris: Fayard.

Mason, H. L. 1952. *The Purge of Dutch Quislings.* The Hague: Martinus Nijhoff.

McAdams, A. J. 1997. Communism on Trial: The East German Past and the German Future. In A. J. McAdams (ed.), *Transitional Justice and the Rule of Law in New Democracies.* Notre Dame, Ind.: University of Notre Dame Press, 239–67.

McAdams, A. J. 2001. *Judging the Past in Unified Germany.* Cambridge: Cambridge University Press.

Müller, I. 1991. *Hitler's Justice.* Cambridge, Mass.: Harvard University Press.

Norges Offentlige Utredninger. 1997. *Inndragning av Jødisk Eiendom i Norge under den 2. Verdenskrig.* Oslo.

Novick, P. 1968. *The Resistance versus Vichy.* London: Chatto and Windus.

Pogany, I. 1997. *Righting Wrongs in Eastern Europe.* Manchester: Manchester University Press.

Pross, C. 1998. *Paying for the Past.* Baltimore, Md.: Johns Hopkins University Press.

Quint, P. 1997. *The Imperfect Union.* Princeton, N.J.: University Press.

Rochebrune, R. de, and J.-C. Hachera. 1995. *Les Patrons sous l'Occupation.* Paris: Editions Odile Jacob.

Sa'adah, A. 1998. *Germany's Second Chance.* Cambridge, Mass.: Harvard University Press.

Schwartz, H. 2000. *Constitutional Justice in Central and Eastern Europe.* Chicago: University of Chicago Press.

Sheppard, B. 2000. *A War of Nerves: Soldiers and Psychiatrists 1914–1994.* London: Cape.

Tamm, D. 1984. *Retsopgøret efter Besættelsen.* Copenhagen: Jurist- og Økonomforbundets Forlag.

Taylor, T. 1992. *The Anatomy of the Nuremberg Trials.* New York: Knopf.

Thaler, R. 1980. Towards a Positive Theory of Consumer Choice. *Journal of Economic Behavior and Organization* 1: 39–60.

Tucker, A. 1999. Paranoids May Be Persecuted: Post-Totalitarian Retroactive Justice. *European Journal of Sociology* 40: 56–100.

Walicki, A. 1997. Transitional Justice and the Political Struggles of Post-Communist Poland. In A. J. McAdams (ed.), *Transitional Justice and the Rule of Law in New Democracies.* Notre Dame, Ind.: University of Notre Dame Press, 185–238.

14

Do Conflicts Make Us Free?

Barbara Guckes

Sometimes we wonder whether we should act in one way or another; we are unsure whether we should do A or B. In situations such as these, different reasons count in favor of different actions, and in our view the different reasons are so strong that we do not quite know which of these reasons should guide our actions. If this is the case, we are in a practical conflict.

Being in a situation of this type[1] seems to be an exception, and yet, in my view, it is situations such as this that nourish our hope that we can act freely. This is so because in general we believe that in order to be free in the way relevant to responsibility, the agent has to be able to do A or the alternative B in a controlled manner. And since we can act in a controlled manner only if we act in accordance with reasons, this implies that we can act freely only if we can act in one way or another in accordance with reasons. We see below that we cannot perform alternative controlled actions unless we are in a conflict situation. Therefore it would appear that we can act freely only in conflict situations. In the following sections I shall begin by arguing that we cannot be free unless we are in a situation of conflict. I will then discuss whether conflicts really are the pockets of freedom we seek.

Intuitively, we tie freedom to the following three conditions:

(1) To be able to act freely, we have to be able to control our actions.
(2) We have control over our actions only if we act in accordance with reasons.
(3) We have control over our actions only if we have an alternative way of acting.

Statements (1) and (2) are accepted as true by most participants of the discussion, compatibilist and incompatibilist alike.[2] However, statement (3) is controversial (and has been so for the last three decades). That is to say, no agreement exists regarding the question of whether we have to be able to act otherwise in order to be free. The answer to this question is of paramount importance, however, since in a deterministic world[3] we do not seem to have the possibility of acting in alternative ways.[4] Therefore, if one is committed to (3), one has to reject compatibilism. The majority of the current compatibilists hold the view that if one ties freedom to the existence of an alternative possibility, one is forced into incompatibilism, but that one does not have to be able to act differently than one actually does in order to be free. They argue that our everyday intuition that freedom is bound up with the possibility of acting otherwise is misguided.

In this chapter I do not wish to enter this debate;[5] rather, without further argument, I opt for one of the two sides. I assume (in my view in keeping with our everyday intuition) that one can be free only if one is capable of acting differently from the way one actually acts.[6] Thus, I make an incompatibilist assumption and ask what are the implications of embracing this thesis.

One implication is obvious: Since in a deterministic world there are no alternative possibilities of acting, freedom requires that actions are not determined. Since freedom is bound up with control, however, one has to offer a plausible account of how indetermined actions can be controlled actions. One can act in a controlled manner only if one can act otherwise and one acts in accordance with reasons. To be able to act in a controlled way, one therefore has to be able to do one thing or another in accordance with reasons. But is the reverse also true, that is to say, have we just formulated an equivalence? If we can act in accordance with reasons either in one way or in another way, do we thereby act in a controlled way? How do situations have to be structured so that one can do one thing among different possible things in a controlled way? Can such situations be situations in which one is not in a conflict concerning how one should act? And if this turns out not to be the case, is it possible in certain conflict situations to have control over whether one does one thing or another?

I answer these questions by discussing Dennett's, Wiggins's, and Kane's theories. All three try to show how it is possible that an agent controls an indetermined action.[7] They also have in common that they restrict themselves to the causal relations of events in their explanation of the causation of the action. I therefore discuss only theories that suppose that events can be caused only by events.[8]

Dennett argues that in certain conditions one can act in a controlled manner in accordance with reasons in one way or another, without being in conflict regarding one's course of action.[9] If he could make his claim plausible, this would support the widely held view that one also can act freely outside conflict situations. He would have shown that we can uphold this position even if we subscribe to the view that freedom is tied to the possibility of an alternative action. Dennett believes that there are some reasons relevant to the action such that it is determined that the agent is consciously aware of them. Regarding other reasons that are relevant to the action, however, it is indetermined whether the agent is consciously aware of them prior to the action. Everything else is seen as determined – the agent's character, his desires and beliefs,[10] as well as his preferences and dislikes. Supposing someone acts in a certain way A. With regard to some reasons that are relevant to A, it is determined that the agent is consciously aware of them; with regard to other reasons relevant for A, however, it is indetermined whether the agent is consciously aware of them. It is determined that a certain number of reasons influence how the agent acts; if the agent does not become aware of a further reason, he will do A. However, he can become aware of further reasons that belong to another set of reasons and that are also relevant to how he acts and that influence the action. Whether he becomes aware of these further reasons, however, is seen as indetermined. However, if he becomes aware of these reasons, he decides not to do an action A but a different action B.

Let me illustrate the situation with an example: The weather is splendid and John decides to go sailing. Ever since he was a boy, John has enjoyed sailing and there is nothing he likes to do better in his spare time. As soon as the weather allows, John becomes aware of a whole set of reasons in favor of going for a sail. His becoming aware of these reasons is assumed to be determined. Suppose, moreover, that it is determined that if John does not become aware of other reasons relevant to his actions, these first reasons are efficacious in guiding his action. John is a passionate sailor, but he is also an ambitious and conscientious philosopher and he would never prefer his hobby to the fulfilling of his duties. If there are strong reasons counting against sailing and in favor of completing his latest article, instead, he invariably chooses the latter. Now, suppose John has agreed to send off his article tomorrow. This promise is a reason against sailing and for John it is a sufficient reason to do without the sailing trip. Indeed, to put it more strongly, it is determined that if John becomes aware of the reason against sailing, he will stay at home and finish his article. However, whether he becomes aware of this reason is indetermined. We can imagine a situation in which it is equally probable that John remembers the deadline or fails to do so. If he forgets the deadline, he will go sailing. If he becomes aware that he has to submit the article tomorrow, he will spend the day at his computer. According to Dennett, which reasons John becomes aware of determine how he acts.

Dennett compares this with a person who makes a decision in accordance with a computer running a mathematical calculation on the basis of randomly selected numbers. The computer here has a hegemony over the "process of consideration," although it cannot be explained completely why one "action" rather than another one is carried out in the end, for the numbers on which the calculation is done appear purely randomly.

Dennett maintains that in the scenario described, all conditions to which incompatibilists tie freedom are fulfilled. The agent acts in accordance with reasons that he himself has weighted, he could have acted differently and he controls his action. According to Dennett, he could have acted otherwise because it is indetermined which of the reasons that finally guide his action will enter his consciousness; he acts in accordance with reasons, because he has reasons for his action, regardless of whether he does A or B, and he controls his action because the reasons that he becomes aware of determine the action.

Does the agent really have control over his action, as maintained by Dennett? The action in Dennett's scenario is doubtless guided by reasons, in the sense that the action is determined through reasons. Moreover, the agent can act in accordance with reasons in one or in another way, because he can become aware of different reasons, and depending on which reasons he actually becomes aware of, he will do one action or another. Either set of reasons can determine the action. However, does the agent have an alternate possibility of the kind that is relevant to freedom? And does he have control over his actions? Not every possibility of acting otherwise fulfills the condition mentioned above, namely, that the agent has to be able to do otherwise.

Given the reasons of which the agent is conscious, there is only one possible action that he can do in accordance with reasons. Granting that the agent could do something else on the basis of the reasons of which he is aware that is in accord with them, one gains an alternative possibility, but such a possibility is irrelevant when we are interested in the question of whether the person has acted freely. This possibility consists only in the possibility either that the agent acts in accordance with reasons to which he has given a certain weight or that he does something different in spite of the reasons. Presumably, this second action also accords with reasons, albeit with reasons that the agent does not want to be efficacious. In this case, however, something would be happening to the agent, rather than him actively causing what is happening. Something would be happening to him that is contrary to what he himself views as an action-guiding reason. He would not do what he does in a controlled manner. This kind of freedom would be a freedom of chance rather than a kind of freedom that we value as responsible agents.

If I decide on the basis of good reasons to choose an option A, then these good reasons count against deciding for another option B, in favor of which there are fewer good reasons. And I do not care to choose option B, rather the opposite. If I now decide for option B instead of A due to some indetermined events, then I do not decide in accordance with reasons I have given a certain weight, but rather against those reasons. Such a possibility of acting otherwise cannot carry the weight of freedom in a sense relevant for responsibility.

In Dennett's scenario there is also an alternative possibility in the sense that the agent could act differently *if* he were aware of a different set of reasons. However, this is not an interesting alternative if we are concerned with the ascription of freedom, since the agent cannot act differently in his actual concrete situation, which includes the reasons of which he is aware. He can act differently only in the sense that, if something else were the case, that is, if the state of the world were a different one, he would act differently. However, the incompatibilist assumption, which I endorse in this article and which is also among Dennett's assumptions, is stronger. It demands that the agent could act differently in the concrete situation. Only if this is the case can the agent act freely in a sense that is relevant for responsibility on the incompatibilist view and, I submit, in the quotidian intuition. However, this does not seem possible if the agent is aware only of sufficiently strong reasons for a single action. Rather, the agent must be aware of different reasons of sufficient weight that count in favor of different possible actions. Since a free agent has to be able to control his actions, the reasons for the different actions have to be given sufficient weight by the agent. It must be possible for the agent, regardless of whether he acts in one way or another, to act in accordance with reasons that are not countered by other reasons that are given more weight by him. However, this can happen only in a situation of conflict.

In the case sketched by Dennett, however, the indeterminacy is in the wrong place, because the agent does not even become aware of the reasons that count in favor of one option or the other. He is not aware of alternatives from which he might choose an action. The indeterminacy is constituted by the reasons of which the agent happens to become aware. However, once he is aware of the reasons, he can act only in one way. Thus, it is clear that the agent himself does not have any control over whether he does one thing or another. Dennett does not succeed in showing how it is possible for the agent to control an indetermined action. The condition that we have to be able to act in accordance with reasons in more than one way has to be given a stronger interpretation.

The agent has to be aware of different options and – regardless of which option is chosen – the action has to be understandable in the light of the reasons of which the agent is aware. Under which circumstances is this possible?

TELEOLOGICALLY INTELLIGIBLE INDETERMINED ACTIONS IN CONFLICT SITUATIONS

Wiggins describes a situation in which an agent is aware of different possibilities of acting and in which, regardless of which option is chosen, the action is teleologically intelligible:[11] The agent accords equal weight to different reasons that count in favor of mutually exclusive actions. These reasons, all of which are potentially action-guiding, cause the action in a probabilistic manner. Therefore, the agent is in a situation of conflict. Only in a situation of conflict can the agent act in more than one way in accordance with the reasons that he is aware of. Let me illustrate Wiggins's point with the following example: Suppose, I am going to the kitchen to quench my thirst. While walking to the kitchen, I wonder whether I should drink a glass of milk or a glass of water. On the one hand, water is more refreshing: a reason to drink water. Milk, on the other hand, will also make me feel less hungry, which is a reason to choose milk. Once at the kitchen, I drink a glass of water. Whether I drink milk or water is indetermined. There are reasons for both courses of action that incline me to the respective action, but – to borrow Leibniz's phrase – none of the reasons forces me to the action in question. Wiggins assumes that the reasons for both actions are equally strong for me so that the probability that I do one thing is exactly as high as the probability that I do another.

In such a case, my actions can be explained teleologically, although there is no deterministic explanation. Regardless of which action I choose, both actions can be explained with reference to the reasons that I have. From the agent's practical point of view, the choice of both actions is understandable.

Taking Foot[12] and Anscombe[13] as his point of departure, Wiggins succeeds in making it plausible that indetermined actions do not have to be completely arbitrary and hostages to randomness but that under certain circumstances we can explain them by citing underlying reasons to which the agent gives certain weights.

Wiggins describes a situation in which it is rational to choose A as well as to choose not-A, while nothing changes with regard to the reasons the person has. At least it is rational in the sense that in both instances the person acts in accordance with reasons, which are not counteracted by reasons to which the agent gives stronger weight. Thus, Wiggins endorses a strong interpretation of the condition that in agreement with reasons one can act in more than one way.[14] If one reads this condition, which I call the *condition of plural agency for reasons*, in such a strong way, one can ascribe freedom only in those cases in which freedom of indifference exists, for example, in which we are equally inclined to A and to B (and B is incompatible with A).

Here we have a special type of conflict, namely, a conflict that exists because we accept the reasons for different actions as being of the same strength and thus cannot, with good reasons, do one thing rather than the other. We waver, we do not know which option to choose, since the reasons we are aware of do not tip the balance in favor of any particular action. This situation has been classically embodied by Buridanus's ass, which starves to death between two heaps of hay that resemble each other exactly. We do not share its fate because we know that it is better to choose any of the actions on offer than to abstain from acting. However, we also know that we are not aware of any reason that is more important and counts against one of the actions. What we finally do, then, is a matter of pure chance;[15] it does not lie in our hand. If all decisions, which are free in an incompatibilistic sense, have this structure, we have not made any headway toward responsibility with this indeterministic type of freedom.[16] However, not all conditions for incompatibilistic freedom that were mentioned earlier are fulfilled in Wiggins's scenario. Wiggins merely assumes that the action is indetermined and can be explained with reference to reasons on the basis of which the agent decides, that is, that there are different actions that are in accordance with reasons given a certain weight by the agent. However, this does not guarantee that the agent has control over which of the reasons will be efficacious in the action, that is, which of the different actions that are in accordance with the reasons the agent will actually carry out.

The agent may be able to perform each action for which there are reasons given a certain weight by the agent, but he does not control which of these different possible actions he chooses. This is akin to the situation in which someone lets a plane fly left- or right-hand curves with a remote control, but does not have any control over *which* of the directions the plane takes. Such a pilot causes the plane to fly in a particular direction, but he does not have control over whether he causes it to fly in this direction or that. Thus, he does not cause a controlled flight in any particular direction.

This is similar to the situation in which an agent acts in accordance with reasons, but does not cause in a controlled way any particular action of the different actions that are possible and in agreement with reasons. To act freely, it must not be a matter of mere chance which one of the possible reasons one acts in accordance with, but rather, this has to be linked to the agent's deliberations. Otherwise, the agent is not responsible for doing one thing rather than another. In the situation described by Wiggins, the fact that the agent does one thing rather than another is not guided by reasons, rather, this simply happens; it seems more appropriate to say that it simply happens to the agent, rather than that he is the origin of the action in question. Therefore we cannot ascribe control over whether he acts in one way or another to the agent, even if his decision is not completely arbitrary in the sense that he acts in accordance with reasons that he has accorded a certain weight.

This also seems to be in agreement with the phenomenological observation that in such a situation we feel less as active agents who are in control of our actions, than as persons to whom our actions happen. We cannot make up our mind between the different options and we feel uncomfortable, for we realize that none of the conscious reasons that count in favor of the different actions takes precedence. And thus it is also obvious to us that we do not control whether we do one thing or another. Whatever is responsible for our carrying out one action rather than another, we feel that we could just as well have done the other thing. Often it may not even be transparent to ourselves why we have acted the way we have.

With Wiggins, I have assumed that the agent has reasons of equal strength for each of the different possible actions A and B. Therefore, the probability that the agent does A is as high as the probability that he does B. Now suppose a slightly different situation, in which it is more probable that a person does A than that the person does B. Let assume that it is more probable that the person chooses water than a drink of milk (say, the probability for his choosing water is .7 and for his choosing milk is .3). The only reason for this distribution of probabilities is that in seven out of ten cases the reasons for drinking water are more important to the subject and thus prevail so that the person chooses to drink water.

The conflict sketched here is not the conflict of Buridan's ass but the conflict of someone who struggles to accord the right strength to different reasons. Finally, the conflict is solved and the person gives a stronger weight to one set of reasons. However, this process could also have resulted in a different decision, since according to the assumption it is indetermined to which decision the agent comes in accordance with his reasons,[17] and this can be the case only if it is indetermined to which reasons he accords the greater weight.

If this is so, however, one cannot rationally explain why the agent does A and not B, because this merely happens to the agent. Still, the action is intelligible before the background of the balancing of the reasons. If the agent had given greater weight to the reasons for A than for B, and if he had done B, then this action would not have been teleologically intelligible. The action has to be guided through the reasons that have been accorded the greatest weight. It is not determined which reasons these are. Although here the action A as well as the action B can be guided by reasons, since due to the indeterminacy both A and B are congruent with the reasons given the strongest weight, the agent does not have control over whether he does one thing or the other, because the balancing of the reasons is not under his control, but only happens to him. This implies that the action may still be congruous with reasons that have been weighted accordingly, but that the agent does not have control over which of the different possible actions that are in accordance with the reasons he carries out.

Even if we do not agree with Wiggins that the reasons for the different actions are accorded the same weight by the agent, but hold that the weights accorded to the reasons may differ, then as long as it is still indetermined how the reasons are weighed, we are subject to the same criticism as Wiggins.

Wiggins made it plausible that indetermined events can be teleologically intelligible. However, the ex post facto explanation that is provided for an agent's particular decision by pointing to reasons that have been given a certain weight and that accord with the agent's decision does not contribute anything to the explanation of why the agent has chosen this particular action out of the different possible actions that could be in accordance with these reasons. Therefore, Wiggins's considerations fall short of showing how indetermined acting can be controlled agency. The mere fact that a conflict in Wiggins's sense obtains does not guarantee freedom, since in this way we still have not gained control over what we do. The reasons of which the agent is conscious have to be such that the agent can do A as well as B in accordance with reasons, and the agent must be in a position to choose each option in a controlled fashion.[18]

We have now reached the following preliminary result. Under the assumption that freedom requires an alternative possibility for acting, free agency – if possible at all – is limited to far fewer situations than we normally believe. For it is uncontroversial that only controlled actions can be free actions, and control over the actions demands that one acts in accordance with reasons that are not counteracted by reasons to which the agent attaches greater weight. Thus, one has to be able to do A in accordance with such reasons as well as to refrain from doing A. Therefore, it is obvious that one cannot be free in one's doing A unless one is in a conflict over which of the opposing reasons one should act in accordance with. Moreover, it seems necessary for freedom that we can control which of the reasons that incline us to different options will guide our actions. For only if the latter is the case do we not just decide by chance to do one thing rather than the other.

A situation in which freedom is possible therefore has to have the following characteristics: We have different options A and B for our actions, and different reasons count in favor of each of these options. We consider which reasons are stronger, arrive at a certain result, and on the basis of this settle for one of the options. Only in such a case it is down not to chance to which reasons we attach the greater weight but to our own considerations. The agent thus has to be in a situation in which he wonders which reasons should guide his actions, and in the end he has to decide on the basis of his own considerations. Therefore, the original condition that a free agent has to be able to do A as well as to refrain from doing A in accordance with reasons must be restricted: The agent not only has to be able to do A and refrain from doing A *in accordance with reasons*, but he has to be able to act either in one way or another *for reasons*. But how is it possible to do A as well as refrain from doing A not just in accordance with reasons, but for those reasons? The fact that the reasons that guide our actions are those that count in favor of doing A, but not those that count in favor of refraining from doing A, must neither be determined by anything outside our control nor be a matter of mere chance – rather, it has to be determined by ourselves. It is that which according to the incompatibilist amounts to freedom of the will, and it is exactly this that renders freedom of the will so mysterious.

WE ARE NOT FREE UNLESS WE ARE IN A CONFLICT – BUT WHICH CONDITIONS HAVE TO BE FULFILLED FOR US TO BE ABLE TO ACT FREELY IN A CONFLICT SITUATION?

The most interesting answer to this question, in my view, is supplied by Robert Kane.[19] Like other incompatibilists, Kane assumes that freedom is possible only if the agent is aware of conflicting reasons that count in favor and against an action A so that the agent is able to act in accordance with reasons weighted by himself in more than one way. In addition, according to Kane, it has to be partially indetermined which of the conflicting reasons the agent becomes aware of as well as which of the conflicting reasons finally guides the action. So Kane combines the suggestions of Wiggins and Dennett where in the processes leading to the action the indeterminacy has to take place.

Indeed, the condition that there can be several actions that can be taken for reasons can be fulfilled only in conflict situations, since only in conflict situations can the agent choose between different actions for which he has sufficiently strong reasons. Conflict situations seem to be a necessary condition for the agent to have control over which of the different reasons that count in favor of different actions should guide the action, and therefore a person who is not in a conflict situation seems to be incapable of deciding and acting freely and responsibly.[20] Only if reasons stand against reasons, which the agent considers as being able to guide his actions, is it possible that it is the agent himself who determines which action he carries out. Conflict situations of this kind occur, for example, when short-term interests stand opposed to long-term interests (prudential conflicts), when the wish to satisfy one's own interest is in conflict with a moral obligation contrary to one's interest (moral conflicts), or when the agent is of two minds regarding which of two morally indifferent actions he should prefer (practical conflicts). What happens in these conflict situations and where could there be room for freedom?

I discuss Kane's suggestions by means of an example for a prudential decision. Suppose, I resolve to rise at 7:00 A.M. from now on in order to manage all the work I have to do. Shortly before 7:00 A.M. my alarm goes off and I remember my intention to get up at 7:00 A.M. I have good reasons for rising, and I also want these reasons to guide my actions, because I want to achieve my goal. However, I am not an early-morning person and I am also notoriously lazy, so it requires a considerable effort of the will not to succumb as usual to my wish to stay in bed for another couple of hours. This is a conflict situation, since my aim to achieve a certain long-term goal stands against my inclination to give in to slumber. My decision to get up early, which is based on good reasons, explains my attempting to get up; my inclination to sleep in explains why it is so difficult for me to resist the temptation to stay in bed. My character and the conflicting reasons for the different actions explain, on the one hand, why I try to act prudently and, on the other, why this is so difficult for me.[21]

If the world in which I live were universally determined and thus my character and my strongest motives as well as the events of the past and the laws of nature determined my decision and subsequent action, according to the incompatibilist I could not act freely for I could not act differently and therefore I could not act in a controlled manner. Is freedom possible if we suppose that indetermined events play the role in the decision process that has been suggested by Kane?

In the situation described by Kane, the character, past events, and the laws of nature are factors that influence the agent's decision without determining it. The agent's character, beliefs, desires, preferences, and dislikes, but also the process of considering, determine which reasons for and against a decision are perceived by the agent and thus can be weighted by him. But both which reasons the agent becomes aware of (or at least for some of them) and which of these reasons guide his actions are undetermined.

Kane realized that the mere fact that a conflict exists and that it is indetermined which reasons the agent acts according to does not guarantee free agency. However, do we gain freedom if we add an indetermined event where Dennett suggests? In other words, do we achieve freedom if it is also partially indetermined of which reasons the agent becomes aware?

Before discussing whether the combination of determined and indetermined events as suggested by Kane can explain how controlled indetermined decisions are possible, I examine more closely the circumstances under which free decisions and actions are possible in Kane's view.

A conflict exists only if the subject of the action is of two minds regarding which of the different options, for which he has reasons, he should choose. This type of conflict situation has already been discussed by Wiggins as possibilities of free actions. Such a wavering between choices is necessary for freedom, since only in such a situation can we act in one way or another in accordance with reasons. In addition, Kane assumes that it is partially indetermined which reasons the agent becomes aware of, that is, on which basis the agent makes his decision. In this way, he integrates Dennett's suggestion into his account. Let me explain the situation by using the early morning example once more. The conflict arises in that the fulfillment of the desire to get up early has reasons against it, which make it difficult for me to act in accordance with this desire. Different reasons enter my mind that count for getting up and for staying in bed; according to Kane which reasons enter my mind is indetermined. Moreover, it is also indetermined which reasons finally guide my action, since it is also indetermined how I balance the different reasons. And therefore, the decision, or the respective action, is indetermined. Even if we know the person's character, the motives, and all the reasons that play a role in the decision process, we may not be able to predict with certainty how the conflict will be resolved. In this situation, the character, the reasons, and the motives influence the decision without determining it.

Let us consider this case: Are all conditions relevant for freedom fulfilled? That is to say, does the agent have an alternative way of acting, does he act in accordance with reasons and does he have control over how he finally acts? There really is a possible alternative way of acting. Although the reasons of which the agent is conscious together with the weight attached to them determine the action, different actions are possible, because it is indetermined which reasons the agent becomes conscious of as well as how he balances them.

Compared with Dennett's account, in which only the awareness of relevant reasons is left indetermined, Kane's account has the advantage that the agent can be said to be able to act differently on the basis of the reasons he is aware of.[22] This is indeed a necessary condition for freedom – at least if we assume that in order to act freely, a person has to be able to act differently and that he or she has to have control over whether he does one thing or the other. The person sleeping in decides according to the reasons which he takes to be the strongest in the concrete situation and his evaluation of his options is not determined, so that the other option, which is contrary to the one he actually chooses, could have been accorded the greater weight. In this sense, he seems to be able to act in accordance with reasons in two or more different ways.

However, does he also have control over which action he chooses? In my view, this is not the case, since he has a controlling influence regarding neither which reasons he bases his decision on nor the balancing of the reasons that he happens to become aware of, nor can he control whether his efforts to decide in a particular way are successful. To have control over our actions, we seem to have to be able both to influence our evaluation of the different options and to act according to our evaluation. Otherwise, the action cannot be rationally explained in the light of the reasons, the weight attached to them before and after the action, and the agent's desires and beliefs. It has been proposed that it might be determined which reasons count among those on the basis of which the decision is made. Further, it has been suggested that it is partly determined and partly indetermined which reasons enter the agent's consciousness and that both the weighting of the reasons by the agent and how much the agent strives for a particular action is indetermined. However, this account cannot explain why the agent attaches the weight to the reasons that he does attach to them – the agent does this without a reason, that is to say, the weighting is simply something that happens to him. He cannot avoid weighting the reasons in the way he does. Thus, the indeterminacy here seems to play just the same role as coercion, which, however, we take to be incompatible with freedom.

In Kane's model, the character, the agent's earlier motives, and past events influence the agent's decision without determining it. In this way, it is guaranteed that nothing but the weight the agent attaches to the reasons and the degree of his effort of will finally decide how the agent decides. Compatibilist approaches and other incompatibilist theories that try to make do with causation of events cannot measure up to this. Kane explains how it is possible that the agent is the final cause of his decisions – in a deterministic world nobody can have this ability. But even if the agent is the ultimate cause of his decision and action, he still does not determine how he acts – this, again, only happens to him. The agent is the cause of his actions without being their origin; he is a passive object, not an active author.

Kane believes it is possible to achieve control by allowing the agent's character and past events (including mental events) to influence the decision. Different possibilities of acting exist because within this framework different things can happen. However, that the agent chooses in accordance with one set of reasons or another can only be determined or indetermined. If it is determined, then the agent is not free in his choice; he cannot but act the way he does. The situation does not improve if it is indetermined according to which set of reasons the agent acts. For then he does not have control over his actions, either.

It is not teleologically intelligible why the agent decides according to one set of reasons rather than another. His weighting of the reasons happens as it does without reasons and is thus not under the agent's control. This is why in my view the agent cannot be responsible for the weight he attaches to the reasons, any more than he can be responsible for the options that exist, since this is determined by his character. Of course, his character can change, but it changes because of indetermined events outside the agent's control. And therefore Kane has not achieved what incompatibilists need in order for them to explain the possibility of freedom. The combination of determined and indetermined events is of no help here.

For freedom there needs to be some determining control through the agent preceding his decision. However, the demand for such a control determined by the agent cannot be fulfilled because it leads into an infinite regress: We have to weigh the reasons as we do. For us to have control over our weighting of reasons, this weighting of reasons has itself to be done on the basis of reasons. However, these reasons must themselves be under our control. This they can be only if they are weighted in accordance with a further set of reasons and so on ad infinitum.

Incompatibilist accounts of freedom that try to limit themselves to the causation of events fail to make the possibility of freedom intelligible. Indeed, the incompatibilist view that we cannot be free unless we are in a conflict regarding how to act seem to me to be correct. To act freely, we have to be able to act with reasons in more than one way. However, I have tried to show that it cannot be made plausible that in conflict situations we can act freely in the way that is relevant to responsibility. For although in conflict situations – as opposed to situations where there is no conflict – we can act in accordance with reasons in one way or in another, we still cannot act in a controlled manner in these situations. Therefore, we cannot act freely in a way that is relevant to responsibility – even in conflict situations.

Notes

For many helpful comments on earlier versions of this chapter I am very grateful to Monika Betzler and Gottfried Seebass. I also benefited from discussions of my paper at the ethics workshop at the University of Constance. Many thanks to Antonia Barke, who translated this chapter from German into English.

1. As we shall see, different kinds of conflict situations belong to this type.
2. Compatibilists hold that freedom is compatible with determinism; incompatibilists hold the opposite position, namely, that freedom is not compatible with determinism.
3. The central thesis of determinism is: All possible worlds in which the same laws of nature hold and the train of events of which is exactly the same up to some point in time t also have the same train of events after t.
4. Or, to be precise, in a deterministic world we do not seem to have an alternate possibility in a way, which is relevant to freedom and responsibility.
5. For a discussion of this point, see Guckes 2003.
6. For the discussion of this question, see Guckes 1998, 1999, 2000, 2001.
7. Dennett, of course, is a compatibilist. He merely aims at showing that indeterminacy is compatible with freedom but not necessary for it.
8. Watson aptly termed theories of this kind "teleological intelligibility theories." See Watson 1982: 11. So-called agent causation theories, which for a long time dominated the discussion of freedom and are still defended by some authors today, I disregard. See, e.g., Clarke 1993, 1994; O'Connor 1993; Rowe 1995.
9. See Dennett 1978: 286–99.
10. Thus the weight of the reasons is determined, too.
11. See Wiggins 1973.
12. See Foot 1966.
13. See Anscombe 1971.
14. Interpreted in such a way, this condition is equivalent to the condition that is termed "condition of plural rationality" in the literature; see Kane 1996: 107.
15. In such a situation we may draw lots.
16. See, e.g., Hobbes 1966: 42f.; Hume 1975: ch. 8.
17. We incompatibilists demand that this is indetermined, but not that the agent acts in accordance with the strongest reasons, because we take it that for freedom the condition of plural agency for reasons is necessary.
18. This condition is aptly called "the condition of plural control" in the literature. See Kane 1996: 107.
19. See Kane 1988, 1989, 1993, 1994, 1995, 1996.
20. Cf., among others, Campbell 1967, but Kant may also be interpreted in this way.
21. See, among others, Kane 1988: 449f.
22. However, the condition is not categorically fulfilled during the whole process; for Kane the indeterminacy does not occur in the moment of the decision but before that. As soon as one knows which reasons the agent is aware of and how he weights them, one can predict with certainty how he will act.

Herein lies a difference from so-called agent causation theories, which hold that up to the very moment of the decision and under exactly the same circumstances, it is possible that the agent acts in one way or in another.

Bibliography

Anscombe, G. E. M. 1971. *Causality and Determinism.* Cambridge: Cambridge University Press.

Campbell, Charles Arthur. 1967. *In Defence of Free Will.* London: Allen & Unwin.

Clarke, Randolph. 1993. Toward a Credible Agent-Causal Account. In Timothy O'Connor (ed.), *Agents, Causes, and Events: Essays on Indeterminism and Free Will.* Oxford: Oxford University Press, 201–11.

Clarke, Randolph. 1994. Ability and Responsibility for Omissions. *Philosophical Studies* 73: 195–208.

Dennett, Daniel. 1978. *Brainstorms.* Cambridge, Mass.: MIT Press.

Foot, Philippa. 1966. Free Will as Involving Determinism. In Bernard Berofsky (ed.), *Free Will and Determinism.* New York: Harper & Row, 95–108.

Guckes, Barbara. 1998. Anmerkungen zur Gültigkeit des Prinzips alternativer Möglichkeiten und verwandter Prinzipien. *Logos* 5: 334–54.

Guckes, Barbara. 1999. Bemerkungen zu Frankfurts und Dennetts Interpretation von "x hätte anders handeln können." *Zeitschrift für philosophische Forschung* 53: 188–213.

Guckes, Barbara. 2000. Kontrolle als Bedingung für Verantwortlichkeit. *Logos* 6: 319–40.

Guckes, Barbara. 2001. Willensfreiheit trotz Ermangelung einer Alternative? Harry G. Frankfurts hierarchisches Modell des Wünschens. In Harry Frankfurt, *Freiheit und Selbstbestimmung*, ed. Monika Betzler and Barbara Guckes. Berlin: Akademie, 1–17.

Guckes, Barbara. 2003. *Ist Freiheit eine Illusion? Eine metaphysische Untersuchung.* Paderborn: Mentis.

Hobbes, Thomas. 1966. *The English Works of Thomas Hobbes*, ed. William Molesworth. London: John Bohn 1839; 2nd rpt., Aalen: Scientia 1966, vol. 5.

Hume, David. 1975. *An Enquiry Concerning Human Understanding*, 3rd ed., ed. L. A. Selby-Bigge and Peter H. Nidditch. Oxford: Clarendon.

Kane, Robert. 1988. Libertarianism and Rationality Revisited. *Southern Journal of Philosophy* 26: 441–60.

Kane, Robert. 1989. Two Kinds of Incompatibilism: In Timothy O'Connor (ed.), *Agents, Causes, and Events: Essays on Indeterminism and Free Will.* Oxford: Oxford University Press, 115–50.

Kane, Robert. 1993. The Ends of Metaphysics. *International Philosophical Quarterly* 33: 413–28.

Kane, Robert. 1994. Free Will: The Elusive Ideal. *Philosophical Studies* 75: 25–60.

Kane, Robert. 1995. Acts, Patterns, and Self-Control. *Behavioral and Brain Sciences* 18: 131–2.

Kane, Robert. 1996. *The Significance of Free Will.* Oxford: Oxford University Press.

O'Connor, Timothy. 1993. Indeterminism and Free Agency: Three Recent Views. *Philosophy and Phenomenological Research* 53: 499–526.

Rowe, William L. 1995. Two Concepts of Freedom. In Timothy O'Connor (ed.), *Agents, Causes, and Events: Essays on Indeterminism and Free Will.* Oxford: Oxford University Press, 151–71.

Watson, Gary (ed.). 1982. *Free Will.* Oxford: Oxford University Press.

Wiggins, David. 1973. Towards a Reasonable Libertinarianism. In Ted Honderich (ed.), *Essays on Freedom of Action.* London: Routledge, 31–61.

List of Contributors

Peter Baumann is Lecturer of Philosophy at the University of Aberdeen, UK.

Monika Betzler is Assistant Professor of Philosophy at the University of Göttingen, Germany.

Ruth Chang is Assistant Professor of Philosophy and Law at Rutgers University, New Brunswick, New Jersey.

Jon Elster is Robert K. Merton Professor of Social Science at Columbia University, New York, and Research Director at the Institute for Social Research in Oslo, Norway.

Barbara Guckes is Associate Professor of Philosophy at the University of Constance, Germany.

Christine M. Korsgaard is Arthur Kingsley Porter Professor of Philosophy at Harvard University, Cambridge, Massachusetts.

Isaac Levi is John Dewey Emeritus Professor of Philosophy at Columbia University, New York.

Alfred R. Mele is William H. and Lucyle T. Werkmeister Professor of Philosophy at Florida State University, Tallahassee.

Joseph Raz is Professor of the Philosophy of Law at the University of Oxford, Fellow of Balliol College, Oxford, UK, and Visiting Professor of Jurisprudence at Columbia University, New York.

Henry S. Richardson is Professor of Philosophy at Georgetown University, Washington, D.C.

Peter Schaber is Associate Professor of Practical Philosophy at the University of Zürich, Switzerland.

J. David Velleman is James B. and Grace J. Nelson Professor of Philosophy at the University of Michigan, Ann Arbor.

Nicholas White is Chair and Professor of Philosophy at the University of California at Irvine.

Name Index

Subject Index

338